Video Production

The McGraw-Hill Series in Mass Communication and Journalism

Video Production

Disciplines and Techniques

Eighth Edition

Thomas D. Burrows

Professor Emeritus

California State University–Northridge

Lynne S. Gross

California State University–Fullerton

James C. Foust

Bowling Green State University

Donald N. Wood

Professor Emeritus

California State University–Northridge

Boston   Burr Ridge, IL   Dubuque, IA   Madison, WI   New York   San Francisco   St. Louis
Bangkok   Bogotá   Caracas   Lisbon   London   Madrid
Mexico City   Milan   New Delhi   Seoul   Singapore   Sydney   Taipei   Toronto

McGraw-Hill Higher Education

A Division of The **McGraw-Hill** *Companies*

VIDEO PRODUCTION

Copyright © 2001, by The McGraw-Hill Companies, Inc. All rights reserved. Printed in the
United States of America. Except as permitted under the United States Copyright Act of 1976, no
part of this publication may be reproduced or distributed in any form or by any means, or stored
in a data base or retrieval system, without the prior written permission of the publisher.

 This book is printed on acid-free paper.

4 5 6 7 8 9 0 QPD/QPD 0 9 8 7 6 5 4 3

ISBN 0–07–231452–4

Editorial Director: *Phillip A. Butcher*
Sponsoring editor: *Valerie A. Raymond*
Marketing manager: *Kelly M. May*
Project manager: *Christina Thornton Villagomez*
Production supervisor: *Heather Burbridge*
Designer: *Kiera Cunningham*
Cover image: © *TSM/John Henley, 2000*
Photo research coordinator: *Judy Kausal*
New media project manager: *Kimberly Stark*
Supplement coordinator: *Marc Mattson*
Compositor: Shepherd Inc.
Typeface: 10/12 Palatino
Printer: Von Hoffman Press

Library of Congress Cataloging-in Publication Data

Burrows, Thomas D.
    Video production: disciplines and techniques / Lynne S. Gross, James C. Foust,
Thomas D. Burrows
        p. cm.
    Includes index.
    ISBN 0–07–231452–4
    1. Television--Production and direction. I. Foust, James C. II. Gross, Lynne S.
III. Woods, Donald N. IV. Title

PN1992.75 .B8 2001
791.45´0232--dc21   00–039434

http://www.mhhe.com

Dedication

To our many students who
have helped make teaching
the most rewarding
of all professions.

About the Authors

Thomas D. Burrows

He now holds the title of Professor Emeritus in the Radio, TV, and Film Department at California State University–Northridge. Retirement from full-time teaching has provided him the opportunity to pursue a number of activities relating both to his academic background and to his work as a professional broadcaster. He continues to work with the Radio, Television, and Film Department at California State University–Northridge, several community broadcasting projects, and the Broadcast Education Association. During his earlier career as a producer and director in commercial and public broadcasting, he received the Christopher, Emmy, and Peabody awards. He holds an M.A. degree from the School of Journalism at the University of Southern California.

Lynne Schafer Gross

She has taught television production full-time at a number of U.S. colleges, including California State University–Fullerton, Pepperdine University, UCLA, Loyola Marymount University, and Long Beach City College. She has also taught production internationally in Estonia, Australia, Guyana, Swaziland, and Malaysia. Her professional experience includes serving as director of programming for Valley Cable TV and producing series for commercial, public, and cable television. She is past president of the Broadcast Education Association and has served as governor for the Academy of Television Arts and Sciences. Her honors include receiving the BEA's Distinguished Education Service Award and the IRTS Frank Stanton Fellow Award. She has published 10 other books and numerous journal articles.

James C. Foust

He is an associate professor and head of the Broadcast Journalism sequence in the Department of Journalism at Bowling Green State University. He has worked in commercial video production and as a television news videographer and editor. He currently works on freelance video and interactive media production, and has published several journal articles and book chapters. He also has written a book, *Big Voices of the Air: The Battle over Clear Channel Radio.* He holds a Ph.D. and M.S. degree from Ohio University.

Donald N. Wood

A Professor Emeritus of Radio, Television, and Film at California State University–Northridge, he was given the university's "Distinguished Teaching Award." He is the author of *Mass Media and the Individual* and *Designing the Effective Message,* and he is coauthor of *Educational Telecommunications.* His most recent book is *Post-Intellectualism and the Decline of Democracy,* which won the 1997 *Choice* award. His M.A. and Ph.D. are both from The University of Michigan. He is currently living in North Carolina and is teaching at the Duke Institute for Learning in Retirement.

Preface

This edition of the text has been greatly revised and reorganized to take into account the many changes that have occurred in video production. Updating is nothing new for this text because it covers a very dynamic field. When the first edition was published in 1978, television was dominated by three TV networks and some local stations. As the years have passed, TV has added cable TV, corporate video, direct broadcast satellite, CD-ROMs, the Internet, and various other distribution technologies. Equipment, too, has changed from analog-based to digital-based while all the time getting smaller, cheaper, and more user friendly.

Underlying Disciplines

While the techniques and equipment of television may be changing, the disciplines that serve as the underlying strength of any operation remain much the same. The basic concepts of *advance preparation,* the constant *checking of detail,* and the *necessity for teamwork* assume a position of even more importance as technology progresses. Disciplines involve a number of attitudes and behaviors such as responsibility, self-control, initiative, and respect for the work of others. These disciplines are, in many ways, the most important part of any university-level production course. The authors firmly believe that these disciplines can be learned only within the structure of production exercises that involve full class participation and the rotation of students within the various crew positions.

State-of-the-Art and Real-World Equipment

As in previous editions, we have presented equipment that in our view serves as an example of the technologies that students work with in their institutions or will work with as they first enter the job market. Some equipment used for illustration will be close to state of the art, but in other cases, we have deliberately shown some older, proven units because they are typical of the technology in general use.

Chapter Organization

New! 13 Chapters

The text is organized into 13 chapters, down two from the last edition because of the consolidation of material on audio and cameras. We hope that this text will fit better into the semester and quarter structure of colleges.

Chapter 1 is introductory, covering the basic concept of disciplines and techniques as well as a history of production in order for students to know from where the processes have come and also where they may be heading. Chapter 2 gives an overview of the duties and responsibilities of cast and crew and should be useful as students begin production exercises.

Extensive Rewriting!

The next five chapters cover various forms of equipment—audio, lighting, cameras, the switcher, and video recording equipment. These chapters have received extensive rewriting in order to bring them up to date in terms of digital and high-definition TV applications while still covering concepts and equipment related to the older, but still used, technologies.

New Computer Concepts

Likewise Chapter 8, which deals with video editing, now emphasizes nonlinear editing but also covers linear equipment and techniques. Some of the newer computer concepts, such as virtual sets, have been added to Chapter 9 on graphics and sets.

Chapter 10 on interactive media was a totally new chapter in the last edition and has been kept fairly similar. The chapters on producing and directing have had minor revisions, but most of the principles related to these concepts stand the test of time. The final chapter on field production serves not only to cover that subject but also as a review of the rest of the book.

The book ends with a bibliography, glossary, and index. The glossary can be particularly helpful as it contains definitions for all the words that are bold-faced within the text.

New Web Material

The book now has extensive interactive Web materials that can be accessed over the Internet. Anyone who purchases this book can access this material at www.mhhe.com/burrows.

For students, Web material includes:

- Audio, video, and teamwork exercises.
- An illustrated glossary.
- Self tests.
- Links to useful sites.
- Updates of the text content.

For instructors, Web material includes:

- Summaries of the scope and purpose of each chapter.
- Training exercises.

This is the first edition to have an extensive Web site to go along with the text. We hope it will help both students and teachers make optimum use of this text.

Test Questions

A set of multiple choice and true/false questions is also available for instructors. Please contact your McGraw-Hill sales representative or call the Customer Service number at 1-800-338-3987.

Authors

Some changes have taken place in the authorship of this textbook. Tom Burrows, who was responsible for the original creation of the text, is now in retirement and decided to take less of a role in the book, turning over the first author position to Lynne Gross. Tom contributed Chapter 1 and also participated in the overall planning for the book. Of course, many of his original words and ideas, such as disciplines and techniques, are still the underpinning for the text.

Don Wood, now in retirement, is no longer actively involved with the book, but we thank him for his many years of dedicated service and his contributions to the structure and content of the book. Jim Foust of Bowling Green State University has been added as a text author. Jim wrote two chapters for the previous edition and was much more heavily involved in this edition.

Acknowledgements

We have had the advice and assistance of many colleagues and students in putting this text together. While we cannot single out everybody, we would specifically like to thank Karen Kearns for her ideas related to audio, and we would like to thank our respective spouses for their cooperative understanding. We also wish to thank those who reviewed the book for us. They are:

James L. Crandall, Aims Community College
John A. Davlin, Hartford Community College
Roger T. Good, Ohio University
Gabriel Giralt, University of Akron
Susan Kehoe, George Mason University
Michael Korpi, Baylor University
Joseph Lanthier, College of the Canyons
John P. Malcom, SUNY Fredonia
Tom Mullin, Eastern Washington University
Sundeep R. Muppidi, University of Hartford
Tom Streeter, Temple University
Sandra J. Thompson, University of West Florida
Richard E. Worringham, Radford University
David A. Wright, Drake University

Again, we wish to provide a text that serves as an efficient teaching and learning vehicle for introductory and secondary courses in television production. As always, we welcome suggestions and corrections from our colleagues.

Contents

chapter 1

Introduction to Video Production

Video production is an exciting field. Whether you are putting together a video of your college graduation ceremony or directing a hit show for network TV, you will find that the art of combining elements into a meaningful whole is a creative process that is both stimulating and rewarding. In order to undertake production, you must interact with both people and equipment. It is the purpose of this book to give you the skills to do both. That is why the book is subtitled "Disciplines and Techniques." Disciplines will make you a valued member of a crew, and techniques will enable you to do your job, especially as it relates to equipment operation.

Starting with Chapter 2 and throughout the text, the creative aspects of the relationship with equipment will be examined within the context of the practical operational requirements of successful video production. This first chapter, however, will be devoted more to an overview of some of the factors that have brought us to the current state of video production and a look into the impressive future that most professionals see for the *new electronic media* of the 21st century. The chapter starts with a definition of the *disciplines* and *techniques* that underlie a successful career in video production (section 1.1). It then goes on to discuss:

- What is meant by a professional attitude (1.1).
- How attitude and self-image can affect your work (1.1).
- The convergence of developing technologies (1.2).
- A historical background of video production, particularly in terms of early programming, the use of film, live TV, the VTR, editing, and portable equipment (1.3).
- Recent digital innovations such as digital formats, compression, interactive video, and the server (1.4).
- Aspects of employment in the video industry (1.5).

1.1 Personal Disciplines in Support of Technique

In the study of media production, it is important for students to develop an early understanding of two differing but related aspects of the creative process. First of all, definite operational *techniques* are put into practice during such diverse activities as equipment operation, script writing, and team organization. Some of these are precise physical actions; others are a matter of often-repeated mental patterns. Secondly, there are some equally important individual *disciplines* that relate more to personal attitudes in such matters as an acceptance of responsibility and an extra careful manner of performance that the person can bring to these techniques.

To define these terms further, let's take the example of one camera operator who uses off-air time to double-check all aspects of focus for upcoming shots, allowing for possible unexpected variables in camera-to-subject distance. Another operator does only a cursory check and makes last-second adjustments if changes occur. Both individuals may know the specific *techniques* needed to operate their cameras equally well, but only the first one will be prepared for the surprises that so often occur.

To go a step further, let's say that, with prior permission from the director, our camera operator has the discipline to look for special but unplanned shots during a rock concert. One shot he or she gets is based on a special technique in using the camera lens and a light source to create a flare effect around a rock performer. Here we have an example of creativity relating to both discipline and technique. Professional directors would be the first to admit that when these qualities are put into practice by motivated and trained camera operators, the result is a considerably improved program. It is what makes "live" and "live-to-tape" sports, news, and music television possible. This text takes a number of opportunities to extend the idea of self-discipline into the related concept of *teamwork* and to discuss the skills you need to function in efficient video production teams. (See Figure 1.1.)

As a video production student, you have entered into a long process of *individual development* that must continue throughout your career. You must be con-

Figure 1.1

Field production work puts a certain pressure on both equipment and personnel. Time is always very precious because unforeseen events invariably occur. It is a test of individual skills and teamwork. Interviews such as this are often the culmination of weeks of planning, which include research, location surveys, and script writing.

cerned with the *techniques* of knowing precisely how to use all of the equipment as well as developing your own sense of production *discipline* so that others will be able to depend on you with confidence. In fact, one of the most revealing tests of your production capabilities will be to answer this simple question: Do other people really want you on their production team? Attitudinal qualities have much to do with how this question is answered.

Development of a Professional Attitude

When people work together in what sociologists call *task-oriented groups,* ongoing success is very much a matter of what other people think of you (especially those in charge of getting things done). In these circumstances, we are judged by a set of values that are usually summed up under the term *professional attitude.* How do others view your manner of approaching tasks that fall within your area of responsibility? (See Figure 1.2.)

Dependability is probably the most basic virtue in a time-oriented industry like telecommunications. Do you make a conscious effort to be on time and to be in the physical and mental condition that enables you to give your best effort? Do you handle your equipment with proper care to avoid costly maintenance work? Do you meet deadlines? Do you make an attempt to communicate your suggestions as well as your uncertainties to those in charge? Do you show respect for the work of others and for their operational needs during the production sequence? Finally, and of great importance, have you learned to discipline yourself to remain calm and focused on your tasks, especially when difficulties occur? The answers to these and similar questions are what determine how you rank with your peers. For many students, their most important career contacts will go back to the people with whom they worked closely in their production courses.

In terms of future employment, it is not so much *who you know* as it is the status of the people *who think well of you.* It therefore behooves any student, beginning on the first day of class, to quietly but confidently start doing those things that go into creating the impression of being one who is articulate, reliable,

Figure 1.2

Successful planning sessions usually result when there is sharing of ideas within a clearly defined structure of leadership and areas of responsibility.

Figure 1.3

For many students the early experiences of working with a well-organized team, such as in this audio session, can produce strong feelings of reward and career direction.

and skilled. Yes, big talkers for a while can make an impression without much to back it up, but eventually the realities of production are their undoing.

Attitudes and Self-image

In this process of interpersonal relationships, it is important to keep in mind that others' opinions about us relate in many ways to what we think of ourselves. There has been much discussion recently about how young people need *self-esteem.* A reality, too often ignored, is that people do not simply *get* self-esteem . . . they must *earn* it. On a production crew, you earn the good opinion of others by consistently doing the sort of job that brings approval and, along with it, self-satisfaction. People know, and the word gets out. Good work does not just happen. It comes from thinking through the things you must be prepared for in order to function in any given position.

(See Figure 1.3.) Do you really understand the signal flow through the audio board, or are you planning on figuring it out during the setup period? Where are the tight places in the script when a great deal happens at once? Do the others working in your area of responsibility really understand their duties, or should you double-check them on equipment and procedures? A few minutes spent in preparation can save a tenfold wasting of precious time during final production.

An interesting process of interaction becomes evident as groups of four and five people begin to work together on a project without a specific leader. Such teams quickly find that it is difficult to function properly when everyone tries to have an equal say on all matters. One designated person must be responsible for final decisions. Those decisions are best made after the leader makes sure there has been an open exchange of ideas and opinions on every aspect of the

Figure 1.4

A three-person editing team combines both technical skill and creative imagination to pull all of the diverse elements of a project together into a meaningful whole.

production. The successful leader maintains the position not only by consistently presenting a good plan of action but also by acknowledging and adopting other team members' ideas when they are appropriate. Teams usually function best when everyone has a chance to exhibit creative thinking as well as production-related skills. The ability to balance both the competitive and cooperative aspects of human nature successfully within a group is one of the surest tests of good leadership. (See Figure 1.4.)

Another balancing process can be observed as each new semester begins. A course starts out with a new mix of students. Some are old friends, while others are going through the process of proving themselves. Some who have done well in earlier classes tend to take their status for granted. During the normal competitive process of crew performance during production exercises, new people begin to emerge both as leaders and/or as persons with other production-related talents. It is then that the student who is sim-

ply coasting either works extra hard to catch up or loses status. The ability to respond positively in these situations says a lot about a person. In the long run, the individual with a firm *ego energy drive,* balanced with an ability for honest *self-evaluation,* will be sought after not only for school projects but also throughout a professional career.

1.2 The Move to Convergence

During anyone's professional career in video production, one thing is certain—there will be change. For example, much of the recent talk among those having any connection with the electronic media has been the coming **convergence** of media forms made possible by the wonders of **digital** technology. Television signals that were previously an **analog** of the original frequency patterns of light and sound waves can now

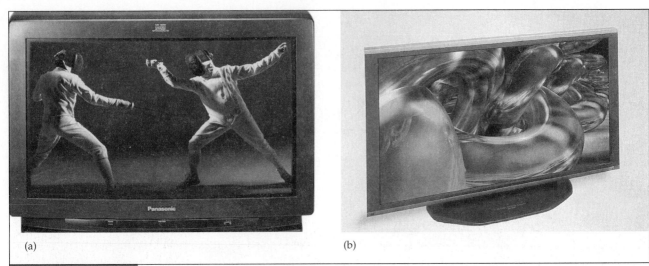

(a)   (b)

be **sampled** at an incredibly rapid rate and then transformed into groupings of digital **bits** of information that are almost impervious to outside interference.

Starting in the 1980s digital equipment, such as switchers with built-in visual effects, computer-controlled graphic generators, and nonlinear editing, was making definite improvements in the visual aspects of all types of video production. During this same period the digital signal was also making possible a whole new series of techniques that greatly enhanced sound recording and editing. Not to worry if the digital signals that had been instrumental in creating all of these eye-catching visuals and stunning sound effects still had to be reconverted back into the old analog form for transmission to television sets at home. The FCC had set up a definite timetable for converting American TV into the new digitally based high-definition form (**high-definition** TV) that could look and sound at least as good as 35mm film in a theater. (See Figure 1.5.)

Convergence would mean the coming together of the telephone, television, and personal computer into one impressive medium. The necessary replacement of all older analog equipment with the new and more expensive digital equipment could mean enormous profits for many segments of the entertainment and information industries. To help the process along, the U.S. Congress granted all existing broadcast stations electronic spectrum space estimated to be worth some $70 billion so that new digital channels could operate along with the older analog facilities during a 10-year transition period.

The movie business, too, was influenced by convergence. Hard on the heels of his successful release of *Star Wars: Episode I—The Phantom Menace* (see Figure 1.6), George Lucas announced that this installment of the *Star Wars* sagas would be the first film to be projected digitally. The digital projection, which ran for four weeks, took place in four theaters in Los Angeles and New York. Lucas sees the entire motion picture process, from the camera through projection, as eventually being done with digital electronic components. Lucas shot *The Phantom Menace* on film, scanned the film into a computer for all the special-effects work, and transferred the digital material back to film. He is hopeful to be able in the near future to shoot in the digital format and have the film remain in this format through the final stage of projection in theaters. When Lucas announced showings in digitally equipped theaters, some in Hollywood compared its potential to that of sound film 70 years earlier.

On another front, the public was attracted to the idea of viewing TV with an **Internet** connection, providing all of the benefits of **interactive** video options. The signal would be brought into the home through the use of satellite transmission, high-speed cable TV **modems,** or high-capacity video cable or telephone lines. People in the various electronic media began to think in terms of the sort of production, manufacture, and distribution structures that would be needed to bring the concept together. Powerful corporations then began a series of multibillion-dollar buyouts, takeovers, and bidding wars to gain control of all aspects of the media of the future, especially its distribution. (See Figure 1.7.)

Reading about all of these corporate plans and advances in technology, the public felt certain that a new media revolution was close at hand. However, while these first multibillion-dollar deals were being made, those who had been close to the early development of the technical side of the convergence were more cautions. Trade magazine articles and editorials began to express some concern about compatibility problems that would have to be solved before all of the technologies could work together.

Earlier, during planning for the digital changeover, movie, computer, satellite, cable, and broadcast manufacturers all held out for operating standards that would give their own particular technologies an advantage. Fearing a delay of the scheduled beginning of digital broadcasting in the fall of 1998, the FCC failed to force an agreement on standards for equipment and signals. This lack of definite standards was disruptive for all segments of the electronic media industry.

For example, some favored different screen shapes and resolution standards. TV set manufacturers wanted to stay with the older system that **interlaced** the odd -and even-numbered horizontal lines of the picture, but the computer people preferred their own **progressive** top-to-bottom scanning system. Equally intense were the arguments about how many of the minuscule color- and light-emitting **pixels** would be used to make up the screen. The result of all this indecision was that early digital sets had to be designed to receive a wide variety of screen designs, ranging from the 1,080-line interlaced scan system with a 16:9 aspect ratio to the 480-line system with progressive scanning and narrower proportions.

Steve Orlandella, director with KTLA-TV Los Angeles, is seen here directing the first digital telecast of the Rose Bowl Parade from Pasadena, California, January 1, 1999. Note the 16:9 size of the primary monitors in the digital control truck. *Photo courtesy of Joseph Marr/Television Broadcast.*

Other problems occurred when the first digital programs were aired in test areas. The very nature of the basic digital signal became an issue. When side-by-side tests seemed to show that the European process of digital modulation known as COFDM was superior to the U.S. version (known as 8-VSB), industry voices began to call for another shift in American standards.[1] One early form of the signal that was used successfully was considered by the motion picture industry as only an interim solution. They insisted that a more complex signal (with a much bigger cable) would eventually be needed to accommodate copyright protection. Otherwise, pay-per-view movies could be easily pi-rated right at the set and bootlegged all over the world.

To make things even more complicated, cable company owners were fighting with most of the major telephone companies, which also wanted to control the new multipurpose cable going into the home. Each had its own version of the signal and related modem it wanted to use. While agreement on many of these problems has been achieved, some continue to defy resolution. At the beginning of the new century, most industry professionals were busy working toward the digital future, but there was also growing concern about the 2006 deadline for complete conversion to digital broadcasting.

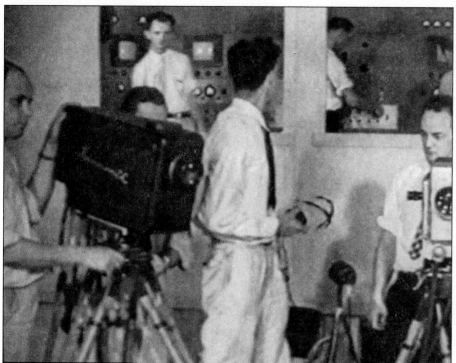

Figure 1.8

Older studios had great numbers of heat-creating lights and big clumsy cameras that carried fixed-focal-length lenses, but to those who worked there, they were an exciting place where something new and wonderful was being created.

1.3 Historical Background

The challenges being caused by convergence are not new to the history of media. Throughout the past several centuries the creation of any medium of expression has been a source of turbulence. The history of books and newspapers is largely one of a fight for freedom of the press. Early radio and television in Europe was largely owned and controlled by government. In the United States, after some early advertising excesses such as medical fraud and what many considered religious and political exploitation of the audience, the government provided a firm, guiding hand to commercial radio. There was a considerable gain in early technical development when the Federal Radio Commission encouraged the sharing of patents.

Early Television

During a brief period in 1941 prior to America's entry into World War II, the FCC granted permission for a few television stations to do experimental broadcasting. (See Figure 1.8.) Many people had seen television at the RCA (parent company to NBC) exhibit during the 1939 New York World's Fair. Some people were eager for this new innovation, but this early broadcast period was cut short by the demands of war. Postwar television again needed a firm government hand both to set technical standards and to reduce a tendency on the part of advertisers to overstate the virtues of their products. Limits on commercial time meant that audiences heard fewer than half the advertisements that are on the air today. Two radio networks, NBC and CBS, used all of their financial and technical expertise to develop successful commercial television networks and affiliate

Figure 1.9

One of the earliest network children's shows featured puppets talking to a grown-up lady in conversations that expressed both wisdom and humor.

structures. Production talent for the new medium came largely from radio. ABC, which had been formed out of the prewar NBC Blue Radio network, was soon giving NBC and CBS competition as a third television network. (See Figure 1.9.)

The earliest television programs broadcast in 1948 fell into two basic categories. There were live-camera versions of already existing events such as *Rollerderby*, a rough game played on roller skates in which one team tries to get ahead of the other on a circular track. Boxing and wrestling from a local arena were also favorites. Bands like that of *Lawrence Welk* did remote broadcasts from a local ballroom with a few acrobatic or dancing acts thrown in. The second program type was programs made specifically for TV in much the same way that programs had been made for radio. *Jack Benny*, *Amos 'n' Andy*, and other shows that had been popular on radio were brought to TV with varying degrees of success. During the day there was often a host on camera introducing some really old bad movies or kid's serials such as *Hopalong Cassidy* and *Flash Gordon*. For a while the movie studios would not release a movie that was less than 15 or 20 years old for broadcast because they were fearful of

TV taking away their movie-going audience. TV sets were relatively expensive, so a lot of the viewing was done on a stool looking down toward the end of a bar. People loved it, and things did improve . . . gradually.

When one of this text's authors was first working in television in the late 1950s, much of daytime programming on a major city station was local kids' shows such as *Chucko the Clown* (see Figure 1.10), cooking programs, or even musical productions aired between reruns of filmed sitcoms or more old movies. Commercials for locally advertised products were usually done live from the studio by freelance announcers with a few slides, maybe some film clips, and a hand prop such as a vegetable slicer or a knife set. Most nationally advertised products were viewed locally as well as on the networks by means of film. At this time ABC-TV's most popular daytime program was *The Mickey Mouse Club*. It aired daily at 5:30 P.M. and was produced on film at the Disney Studios in Hollywood.

Uses of Film and Live Camera

Film was an important part of local news programs, but it was used carefully because of the cost. Local newscasts would show a lot of still photos that came over the syndicated news wires to cover stories that had not been covered on film. Until the mid-1960s most stations shot their news footage as black-and-white negative film. Editors and reporters had to do their work while looking at pictures in the negative. For broadcast it was projected on the air as a positive picture through the action of a polarity reversal in the **telecine** camera, which was also used to air still slides. Sound was recorded on a magnetic strip on the side of the film. Because of the location of the sound pickup head in the projector, editors had to leave an extra second of picture on the film before making an edit. This meant that the audience would often see a moment or so of a speaker's lips continuing to move at an edit outpoint. With the later introduction of color film, a *double system* was used in which sound was recorded and played back on the air from a synchronized audiotape.

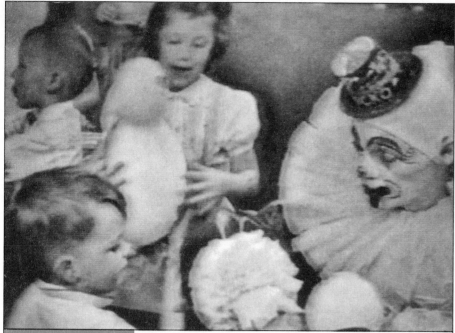

While much local programming was technically and creatively primitive at this time, a number of excellent musical and dramatic programs were being produced in New York using a multiple video-camera technique. They were aired "live" to those fortunate eastern cities that were on the early **coaxial cable.** *Milton Berle* and *Ed Sullivan* reigned supreme as kings of the comedy and variety shows, but dramatic programs captured the hearts of all America. Writers such as Rod Sterling were responsible for such excellent hour or 90-minute programs as *Requiem for a Heavyweight,* which won a number of awards. Done straight through from start to finish with only short breaks for commercials, the actors responded to the challenge and gave gripping performances with the feel of an actual stage performance. Many later film stars such as Robert Redford emerged from this creative period, which is still thought of by many as *"the Golden Years."* A top network show would occasionally draw over 60 percent of the total viewing audience. It must be kept in mind, however, that on any given evening the three networks together had 90 percent of the total audience. Coverage of national events and holiday programming also gained large audiences.

The only way to record a live program in these early years was through the use of the **kinescope** film process. With few refinements, this was basically a matter of placing a film camera in front of a TV set. (See Figure 1.11.) In the late 1950s, many people in the western states were still seeing prime-time network studio productions by means of these filmed recordings as they awaited the arrival of coaxial cable in their towns. Programs had to be aired one week late in these areas. To make things worse, the "kine" process caused a noticeable loss of audio and picture quality.

Figure 1.11

The lack of resolution seen in this kinescope of a late 1950s live KABC-TV program resulted in equally weak audio as a result of the recording process.

In the early 1960s local live programming began to have a vitality all its own, as seen in the youth-oriented rock and roll dance-show craze. In the mid-1960s every local station and network had its own "rock" program on the air. (See Figure 1.12.) For the most part, however, *prime-time* viewing was being taken over more and more by *westerns, situation comedies,* and *movies of the week* that were being produced on film in Hollywood studios. The profits were higher because of the improved market for repeat broadcasts of these shows in the United States and the growing markets around the world.

Further complicating the technical side was that by the early 1960s the three networks were making the transition to color. NBC led the way because its parent company (RCA) held many of the patents for color components in cameras and TV sets. CBS lost money producing color shows to compete with NBC and, for a while, pulled back on subsidizing color programs. ABC, strapped for money at the time, broadcast only color shows produced by the movie studios on 35mm film and did not convert the

first of its many multiple-camera studios to color until 1966.

The Impact of Recorded and Edited Video

Even as many of television's entertainment programs moved under the control of the film studios in the 1970s, new program techniques were being developed in the areas of sports, news, and public affairs. Most of these changes were made possible with the invention of videotape and the follow-on advances that it made possible. The first **videotape recorders** (VTRs)[2] were as tall as the operator and more than three feet wide. (See Figure 1.13.) They were indeed an impressive piece of equipment in their time. CBS first began to use them in 1956 for delaying the feed of news programs to the western states. It took much of the next decade, however, before videotape was in general use. At first, editing was done with razor blades and plastic adhesive tape. This process was quickly replaced by electronic **transfer editing** that recorded selected segments

Rock and roll music was riding high and wide by the middle of the 1960s. Now seen as "Golden Oldie" performers, Shivaree and others were constantly seen on local and network programs in those days.

from a playback machine to an edited master tape on a second machine.

By the early 1970s, two developments, now considered the basic essentials of editing, were being put into use. First,. the **helical scan** videotape format permitted a slow-motion or freeze-frame picture. Each single slanted top-to-bottom scan of the tape produces a viewable 262 1/2-line top-to-bottom picture **field,** allowing editors to move a picture back and forth in slow motion as they locate a precise frame for the edit point. (A complete analog **NTSC frame** contains 525 lines). Secondly, **SMPTE[3] time code** provided editors with an accurate location system by designating a numbered position for each hour, minute, second, and frame on a tape. It is now only one of several different methods of numbered frame location. This time code information is recorded on the tape or on a digital disk and is essential for all computer-controlled editing.

Portable Video Equipment

Three-quarter-inch (and later one-half-inch and smaller) videotape (packaged into a cassette) gave rise to small portable video recorders, which were a definite boon to what was becoming known as **electronic news gathering** (ENG) and **electronic field production** (EFP). Along with new lightweight cameras, movable lights, and a crew of three in a panel truck, they replaced the converted bus, heavy studio cameras, and large videotape recorder for out-of-studio (remote) broadcasts. (See Figure 1.14.) For news production there was no waiting for film to be delivered back to the lab to be developed before editing. Small videotape recorders, and later the very portable **camcorder,** changed the way that field production was done. ABC's *Wide World of Sports,* with preproduced video segments inserted into a live broadcast, is possibly the

Until the late 1960s many stations were still using large standing models of video recorders for basic playback and recording purposes. Compare the size of the recording unit inside a camcorder to this VTR, which was about as tall as its operator.

best example of how far field production had progressed in several decades. (See Figure 1.15.) The equipment improvements described above were always eagerly awaited by those who struggled to get programs produced.

1.4 Recent Innovations

Most of what has been discussed in the previous section will not be dealt with in this textbook because it is no longer state of the art. Film is not used for news;

drama is rarely shot live; the three-quarter-inch tape format has been phased out; kinescopes are no longer needed. Some of the innovations from the 1980s and 1990s, however, are still in constant use and will be discussed in other chapters throughout the book.

Digital Formats

During the 1980s, the major companies were producing VTR machines in a number of competing digital formats that were differentiated by whether the brightness and color were combined (**composite**) or separated (**component**). The large number of formats on the market (labeled D1, D2, D3, etc.) began to cause compatibility problems. Ultimately, most professional video machines of that period had to be designed to convert between analog and digital as well as between composite and component signals.

In the 1990s, even more digital formats arose, such as Digital S (from JVC), DVCAM (from Sony) and DVCPRO (from Panasonic). These are basically camcorder formats being marketed for consumer and professional use. Digital cameras and recorders are discussed further in Chapters 5 and 7.

Computer-Controlled Editing

The computers that earlier had made impressive graphics possible were put to work to roll videotape into position for edit transfer. Through the use of a number of display screens, as shown in Figure 1.16, editing equipment could be programmed to remember a list of precise segment in and out times on the EDL (**edit decision list**). The technology of recording digitized information increased its practical limits from megabytes to gigabytes. Sufficient audio and video could now be stored on a hard-drive disk, thereby providing a workable edit playback source. (See Figure 1.17.)

This, in turn, made possible the concept of **nonlinear** editing, discussed further in Chapter 8. The computer controls instant access to any point on the playback or edit master disk just as a person with a personal computer can almost instantly find the beginning of a sentence and then add or subtract any amount of copy on a document. The time previously spent rolling tapes back and forth has been elimi-

Figure 1.15

The competitive nature of both news and sports production has meant a never-ending search for ways that allow maximum camera movement while on location.

nated. Once an edit decision list has been created, all planned edits (cuts, dissolves, or special-effect transitions) are viewed in a continuous trial sequence that permits changes of varying lengths to be made on a revised edit decision list before final assembly is made.

Video Compression

Further improvements on these impressive achievements are now rapidly arriving on the scene. The next major development in the area of editing and storage is the rapidly developing technology of signal **compression**. This process encodes digital signals in such a way that sound and picture can be reduced to a form that occupies much less "cyberspace" than it did in its original form, whether on disk or tape. Called *bit rate reduction*, it is possible only with a digital

Figure 1.16

This computer-generated control screen typifies one of many different work screens that would be used during various aspects of a computer-based editing session

Figure 1.17

The almost instant access to any part of the hard-drive disk is made possible through computer control of the access area. The digital signal can be either picked up from the disk or recorded onto the disk by means of a laser beam emitting from the tip of the arm.

signal and is currently being done in several different ways. The best known method operates on the principle that in the 30 frames per second that make up an NTSC (American) television picture, more of the picture stays the same, from frame to frame, than changes with each new frame.

That approach, the **MPEG-2** compression system,[4] analyzes a group of frames at one time and uses specially designated frames to predict the degree to which parts of the picture will change or stay the same. This analysis process starts with the smallest measurable part of the picture, the *pixel*, and then works with eight-by-eight blocks of pixels. When you consider that there can be more than a million pixels to deal with, the process operates on an impressive scale. Because it is compatible with the HDTV system, the MPEG-2 encoding method (or an improved successor) will probably end up being used in a large number of video applications.

Interactive Video

As digital TV became a reality, a number of people in the electronic media field spent considerable time and money examining the benefits of combining the Internet, along with the benefits of interactivity, on home television screen. At the same time others said that while watching video is largely passive, the active and participatory nature of on-line activity was such a different experience that the two could not be successfully combined. Some of the early experiments in this area seemed to reinforce this feeling. However, now that many of the technical problems have been solved, a number of viable program options are being considered—such things as e-commerce sales, movies-on-demand with multiple starting points, and instant audience feedback (in terms of both issue-oriented programs and commercials).

A New Technology for Playback and Recording

Perhaps the most promising example of technological convergence is the large multipurpose, multifunction video storage and delivery channel file server, known more simply as a **server.** (See Figure 1.18.) Although some models have been used at networks and major TV stations since the late 1990s, the concept is still being developed. This one piece of equipment can serve as the master recipient of all incoming station video such as programming, news clips, and commercials while at the same time dispensing multiple video feeds to sustain on-the-air programming and commercial inserts. As with so much of the new equipment, the cost factor initially caused some concern, but the obvious benefits to large stations, production houses, and Internet providers have overcome much of this problem.

1.5 Aspects of Employment in the Video Industry

To the outsider, and probably to some newer entry-level workers, video production might seem to be an endlessly fascinating combination of glamour

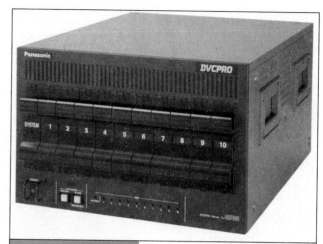

Figure 1.18

The compact AJ-DR7000 Video Server from Panasonic provides a 90-gigabyte (6-hour) hard-disk storage capacity for DVCPRO digital video format. It is designed for every step of the broadcast process from news production to time-shifting applications. *Photo courtesy of Panasonic.*

and excitement. While it is true that status and income levels are often impressive and that the intensity found in many production situations can make the pulse race, other aspects of a video production career make it very attractive. (See Figure 1.19.) Most video professionals feel a definite sense of pride in functioning as a part of a team that creates a product generally valued by our society. Whether you work on a TV news program or on developing an industrial training tape, a number of things about being part of a communications team strongly appeal to intelligent, highly motivated people. Because the effort requires many different and exacting skills, the process of working together and creating this worthwhile and rewarding end product provides a strong sense of continuing inner satisfaction as well as a good deal of mutual respect among colleagues.

Work Patterns and Locations

While many prime network and cable shows are still produced in large, fully equipped video studios often located on movie lots, an increasing number of programs are done in smaller **production houses,** with or

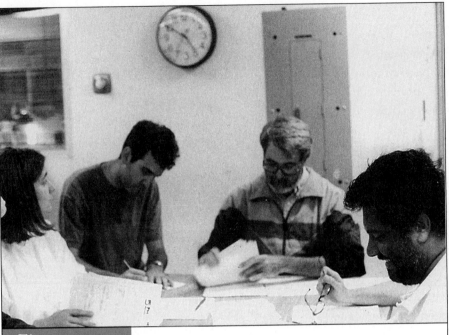

Figure 1.19

Fast-breaking stories can create a number of last-minute and even on-air changes in a five o'clock newscast. These updates are possible because the director has calmly talked through the basic structure of the program with key personnel in a session that goes right up to airtime. Note the clock.

without union sanction. They employ many recently graduated students working at entry-level wages. The reality is that all too often during the early years of a media career, you must make the decision to trade experience for the kind of salary you would prefer.

Another problem is that your work may not be steady. Often people in the video business are employed on a **daily hire** basis. These workers are not on staff, and even though they may work three or four days a week, they are not eligible for health care or other benefits. The result of this **freelance** employment is that many people now make their living working simultaneously in cable, corporate, and broadcast production. The production techniques and equipment are very much the same. Except for larger unionized broadcasting stations and networks, crew members are often called upon to perform a wide range of engineering tasks such as audio, lighting, camera, and graphics. Those wishing to direct and produce are usually selected from the crew positions.

For those about to graduate, the good news is that in many areas of employment there is a healthy rate of expansion. Most of those who can survive the difficult early years find themselves in responsible positions with a fairly secure future. You can take heart in the knowledge that those early career problems facing today's students are not very different from those entry-level people faced over the past four decades. The oversupply of young people wanting to get into TV has always existed.

One of the burgeoning areas for jobs today is *corporate video*. Large and small companies produce a variety of material such as orientation tapes for new employees, training tapes for new products, and video "newsletters" to keep employees up-to-date. Sometimes these companies have staff people who use company equipment to produce the material in house; other times they hire freelancers or people who have small production houses. In both cases jobs are created for people with television production skills.

Educational institutions also employ people in media-related jobs. Today many universities use **Instructional Television Fixed Service** (ITFS) to transmit courses over specially designated channels. At many universities this service is a part of a media center that also trains instructors in the use of video in their own classrooms.

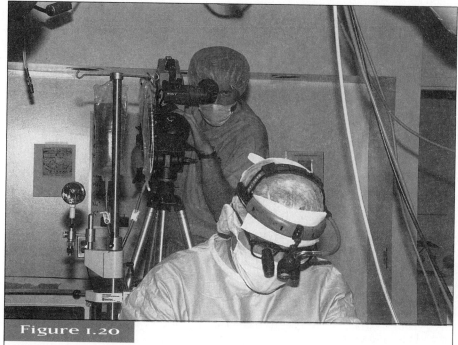

Figure 1.20

Many former broadcasting students have turned corporate video internships into fulfilling careers.

Interactive video, made possible by the instant access possibilities of **CD-ROMs** and other digital technologies, is having an important impact on the variety of new jobs that have been established related to designing Internet **Web** pages and developing interactive products for both large and small companies.

During the 1980s the FCC approved the use of commercial **low-power television** (LPTV) by educational institutions and other organizations. With a transmission distance of only 15 to 20 miles and the difficulty of competing with an ever-increasing number of cable channels, its ultimate success remains in question, but it provides excellent entry-level jobs.

One of the largest employers of media people is the government. Local, state, and federal agencies are involved in a myriad of telecommunications projects. The federal government is probably the world's largest television and film producer. Military applications, including the Armed Forces Radio and Television Services, account for worldwide operations.

One of the most rapidly expanding areas is in the field of *medical and health services*. More than 80 percent of the 7,000 hospitals in the country use television and related media for patient education, in-service training (staff development), and/or public and community relations. (See Figure 1.20.) Another specialized field is *religious production*. The production level seen on many broadcasts of evangelical groups rivals that of many network programs. At least five such church bodies operate their own satellite networks.

One of the more intriguing applications of video and computer technologies is **event video** wherein entrepreneurs produce videotape recordings of weddings, birthdays, school yearbooks, and other significant events.

Final Notes On Employment

While a first-year video production course may seem a little early to be thinking about a job résumé, consider that you could be writing a short *résumé* for an internship with some production-related company sooner than you think. Many schools coordinate just such programs. Also keep in mind that some of those final projects in more advanced video classes such as *audio and video editing, computer graphics,* and *interactive video* may well give you material for the first edition of that all-important *portfolio* that shows what you can do. If the competition is tough for the kind of job you want, start working part-time while you're in school and you will have some professional projects to show. If you can handle simple school projects well, the people interviewing you for jobs will spot it. Don't forget, most of them started much the same way you are and they haven't forgotten. Also keep in mind that many of your classmates, especially those with whom you have worked on a team project, are people who may help you get a job or are the ones you may hire someday. It happens.

Discussion Questions

1. Discuss the concept of disciplines and techniques in terms of your own athletic participation, hobbies, schoolwork, and/or employment experiences.
2. Discuss the concept of convergence and all of the various technologies that are being brought together to create the new digital video media.
3. Discuss the potential impact of the all-electronic digital movie projector upon the video and motion picture industries.
4. Listing positive features as well as disadvantages, briefly trace the development of videotape over the last 40 years.

Footnotes

1. Joe Flint, "STAY TUNED: High-definition TV Was Going To Reinvent the Medium, So Where Is It?" *The Wall Street Journal*, March 20, 2000, p. R10.

2. The first videotape machines utilized a reel-to-reel technology borrowed from existing audio equipment. VTR stood for video tape recorder. The term VCR came into use with the advent of the cassette, first used in the portable three-quarter-inch Sony U-Matic Recorder.

3. The initials SMPTE stand for the Society of Motion Picture and Television Engineers. It is the preeminent organization for those who work to design and bring about the proper implementation of the technical base that underlies the electronic media.

4. MPEG and its subsequent numbered versions of compression standards were developed by the Motion Picture Experts Group. Another compression method, M-JPEG, is a motion application of a standard for still pictures developed by the Joint Photographers Experts Group.

Chapter 2

Cast and Crew

When television was first being introduced, radio comedian Fred Allen quipped, "Television is the triumph of equipment over people." There are times (when the camera focus goes out and the computer graphics generator crashes and the audio cable develops a short—all in one day) that cast and crew members may feel that equipment has, indeed, triumphed over them. But as important as equipment is to the production process, it is really the *people* behind and in front of that equipment who are the driving force and the deciding factor regarding the quality of any TV production.

This chapter will give an overview of the duties of the various people involved in production. For the most part, it will discuss the positions and tasks required for studio production where several camera operators frame shots in a **studio** (see Figure 2.1) and a bevy of people operate equipment in a nearby **control room** (see Figure 2.2). The assumption is that the program is being sent out live over the airwaves or is being recorded from beginning to end with very few, if any, stops. This type of production requires a large crew because many things must be done all at once.

Other types of production, such as **field production** or the producing of **interactive** media, can be undertaken with fewer people, because various portions of the programs are constructed in small increments and then joined together after the fact during editing. Although this chapter will make some comparative references to field and interactive productions, these subjects are covered in depth in Chapters 10 and 13. Beyond this, the cast and crew for studio productions, too, vary from place to place and time to time. Facilities that are unionized are likely to have more people than nonunionized shops where people switch jobs and often undertake several functions. Other factors that can affect crew positions are the degree of the production facility's automation and the health of the economy.

Figure 2.1

A TV studio. The anchors for a newscast sit on the news set that is placed in the studio. Cameras, lights, and microphones are also in the studio.   *Photo courtesy of KABC-TV.*

Figure 2.2

A TV control room. While the anchors are reading the news stories from the studio, these people in the control room are making sure that the right picture and sound are broadcast.   *Photo courtesy of KABC-TV.*

The crew positions covered in this chapter, however, are the ones that are at least somewhat standard in the business. Each crew position will be discussed in terms of what you would need to do before the actual production process begins, what you do during rehearsal and while the program is being recorded (or aired live), and what you do after production is over. This should give you a general overview of what you should do for your very first production exercise. Because many of these positions are involved with producing or directing or with operating specific pieces of equipment, the chapters that follow will, by nature, give even more detail about the jobs. But this chapter should allow you to get started with production, and then you can hone your skills as you learn more details.

You and all the other people involved in a production must undertake certain *techniques* in order to accomplish the given tasks. A technical director must know which buttons and levers to push in order to dissolve from camera 1 to camera 2; the VCR operator must know how to check various meters to make sure picture and sound are actually being recorded; an actor must be able to memorize lines. But you also need the *disciplines* that will ensure a smooth production. There can be a great deal of "hurry up and wait" involved with TV production, and cast and crew members need to be at the ready so that they can undertake their duties when the need arises. To delineate the techniques and disciplines of all involved with production, this chapter covers:

- The intensity of the producer's work during preproduction (2.1).
- The "orchestra conductor" role of the director (2.2).
- The timing of a production and the other duties undertaken by the AD (2.3).
- The various ways the stage manager keeps control in the studio (2.4).
- The basic functions of the camera operators and the shaders who assist with camera controls (2.5).
- The TelePrompTer operator's role in relation to the script and the talent (2.6).
- The strong preproduction role of the lighting director (2.7).
- The audio operator's duties in terms of both the studio and the control room (2.8).
- How the technical director assures that the proper picture gets on the air (2.9).
- The technical and aesthetic duties of the graphics operator (2.10).
- The video operator's responsibilities in terms of recording and playing back (2.11).
- Work that the editor does, especially after the production (2.12).
- The difference between performers and actors (2.14).
- Performing tips for people who are in front of the camera (2.14).
- Clothing, makeup, and hairstyling considerations for those on camera (2.14).

2.1 Producers

Producers are in charge of the *overall organization* of a production, be it a network comedy, a local station newscast, a cable TV sportscast, a syndicated soap opera, a public broadcasting music concert, an interactive video game, or a corporate training tape. As a producer, you are responsible for seeing that all the elements of a program are in the right place at the right time. Have the actors been cast? Has the fog machine been ordered? Where will the cast and crew eat? Producers often initiate a project and see that it is finished *on time* and *on budget* (see Chapter 11).

Before Production Begins

Your most intensive work as a producer is accomplished during **preproduction.** This is the period when everything must be carefully planned so that **production** (shooting) and **postproduction** (editing) can progress smoothly. You oversee the script (see section 11.2) and the budget (see section 11.3), make sure all the necessary people have been hired and scheduled (often in conjunction with the director), attend to legal matters, and see that all facilities and equipment are available.

In general, a producer handles logistics of a production while a director makes the creative and aesthetic decisions. But sometimes a producer will be a **hyphenate**—a producer-director. In this case, the producer will handle organization (primarily during pre-production) and then lead the cast and crew through the creative process of production and postproduction.

During Rehearsal and Recording

For most student productions, a producer who is not a hyphenate is present during rehearsal and recording to give the director moral support and to handle any last-minute details. On the professional level, a producer's role during rehearsal and recording varies according to the nature of the project, the relationship between the producer and director, and how smoothly things are going. If a drama is shot outside the country, the producer may stay home and not even witness a single day of shooting; if a talk show is taped in the same building where the producer works, it is a good idea for that person to stop in and at least welcome the guests. Producers are usually in the control room during the entire broadcast of a live news program, because so many decisions must be made at the last minute.

When producers and directors work together frequently and harmoniously, the producer comes to trust the director and may never appear on the set. A producer will exert more control if the director's ability is uncertain. Related to this, a director who is still shooting two days after production was to have finished can most assuredly expect a visit from the producer. So can one who is spending money at a rapid clip.

After the Production

The producer's role if a program needs editing has the same variations as the role during production. A producer stationed at some distance from the editing facility who trusts the director may never appear in the editing room, although the producer almost always looks at a rough cut of an edited program and gives opinions as to what needs to be changed. A student producer will be more involved.

As producer, you should handle the social and legal aftermath of the production. Have the guests been sent thank-you notes? Have the music copyright fees actually been paid?

The producer also oversees the distribution and promotion of the program and evaluates the program and the process so that things can operate more smoothly (or as smoothly) next time.

2.2 Directors

A director has been likened to a symphony conductor. The various crew members are each playing their own "instruments" (camera, audio board, video recorder, etc.), and it is the director who coordinates them and sets the overall pace of the program.

In some situations, especially when the director is a producer-director hyphenate, the director will have helped to shape the script. In many other situations you, as director, will have the script handed to you and will take the production from there.

Before Production Begins

Your first concern should be to determine the *specific purpose* of the script. Ask yourself several questions: What is the objective of the program? How do you want the audience to be different when this program is over? Then you can begin to think in terms of the overall "feel" and image of the program. What kinds of settings, lighting, and graphics would be most effective in this particular *communication* process?

Next, you should check the script for rough timing. Is the length all right or does the script need to be cut or lengthened? The script should be put in its final television production format and duplicated for all personnel involved. How many copies do you need?

Once you are completely comfortable with the script, you should be able to start specific *facilities planning*. In the case of a remote coverage of some event, you have to scout the location (often in conjunction with other crew members). In other professional situations, you may have to rent studio facilities. In most academic and training situations, the studio will be assigned to you for a definite period of time. In many institutions—even for training purposes—you will still have to fill out a **facilities request form** (often abbreviated FACS) reserving specific equipment or a specific studio and control room.

```
FACILITIES REQUEST FORM
YOURTOWN UNIVERSITY

Date Facilities Are Needed _____

Time Facilities Are Needed _____
   (Maximum is 4 hours unless special permission has been obtained)

Your Name _____

Address _____

Phone Number(s)_____

Student ID Number _____

FACILITIES REQUESTED
_____ Studio
          _____ number of cameras needed (maximum=3)
          _____ number mics needed (maximum=5 lav, 3 stand, 1 boom)
                     Indicate type(s) _____
          _____ number of lights being used (maximum=20)
          _____ news set
          _____ talk show set
          _____ other. Specify _____
_____ Control Room
          _____ audio board
          _____ graphics generator
          _____ switcher
          _____ teleprompter
          _____ record VCR
          _____ roll-in VCR
          _____ other. Specify _____
_____ Editing Suite A
          _____ nonlinear editing system
          _____ CD player
          _____ microphone
          _____ other
_____ Editing Suite B
          _____ linear editing system
          _____ graphics generator
          _____ CD player
          _____ audio cassette player
          _____ microphone
          _____ audio/video mixer
          _____ other
```

Figure 2.3

A sample facilities request form that might be used by a university.

(See Figure 2.3.) Failure to attend to such paperwork carefully at this stage can result in costly problems and misunderstandings later.

In most academic situations, you may not have to be concerned with securing personnel. The tech-nical crew may be assigned from your class or from some other participating class. There may be some occasions, however, when you will be involved in selecting specific individuals for particular crew assignments.

Figure 2.4

Prior to production, the director holds a conference with the associate director, stage manager, technical director, and lighting director.

Casting for actors or other performers may also be done on an informal basis in the academic setting. You may work through the drama department, or you may prevail upon your personal friends. In securing such volunteer help, make certain that you have a firm commitment; many a student production has been ruined because some friend or casual acquaintance backed out of a production at the last moment. In professional situations, of course, casting is quite an involved process (see section 12.4).

Next comes the job of pulling the production together. In any kind of major production, the director should plan on holding one or more *production conferences* involving the chief production personnel. (See Figure 2.4.) You must now make sure that all the preproduction elements are properly requested and constructed. The lighting and staging plans are developed at this stage. If any special costumes or props have to be ordered or fabricated, the process is initiated now. Music and other special audio or video material must be chosen and/or produced.

During the entire preproduction process, you have to be working within a very tight interlocking schedule of *checkpoints* and *deadlines*. Many production elements cannot proceed until other items are taken care of first. The costumes must arrive before the exterior videotape can be shot. The set must be designed before set pieces can be constructed.

In the midst of this activity, you also must be concerned with preparing your script for the day of pro-

duction. How are you going to use your cameras? What will be the pacing you want to achieve? In short, what images and sounds do you want to create to achieve your purpose? You should *mark* your copy of the script indicating which cameras you are going to use for which shots and what instructions you are going to give cast and crew (see section 12.1).

During Rehearsal and Recording

The director is *the* person in charge during rehearsal and recording. During rehearsals (see section 12.1) you must make sure that both the people behind and in front of the camera know what they are to do. Never assume that people can read your mind. Some programs, such as dramas, need extensive rehearsals, because everything must take place in a very precise manner. Other programs, such as talk shows, require less rehearsal. In fact, rehearsing a talk show too thoroughly can ruin its spontaneity, because all the participants will know what everyone else is going to say. For these types of programs, it is often best to discuss only the general topics and the logistical aspects, such as when you will be cutting away for commercials.

After rehearsal, you are ready to start calling shots on your production. No doubt you will feel some anxiety. However, regardless of what might be churning inside, try *not* to let it show. Force yourself to sit back and take a deep breath, let it out slowly, and coolly tell all the crew and the talent that everything will proceed confidently. Remember that the composure or anxiety you communicate to the crew will surely be returned to you.

Your actual commands will depend on the type of production, but usually you must do the following: make sure the video recorder starts so that the program is recorded; call up the music and graphics needed for the opening credits; make sure the cameras are on shots you are likely to need as the program progresses; call for the proper camera to be on the air at the proper time; bring in prerecorded video or audio material as it is needed; execute the closing credits; and make sure the recorder is stopped at the end of the program.

During the course of your program, always be *looking ahead* two or three minutes. What possible problems lie ahead? Did the mic boom get repositioned all right? Are the dancers prepared for their entrance? Are the closing credits ready to roll? Usually, it is a good idea to delegate many of these "look-ahead" duties to your associate director, but you, as director, have the ultimate responsibility to make sure everything goes as planned.

After the Production

When the program is finished, don't let either talent or crew leave their positions until the video recorder operator has played back a bit of the program to make sure it recorded. Then use the **studio address** to thank the crew and talent. Assure them that everything went well. Keep your composure until you have a chance to collapse in private. Make certain you and your crew clear the studio and control room of all scripts, notes, props, and everything else connected with your production. Don't expect the next group using the studio to clean up your mess.

If there is any postproduction editing to be accomplished, your job is far from done (see Chapter 8). If it is a simple matter of inserting a clean shot to cover the one bad blunder, you may be able to get it done right away. If it is a major postproduction editing job of assembling video pieces from several different sources, you will need to schedule editing sessions.

Figure 2.5

The associate director (*front*) sits next to the director (*center*) during taping.

shown to the audience so they understand how the story progresses.

With just about every kind of studio operation, however, one of the AD's primary jobs will be that of timing the production. You will time individual segments during rehearsals, get an overall timing of the program, and then be in charge of the pacing of the program—speeding up or stretching as required—during the actual recording.

Before Production Begins

In any major production undertaking, the AD will work with the director well in advance of the actual production period—attending production conferences, working with talent, and assembling props and other materials. You may be in charge of the rest of the crew—checking to make certain that everyone is present and reporting this to the director. In nonunion or corporate productions, you may well be in charge of arranging substitute assignments, thus ensuring that every position is covered.

During Rehearsal and Recording

During the rehearsals, the director will mention various production items that need attention before the actual take. You will jot down the "critique notes," as the director spots problems. Additionally, you should be making notes of similar items that might have

2.3 Associate Directors

The **associate director** (sometimes referred to as the **assistant director,** or AD)[1] helps the director with various tasks. For this reason, some of the duties the AD is assigned differ from program to program, depending on the philosophy and work style of the director. One director may want you to set up all the on-air camera shots so he or she can concentrate on last-minute details, aesthetic decisions, and the actual takes on the air. Other directors want you just to sit nearby to remind them of what is coming up next. (See Figure 2.5.) If a show is taped in front of an audience, but the scenes are not taped in order, the director may ask the AD to prepare taped material compiled from rehearsals that can be

escaped the attention of the director. If you notice a major item, such as a missing prop, it should be called to the director's attention before the rehearsal proceeds. Minor items, such as a distracting shadow on the talent's shoulder, are simply written down to be cleaned up later.

You will be especially concerned with noting all the script changes that are made. If any segments are going to be taped out of order, you should note any **continuity** problems that could arise. For example, if a vase of flowers is needed for the first segment and is removed during the second segment but is needed again for the third segment, you should make a special note to double-check that the flowers are returned before the taping of segment three begins.

You may also use the rehearsal period to time as much of the program as possible, including individual segments, tape inserts, and opening and closing elements. All of these will help you with crucial timing that will be needed during the actual production of the program. For example, the final segment of a program might be very crucial to the understanding of the entire program and need to be aired in a specific way. You can time that segment during rehearsal and then **backtime** (count backwards from the end of the program). Thus, you will know exactly when the preceding segment must end so that the final segment can be completed properly. Then during production, you can give time signals to the talent regarding when they should wind up the next-to-last segment and begin the final segment.

After the rehearsal and before the actual take, it is your job to make certain that the director *follows through* on all production notes that were jotted down during rehearsal. Often, at this point, the director has a meeting with the entire crew to go over what needs to be changed before the program is actually taped or broadcast. This meeting is based largely on your notes.

Next, you must make sure that everybody involved has all script changes marked down. As surely as one person did not get a crucial script change, that omission will lead to an on-the-air mistake. Additionally, you should remind the director of how much time is remaining before recording is scheduled to start or before the live program goes on the air.

Just prior to production, you will "*read down*" the clock, letting the director know how many minutes or seconds until air or until recording is to begin. Once on the air, you should follow the script and remain alert to any and all potential problems—ready to call major troubles to the attention of the director. You must show *initiative* in this regard.

Your primary job, however, is handling *timing*. The AD must ensure that the entire production is the right length. If the program is to be edited, timing all of the segments to be electronically glued together is an important consideration here. You need some way of keeping track of the various timing notes and reminders. The digital clock readouts available in most control rooms are essential, but many ADs also use timing sheets (see section 12.1).

As AD, you are also in charge of making sure the talent receives proper time cues. Either directly or through the director, you will tell the stage manager when to give each time signal to the talent. Time signals are given to the talent in terms of *time remaining*. Thus, as you approach the end of a program, you will have the floor director signal the performer that there are "five minutes remaining," "one minute to go," "30 seconds left," and so forth.

Also during the production, you will be taking notes for postproduction editing—both those items that the director points out that need to be taken care of (a missed shot, timing that was off a little, an opportunity to insert a reaction shot) and the items that you notice need to be corrected. Finally, you must be ready to take over at any time. The AD is literally the standby director. Should the director be unable to complete the program, you will assume responsibility for calling shots, and the production will continue.

After the Production

Once the production is completed, you still have a few obligations. You should help clean up the control room of extra scripts, notes, and other materials, and debrief the director on any errors that occurred during the program.

A crucial postproduction job of the AD in many situations is the final editing session. You may need to set up a schedule with the director for any planned editing. You may simply continue as the director's

Figure 2.6

This stage manager is using flipcards to give the talent time cues.

right-hand assistant in these assignments or, depending upon the nature of the production arrangements, you may be substantially in charge of the postproduction editing session—following the director's instructions, of course.

2.4 Stage Managers

The **stage manager** (also called the **floor manager** or the **floor director**)[2] is the director's key assistant in charge of what is happening in the studio. When you assume this role, your main job is to communicate with the talent. The director is in the control room during the actual production and cannot give instructions directly to the performers, who, generally,[3] are not wearing headsets. Therefore, such instructions are relayed by the stage manager, mainly through hand signals, but sometimes with flipcards. (See Figure 2.6.)

Before Production Begins

Prior to actual production, you should attend to the *emotional-physical* needs of the talent. Is the talent physically comfortable? Can you offer a glass of water? Can you get the talent out of the lights for a few minutes? What production mysteries should be explained to the talent?

This last point is important. Because the performers are not tied into the intercom, they are not aware of what is going on most of the time. Explain to the talent why there is a delay (a result of a computer malfunction—not because the talent sat in the wrong chair); explain why the crew is laughing (at the AD's story—not at the talent's clothing). Try to

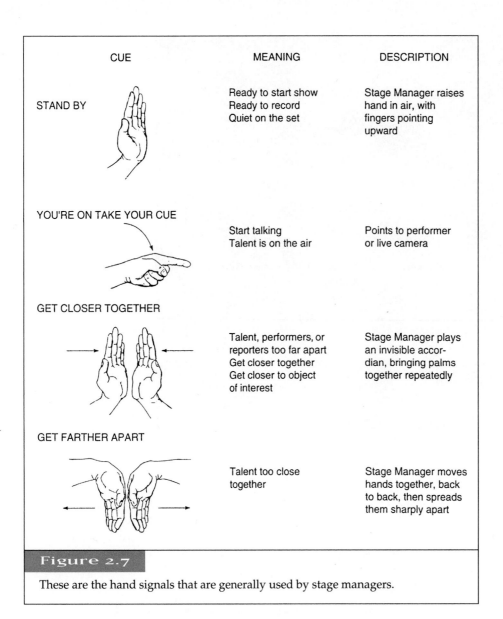

CUE	MEANING	DESCRIPTION
STAND BY	Ready to start show Ready to record Quiet on the set	Stage Manager raises hand in air, with fingers pointing upward
YOU'RE ON TAKE YOUR CUE	Start talking Talent is on the air	Points to performer or live camera
GET CLOSER TOGETHER	Talent, performers, or reporters too far apart Get closer together Get closer to object of interest	Stage Manager plays an invisible accordian, bringing palms together repeatedly
GET FARTHER APART	Talent too close together	Stage Manager moves hands together, back to back, then spreads them sharply apart

Figure 2.7

These are the hand signals that are generally used by stage managers.

put yourself in the position of the talent—isolated, in the spotlight, and receiving no feedback as to what is going on.

Prior to production, you should also work out with the talent the *technical-production* requirements. What props must be available and where? Where is the talent to stand for the demonstration? What kinds of special cues might be needed? All these details should be considered carefully, so that both you and the talent know what to do during the actual taping.

One inevitable production requirement is the communication of information to the talent through various hand signals and/or flipcards. Prior to rehearsal, you should demonstrate the various hand signals (stand by to start, begin talking, talk to this camera, speed up, 30 seconds to go, cut, and so forth) to the talent and decide exactly what time cues will be given. (See Figure 2.7.)

In addition to handling talent, the other main job of the stage manager is that of handling all production details on the studio floor. This area includes a

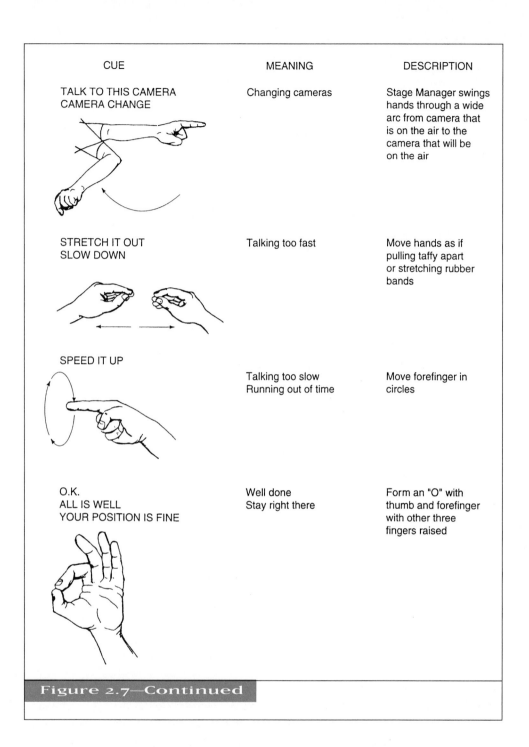

CUE	MEANING	DESCRIPTION
TALK TO THIS CAMERA CAMERA CHANGE	Changing cameras	Stage Manager swings hands through a wide arc from camera that is on the air to the camera that will be on the air
STRETCH IT OUT SLOW DOWN	Talking too fast	Move hands as if pulling taffy apart or stretching rubber bands
SPEED IT UP	Talking too slow Running out of time	Move forefinger in circles
O.K. ALL IS WELL YOUR POSITION IS FINE	Well done Stay right there	Form an "O" with thumb and forefinger with other three fingers raised

Figure 2.7—Continued

variety of concerns: broadly supervising staging and lighting setups,[4] directing studio traffic, distributing scripts to everyone who needs them, making sure props are in their right positions. You must have a great deal of authority, because virtually every other floor position is concerned with the production from only one specific viewpoint. For example, the camera operator, the audio technician, and the lighting director all have their particular perspectives to take care of. Perhaps each of these three will have selected the same spot on the floor to position a camera, a mic boom, and a light stand. It is up to you, working from

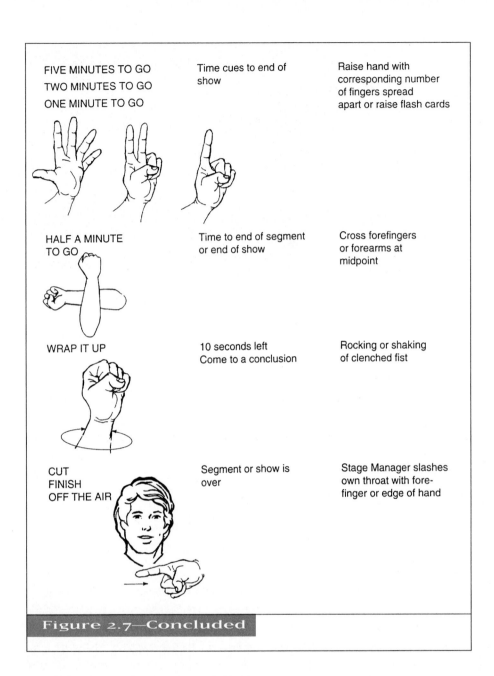

FIVE MINUTES TO GO TWO MINUTES TO GO ONE MINUTE TO GO	Time cues to end of show	Raise hand with corresponding number of fingers spread apart or raise flash cards
HALF A MINUTE TO GO	Time to end of segment or end of show	Cross forefingers or forearms at midpoint
WRAP IT UP	10 seconds left Come to a conclusion	Rocking or shaking of clenched fist
CUT FINISH OFF THE AIR	Segment or show is over	Stage Manager slashes own throat with forefinger or edge of hand

Figure 2.7—Concluded

a broader perspective, to coordinate these needs and decide what goes where.

During Rehearsal and Recording

During rehearsal, the stage manager should give the talent hand cues so they can become familiar with them. In doing this, you should always be in a position to be spotted easily by the talent. The performers should never have to turn their heads or search the studio with their eyes to find you. Often it is good to crouch below the camera that the talent should be addressing. You must, however, make sure that you stay out of the way of the camera lens. You are not one of the performers, and you do not want your head or arm to inadvertently pop up in the shot.

During rehearsal, you should also make sure of what your other duties will be. Do you need to move a prop? Do you need to hold up a chart? Do you need to replenish a bowl of fruit?

Once the production begins, the stage manager is the primary contact the talent has with the rest of the world—the studio door is shut; the director is in the control room; all lights are focused on the talent who face the cameras alone—except for the support of the stage manager. At this stage, your main job is to give hand cues to the talent and possibly move elements on the set, such as props or charts. You must remain extra alert for any problems and double-check to ensure that all crew and talent are in their places, executing their cues. In general, you must guarantee that everything for the studio that was worked out during the rehearsal period is executed during production.

Figure 2.8

The camera operators practice their shots during setup time.

After the Production

When the taping is over, the stage manager helps collect props, assists the staging and lighting crew in getting their elements properly stored, and generally polices the studio to see that everything is returned to where it belongs, ready for the next production. After the production, as well as before and during it, you must think of yourself as *the* pivotal individual in charge of the studio—the person who must take the initiative in getting things done.

2.5 Camera Operators

Camera operators are the people who, based on instructions from the director, frame the shots for the program. To do this job, you must understand the operation of the camera thoroughly (see Chapter 5) so that you can physically move the camera while keeping the image steady and in focus. You must pay particular attention to how the camera interacts with the lighting so that the picture is not overexposed or underexposed. In addition, you must have an aesthetic sense so that the pictures are properly composed. The camera operator frames, from a broad panorama, what the viewer will see.

Most studio productions require at least three camera operators who stand behind their cameras and operate them throughout the taping. Some productions use **robotic cameras;** the cameras are located in the studio but have no operators. One person in the control room or on the floor operates all the cameras by handling levers that focus and move the camera parts remotely.

Before Production Begins

Before the production begins, camera operators ready the cameras for operation. Often this involves wheeling the camera out from beside a wall where it is stored, turning it on, taking a cap off the front of the lens, opening and adjusting a number of levers and knobs that allow the camera to move freely, and generally checking to make sure everything is working properly. (See Figure 2.8.)

Once all the lighting is set, you often need to make some adjustments to the cameras so that their pictures will be optimized for the lights. Sometimes an engineer in the control room, usually referred to as a **shader** or a **camera control unit** (CCU) operator, assists the camera operators with some of the more technical adjustments for their cameras. For example, this person operates remote controls on the CCU that govern the relationship of the cameras to the lighting.

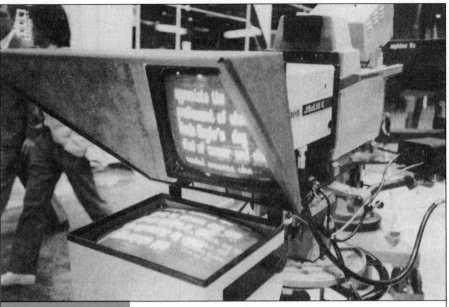

Figure 2.9

Like many other prompting systems, this on-camera display unit reflects copy from a monitor onto a mirror positioned in front of the camera lens. The camera shoots through the mirror to pick up the talent's image.

During Rehearsal and Recording

Rehearsals are when you find out exactly what will be required and iron out any potential problems. If the program is not rehearsed, you should definitely meet with the director before taping to find out what shots you will be covering. Then during the production, you follow the instructions given by the director over the **headsets.**

You should always try to think ahead to your next shot. Is the talent going to rise, and, if so, have you unlocked the lever that allows you to tilt the camera up? Are you going to need to get out of the way of another camera operator who has to make a wide move? Are there any cables or other obstructions that will get in the way of your own camera move?

After the Production

After the production is over, you should put the cameras away properly. Usually this involves coiling the cable attached to the camera and moving the camera back to where it is stored. You should cap the lens and lock down all levers and knobs. It is not always necessary to turn the camera off. If it is going to be used again within a short period of time, it should be left on, because turning electronics off and on too frequently shortens a camera's life.

2.6 TelePrompTer Operators

TelePrompTers[5] are mirrors that fit over the front of a camera lens and show the talent the script. (See Figure 2.9.) Usually all the cameras are equipped with a TelePrompTer so that talent can turn from one camera to another and still see the same script. The viewer does not see this script, but the talent can read it while looking directly at the camera lens. Someone has to control the rate that the script crawls up the TelePrompTer so that it does not get either ahead of or behind the talent. That someone is the TelePrompTer operator, although in some situations the talent controls the operation of the TelePrompTer.

Figure 2.10

This lighting crew member has climbed a ladder to position a light so that it covers a precise area.

Before Production Begins

Most TelePrompTers are computerized so that whatever script is written for the program can also be fed into the TelePrompTer computer without having to be retyped. If the script must be retyped, however, it is your job, as TelePrompTer operator, to do that before the production begins. Even if the script does not need retyping, you should check it carefully before taping to make sure it is formatted properly and does not contain anything that will confuse the talent. Are stage directions included in such a way that the on-camera person might accidentally read them? Are there any commas missing that could cause the talent to stumble over words?

During Rehearsal and Recording

During rehearsal and production, the TelePrompTer operator (who may be physically located in either the control room or the studio) must position the script properly. Many TelePrompTers have a variable speed knob that the operator uses to move the computerized copy. The words that a performer is reading at the moment should be close to the center of the screen with enough of the upcoming script showing so that there is no chance the talent will need to hesitate.

After the Production

After the production is over, you should delete the script from the computer so that it does not clog up the storage capacity. If production is over for the day, you may want to turn off the computer, although in some facilities the computers are left on most of the time.

2.7 Lighting Directors

The **lighting director** (LD) is in charge of seeing that the lights are properly set for the telecast and that any lighting effects needed during the telecast are executed. Usually this person has a crew that actually places and adjusts the lights while the LD makes sure the overall effect is accomplished. (See Figure 2.10.)

Before Production Begins

Most of the work that you do as lighting director takes place well before the production begins. For a studio shoot, you and your crew members make sure that the proper amount and type of light reach all the studio locations that need it (see Chapter 4). For studios that can afford a large number of lighting instruments, this may involve identifying, from the many lights on the **grid** (a series of interconnected pipes that hang just below the ceiling), the lights that are needed and then turning them on. If a studio does not have a large number of lights, then the crew members may have to climb ladders and reposition lights on the grid so that they illuminate the proper areas.

Whether the lights are moved or prepositioned, crew members may have to readjust them slightly so that they cast the best possible illumination. Lights are usually plugged into a **dimmer board** that is used to control the total amount of light hitting the set. As LD, you must make sure that the lights give the proper amount of illumination and the proper emotional feeling.

During Rehearsal and Recording

During rehearsals, you and your crew make whatever adjustments you or the director deem necessary. During the production, the LD and crew may have nothing to do. If the same lighting is needed throughout the taping, they may actually leave the studio to work on another show. Often for student productions, these people assume other positions during the production. However, if lights need to be dimmed or changed in some other way during production, then at least the lighting director will remain to execute these changes.

After the Production

After the production is over, someone must make sure that all the lights are turned off. If studio procedures so require, any lights that were moved should be put back where they were.

2.8 Audio Operators

Some of the work that is done in connection with audio is undertaken in the studio and some is in the control room. (See Chapter 3.)

Before Production Begins

Someone must select the appropriate microphones and position them in the studio before the production begins. Do you need to attach a mic to the talent's clothing? Will you be placing any mics on stands, and, if so, do you have the stands? Will you be hanging any mics from the lighting grid? The mics must be connected to receptacles located somewhere in the studio that send the audio signal to the **audio console** in the control room.

Once you have positioned and connected the mics, you must test them to make sure they are working properly. Usually this job involves two **audio operators,** one talking into each mic in the studio and another adjusting it through the audio console in the control room. If only one audio operator is available, the floor manager can talk into the mics. The talent can also talk into the mics (and should in order to set levels), but it is a good idea to make sure the mics are actually working before the talent arrives. You do not want high-priced talent sitting around while you replace a mic battery or trace down a bad cable.

Once the talent is in place, you should make sure each miked person talks as they will during the production and everyone else (including crew) should be quiet so that you can set the volume of the mic as it will be needed during the taping.

If the program is going to contain music, sound effects, or other audio elements, you should also check these out and cue them up before production so that when they are needed during rehearsal or taping, they will come in exactly as the director desires.

It is a good idea to mark on the audio board, with tape that is easily removable, what each of the inputs is handling. For example, for each mic input you can write the name of the talent using the mic. This will help you bring up the right person's sound at the

Figure 2.11

Working at the audio board, the audio operator combines sounds and adjusts their volume.

right time. Similarly the inputs from the CD, DAT, and such should be clearly marked.

During Rehearsal and Recording

During rehearsal and/or production, there may be a need for audio operators in both the studio and control room. If a mic needs to be moved (on a **boom** or other apparatus) during taping, then someone must be in the studio to do this job. If all the mics are attached to talent's clothing, then there is really nothing for a studio audio operator to do. There may be a need for two operators in the control room, however. If a show has complicated audio (and if the control room audio area is large enough), one person can operate the audio console while another starts and stops tape recorders, the CD player, or other equipment. More common, however, is one audio operator handling all the control-room audio. (See Figure 2.11.)

During rehearsal you should make sure to have all performers speak at the voice level they will be using during performance so that you can set the levels of their mics. All too often beginning audio operators say, "Have him speak louder," or "Have her move closer to the mic." This is the wrong approach. The person (especially one who is seated) who moved into the mic or speaks louder during the test will probably lean during the show to a more natural posi-

tion. Also, the speaker's volume will probably return to its normal level. It is the audio operator's responsibility to get consistent quality sound. Can you move the mic closer to the person? Can you increase the volume without creating distortion?

Once the production begins, you should bring in sounds when the director calls for them. Your main job is to make the sound audible and consistent. For example, in most instances you should make sure the music does not drown out what someone is saying, and you should make sure that someone who talks softly can be heard as well as someone with a booming voice.

After the Production

After the production is over, the audio operator(s) should coil the audio cable and put away all the microphones, generally in boxes that are specially made for them. Some microphones have batteries that need to be removed when they are not in use. Any CDs or tapes used during production should be stored away or given to the director or producer.

You should put the board in the generally agreed-upon configuration for the facility. Because audio boards contain a large number of buttons, knobs, and faders, the audio personnel of a facility should agree on commonly used settings for everything and then set the board that way at the end of each production. An enormous amount of time can be wasted if one operator has a need to turn on a little-used knob and then doesn't turn it off again and the next operator can't figure out what is wrong. This is a particularly common problem in colleges where many students who are just learning the board use it during the course of a day. For this reason, college facility engineers often make drawings of how the board should be set or carefully indicate the desired positions of the various controls.

2.9 Technical Directors

The **technical director** (TD) operates the **switcher,** the piece of equipment that selects which video signal (camera 1, a videotaped segment, camera 2 with graphics over it, etc.) will go out over the airwaves or onto videotape. This piece of equipment can be used simply to **cut** from one picture to another, but most modern switchers are capable of executing a large number of special effects—wipes, swirls, squeezes, and so on. (See Chapter 6.) Like the audio console, the switcher has a large number of buttons, knobs, and levers, and you must become adept at operating them quickly.

The technical director is also the head technical person for most studio productions. Although the director actually gives the commands to the various equipment operators, the technical director oversees and assists the crew members if they are having trouble executing something the director wants done or if the equipment is malfunctioning.

Figure 2.12

The technical director (*front*) sits near the director (*center*) during taping. On the other side of the director is the associate director.

Before Production Begins

Before the production begins, you as the technical director are responsible for ensuring that all the equipment will work throughout the production. If one of the monitors is flickering, should you replace it, try to fix it, or leave it as it is? You also make sure you know about any particularly difficult picture-switching maneuvers the director might want. Often special effects can be partially set up ahead of time so that they are easy to execute when they are needed.

During Rehearsal and Recording

During the rehearsal and recording the TD operates the switcher. As with many other crew members, you follow the instructions of the director. Usually you sit right next to the director so you can communicate fairly easily. (See Figure 2.12.)

After the Production

After the production, you set the switcher to its normal configuration in the same manner that the audio operator sets the audio board. Usually resetting the switcher involves pushing all the buttons that indicate "black" so that there are no pictures coming through the switcher. You have the responsibility for the technical **strike** (the turning off and putting away) of the equipment and, as part of this duty, should note any

equipment that needs repair or adjustment and inform the studio engineer.

2.10 Graphics Operators

The **graphics operator** is in charge of the computer system that is used to create words, drawings, and various visual effects. (See Chapter 9.) These include such things as opening and closing credits, temperatures used for the weathercasts, short animated sequences used in commercials, statistics for sportscasts, and bar graphs used for corporate productions.

Originally graphics operators were called **character generator** (c.g.) operators, because the early graphic computer systems were capable of displaying only characters such as letters and numbers. As the sophistication of the equipment has grown, so have the duties of the c.g. operator, so although that term is still used, *graphics operator* or *graphic artist* is becoming commonplace.

Before Production Begins

While the rest of the crew is setting up, you must create the visuals needed for the program. (See Figure 2.13.) If these are extensive, you may have to come in a day or two early to create them and store them in

The graphics operator prepares material for broadcast.

the computer or on a floppy disk. If they consist only of opening and closing credits, the job is fairly simple.

Most computer systems are capable of special effects that look very much like those that can be executed with the switcher. The graphics operator, the director, and the TD must plan together so each does what is needed to achieve the proper effect. You, as a graphic artist, should have a good sense of composition and color, because you usually are creating something that will make an aesthetic statement.

During Rehearsal and Recording

During rehearsal and recording you must make sure that the proper graphic is ready when the director wants to display it and that it is displayed in the manner requested. Should it roll or blink? Do credits come on one after another or is there time in between?

As with other positions, you should exhibit the *discipline* of thinking ahead so everything you are responsible for comes off smoothly.

After the Production

After the production, you should remove at least most of the graphics from the computer so that they

do not clog up the hard drive. Some stations or studios use the same graphics over and over. Those graphics are usually stored permanently on the hard drive. One of the graphics you constructed for a particular program may be something that another program wishes to use with slight modifications. In that case, you should save the graphic in a predetermined file so it can be found easily.

2.11 Video Operators

The person who plays back and/or records video signals is often referred to as the *VCR operator* and operates a **videotape recorder** (VTR); these are often referred to as **videocasette recorders** (VCRs) when the tape is on a self-contained cassette, as it is for many consumer formats. However, devices other than VTRs, such as **video disk** recorders and computer drives, are now used to record video and audio (see Chapter 7), so the term **video operator** is frequently used.

The video operator is responsible for recording the program being produced. Sometimes even programs that are shown live (such as news or sports) are recorded for archival purposes or so the footage can be used in other programs. In addition to recording, the video operator often plays back video material that was previously recorded. For example, the video operator may play back a news story that was edited in the early afternoon into a newscast going out live at 6:00 P.M.

Before Production Begins

Before the program begins, you, as the video operator, must make sure each playback tape or other recorded material is properly cued up so that when the director calls for it, the right material will play. In line with this, you should also make sure the machine playing back the tape is properly set up so that the signal will go where it is supposed to go. You must also make sure to insert a blank tape in the machine that is to record and you should check that all the VCR controls are properly set. If the tape has a button or tab that can be set so that the tape is not accidentally erased, you should set that tab or button so the tape will actually record.

During Rehearsal and Recording

During rehearsal, you are likely to play back tapes but not record the rehearsal itself, although sometimes final dress rehearsals are taped so that material from the tapes can be used if something goes wrong during production. During production you start the record tape when the director so instructs and monitor all the vital signs to make sure the tape is actually recording. Are the audio signals going to the right channels? Is the video meter indicating that the machine is getting a strong enough signal? You also play back any prerecorded material when it is needed. If a program calls for many roll-ins, you may have an assistant to play back some of the tapes. (See Figure 2.14.)

After the Production

After the production is over, you should carefully label the master tape on which the program is recorded. Most studios have a standard labeling system that includes the title and length of the program, the date on which it was recorded, and the name of

Figure 2.14

This video operator readies the tape so that the program can be recorded.

the director. Usually it is a good idea to label both the tape and the box. You should file the tape in the appropriate place or give it to the appropriate person. The same is true for all the tapes that were rolled into the program.

2.12 Editors

The **editor's** job is to piece together different shots or scenes taped in the studio or the field to create a unified piece of work. Sometimes all the editor's work occurs before a production is taped and sometimes it all occurs afterwards. With some of the newer editing systems, editors can even edit while a program is in progress. Of course, some shows, such as a live telecast of a telethon, do not require an editor at all.

Figure 2.15

The editor, under the guidance of the director, is in the editing suite assembling footage.

Before Production Begins

An editor works before a program is taped to piece together material that will be rolled into a production. For example, you may assemble a background piece about an Olympic athlete to include in a magazine show. You usually work alone in a small room called an editing suite (see Figure 2.15) that contains all the equipment needed for editing. (See Chapter 8.)

Sometimes the director (or a reporter, in the case of news) is also present for editing. Editors who work alone are usually given a script or a list of shots so they have a general idea of what they are to assemble, but they also use their own creativity to present material in an aesthetically pleasing manner.

During Rehearsal and Recording

If editing occurs during production, it is often so that a summary of something that has happened during the course of the telecast can be presented. For example, you might pull together a collage that shows a basketball player sinking six baskets at six different times during the first half. Then the sportscasters could comment on these during halftime.

After the Production

Most editing, however, occurs after the production has been shot when you place shots in juxtaposition with each other. There may be hours of footage that must be cut down to a 30-minute show. You and the director (and/or associate director) must organize the footage, decide what to use, and assemble it.

Often the editing job is broken down, with one or more people editing the picture and several others working on the sound. This is most likely to be the case for dramas and comedies, which often need special audio enhancements such as a laugh track or sound effects. Other editing is much simpler, with both sound and picture being edited by the same person. As an editor, you may need to shorten a game show that ran too long, or piece together parts of a variety show taped stop-and-go fashion over the course of an afternoon, or eliminate some dull parts of a talk show.

2.13 Other Positions

A raft of other people are needed for TV production. Sometimes people called *production·assistants* undertake all the little jobs that need to be done—distributing scripts to cast and crew, moving flower pots, getting coffee for everyone, and so on. For a large unionized production, specialists undertake specific jobs—a *propmaster* places and handles all props, *painters* and *carpenters* are available to touch up sets, *makeup artists* apply makeup to talent, *grips* carry cable and other things. All of these people are usually around before, during, and after production to handle setup, production miscellany, and cleanup on an as-needed basis.

The overall look of a production comes under the province of the **art director, production designer, and/or set designer.**[6] These people work to ensure that all the artistic aspects of a program (set pieces, props, graphics, costumes) work together without clashing or giving different psychological messages. Most of this work takes place before the production is begun, as does the work of *set builders* and *costume designers.*

Different types of programs require various specialists. Are you featuring dogs, monkeys, or more exotic animals? If so, you need an *animal handler.* Are real plants and flowers in evidence? A *greensperson* will keep them looking fresh. Do you have children in the class? Then you must hire a *teacher.* Are there dance numbers? *Choreographers* stage these. Is the end product of the production going to be an interactive program? If so, you will need someone with *computer programming* skills.

People who execute *special effects* have been in great demand in recent years. Even for studio shoots, pyrotechnic effects are used more frequently than in the past, and many shots that used to be shown fairly straight are now enhanced through digital manipulation. Just about every frame of the movie *Babe* underwent manipulation so that the real animals used throughout the movie looked more peoplelike. The credits include such jobs as Fleece Fabrication Assistant and Feather and Anatomy Designer.

Overall, job classifications are in a state of flux. Technological advances eliminate jobs (e.g., camera operators eliminated by robotic cameras), but just as quickly other technological advances create new jobs (e.g., digital manipulation). The people most likely to succeed in behind-the-scenes employment are those who have a variety of skills and who are willing to learn new tasks and new equipment.

2.14 Cast

This book, because it is aimed more at the behind-the-scenes aspects of video production, will not dwell on acting techniques, which are covered very well in the many books written on the subject.[7] However, people who are in the television business often have to appear on the screen, and certainly, within the classroom setting, producers and directors often call upon their classmates to appear in front of the camera. Therefore, in this chapter, we will give some rudimentary tips on what you should do when you are talent for a TV show.

A distinction is often made between two groups of talent: (1) those who serve essentially as communicators, portraying no role except as a host or reporter; and (2) those in dramatic roles who are portraying some theatrical character. The first category is referred to as **performers,** while the second group is referred to as **actors.** Although the two groups share many characteristics and concerns, it may be helpful to look at them separately in terms of what you need to do when you are in one of these roles.

Television Performers

The category of performer includes announcers, hosts, narrators, reporters, interviewers, demonstrators, panel participants, and the like—talent who are communicating personally with the audience, usually addressing them directly.

You, as a performer, must realize that your primary responsibility is to the audience. Even though millions of people may be watching a particular TV program, television is an intimate medium. It is usually received on a small screen, in the privacy of the home, as a rule by an audience of one or a few people.

You will be most successful when you conceive of the audience in that manner—one to four people sitting just a few feet away.

Voice and Eyes

For this reason, a natural conversational speaking voice is best. The mic is usually clipped on your shirt or blouse so there is no need to speak to the camera or some far-off viewer. If you can project the feeling of spontaneity and intimacy in your speaking style, you will be on the way to capturing one of the most sought-after qualities of any television performer—*sincerity*. (As one comedian wisecracked, "If you can fake sincerity, you got it made.")

Just as important as vocal directness is the intimacy of specific visual directness—eye contact with the TV camera. When you are speaking to the audience, you should maintain a direct and personal eye contact with the camera lens at all times, looking straight into the heart of it. This direct eye contact is the secret of maintaining the illusion of an exclusive relationship with each individual member of the audience.

In maintaining the illusion of direct eye contact, you must become skilled, of course, in some of the artifice and techniques of the medium. In many productions, the director will cut from one camera shot of the performer to another. You will have to reestablish eye contact with the new camera immediately. One way to make this transition look as natural as possible is to glance downward—as if glancing at some notes or trying to collect your thoughts—and then immediately establish eye contact with the new camera.

The director should inform you if one camera is being used exclusively for close-ups of some object you are demonstrating or discussing. Then you won't need to worry about ever having to look at that camera, even though it is on the air.

Mannerisms

Because television is such an intimate, close-up medium, any visually or vocally distracting mannerism you have will certainly be captured with full impact. Some nervous mannerisms, such as a facial twitch or the unconscious habit of licking lips, may be hard to control. On the other hand, some fidgety dis-

tractions, such as playing with a pencil or pulling an earlobe, can be corrected if someone calls them to your attention. Ask for such advice; it will help you come across better on the tube. Besides, many an audio operator has had a few hairs turn gray when a performer thumped his or her fingers on the table next to the desk mic while pondering a weighty question.

Vocal habits and mannerisms can also be distracting. The use of vocalized pauses (saying "um" or "ah") every time there is a second of dead air is a problem many of us share. The ubiquitous "I see" somehow always becomes part of the interviewer's basic vocabulary. Try to avoid these mannerisms.

Handling the Script

Depending upon the specific program, you may be working from a full script, speaking extemporaneously, or something in between. Some performers, such as guests on a talk show, may speak spontaneously or *ad-lib* with no preparation at all. Many performers think they have to work from a full script—when they probably would be better off working from rough notes. These enable the talent to have enough of a solid outline to speak with confidence; yet, by composing the exact words on the spot, they can add vitality and sincerity that is difficult to achieve with a prepared text.

You can handle fully scripted material in one of several ways. *Memorization* usually is required only for dramatic works and is best left to actors. Seldom can typical television performers deliver memorized copy without sounding artificial and stiff. You are better off reading from a physical script in your hands, from cue cards held next to the camera, or, better yet, from a prompting device.

Reading directly from a *script* is satisfactory if you are quite familiar with the material and do not have to keep your eyes glued to the script. Some people can handle a script very well, glancing down only occasionally. Others, because of insecurity or nervousness, get completely buried in the script and never establish eye contact. If you do use a script, you should make sure the pages are unstapled so you can slide the pages to the side unobtrusively without creating noise on the microphone. Also, make sure the pages are in the right order before starting the final take.

This cue card is being held next to the lens so that the talent can see it easily.

The difficulties of working with a script can be avoided by using **cue cards,** but they have their own problems. Either you or some crew member will have to transfer the entire script onto large cue sheets. The person holding the cue cards has to be trained to raise each card to keep the exact line being read next to the lens. With a hefty stack of cue cards, holding them can become a very wearisome and demanding assignment. (See Figure 2.16.) Cue cards allow for better eye contact than many performers can muster if they use handheld scripts, but because they are beside the camera, the performers often appear to be looking slightly off camera.

For studio productions, cue cards have been largely replaced by the TelePrompTer (review Figure 2.9), which enables you to read the copy while staring directly at the lens. The direct spot on the script can always be positioned directly in front of the lens so that your eyes cannot wander away from the lens. You should try to keep your eyes from going back and forth across the screen so you do not look like you are reading.

Other Performing Tips

In order to achieve good camera angles, performers have to work close together. One old television adage is, "If you ain't touching, you ain't close enough." Some performers feel uncomfortable with the close physical proximity they must maintain to other talent. As a result, they will start out in a chair close to the other talent but gradually, during the course of rehearsal and taping, move further and further away. The result is that a gap develops that looks inappropriate in the TV frame. (See Figure 2.17.) As a performer, try to get used to this "closeness" and check every once in a while to make sure you and the other performers are positioned properly.

Make sure you know where the microphones and lights are, and don't walk out of the light or out of the range of the sound pickup.

Don't acknowledge the floor manager's hand signals in any way (such as nodding your head), because this will show on camera. You should be aware of where the stage manager is, but it is the stage manager's job to stand where you can easily see him or her.

Figure 2.17

Although these two people are sitting at what is normal distance for ordinary conversation, when the television camera frames both of them, there is an undesirable gap between them. They should sit closer together.

Don't make any big or sweeping gestures, because the chances are that the camera will be on a fairly tight shot. Similarly, be careful with facial grimaces; there is a likelihood that the camera has a close-up of you.

Whenever you can, help the director prepare for important shots by telegraphing them ahead of time. Say, "Now let's look at the first demonstration . . . ", as this will warn the director that you are going to move to the demonstration area. However, don't give direct instructions such as "Now, if I could just get a shot of this wristwatch!"

In a similar vein, if you are going to make a big move, you should lean into it gradually, giving the director and the camera operator ample warning. For example, if you are sitting in a chair and are ready to stand and walk over to the demonstration area, place both feet firmly on the floor, lean forward, put your hands on the sides of the chair, and *slowly* lift out of the chair. The camera is then able to follow you smoothly. In general, you should develop a habit of moving slowly as you go from one area of the set to another. This gives the camera operator a good chance of moving along gracefully. (And it always looks fast enough to the viewer.)

If you hold up some object in front of the camera for a close-up, hold your arm tightly against your body to steady the hand. Even better, rest the object on a table or stand so there is no possibility of it moving.

Don't handle microphones, except hand mics, and avoid playing with the mic cords, because both can ruin audio. When you are asked to give an audio level, speak as you will speak during the program. Some performers will mumble a relatively weak audio check and then boom out on the air with their best basso profundo. A few will do just the opposite.

Clothing

Usually performers wear their own clothes, not specially designed costumes. If you are going to perform on a program, you should try to find out something about the set so you do not clash with it. If you are going to be sitting in a tan chair, you should not wear a tan shirt or dress because you will disappear. If the set is basically green, don't wear red clothing—unless you want to give the impression of Christmas.

Unless a spectacular, deliberately colorful, dazzling effect is advised, stick to clothing of a *dull saturation*—muted aqua rather than chartreuse, tan rather than brilliant yellow. Brightness and tonal balance also should be considered in terms of the overall emotional effect that is desired. Would dark, somber grays and browns be more or less appropriate than lighter shades and pastels?

Line is also an important design consideration. Vertical lines tend to emphasize tall and slender proportions; horizontal stripes tend to exaggerate weight and mass. Performers who are concerned about appearing too heavy (and television has a tendency to make people appear a little heavier) are advised to stick to vertical lines.

You should also avoid high contrast and extremes in color brightness. Television cameras have a relatively limited contrast ratio, which makes it difficult for them to handle white shirts against a dark suit. Try also to avoid high contrasts with skin tones. Dark clothes will make a pale person look even more pale; light-colored clothes next to a tanned complexion will make the skin appear darker. Blacks and other dark-skinned performers should be careful of light-colored clothing that would tend to heighten the tonal contrast and wash out facial details in the dark areas.

Generally, finely detailed patterns should be avoided. Whereas clothing with a rich thick texture will photograph well on television, clothing with a fine pattern usually will not, because it is too busy and distracting and hard to make out once it has gone through the TV process. Thin stripes, herringbones, and small checks can also create the **moiré effect**—a distracting visual vibration caused by the interference of the clothing pattern and the TV scanning lines. **High-definition** television cameras, when they become widely used, will be able to reproduce contrast extremes and fine detail better than conventional cameras.

One other minor clothing consideration involves **chroma key.** This is an effect wherein talent is taped against a colored background, usually blue; then the blue is removed and something else, such as a picture of a building, is inserted in its place. (See Chapter 6.) The problem is that anything, even a tie, that contains the blue used for the chroma key will disappear, and the background picture will show through. Imagine the effect if you have a scene from the fire keyed in behind you—and we see flames coming through your shirt. Ask if chroma key is going to be used, and, if so, avoid wearing chroma key blue.

Makeup

Many productions (such as public-affairs shows) do not require formal makeup. Guests can "come as they are" and look perfectly fine. However, many guests will look better if makeup is used to enhance or correct appearance. In addition, HDTV will make the need for makeup more crucial, since the higher resolution is more likely to show skin blemishes. For this reason, makeup to cover the body as well as the face may also become more in vogue.

The object of television makeup for performers is to have them look as natural as possible. A good, basic, unobtrusive makeup job should help enhance normal colors (evening up flesh tones, cutting down on the shine of a bald head), minimize any blemishes or distortions (covering up birthmarks, eliminating bags under the eyes), and emphasize good points. However, with the close-up lens, any exaggerated makeup certainly would be perceived as unnatural.

If you are performing at a TV facility, there may be a makeup person available to apply the makeup, but often, if you want to wear makeup, you will have to apply your own. Such applications are not all that difficult. Before applying any makeup, clean your face with either a moisturizer for dry skin or an astringent (such as alcohol or witch hazel) for oily skin. Then apply the *base.* This is the initial covering that is usually applied to the entire face or exposed area (arms and hands) being treated. This base is to provide the color foundation upon which all the rest of the makeup is built.

Next, apply *powder* to help keep the base from smearing. Usually, powder that is a little lighter than the base color is best. You can use *highlights* and *shadows* to emphasize or minimize facial features. Your forehead, nose, cheekbone, and jaw can all be highlighted with lighter shades or de-emphasized with darker tones. Normally, *rouge* is next applied to the cheeks, nose, forehead, and chin as needed to give you a healthy complexion and to counteract the flatness of the base color.

Finally, you should give special attention to those most expressive features of the face—the eyes and the lips. Use specific drawing tools and accessory items as necessary: *lipstick, eye shadow, eyeliner, eyebrow pencil, mascara,* and possibly *false eyelashes.* The extent of the use of these accent items depends upon the need for remodeling and your individual taste.

Hairstyling

Hairstyles with a definite shape or firm silhouette usually compliment the performer more than wispy, fluffy hairdos. You should comb your hair carefully, because backlight will tend to make loose strands stand out. Avoid fancy hair treatments and fresh permanents, because they will make you look unnatural.

Handling all these aspects of performing is part of the overall *discipline* of being in front of the camera.

Television Actors

Many of the observations made regarding television performers apply equally to television actors. Actors, too, must be concerned with their relationship with the audience. Are you talking conversationally as your character would talk? Are you aware of the demands of the mics and lights? Do you understand the stage manager's hand signals?

However, acting involves special considerations. First, actors have to learn to adjust to the concept of a moving audience perspective. Unlike theater, there is no **proscenium arch;** there is no firm boundary separating the audience from the actors. The audience perspective is switched every time the camera is changed. The viewer can be transported sideways, in or out, or into the mind of the actor. Actors must, therefore, be aware of how their actions will appear from all angles.

Gestures and Voice

As an actor, you must limit sweeping gestures, because you are playing to a camera that is only about 10 feet away. Likewise, you must restrict voice volume level—without losing emotion or intensity—for a pickup point only three or four feet away. Television is a close-up medium, and actors must play to this intimacy.

Precision

Actors must move very *precisely,* because they must be within the bounds of what the camera is shooting. If the actor's head is tilted at the wrong angle, the framing for a given shot may be off. If a moving actor does not "hit his mark" at exactly the right spot behind the sofa, he may ruin the impact of an emotional close-up. Sometimes directors have actors "cheat to camera." An actor, in a two-shot for instance, will be directed to turn his or her face slightly toward the camera—rather than looking directly at the other actor straight on. Such *cheating* is not perceived by the viewer, but it does result in more of a head-on shot into the camera.

Television exists generally in a demanding and nonflexible time frame. Most dramatic programs have to be squeezed (or stretched) into given time slots—multiples of a half hour, minus requisite time for commercials. This means that you, as an actor, may need to adjust pacing very precisely, speeding up or slowing down delivery of lines or action. This is especially a major concern with soap operas and situation comedies where there can be little flexibility in timing. It is less of a concern for filmed dramas, however, where

the exact timing can be worked out in the editing process by cutting or augmenting silent footage, panoramic long shots, and chase sequences.

Quick Study

Compared to the stage and to theatrical motion pictures, television drama is a quick-study medium. Whether working with single-camera or multiple-camera techniques, regular actors in a continuing series must learn up to an hourlong script every week—the equivalent of two feature-length motion pictures every month. For the actor in the hourlong daytime soap opera, the pace and discipline is even more demanding—up to an hour of dialogue every day!

Performers and actors are very important to any video production. They are what the home audience sees. All positions are important, however. A mistake by anyone, cast or crew, affects the overall quality of the production.

Discussion Questions

1. Of all the jobs listed in this chapter, which would you prefer? Why?
2. Discuss what you think would be the main disciplines needed by stage managers, camera operators, audio operators, graphic operators, and video operators.
3. If a friend who was going to be on a television talk show for the first time asked you for some helpful hints about what to wear and how to perform, what would you tell him or her?
4. What are some of the major differences between being a television performer and a TV actor?

Footnotes

1. Depending on the actual production setup and the traditional organization of the studio/station, the AD may be labeled either "assistant director" or "associate director." The Directors Guild of America officially refers to the position as "associate director" because the "assistant director" title is traditionally used in the film industry.

2. "Stage manager" is a term brought over from the theater. The first TV term used for this person was "floor manager," but

because the person is the director's studio representative, some studios/stations use the term "floor director." "Stage manager" is now probably the most commonly used term, but all three terms are used interchangeably.

3. Sometimes performers are tied into the communication system because they are wearing an earphone for an interrupted feedback system through which the director can communicate with them. News reporters, for example, often wear these when they are in the field so they know when to start talking.

4. In union situations, the stage manager may be restrained from crossing jurisdictional lines, such as giving orders to the lighting crew.

5. *TelePrompTer*™ is a registered trademark of the Teleprompter Corporation. Many companies now produce prompting equipment, but the word *teleprompter* has stuck, and devices manufactured by other companies are often generically referred to as teleprompters.

6. For most TV shows, the term used for the person who designs the overall look of the show is "art director." "Production designer" is used for highly stylized productions that need a great deal of design coordination—mostly science-fiction movies such as *Star Wars* and *Jurassic Park*. The "set designer" just works with the elements of the set, not the overall look.

7. Several books that can be consulted for overall information on acting are: Patrick Tucker, *How to Act for the Camera* (New York: Routledge Press, 1993); John Harrop, *Acting* (New York: Routledge Press, 1992); Tony Barr, Eric Stephen Kline, and Edward Asner, *Acting for the Camera* (New York: HarperCollins, 1997); and Hayes Gooden, *A Complete Compendium of Acting and Performing in Two Parts* (Sydney: Ensemble Press, 1992).

Chapter 3

Audio

The audio system is a natural place to begin the study of audio/video production. The basic principles of equipment function and operation are easy to understand, and they provide a convenient frame of reference for the later study of multiple-camera video. The concept of how both *disciplines* and *techniques* relate to production can be clearly applied to the field of audio. For example, knowing the steps needed to connect a microphone so that it functions through an audio console is a matter of applying several basic *techniques*. However, the care with which the operator then works to test the quality and loudness parameters of that mic for its eventual use is very much a matter of individual *discipline*.

This chapter includes a simple explanation of how sound is controlled. It starts with how a microphone can transform the human voice into an electronic signal and then describes the functions that act on sound as it progresses through the studio and control room. Following that, it discusses, in some detail, the major pieces of equipment that you, as an audio operator for a studio production, are likely to work with—namely, microphones, recording equipment, connecting equipment, and the audio console.

The material in this chapter should enable you to build both audio techniques and disciplines and to understand both the technical and creative aspects of sound. It includes:

- A description of the basic control functions of transducing, channeling, mixing, amplifying, shaping, monitoring, and recording (3.1).
- How dynamic and condenser mics differ in their transducing methods (3.1).
- How digital technology encodes the analog signal (3.1).
- Knowledge needed for troubleshooting sound problems (3.1).
- Types of signal-processing equipment used for shaping (3.1).

- Types of audio monitors, including those used by cast and crew (3.1).
- Pickup patterns and other characteristics related to mics (3.2).
- Microphone holders (3.2).
- Characteristics of different types of recording and playback equipment (3.3).
- How to care for cables and connectors (3.4).
- Types of connectors (3.4).
- How to use a patch bay (3.4).
- Functions of a simple production console that might be used for studio production (3.5).
- More advanced audio board functions (3.5).
- The flexibility of digital audio workstations (3.6).
- Methods for ensuring proper sound reproduction (3.7).
- The concept of commands of preparation and commands of execution (3.8).

3.1 Seven Basic Control Functions

Each piece of audio equipment in the **control room** and **studio** is designed to move, modify, or otherwise control a signal in one or more of the following seven ways:

1. **Transducing:** converting sound waves into electrical energy and back again.
2. **Channeling:** routing the signals and sending them wherever necessary.
3. **Mixing:** combining two or more sound sources.
4. **Amplifying:** increasing (or decreasing) the signal strength.
5. **Shaping:** creatively improving or, for other reasons, changing the quality of a sound.
6. **Monitoring:** hearing or seeing an indication of the quality and volume of sound sources at various stages of control.
7. **Recording** and **playing back:** retaining a sound in permanent electronic form for later use.

Some components perform more than one function. For example, the speaker that *transduces* a signal into listenable sound is obviously also a *monitor.* The audio board used to *mix* sound sources often includes controls that *shape* the quality of the sound. Understanding the essential elements of the audio system in your own facility is the necessary prerequisite for successful equipment operation in any production situation.

Transducing

The process through which sound (voices, music, etc.) is converted into an electrical audio signal is referred to as *transducing.* The tone production of a human voice or musical instrument creates pressure waves in

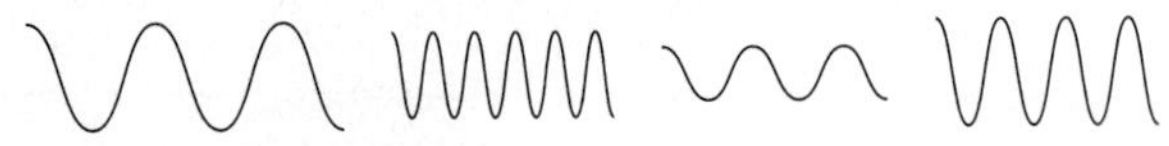

Figure 3.1

Frequency and amplitude. The second wave would be a higher pitch than the first wave because its frequency is greater. The fourth wave would be louder than the third one because its amplitude (height) is greater.

air molecules. If, for example, these waves are produced at a constant rate of 440 **hertz (cycles per second),**[1] the result is the musical tone of A above middle C on the piano.[2] Bass sounds have fewer cycles per second than treble sounds. Another way of saying this is that treble sounds have a higher **frequency** than bass sounds.[3] Men's voices have frequencies around 500 hertz, while women's voices are more likely to range in the area of 1,500 hertz. The higher the frequency, the higher the **pitch.** Another characteristic of a sound wave is its height, or **amplitude.** The higher the wave, the louder the sound. The sound of someone screaming will have a higher amplitude than the sound of a whisper. Figure 3.1 shows frequency and amplitude characteristics of sound waves.

Types of Microphones

When sound is transduced by a microphone, audible sound pressure waves, with their particular frequencies and amplitudes, move through the air and come in contact with the **diaphragm** of the microphone. Some types of microphones, referred to as **dynamic** mics, contain a **magnet** and a **coil.** The sound waves cause the diaphragm to vibrate within the magnetic field,

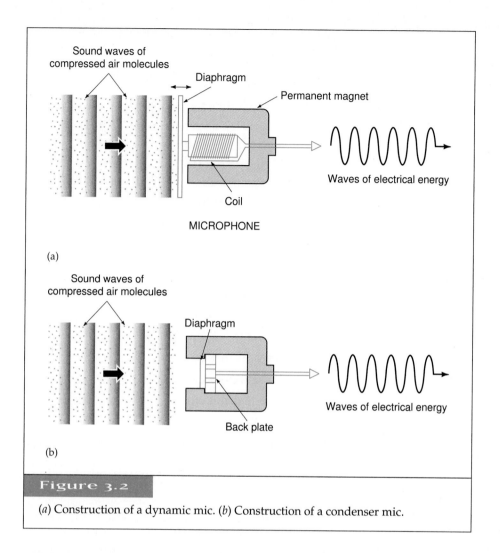

Sound waves of
compressed air molecules

Diaphragm

Permanent magnet

Waves of electrical energy

Coil

MICROPHONE

(a)

Sound waves of
compressed air molecules

Diaphragm

Waves of electrical energy

Back plate

(b)

Figure 3.2

(*a*) Construction of a dynamic mic. (*b*) Construction of a condenser mic.

and this sets up a current in the coil. (See Figure 3.2a.) In this way the sound signal is transduced into an electronic form that retains its original frequency and amplitude information. The structure of a dynamic mic makes it able to tolerate rough handling as well as temperature and humidity extremes.

Other microphones, know as **condenser** mics, also have a movable diaphragm to receive sound waves. The difference lies in the condenser mic's use of an electrically charged **backplate** just behind the diaphragm. The two elements form what is called a **capacitor,** enabling the unit to generate voltage in response to sound wave pressure. (See Figure 3.2b.) This structure not only produces very high quality sound but also allows the unit to be as small as a clip-on *lapel* mic. While a dynamic mic can generate its own charge, this condenser unit must have a source of electricity to function. One way is to have batteries located in the handle or in a portable battery pack. Another solution to the need for power is using what is called **phantom power.** In this case, the power is a small current sent to the mic through its cable from the audio console. Condenser microphones that have a permanently charged backplate are another option. A condenser mic is not quite as durable as a dynamic mic, but it has slightly better frequency response. Other characteristics of mics are discussed in section 3.2.

Analog and Digital

Once the microphone has transduced the sound (changed it from audible sound to electrical energy), the electronic **waveform** is said to be an **analog** of the original sound pressure wave, since the electronic wave retains essential elements, such as frequency and amplitude, that characterized the original sound pressure wave. At this point it can be

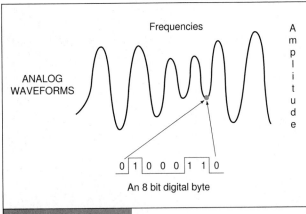

ANALOG WAVEFORMS

Frequencies

Amplitude

0 1 0 0 0 1 1 0

An 8 bit digital byte

Figure 3.3

The location of this digital byte roughly illustrates that it could be serving as part of a sample of the amplitude of a particular analog wave. It would be one of a large number of samples taken of that wave in the process of converting to a digital signal.

routed through analog equipment such as analog cassette tape recorders.

With **digital** playback and recording systems, the signal goes through an additional encoding (and later decoding) stage. Using computer technology, the characteristics of the analog wave are analyzed, or **sampled,** at numerous points of its structure. The resulting encoded information describing such factors as frequency and amplitude is now in the form of groups, or **bytes,** of on (1) or off (0) pulses called **bits,** as shown in Figure 3.3. Commonly a byte is composed of eight bits. Bytes can be further combined into two- and three-byte groups. A 16-bit grouping (two bytes) is often used for recording sound on a *digital audiotape (DAT)*.

One of the advantages of a digital signal is that it retains its quality as it is duplicated, or **dubbed,** and moved from point to point. This is because the digital signal is discrete on and off pulses that can always be duplicated, whereas an analog signal is a wave that changes slightly each time it goes through a process. This is akin to trying to redraw the waves of an analog signal—you are bound to draw them a little differently when you redo them—as opposed to copying down the numbers 1 and 0 in the correct order. When digital signals are transmitted, they are **transparent** because the quality of sound stays the same as the bytes move from one place to another.

Speakers

Whatever the sound's final destination, it will probably also be heard on a speaker in the audio booth. The speaker is also a *transducer,* something like a microphone, with the diaphragm, coil, and magnet now operating in reverse order. (See Figure 3.4.) The electrical energy of the signal puts the diaphragm into pulsating motion, pushing against the air molecules. When it moves at a rate of 440 hertz, for example, it creates sound pressure waves reproducing the original tone of A above middle C. If the signal is digital, it must be decoded from its digital form back into analog before it can be heard from the speaker.

Channeling

Channeling refers to moving sound from one place to another. In television studios, this is usually accomplished over wires, although obviously sound can be moved through the airwaves in a **wireless** manner. The sound from someone's lips is "channeled" to the microphone through the air. **Wireless mics** send the signal from a small antenna on the mic to a nearby receiver that then attaches to other equipment through wires. Signals from the television station **antenna** travel through airwaves, as do signals from a **satellite.**

But within a TV studio, where distances are short and most equipment stays in the same place, channeling is generally done through cables. Both the cables and the equipment have **connectors** so that sound can be channeled a number of ways. For example, most microphones have a connector at the end so that the mic can be connected to a cable with a similar connector. (Types of connectors are discussed in section 3.4.) This cable has a connector at the other end that can plug into the audio board or, if preferred, into some other piece of equipment such as a tape recorder.

Channeling Paths

In reality, cables rarely go directly from microphones in the studio to the audio board in the control room—the studio floor would be cluttered with wires. More often the mic cables plug into connectors placed in the studio walls near where the talent will be speaking.

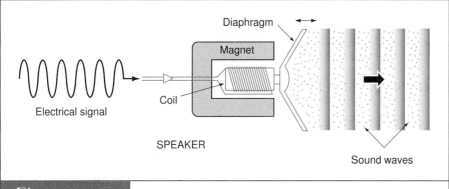

Figure 3.4

The construction of a speaker. When the electrical signal reaches the speaker coil, it produces fluctuations in the magnetic field that then cause the diaphragm of the speaker to vibrate, creating sound waves that reproduce the original sound picked up by the microphone.

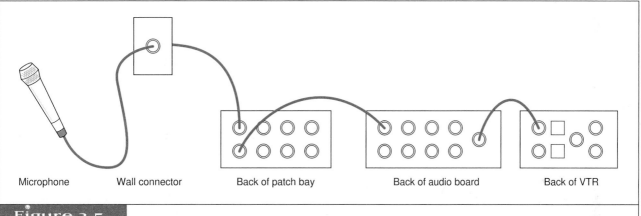

Figure 3.5

The channeling path for an audio signal as it might exist in a TV production facility. The sound goes from a mic to a connector in the wall of the studio. From there it goes by wire through the studio and control room walls to the patch bay. From the patch bay it is routed to the audio board and from the audio board to the videotape recorder.

Sometimes they plug into a **snake,** which is a box of connectors that can be moved about the studio; it has a cable that goes to the studio wall. Then wires go inside the walls to the area of the audio console where, once again, a connector is used to send the signal into the board.

Sometimes the wire inside the wall goes to a **patch bay,** and from the patch bay wires go to a variety of places, such as different inputs on the audio board, an audiotape recorder, a videotape recorder, and the station transmitter. The patch bay (as explained in section 3.4) allows sound to travel to different places without the need to reposition cable.

Once the signal gets from the microphone to an audio board, it is further channeled through the board. Most consoles have an on/off switch for each signal so that unwanted sounds do not accidentally come into the board. Consoles also have switches that channel sound in different ways depending on whether the sound is coming from a microphone or from some other piece of equipment such as a CD player or a tape machine. All of this is discussed in more detail in section 3.5. From the audio board the sound is usually further channeled to a videotape recorder or some other recording or distribution equipment as well as to speakers. (See Figure 3.5.)

Troubleshooting

Understanding channeling is one of TV production's most important *disciplines.* The concept of input/output is very important. As the signal moves through any system, it is repeatedly going into, through, and out of a series of controls and other components. The output of one component becomes the input of the next.

If you are acting as the audio operator and find that the sound going into the microphone is not getting to the audio board, you need to know the input/output path the sound should be taking so you can trace it and troubleshoot. Do you have a faulty connector? Does a wire need to be soldered? Have you connected correctly through the patch bay? Are the switches on the audio board in the correct position? Is the speaker volume up? A disciplined audio operator makes a systematic check of the channeling path and finds the problem. An undisciplined one randomly flips switches and changes cables, wasting precious time.

Mixing

It seems obvious now that the ability to blend and control a number of sound sources and to control separately the volume levels of each would be a primary requisite for any type of audio production. History tell us, however, that early radio studios had only one microphone and that volume control was accomplished by placing people and musicians closer or farther away from one mic. Fortunately, engineers developed the **audio console** (also called the **audio board**), which allows a number of audio sources to be fed into this one piece of equipment.

Within the audio board, sounds can be mixed together. For example, music from a CD can be played at the same time an announcer is speaking, and the two sounds can be joined in such a way that the music does not overpower the voice. At a particular point the sound effect of an airplane can join the other two sounds. The music and sound effects can fade out entirely as the announcer says a particularly important line. All of this, accomplished by adjusting the **faders** (volume controls) of the audio console, is discussed more fully in section 3.5.

Amplifying

The sound that comes from a microphone is very weak. In order to be heard it must be *amplified* a number of times as it is channeled through a system. Audio boards have amplifiers built into them that boost the microphone signal.

The other sounds coming into a board (such as that from CDs, MiniDiscs, or tape recorders) also need to be amplified but not as much as the sound from a mic. Therefore, the board routes mic sound through more amplification than it does sound from other equipment. For this reason most boards have switches to designate whether the sound is a **mic feed** or a **line feed** from some other piece of equipment.

Once sound is out of the board, it often needs further amplification. For example, it may need to go through another amplifier before it can be properly heard from a speaker.

Shaping

Shaping, often referred to as **signal processing,** is a process of altering the tonal characteristics of sound. It is both a technical and a creative function. A number of subtle but important things can be done to affect the quality of a sound signal.

Reasons for Shaping

In both a technical and a creative sense, much of the technique and discipline of a trained audio operator results in the ability to reproduce the same quality and dimension that existed in an original sound pressure wave—replicating the natural sound as we would hear it without electronic intervention. A related goal is that of creating an enhanced version of that original sound so that it sounds like the tone the listener *expects* to hear in a given program situation. The problem of turning natural sound into electronically reproduced sound is that much of what shapes the quality of the sound is strongly affected by the physical conditions of the recording location as well as by the microphones and other audio equipment being used.

In addition, the quality of sound from a musical instrument (or voice) is shaped not only by the main frequency of the sound (called the **fundamental**) but also by the presence of a number of higher frequency

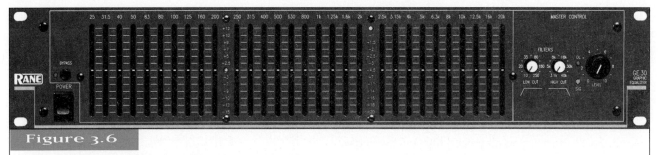

Figure 3.6

A graphic equalizer. The controls are moved up or down to emphasize or de-emphasize certain bands of frequencies. The controls actually form a line graph so it is easy to tell what is boosted and what is not. *Photo courtesy of Rane Corporation.*

overtones produced by the instrument in addition to the fundamental note. While these overtones (also known as **harmonics**) are produced at much *lower amplitudes* (loudness) than the fundamental tone, they are very definitely picked up by the human ear. Humans can hear ranges from a low rumble at 20 cycles per second (hertz) up to a possible high of 20,000 cycles per second. These overtones vibrate at different degrees of loudness according to the resonating qualities of each instrument (**timbre**). Brass reflects differently than wood. A trumpet has a different sound from a clarinet because its overtone pattern is very different from that of a clarinet.

Sound is further affected by a number of other things such as soundproofing on the studio walls and cloth material in a curtain. These surfaces cause the overtones to be absorbed, and therefore lost, or to be reflected and picked up by the mic. In either case, the result definitely alters the quality of sound picked up by the mic.

The electronic components of the audio system further shape the tone of the original sound. This process starts with the selection of the microphone and continues through other components of the console. Mics vary greatly in their designed capacity to capture overtones at varying distances and levels of loudness. They should be used only for the purpose for which they were intended. The all-purpose mic designed for an outdoor public-address system is not able to reproduce the subtleties of musical tones required in a commercial recording studio.

Sometimes sound needs to be changed to fit the creative needs of a TV program. You might want to change a voice recording so that the voice sounds like it is coming from an answering machine or emanating from a cave. This, too, requires shaping.

Shaping Equipment

There are various signal-processing "black boxes" you can use to shape sounds. **Reverberation** units give sound a bit of a bounce or echo.[4] **Equalizers** strengthen certain frequencies to alter pitch relationships of sounds.[5] (See Figure 3.6.) They can give someone's voice a deeper, fuller sound by emphasizing the lower pitches, or they can bring overtones, absorbed by a studio curtain, back up to their original level. **Filters** cut out certain frequencies.[6] If you have picked up a hum from a power line, you can sometimes get rid of it by filtering out the particular frequency of the hum. A **compressor**[7] can be used to compress the distance between the lowest and highest volume levels, in effect raising the lowest levels to bring them up close to the loudest levels the system can handle. Other shaping equipment includes **limiters, flangers, digital delay** units, and noise reduction systems such as **Dolby.**[8] Audio consoles often have shaping functions built in, as will be discussed in section 3.5.

Monitoring

An audio operator who is amplifying, mixing, and shaping sounds needs to know how the final product, or individual segments of it, are going to sound. This monitoring can be done both aurally and visually.

Speakers

The most common way to monitor sound is to listen to it on a speaker. Television facilities usually have a number of speakers. There may be one speaker, called an **air monitor,** through which you can hear the sound as it is broadcast over the air for a live feed. A **program monitor** provides a high-quality reproduction of the sound coming from the audio board and going to a recorder or out over the air.

Sometimes you need to hear one particular sound. For example, you may need to cue a particular spot in some music on a CD while sending other sounds to a videotape recorder. A **cue monitor,** which operates off a cue button on the audio board, can facilitate listening to the CD separately without getting its sound mixed in with what is being recorded.

Talent sometimes needs to hear program audio. For example, dancers need to be able to hear the music they dance to. A **studio monitor** positioned on the walls of the studio brings in this sound. Sound should not be piped into the studio whenever mics are live, however, because the sound feeding back into the equipment through the mics will create the nasty squeal of **feedback.** Most studio monitors automatically cut off microphones when they are activated.

Individual pieces of equipment, such as the VTR, often have their own speakers so that the operators can hear what they are playing.

VU Meters

The **volume unit (VU) meter** provides a visual description of volume levels and the degrees of difference among the ongoing level changes. Some VU meters, such as the one in Figure 3.7, have a needle-sized pointer that is in constant motion as it indicates differing intensities of volume. On other equipment, the VU meter often consists of a column of **light emitting diodes (LED).** The effect is a bar of light that grows and shrinks (either horizontally or vertically) to indicate ongoing changes in volume level. (See Figure 3.8.)

VU meters are most commonly found on audio boards so that the audio operator can monitor the various sound sources. Often they are on other equipment as well so that audio levels can be calibrated to be the same throughout the system.

On VU meters that have a needle, this needle should **peak** (reach the high point of its swing) at the "0" position (refer again to Figure 3.7). On LED VU meters, the color of the lights usually changes from

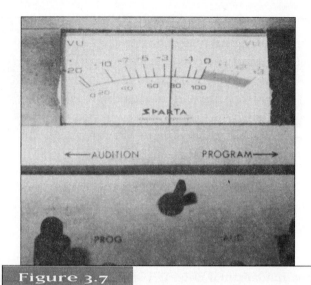

Figure 3.7

Volume unit (VU) meter. The traditional VU meter provides a depiction of continuing peaks and low points of an audio source. Higher decibel readings (beyond the 0) hold the possibility of signal distortion or clipping. The parallel percentage of modulation scale (shown here) is sometimes seen on VU meters. On many consoles there are individual meters for each channel as well as for the final line-out feed.

green to red at the point where the signal should peak. It is very important for an audio operator to pay attention to the peaking point because, as the amplification of the signal is increased beyond this point, not all frequencies are equally amplified. With analog sound this results in **distortion.** Digital sound that is too loud for the equipment often disappears, or **clips.** When levels drop below an acceptable minimum, they are not processed by the system and are lost.

Other Monitoring Capabilities

Often the director needs to communicate with the cast or crew. This type of monitoring is somewhat different from program monitoring because the quality does not need to be as high, but it is still a very important form of monitoring.

The main way that the director communicates to the crew is through an **intercom** system (sometimes referred to as the **PL** for **private line**). It is, in essence, a closed-circuit audio network that connects all primary production personnel by standard headsets

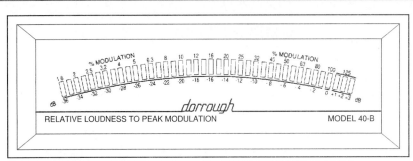

RELATIVE LOUDNESS TO PEAK MODULATION   MODEL 40-B

DORROUGH RELATIVE LOUDNESS TO PEAK MODULATION METER, Model 40-B

Figure 3.8

This meter uses LED bar graphs to indicate sound activity at lower dB levels in addition to peak volumes.   *Drawing courtesy of Dorrough Industries.*

Figure 3.9

The successful use of the intercommunication system both before and during production is essential not only for the director but also for lighting, audio, and assistant director duties.   *Photo courtesy of KABC-TV.*

with earpieces and small microphones. Technically, any crew member with a headset can talk to anyone else. In practice, the audio operator and technical director make heavy use of the system during setup time, but it is the director who is heard most of the time during a production. (See Figure 3.9.)

When directors (or others) need to talk to talent and/or talent and crew during setup, they often use the **studio address (SA)** system. This is a loudspeaker system that uses the studio monitor, usually the same one used for program audio. A talkback microphone (usually there is also one for the audio operator) in the control room enables the director to activate the studio speaker so he or she can talk to everyone regardless of whether or not they are wearing headsets. Most studios also have a talkback feature with a mic hanging in the studio so that anyone in the studio, including lighting crew members up on ladders, can be heard in the control room.

Obviously the studio address cannot be used during production because of feedback problems. If the director needs to talk to talent during the production, the talent can be wired with an **interrupted feedback (IFB)** system. This is a small monitor that fits in the talent's ear. It is often used for news, when the director must tell an anchor about a story change while the anchor is reading another story. Field reporters use them, too, so the director can tell the reporter when to begin a live stand-up.

Sometimes crew or talent need to hear program audio in addition to commands from the director. For example, boom operators need to hear program audio so they know if they are picking up sound properly, but they also need to be able to hear the director. PL, SA, and IFB systems can all be wired so that they can transmit program audio as well as crew comments.

Recording and Playing Back

An array of equipment can record and/or play back audio (see section 3.3). Some of it is older analog equipment, while the rest is newer digital equipment. Generally, audio systems can handle both.

For most television productions, the end result is a video recording that also, obviously, contains audio. Operators must exert *discipline* to make sure sounds travel from the microphone to the recorder in a manner than maintains the quality. Sound that is perfectly fine as it comes from the audio board but is distorted (or not recorded at all) as it goes through the recorder is obviously not acceptable.

Most of the equipment that records also plays back. Playback is important in many circumstances such as when a news story is to be incorporated in the evening news, when music is used for opening or closing credits, or when sound effects are part of a game-show routine.

3.2 Microphones

Microphones differ in how they pick up sound, and there is no such thing as a "perfect" mic for all applications. We have already discussed that dynamic and condenser mics differ in construction and that dynamic mics are more rugged while condenser mics have better frequency response (see section 3.1).

Pickup Patterns

In addition to differences in construction, microphones pick up in different patterns. Some are **omnidirectional,** meaning they pick up sound from all directions, while others are **cardioid,** picking up sound in a heart-shaped pattern. (See Figure 3.10.) Omnidirectional mics are good for picking up crowd noises at a ball game or sounds from a group of people in a circle. Cardioids are better when you want to pick up sounds in one direction while excluding sounds from other directions. They are generally used for TV studio production because they pick up talent voices without picking up the background noise of cameras moving in the studio.

Some mics have very narrow pickup patterns, usually referred to as **supercardioid** or **ultracardioid.** They pick up sound from a great distance away but pick up only a small area. **Bidirectional** mics pick up sound from two sides, making them useful if two people are directly facing each other.

Impedance

Mics (and other audio equipment) also come as high impedance and low impedance. **Impedance** is a type of resistance, measured in **ohms,** that cuts down on the amount of sound that gets through the mic. Low-impedance mics are better quality than high-impedance mics but are more expensive. For this reason, studios use low-impedance mics (600 ohms or less), while consumer equipment usually has high-impedance mics (10,000 ohms and higher). Because sound travels better through low-impedance mics, they can have long cables, whereas high-impedance mics are usually limited to about six feet of cable.

It is not a good idea to mix impedance, for example, to plug a high-impedance mic into a low-impedance

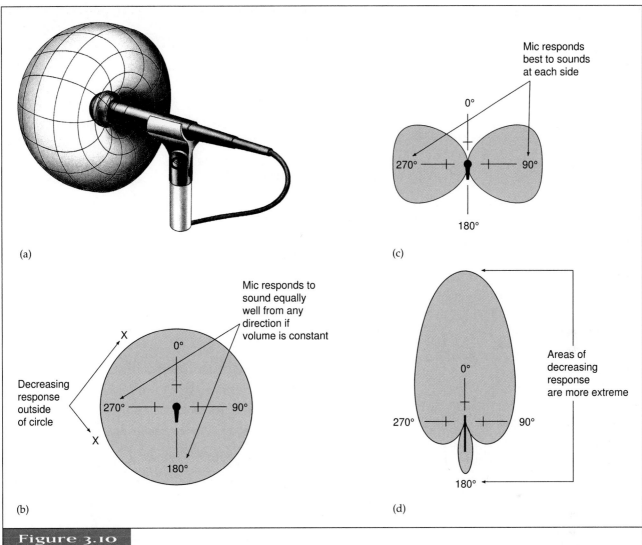

(a)

Mic responds
best to sounds
at each side

(c)

Mic responds to
sound equally
well from any
direction if
volume is constant

Decreasing
response
outside
of circle

(b)

Areas of
decreasing
response
are more extreme

(d)

Figure 3.10

(*a*) Pickup patterns are actually a 3D sphere as depicted in this cardioid pattern. For simplicity's sake they are often drawn in two dimensions as shown for (*b*) omnidirectional, (*c*) bidirectional, and (*d*) supercardioid.

tape recorder. There are transformers (sometimes built into connectors) that change signals from high to low and/or low to high impedance.

Frequency Response

Frequency response also differs from one mic to another—some pick up high pitches better than low pitches and vise versa. A mic that picks up all frequencies equally well is said to have a **flat** frequency response. One that picks up the human voice better than higher or lower frequencies is said to have a

speech bump. Some mics pick up certain pitches better at different positions. For example, the Shure cardioid mic shown in Figure 3.11 picks up 125-hertz frequencies but not 1,000-hertz frequencies toward the back of the mic. If you are producing a discussion program, you can use mics with more limited frequency response than those used in producing a musical show. Microphone manufacturers often provide charts to show frequency response characteristics so that you can choose the mic that is best for your particular application. (See Figure 3.12.)

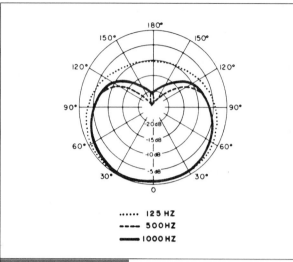

The different lines show the directional sensitivity of the Shure SM 58 mic at three different frequencies. The low 125-hertz sounds pick up better toward the back of the mic than do the 1,000-hertz sounds, which are more in line with the cardioid pattern of this mic.

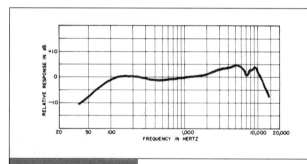

The frequency response chart gives the audio operator an accurate and quick indication of how a mic will perform at all frequency levels.

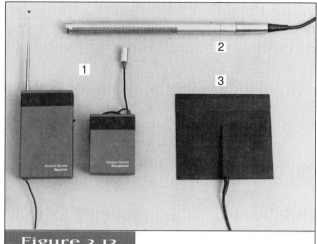

Three very different methods of picking up sound. (1) A lapel mic used in conjunction with wireless transmission and receiver units. (2) A highly directional long-distance "shotgun" mic. (3) A PZM surface-mount mic.

The SM 58 mic is well known in professional circles as a reliable hand/stand mic with a dynamic transducing element. The mic has a windscreen on the top of it.   *Photo courtesy of Shure Bros. Inc.*

Types of Microphones

Because mics are used in such a variety of situations, many types are needed. Very small mics, referred to as **lapel, lavaliere,** or **lav** mics, are meant to attach to a person's clothing. (See Figure 3.13, part 1). For optimum pickup, they are usually positioned slightly below the neck on a tie or blouse. Some come with an inconspicuous cord to put around the talent's neck. They are used for game shows, demonstrations, and other situations where it is undesirable to have an obvious mic.

Larger, more conspicuous mics are often used for news situations, where the viewer expects to see someone using a mic. Reporters often hold them in their hand, but sometimes, especially in news conferences, they are placed on a stand that rests on a podium or table. These mics are also used for many other situations—a concert in which the singer holds a mic by hand or a talk show where the mic sits on the host's desk. (See Figure 3.14.)

Sometimes these larger mics are attached to a **boom** that is moved around by a boom operator.

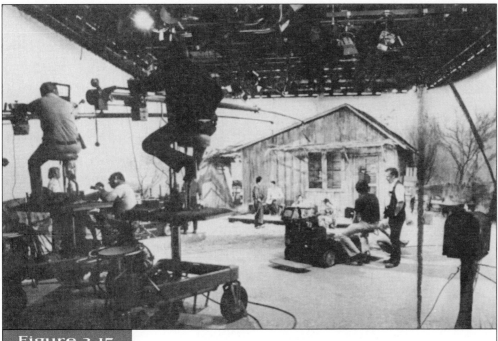

Figure 3.15

Two or more large studio perambulator booms usually are used to cover a drama or other program where hand mics cannot be used. *Photo courtesy of KCET-TV, Los Angeles.*

This is particularly common for dramas and sitcoms, where actors move about but where seeing the mic might spoil the reality. Booms come in various sizes and with varying degrees of maneuverability. Large **perambulator** booms (see Figure 3.15) are motorized and can move the mic into a variety of positions—up, down, left, right, in, out. Usually it takes two people to operate a perambulator—one to drive it and one to position the mic. Smaller booms, called **giraffes** (see Figure 3.16), have wheels and can be operated by one person. Simpler yet is the **fishpole,** a pole with a mic on the end that a person holds and moves above the heads of the people who are speaking.

Long, thin mics called **shotgun** mics (see Figure 3.13, part 2) have a supercardioid pickup pattern and are used when sound needs to be picked up at a distance. They are particularly useful for documentaries but are rarely used in the studio. **PZM** mics are flat mics that can attach to a table or wall to pick up overall sounds. (See Figure 3.13, part 3.)

Mics—be they lavs, handhelds, or any other form—can also be *wireless* (see Figure 3.13, part 1

again). In this case there is no wire going from the mic to the microphone connector in the wall. Rather, the mic has a small antenna that sends the sound through the air to a small receiver—sort of a miniature radio station. The receiver is then connected to the wall outlet. Wireless mics are used when the talent needs to move about—a singer or a talk-show host going into the audience.

Stereo Recording

Often television programs are recorded in **stereo.** There are a number of different ways to accomplish this. The simplest is to take the **monaural** signal from one microphone and send it to both the left and right channels of the stereo equipment. This is not true stereo, however, and does not allow for effects, such as the sound of an airplane that moves across the screen. Another way to record stereo is to place mics several feet from each other to pick up sounds much as the ear does **(split-pair miking).** Mics can also be crossed to form an X so that they pick up sounds from the left and the right **(cross-pair miking).** Another method, **mid-side miking,** picks up sound from the

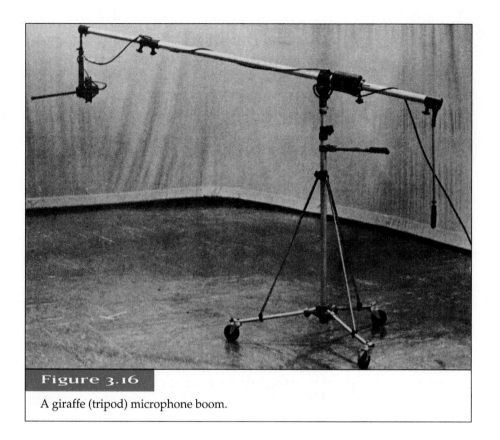

Figure 3.16

A giraffe (tripod) microphone boom.

middle and the two sides. (See Figure 3.17.) This type of miking can use three microphones (usually super-cardioid), or it can use two mics—a supercardioid mic for the middle sound and a bidirectional mic to pick up the sounds from left and right.

All these methods have their disadvantages. Both the split-pair and crossed-pair suffer because very little sound comes from the middle, where much of the action usually is. As a result the pickup can sound "spacey" (in the case of split-pair) or "unfocused" (in the case of crossed-pair). These two methods are also not very compatible with monaural sound because of the lack of center sound. The mid-side method solves the center problem and can easily be converted to monaural sound by using only the sound from the middle mic. However, it is complex to set up because the center and side sounds have to be very carefully balanced.

Some stereo mics are single mics and have elements in them that imitate the various miking patterns. They are not perfect, but they are simpler to set up and use than any of the mic setups described above. (See Figure 3.18.)

Of course, it is also possible to record **surround sound,** so that the final sound can come from five or six speakers located around the room. This type of recording is quite complex and usually beyond the realm of studio recording for student productions.

3.3 Outboard Equipment

Equipment used in conjunction with the audio console is often referred to as **outboard equipment** because it is outside the board. Most of it is used to record and play back. (See Figure 3.19.) The choices in this equipment have expanded in recent years as digital has taken hold. You will no doubt be familiar with at least some of this equipment, having used it in your home. Professional equipment operates much like consumer equipment, but professional equipment is sturdier because it is used in an active way for many hours of the day.

Professional equipment may also provide superior sound in terms of *frequency response* and **signal-**

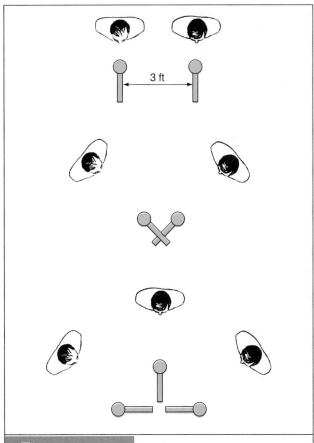

Figure 3.17

Three basic stereo microphone patterns. Top, the split-pair setup. Middle, the crossed pairs method. Bottom, M-S (mid-side) miking.

Figure 3.18

A stereo mic. This self-contained microphone includes the various elements needed to record stereo. *Photo courtesy of Audio-Technica.*

to-noise ratio (S/N). Frequency response has already been discussed in terms of microphones. High-quality outboard equipment is capable of receiving a wide range of frequencies from very low bass sounds to high trebles. The signal-to-noise ratio rates the amount of wanted sound that gets through a piece of equipment in relation to the unwanted noise that is not part of the original sound signal. Usually this unwanted sound comes from mechanical gears or electronic circuits. The higher the S/N, the better. Professional equipment usually has at least 60 units of signal for each unit of noise, whereas consumer equipment may have an S/N ratio closer to 40 to 1.

CD Players

No doubt the most ubiquitous of outboard equipment is the **CD (compact disk) player.** In fact, audio setups often have two CD players so that the audio operator can undertake quick transitions from the sound on one to the sound on the other. CDs used for professional production cue up quickly so that there is no *dead air* when going from one to the other. The quality of the digital sound and the small size and sturdiness of CDs make this an excellent technology for production. Of course, a great deal of music is prerecorded on CDs, and there are also some excellent sound-effects CDs that can be used effectively within programs. Some CD equipment records, but it is more likely to be used for postproduction in radio and music recording than in studio television production.

Turntables

The CD player has essentially replaced the older analog **turntable,** but many people still like the sound of vinyl, so turntables have not disappeared from TV facilities. Cueing a record is harder than cueing a CD.

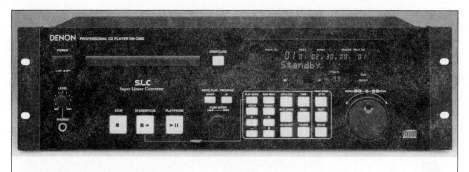

(a)

(b)

(c)

Figure 3.19

A variety of outboard recording/playback equipment. (*a*) A CD player. (*b*) A digital audio tape (DAT) recorder. (*c*) An analog cassette recorder. (*d*) A MiniDisc recorder. (*e*) A bank of cart machines. (*f*) A DigiCart. (*g*) A reel-to-reel recorder.   *Photo* a *and* d *courtesy of Denon Electronics; photos* b, c, *and* g *courtesy of Tascam; photos* e *and* f *courtesy of 360 Systems.*

(d)

(e)

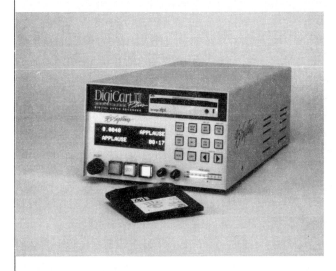

(f)

(g)

Figure 3.19—Concluded

You must find the spot you want and back up half a turn so that the turntable has time to get up to speed when you actually want to use the sound. Then you must make sure the vinyl record stays in that position (either by holding it or by turning off the motor). When it is time to play the selection, you must act quickly to avoid dead air.

DAT Recorders

Digital audio tape (DAT) is taking on an increasing role in studio production. Information in binary form (0s and 1s) is recorded onto the tape in a diagonal fashion, allowing a small 1/8-inch cassette tape to hold several hours of material. Portable units can record in the field, and larger console units can play back the material for studio production. Generally, DAT is used for material specially recorded for a particular program as opposed to preproduced material such as music and sound effects.

Cassette Recorders

Although DAT is increasingly replacing the analog **cassette recorder,** many are still in use. They are very inexpensive, and many people (including students) personally own them and can use them to acquire material to include within a program. At present they are more durable than DAT recorders, but DAT technology is improving in that regard.

MiniDisc Recorders

The **MiniDisc** is a digitally based recorder/player that records material on a special disk that is similar to a computer floppy disk. Again, there are portable and tabletop models. One of the big advantages of the MiniDisc is its editing capabilities. It is possible to edit within the recorder itself, so a reporter, for example, could record a story in the field and edit it on the way back to the studio. For television, this story would need to be accompanied by visuals, but the MiniDisc works well for an audio-based story with graphics.

Cartridge Recorders

For many years the analog **cartridge recorder** (often called the *cart machine*) was the workhorse of production centers, and it still sees use. The **cartridges** (*carts*) that fit into the player contain a continuous loop of tape that can be of short or long duration. When something is recorded on a cart, the machine places an inaudible **cue tone** on the tape that enables the tape to cue itself very accurately to the beginning of the recorded segment. Many studios keep a rack of carts for material they play often (station IDs, program theme music) or for material of short duration that must be cued up quickly (commercials, public-service announcements). Usually at least two cart machines are set up as outboard equipment so that the operator can feed the carts in and out of the machines while going from one to the other. There are banks of cart players that allow an operator to get ready for a whole commercial break by placing a large number of carts in machines and playing them one after another.

Digital Carts

A **digital cart** is not really a cartridge in the same sense as an analog cart. But it is designed to replace the analog cart and seems to be doing so. What it really amounts to is a computer with a great deal of storage that can hold a large number of digital audio files. Commercials, jingles, and the like can be produced in a digital editing system and outputted to a **zip drive.** The disk from the zip can be placed in the digital cart in order to transfer the audio file to the cart. Then the audio operator simply brings up the file and activates it when it needs to air. Or an operator can program a number of files to play one after another and in that way handle a commercial break in the same way that the operator used to do by loading a series of analog carts into cart players.

Reel-to-Reel Recorders

The very first analog tape recorders were **reel-to-reel.** The tape was not on a cassette or cartridge or computer-based disk but rather on a single reel that had to be manually threaded past the tape-recorder heads onto a take-up reel. The material on the tape had to be manually cued by finding the spot where you wanted to start, backing up a bit so the tape machine had time to get up to speed, and then hitting "play" at the appropriate moment. One of the advantages reel-to-reel configurations had over cassette and cartridge systems was that reel-to-reel tapes were easier to edit. The tape was exposed as it went from one reel to another so it was fairly easy to use a razor blade, a grease pencil, and some adhesive tape to edit out portions of tape that were not wanted or move sections of the tape from one place to another. Now, however, editing is more likely to be undertaken in a computer, so reel-to-reel recorders are becoming obsolete.

Videotape Audio Tracks

Many types of productions have videotape inserts, in which short, previously recorded tape segments are incorporated into the body of the program being assembled. The videotape recorder (whether analog or digital) is probably not near the audio console as the other outboard equipment is, so it is the responsibility of the video operator, not the audio operator, to actually start the videotape. The audio operator needs to make sure the sound on the tape is brought up on the audio board at the proper time. The audio operator and video operator should work together before the production to coordinate roll-ins. It is good *discipline* for the video operator to play the tape while the audio operator makes note of the volume to ensure that the volume is correct when the tape is played for the actual production.

Sometimes, rather that a videotape recorder, an audio operator plays back material from a **video disk** machine. This is especially true now that the **DVD (digital versatile disk)** has been developed and is being incorporated into studios.

Synthesizers

Originally **synthesizers** were tied only to the music record business. They were difficult to operate and could produce only one sound at a time, so they were of little value to radio or television production. But they have improved greatly over the years and now can be used by people with no musical knowledge to mimic and create just about any type of sound. As a result, audio operators sometimes encounter the music keyboards or other equipment (such as *drum machines*) associated with them. Synthesizers use a digitally based control system known as **musical instrument digital interface (MIDI)**. This term refers to a protocol that governs the information used to control a synthesizer. Some audio equipment is manufac-

tured so that it is MIDI compatible and can interface easily with synthesizers.

Servers and Other Computer-Based Equipment

Servers (see Chapter 7) are powerful computers with a large amount of storage that can hold video as well as audio. They are usually located at some distance from the audio console, so once again it is the responsibility of audio operators to make sure they can properly record any sound that might come from or go to a server during the course of a production. As time progresses, audio operators will probable be playing more and more computer-generated sound, whether from a server, a digital audio workstation (see section 3.6), or something that is as yet not invented.

3.4 Cables, Connectors, and Patch Bays

As previously mentioned, the sound from the microphone (and other equipment) is channeled through the use of cables, connectors, and patch bays. All of this equipment must be handled very carefully because it can be easily damaged. Cables consist of tiny wires that can be easily broken, but these broken wires are particularly difficult to find because they are inside a plastic casing. To prevent this breakage, cable should be neatly coiled after it is used. One effective coiling technique is to string the cable on the floor in a figure-eight pattern and then fold the two halves together and hang the cable on a peg. When cable is coiled properly, it should look like the cable in Figure 3.20. It takes *discipline* to do this neatly and correctly at the end of a long production, but it pays off in the long run. You should never pull on the cable when you are disconnecting it; use the connector instead. But treat the connector gently; don't force it because the prongs can bend or break, rendering it ineffective or, worse yet, intermittent.

Cables

Cables consist of wires through which the signals are sent. These cables can be either balanced or unbalanced.

XLR Plug to XLR Jack

Figure 3.20

This is how cable should look when it is coiled properly.

Balanced cables have three wires—two to carry the signal and one to act as a ground. **Unbalanced cables** have just two wires—one carries signal and the other carries part of the signal and also acts as a ground. In both cases, the wires are sheathed in an outer cover of plastic. Balanced cables are higher quality (and more expensive) than unbalanced cables because they are less susceptible to the electronic interference caused by, for example, a vacuum cleaner or power tool. Generally, professional studios use balanced systems while unbalanced cables are found in consumer gear.

Connectors

Cables have **connectors** on each end so that they can transport sound from one place to another. One type of connector is the **XLR connector.** It is used with a balanced system because it has three conductors, one for each wire. (See Figure 3.21a.) With the aid of a **guide pin,** the prongs of the male **plug** fit into the female **jack** so that they are tightly connected. The only way to unlock them is to press on the connector lock.

Another type of connector is the **phone connector.** The **sleeve** and **tip** of the male plug fit into the female jack. (See Figure 3.21b.) A **miniphone connector** is similar to a phone connector except that it is smaller. (See Figure 3.21c.) Male **RCA connector** have a prong surrounded by an outer sleeve that fits into the female jack. (See Figure 3.21d.)

There are a variety of connectors because each has a different purpose. As already alluded to, XLR connectors are used in professional situations because they are designed for low-impedance mikes and balanced cables. However, they are the largest and bulkiest of the connectors, so they are not really suitable for most consumer gear, which is more likely to employ miniphone connectors. RCA connectors are versatile in that they are used for both professional and consumer applications and also for both audio and video (although not at the same time). Both phone and miniphone connectors can carry either mono or stereo sound. If the connector has one ring, it can carry only mono; if it has two rings, it is capable of transporting stereo. For both the XLR and RCA connectors, one connector can carry only mono. Two connectors are needed to handle stereo, one for the right channel and one for the left.

Sometimes two pieces of equipment that need to be connected may have different connectors. For example, a DAT with a miniphone may need to connect to a VTR with an RCA connection. Other times the equipment may have a male plug but the end of the cable also has a male plug and the two cannot connect. To solve these types of problems there are **adapters;** for example, the female end is a miniphone and the male end is an RCA, or both ends of the adapter are female RCA. Figure 3.22 shows an array of adapters.

Patch Bays

As previously mentioned, a patch bay is in a system that enables signals to be connected to various pieces of equipment without restringing cables all over the facility. Patch bays are boxes that usually consist of a

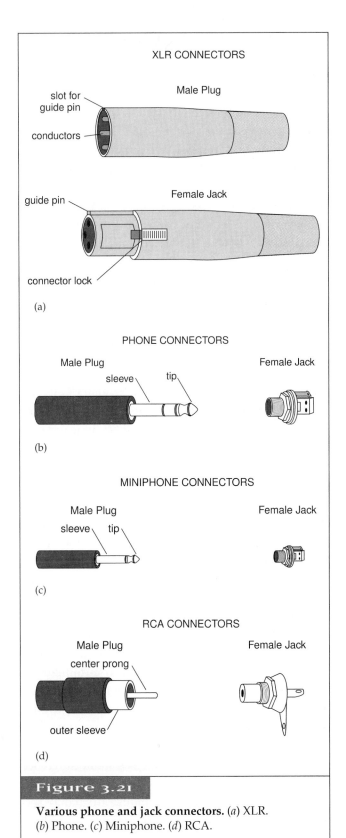

Figure 3.21

Various phone and jack connectors. (*a*) XLR. (*b*) Phone. (*c*) Miniphone. (*d*) RCA.

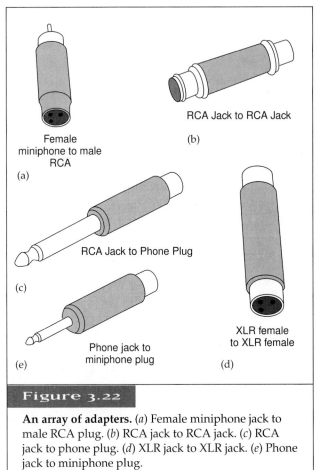

Figure 3.22

An array of adapters. (*a*) Female miniphone jack to male RCA plug. (*b*) RCA jack to RCA jack. (*c*) RCA jack to phone plug. (*d*) XLR jack to XLR jack. (*e*) Phone jack to miniphone plug.

large number of *phone jacks.* One row of jacks is for sounds coming from equipment, and another row is for sounds going to equipment. Each piece of equipment is wired to the back of a particular jack. Some pieces are wired both for a signal to come in and a signal to go out in order to allow for flexibility. For example, sometimes you may want to send the sound from the DAT to the VTR; other times you may want to send the VTR audio to the DAT. When a signal needs to go from one place to another, you simply use a cable (usually called a **patch cord**) with male phone plugs at each end to transfer the audio from the top row to the bottom row. Figure 3.23 shows a patch bay with a patch cord going from the DAT to the VTR.

If, using Figure 3.23, sound needed to go from mic 1 to channel 1 of the audio board, you would not need to use a patch cord. That is because this connection is

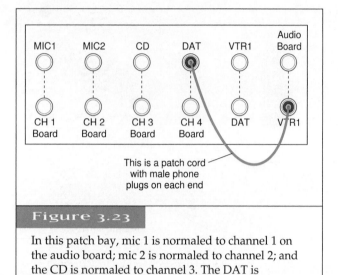

MIC1 MIC2 CD DAT VTR1 Audio Board

CH 1 Board CH 2 Board CH 3 Board CH 4 Board DAT VTR1

This is a patch cord with male phone plugs on each end

Figure 3.23

In this patch bay, mic 1 is normaled to channel 1 on the audio board; mic 2 is normaled to channel 2; and the CD is normaled to channel 3. The DAT is normaled to channel 4, but in this illustration it is patched so that it will go to VTR 1.

normaled. If microphone 1 is not patched into something else, it goes to channel 1 because that is where the engineer has decided it will need to go most often—where it *normally* goes. Most patch bays are wired so that whatever is on the top will normally go to the bottom; this saves time, as the operator does not have to make a patch for setups that rarely change. The connections at the back of the patch bay are usually **hardwired,** which means they are permanently wired in some way, such as *soldering.*

If audio signals within the studio always go to the same places, the facility may not have a patch bay. Mic 2 could be hardwired or connected with an XLR plug to channel 2 on the audio board and never moved. Likewise the output of the audio board could be taken directly to the VTR. But for studios that need flexibility, a patch bay is the answer.

3.5 Audio Consoles

Audio consoles come in many configurations from very basic to very complex. (See Figure 3.24.) Basic ones are usually used for live and live-on-tape television work, while more complex ones are used for postproduction editing and complicated production such as recording musical bands. The more complex

(and more expensive) consoles tend to have a great deal of shaping capability—knobs and buttons for delaying the signal, removing some of the frequencies, and so forth. When you are taping something live, you rarely have time to change these settings, for example, to get just the right amount of echo. In fact, a large number of controls can impede you because something is invariably set in the wrong position for what you want to do and you have to troubleshoot through an array of controls to correct the problem. However, some facilities can afford only one audio board, so they opt for a more complicated board that can be used for a variety of applications. Experienced television audio operators also like to have complicated boards so that they can set up special sounds ahead of time and then incorporate them into programs.

In this discussion of audio boards we will examine in detail the controls of a *generic* audio console that we have "designed." This will acquaint you with the main audio board functions that you will need for your productions. Then we will discuss, in less detail, other functions that you may find on the audio board you use. In all probability we will discuss a number of functions your board does not have and will not mention some that it does have. Also, controls will be in different positions on our make-believe board than on yours. The only way to truly understand the operation of an audio console is to work with it. But once you have mastered one board, it is very easy to transfer your skills to another board because they all operate using the same principles.

Another difference with audio consoles is that some are analog and some are digital. The newer digital boards have been designed to minimize the amount of time someone who has operated an analog board needs to learn the digital board. So digital boards operate in much the same way as analog boards (we've tried to make our generic board applicable to both analog and digital). The main difference with digital boards is that some have a computer screen so that you can click a mouse to change settings. (See Figure 3.25.) For example, instead of having a knob to adjust equalization, you can select frequencies you want to enhance by clicking on them on the computer screen. You can also save settings in the

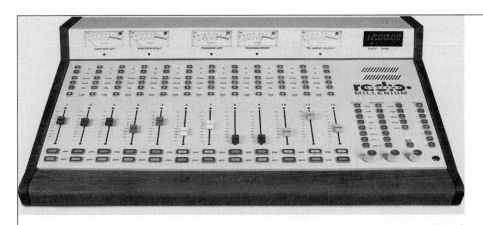

(a)

(b)

Figure 3.24

(*a*) A simple basic board. (*b*) A much more complex board.   *Photo a courtesy of Radio Systems; photo b courtesy of Solid State Logic.*

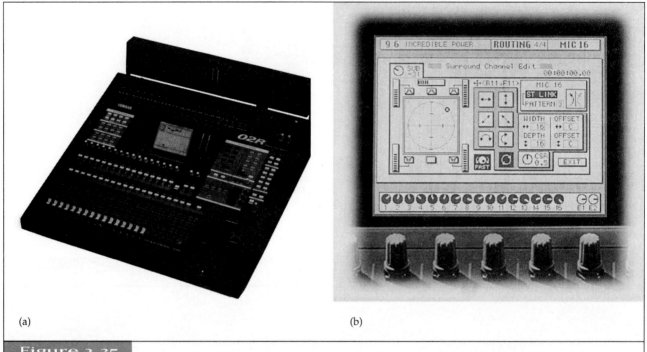

(a)   (b)

Figure 3.25

This Yamaha 02R digital audio console (*a*) contains a screen that displays a number of control settings and other operational information. For example, the screen shown in (*b*) is used to preset conditions for creating surround sound. These settings can be stored in the computer for later recall.   *Photo courtesy of Yamaha.*

computer and then reinstitute them for a program a week or two later.

In addition, some boards are mono and some are stereo. For simplicity, we are going to describe a mono board, but if this board were stereo, we would need two faders for inputs (i.e., one for the CD right channel and one for the CD left channel). Some consoles, though, have stereo buses so that the two sounds are tied together for one fader.

The Basic Board

Our generic board shown in Figure 3.26 is called an *8 in, 4 out* board. It has the capacity to manipulate eight different sounds at the same time. (You can actually wire in 16 sounds, as we will see a little later, but you can't play them all at the same time.) Whatever you bring into the board can be sent to four different places as it leaves the board.

Even this basic board may look a bit intimidating to you because of all its knobs and buttons. But if you look at it carefully you will see a great deal of duplication. Each channel has the same controls. As we dis-

cuss them, you should keep in mind that they all work the same.

You will note that all the inputs can be used for microphones or for some other piece of equipment (a situation that will be explained shortly). We have labeled the channels (it is a very good idea to label the board to whatever extent possible) indicating the use of each. We have arranged our board with the idea that we will generally use the first two or three positions for microphones and the rest for other equipment that we use frequently. We have two CD players so we can go from music on one to music on the other, and we have a digital audiotape player and a MiniDisc that we use often. We also frequently bring in sound from a VTR when we are rolling a tape (such as a prerecorded news story) into a program (such as a newscast). We use our analog equipment (cart, turntable, cassette recorder) less frequently, so this equipment shares a position with the mics we use often.

On/Off switch

At the very basic level, you need to be able to turn this input channel on and off. If you are not using it,

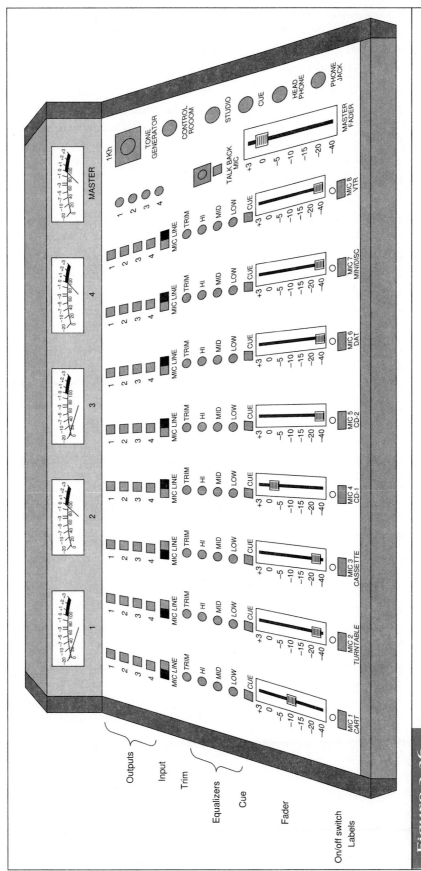

Figure 3.26

A generic audio console.

you do not want to have it on because some sound may accidentally come through. Some boards have two large buttons, one for on and one for off. We have designed our board with one button that toggles on and off. A small red light above the button lights up when the channel is on.

Fader

Faders control the volume of the sound for each particular channel. The 0 position is usually the optimum area for sound, but, of course, the reason you have the fader is so you can vary the volume. If someone with a loud voice is speaking into mic 1, you would want to set the volume lower than you would for talent with a soft voice. You may wonder about the numbers beside the fader. Why is 0 the optimum number? Why are there so many negative numbers? The answer is rather technical. Sound has traditionally been measured in **decibels (dB)**,[9] and 0 decibels has been calibrated to be a comfortable level to hear and a comfortable level for equipment to handle without *distortion* or *clipping*. Sound down from 0 has been marked with minuses, while sound above 0 is indicated with pluses. Some boards use percentages rather than decibels, with 100 percent being equal to 0 decibels.

Some boards do not have faders that move up and down. Rather they have knobs you turn to the right to increase the volume. These knobs are referred to as **pots** (short for potentiometers).

When you are operating the board during a production, you often need to bring a particular fader up to **fade in** a sound and take it down to **fade out** a sound. Faders are also used to mix sounds together. For a **crossfade,** you bring one sound in slowly while you take another out slowly. For example, if you are doing a crossfade from music on CD player 1 to music on CD player 2, you would gradually bring channel 4's fader down while raising channel 5's fader. The other main type of audio transition is called a **segue.** This is an abrupt change from one sound to another. For effect's sake, you might want to move abruptly from the middle of a piece of music to a voice statement coming from a MiniDisc. You would lower channel 4's fader quickly while at the same time raising channel 7's fader. Or you could hit the respective on and off buttons.

Cue

The **cue button** (sometimes called **audition**) is used when you want to get something ready but you don't want it to record. For example, if you push the cue button for channel 6, you can play the digital audiotape to the point where you want it to start and then bring it in at that point later in the program. As already mentioned under the monitoring section, the material that you hear will play through a special *cue monitor.*

Equalizers

We have included a bit of **equalization** on our board so that we can at least alter sounds to some degree. The equalizer unit in this board handles high, mid-level, and low frequencies separately so that we can emphasize or de-emphasize ranges. For example, if we wanted to give someone's voice a deeper sound, we might turn the knob for low frequencies so that they are maximized, leave the knob for mid-frequencies in the center position, and adjust the high-frequency knob slightly to lessen these frequencies.

Trim

Trim (often called **gain**) is a volume control that can be used to supplement the amplification of the channel fader. It increases volume without causing distortion (for analog) and clipping (for digital). It is particularly good to use with people who have soft voices.

Input

This is the control that determines what is fed through the channel—a mic or some other piece of equipment. It enables the 8-channel board to actually accept 16 different inputs. But because the switch must be in either the *mic feed* position or the *line feed* position, both cannot operate at the same time. In the mic-feed position, the sound is routed through a preamplifier to take into account the fact that the mic signal is very low. Line equipment does not go through this preamp.

If a lot of different equipment is going to be used during a production, the audio operator must think carefully about what is used when. If, for example, the production requires eight mics, then the audio operator should make sure the person on mic 8 does not speak right before or after a VTR roll-in so that there is time to change the mic/line switch on channel 8 to accommodate both mic and VTR needs.

Another solution would be to use the *patch bay* to temporarily change where one of the inputs goes. If, for some reason, you had to use mic 8 and the VTR at the same time, you could patch the VTR into channel 5.

Outputs

These four buttons determine where the sound goes once it leaves the board. This is really a function of how the engineer wires the board. In a TV studio, you want one of the outputs to go to the VTR so that the sound can be recorded with the picture. You might want another output to go into the studio for when talent needs to hear program audio. Perhaps you want to send one output to the DAT so you can have an audio-only recording of the program. Or you might want the sound to go to the patch bay so that it can be sent other places, if desired. The signal can go to all four places at the same time; you simply push the buttons for the designations you want. Each channel has its own selection of outputs because you might want to send only part of the sound to a particular place. For example, if you are making a DAT, you might want to record only the voices coming through the mics, but not the music from the CD.

Other Controls

We have now finished discussing all the controls on our generic console that are related to channels 1 through 8. However, you also need to understand a number of other controls on the far right of the board.

Quite a few of them are volume levels. The knobs labeled 1, 2, 3, and 4 are the volume controls for the four outputs. It is conceivable, for example, that you would want to send the sound to the DAT at a lower volume level than what you send to the VTR. There are also volume controls for the speaker in the control room, the speaker in the studio, the cue speaker, and the headphones. There is also a place to plug in headphones so that you can work on setting up the board without disturbing everyone else. This is often particularly helpful before production begins when people in the control room want to be able to communicate with each other and concentrate on their jobs without

the annoying noises of tapes rewinding or the same part of some CD being played over and over.

The **talkback** mic is used to talk into the studio speaker. It is an inexpensive mic that is activated when the button below it is pushed. Again it is used mainly before actual production, when the audio board operator is coordinating sound needs with people in the studio.

The **master fader** controls the sound for the whole board. If it is down, nothing will come through the console. Usually it is set at the 0 (or 100 percent) position and then not changed.

The **tone generator** is used in conjunction with the master fader to calibrate sound levels throughout the system. It creates a steady tone at 1 kilohertz. If the master fader is at 0 and the tone generator is turned on, then all of these other volumes should register at 0, too, so that sound is consistent as it moves from one place to another. For example, when the sound on output 1 has been set to 0, then that sound should be sent to the VTR so that the VTR sound can also be set at 0, using its VU meter. In that way the sound coming from the audio board will be the same volume as it goes into and comes out of the VTR.

VU Meters

As already discussed, *VU meters* show volume levels, so they are used for the calibration discussed above. We have equipped our board with five VU meters, one for each output and one for the master volume coming from the board.[10] The regular procedure we envision for our generic board would be that the master volume would be set at 0, which, if the board is properly engineered, should register at 0 on the master VU meter when the tone generator is turned on. Then the volume controls for all four of the outputs should be used to set those at 0—unless, of course, you have some reason you don't want them all to be the same. At the same time other VU meters throughout the control room (such as the one on the VTR and the one on the DAT) should be set at 0. Once these volumes have been set with the tone generator, they should not be changed. To do so will upset the consistency of volumes from one place to another.

The volume levels for the control room, studio, cue, and headphone monitors are not set with the tone generator and are not tied to a VU meter. Those volumes are independent and do not affect the recording level. Any number of students have been tricked by turning the control room monitor up loud while having the program levels low. They think they are recording good sound, but in reality the only sound that is loud enough is that in the control room.

One way to prevent such a problem (in addition to setting the volumes correctly in the first place) is to keep a wary eye on the VU meters during production. Your sound should *peak* at the 0 point on the VU meters. Going higher is called **peaking in the red** and, as previously discussed, is not good for sound quality or the equipment. If the sound is consistently low (around 20 percent, which is about –33 decibels), it is said to be **riding in the mud.** Such sound will be soft, mushy, and unintelligible.

Advanced Functions

Although mastering what has been described above for our generic board will probably get you through the average studio production, most audio consoles can perform additional functions. Some of these have already been alluded to in other parts of this chapter. For example, some boards have a switch to send 48 volts of *phantom power* to condenser mics. Boards meant for stereo have a **pan knob** that controls the amount of each channel that is going to the right speaker and the amount going to the left speaker. Of course, consoles can have more inputs than the eight on our generic board and more outputs than four.

Two other buttons frequently found on boards are **mute** and **solo.** When mute is pushed, it turns off the sound of that channel. When solo is pushed, the board will shut off all channels except the one on solo. It is possible to mute or solo several channels at once. In all probability, you would not want to engage mute or solo during production. They are more likely to be used when you are setting up sounds and want to know how a particular sound or combination of sounds will play.

A more complicated concept is that of **submastering.** If you have many sources coming into a large console (perhaps a 24-in board), you may want to group some of them together so you can raise one fader to activate all of them. For example, if you have

four mics over the violin section of an orchestra, you will probably want to activate all of them at once. You can use a **group assign switch** to assign the four channels for the violin mics to one submaster fader. Likewise, you could assign the microphones covering the percussion section to another submaster. These submaster faders are used to mix groups of sounds and come before the master fader.

Some boards have an **auxiliary send** feature through which a signal can be sent to external equipment, such as signal-processing gear, and then sent back again into the board. Sometimes each channel will have a **pad** knob that reduces the input signal in 20-decibel increments. This allows an amplified line signal to be played through a mic input. It does this by attenuating the line signal by 40 dB. Sometimes guitars have different amplification than either mic or line feeds, so the pad can be used to accommodate them. The capacity of an audio board can be increased with a **routing switcher** that allows two of more inputs to be fed into any one channel.

Consoles can also have connections for telephones so that people who call in can be included in a live broadcast. Such a console will probably have *digital delay* built into it so that what the person is saying can be delayed for several seconds before being sent to the transmitter. This is so the sound can be stopped if a caller says something that is not fit for air.

Remote controls for outboard equipment are sometimes included with boards. By using them, the operator can start or stop tape recorders, CD players, and other equipment without having to stretch to reach it. Often consoles have *digital timers* that inform the operator how long the program or a specific segment is running.

3.6 Digital Audio Workstations

Digital audio workstations (DAWs) are computer-based systems that can do much of what has been described for other pieces of equipment, all within one box. They lend themselves more to postproduction editing than to studio production because the person operating them must often switch from one part of the software to another in order to accomplish differ-

This computer is incorporated in a radio station studio. The disk jockey can read copy from the screen and use the keyboard to perform numerous production transitions. *Photo courtesy of ENCO Systems.*

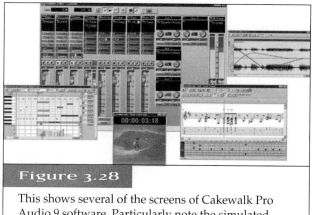

Figure 3.28

This shows several of the screens of Cakewalk Pro Audio 9 software. Particularly note the simulated faders on the big screen and the waveforms on the right screen. *Photo courtesy of Cakewalk.*

ent tasks. The simultaneous needs of live or live-on-tape productions do not lend themselves well to this, but sometimes a digital audio workstation is incorporated into a control room to handle one or several audio functions. (See Figure 3.27.)

Sounds from microphones and various outboard equipment can be recorded into the computer in digital form and then manipulated in a number of ways. Most software programs include a virtual audio board. This is not a piece of equipment but a graphical representation of the board that allows for volume adjustment, equalization, panning of sound, and so forth. Programs also have simulated recorders with play, rewind, pause, and the like in order to help with the manipulation of sounds that have been put into the computer. Most programs have a **timeline** on which representations of different sounds are placed—voice on one line, music on another, sound effects on another. These sounds can then be moved in small degrees—bringing the music in one-half second later, cutting the dog barking three seconds shorter. (The process of computer-based audio manipulation is discussed more in Chapter 8 on editing.)

One of the definite strong points of computer-based audio equipment is in shaping sound. Once

sound is in the digital domain, it can be shaped quite easily because it is broken down into finite bits and bytes that can be individually altered. Software allows you to vary frequency, amplitude, speed, and various other sound characteristics to create a vast array of noises. You can, for example, record several seconds of a man walking on a sidewalk, input the sound into a computer, and manipulate it so that it eventually sounds like 30 seconds of a three horses galloping. Computer technology has taken shaping to a new level. (See Figure 3.28.)

3.7 Tips for Recording Good Sound

The main difference between most student productions and professional productions is the quality of the sound. Students, in their preoccupation with the picture, often forget to consider sound and wind up putting a microphone in some inconspicuous place and hoping for the best. Sometimes professionals give sound second-class status, too, but increasingly sound is coming to the fore because of the improved quality of television set speakers and the very high quality sound that is possible with the new digital television technologies.

One easy method to ensure good sound pickup is to insist on checking the sound carefully during setup and rehearsal. Have the talent speak into the mic as they will speak during the program—not the usual

"Testing 1, 2, 3" routine. If it is a talk show, have each person say a few things as they might say them for the show. If your talent is going to sit up straight and clearly enunciate "Testing 1, 2, 3" for the test and then slouch and mumble during the show, it is better to know it ahead of time than to try to compensate during the taping. Have each person talk separately so you can set the optimum volume level for each ahead of time. This doesn't mean you won't have to make changes during the program, but you will be starting at a better point.

With some talent, their *s*'s hiss and their *p*'s pop. Try putting a **windscreen** (also called a **pop filter**) over the front of the mic. This is a ball-shaped accessory made out of metal or foam. The mics in Figure 3.14 have windscreens on them. If this doesn't work, try repositioning the mic or try a different microphone. As previously mentioned, microphones are built slightly differently, and one brand that makes Talent A's *p*'s pop might work just fine for Talent B.

You want to make sure that your sound has both presence and perspective. **Presence** relates to sound that is loud and clear and sounds like it is coming from the person's mouth. You do not want sound that is **off-mic**—that sounds as if it is coming from behind the person or off to the side. This is usually a matter of placing the mic near enough to the person's mouth—six inches to a foot is a good distance. (See Figure 3.29.) Sometimes, of course, the production is such that you can't position a mic that close. If you must be farther away, at least make sure the mic is pointing toward the talent's mouth. You want to minimize the amount of sound you pick up that has bounced off a wall, creating an echo-type sound. (See Figure 3.30.)

Perspective is the relationship between the picture and the sound. The sound should be what the viewer expects. If a person is being shown in the distance in a long shot, the sound should be different than if the person is seen in a close-up. The best way to achieve proper perspective is to move the mic closer to or farther away from the person. The farther the mic is from the sound source, the farther the audience will perceive the sound source to be.

The distance that a mic is placed from the talent must take into account the **inverse square law.** This is

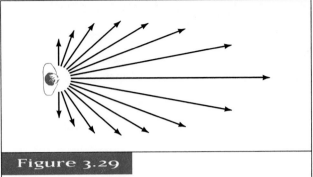

Figure 3.29

The sound pressure waves of the human voice begin to decline in intensity beyond a 45-degree angle from those projected directly to the front of the speaker.

a principle of physics that says that *as the microphone-to-source distance is doubled, the loudness is reduced to one-fourth of its previous strength.* Therefore, if you have an audio source (voice) giving you a constant level of sound at a distance of one foot from the microphone, and then you move the mic back to a distance of two feet, the strength of the sound pressure (loudness) hitting the microphone will be only one-quarter of what it was when the mic was one foot from the source. If you again double the distance and place the mic four feet from the source, it will again reduce the loudness level to one-quarter of what it was at two feet so that the level is now 1/16th of what it had been at a distance of one foot. This same principle applies to lighting, so you can look at Figure 4.27 to get an idea of how the inverse square law works. If you are working with a relatively short source-to-mic position, such as you might have for a talk show, any distance change can be crucial. This is all the more reason to check the sound levels carefully before you start recording a program.

Another problem that can creep into audio recording is **phasing.** If you place microphones too close together so that they are picking up the same sound source, their similar waveforms tend to cancel each other out when they get to the audio console. The result is disappearing sound or sound that goes in and out. To prevent this problem, you should obey the **three-to-one rule** that states that if two singers (or other performers) are standing (or sitting) side by side, each working at a distance of one foot from their

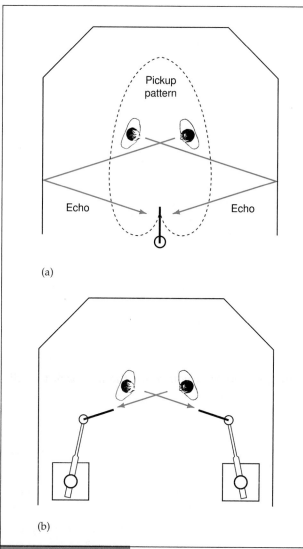

Pickup pattern

Echo   Echo

(a)

(b)

(a) Incorrect placement of directional mic between two performers. Although the two actors are standing "in the pattern" of the directional mic, their voices will be picked up with a hollow "off-mic" quality because they are not facing toward the mic; they are directing their voices away from the microphone. (b) Correct placement of directional mics. To achieve optimum presence from two actors facing each other, it is necessary to use two directional microphones—a separate mic placed directly in the vocal path of each actor.

respective mics, then the two mics must be at least three feet apart. (See Figure 3.31.) If source-to-mic distance is increased, mic separation must similarly be increased. A further application is that if a person

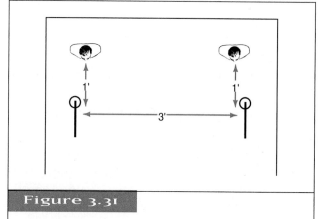

1'   1'
3'

Figure 3.31

The three-to-one rule. If the microphones are one foot from the sound source, they should be at least three feet away from each other to prevent phase problems.

wearing a lavaliere mic walks over to a standing mic, one of the mics must be turned down.

Anyone operating an audio board must pay careful attention to **balance.** This is the relationship of one sound to another. The most common balance problem is that the music is too loud and drowns out the voice. This is fairly simple to fix simply by lowering the volume of the music. Harder to balance are the voice levels of different talent. If one person speaks very loudly and another is soft-spoken, the audio operator should attempt to balance their levels. Sometimes this is simply a matter of having one fader higher than another, but often the position of the mics needs to be changed. If one mic is being used, it can be cheated toward the soft-spoken person; or the soft-spoken person's mic can be placed a little closer to the mouth, taking into account the inverse square law.

Recording good sound requires great discipline on the part of the audio operator because it is very easy for sound to become unintelligible. Some sound operators close their eyes during taping so that they are not aware of the picture and can concentrate on the sound.

3.8 Voice Command Procedure

During production, the director will give the audio operator (and other crew members) voice commands. These commands are divided into two

```
                                    COPY: INTEGRATED SOUND CORP. COMML.

TIME        DIRECTOR COMMANDS

–:10        Stand by music &
            announcer

:00         Music up full           MUSIC:    UP FULL 10 SEC. AND UNDER

:05         Stand by music
            under & annc.

:10         Music under,            ANNC:     THE INTEGRATED SOUND CORPORATION
            cue announcer                     IS PLEASED TO PRESENT ITS NEWEST
                                              HOME STUDIO COMPLETE SOUND SYSTEM
                                              FEATURING A CD PLAYER, DIGITAL
                                              TUNER, DAT RECORDER AND CASSETTE
                                              DECK ALL HEARD ON SPEAKERS WITH 120
:25         Stand by music                    WATTS OF POWER FOR EACH STEREO
            up full                           CHANNEL.  THESE COMPONENTS FEATURE
                                              A REMOTE CONTROL FOR CONVENIENCE.

:30         Music up full           MUSIC:    UP FULL 5 SEC. AND UNDER.
            and stand by
            announcer

:35         Music under,            ANNC:     LISTEN TO THE SOUND IN THE COMFORT
            cue announcer                     OF YOUR HOME AND ADJUST IT TO YOUR
                                              NEEDS. THE FIVE-BAND GRAPHIC EQUALIZER
                                              LETS YOU SHAPE THE SOUND TO YOUR
:50         Stand by music                    TASTE. SPEAKERS EACH HAVE A TWELVE
            up full                           INCH WOOFER, A FIVE INCH MIDRANGE AND
                                              A THREE INCH TWEETER.
```

Figure 3.32

This example shows how each of the director's commands is given at a precise point in time during the ongoing production sequence. Each command requiring some action by a crew member would be given slightly ahead of its actual execution to allow for the normal reaction time of an equipment operator.

phases—preparation and execution. The *commands of execution* are those that directly affect what goes out from the board. "Fade in music" or "Cue the announcer" call for immediate actions at a precise point in time. For a crew member or performer to respond with this immediate action, however, adequate preparation time is required to be mentally ready and physically prepared. For this reason, commands of execution should be preceded at some point by a related *command of preparation*. The term *"stand by"* (music, announcer, CD, etc.) is probably the most functional preparation command. It alerts the audio operator—and all other personnel—to listen carefully for the subsequent command of execution. Figure 3.32 shows how the commands might fit into the time frame of the production sequence for a simple audio exercise.

At this point the members of your class might want to undertake an audio-only exercise to make sure you understand the audio functions before proceeding to video. Figure 3.32 is the beginning of such an exercise. The entire exercise appears on this book's Website.

Discussion Questions

1. Name at least one piece of equipment in your facility that does each of the following:

transducing, channeling, mixing, amplifying, shaping, monitoring, recording.

2. If you were the audio operator for a TV studio-based game show, what kind of mic do you think you would use? Cardioid or omnidirectional? Dynamic or condenser? High or low impedance? Flat frequency response or with a speech bump? Lavaliere, handheld, stand, boom? Would you use balanced or unbalanced cable? What type of connectors would you use? Justify your answers.

3. If the sound from the CD player is not getting through the audio board but the sound from the microphone is, what troubleshooting would you do to get the CD sound operating properly?

4. Assume you are directing a dance number where the music on a DAT fades in slowly, then cuts abruptly to music on a CD. This CD music overlaps briefly with music from a cassette recorder and then the cassette music is on by itself until it fades out. What commands would you, as the director, give to the audio operator?

Footnotes

1. The term *cycles per second (cps)* is used as the basic unit of measure for sound pressure waves and, in the past, for electromagnetic waves. Now, engineering terminology has for the most part replaced the term *cycles per second* with the term *hertz* (abbreviated Hz), in honor of Heinrich Hertz, who first demonstrated the existence of electromagnetic waves.

2. Actually, the tone A above middle C at the frequency of 440 cps in our example is only the fundamental tone. It is by far the most prominent of many tones that are simultaneously produced when a voice or an instrument is sounded. The other tones that are much softer in volume and occur at higher frequencies are called "overtones" or "harmonics" and are discussed in more detail later in this chapter.

3. Waves can also be discussed in terms of their wavelength. The distance between the peaks is the wavelength. Lower frequency sounds, because they are more spread out, have longer wavelengths than higher pitch sounds.

4. Reverb units are constructed in various ways. A plate reverb has a metal sheet suspended within a frame. A transducer at one end of the plate vibrates the plate, and a mic at the other end picks up the vibrations. Today most reverb units are digital, with the signal being electronically processed.

5. Two types of equalizers are the graphic equalizer and the parametric equalizer. The graphic equalizer divides the frequency response range into separate bands that can then be altered. The controls on the equalizer form a graph of what frequencies are emphasized and which are de-emphasized. The parametric equalizer can control individual frequencies as well as a band of frequencies.

6. Filters eliminate frequencies. A low-cut filter eliminates frequencies below a certain point. A low-pass filter lets frequencies below a certain point pass but cuts out other frequencies. A notch filter completely eliminates a narrow range of frequencies or one individual frequency.

7. This term *compressor* should not be confused with compression technology used with video today. It is a term that predates the new use of the word *compression.*

8. A limiter is a type of compressor that keeps a signal from increasing any more once it has reached a particular level. A flanger combines the original signal with a slightly delayed signal to create a swishing sound. A digital delay holds a signal for a set period of time before letting it go forward. A Dolby noise-reduction system increases the volume of the program signal at certain frequencies during recording; during playback, levels that were increased are decreased, but noise in the recording process that was not boosted seems lower in relation to the program level.

9. A decibel is actually 1/10th of a larger unit, the Bel, named for Alexander Graham Bell of telephone fame.

10. VU meters are used in many different configurations. Some audio consoles have VU meters for each input channel; some have VU meters for submasters.

chapter 4

Lighting

In the next chapter we will introduce the camera and its video signal, but before you can really understand how cameras and lenses work, it is important to examine the physical phenomenon that makes all vision possible—light. There are many *techniques* that have been developed over the years to create appropriate lighting, one of the main ones being three-point lighting. But lighting is very much a creative process, and usually there is no one right way to light a set. The techniques serve as a starting point that may then be fine-tuned. Lighting can be dangerous and time-consuming. The *discipline* needed in order to think about safety cannot be overemphasized. In addition lighting must be carefully planned so it can be executed as quickly as possible in order to save time for actual production. Both techniques and disciplines figure heavily in this chapter as it covers:

- The difference between incident and reflected light (4.1).
- General illumination principles such as consistency, contrast ratio, and color temperature (4.2).
- How and when to use a light meter (4.2).
- How to accomplish creative lighting objectives such as shape, reality, mood, and focus of attention (4.3).
- The different types of lamps used in lighting instruments (4.4).

- The differences between spotlights and floodlights (4.4).
- The key, fill, and backlights needed for three-point lighting and their approximate ratios (4.5).
- Set lights and kicker lights (4.5).
- Principles for multicamera lighting (4.5).
- How to mount lights (4.6).
- Equipment principles used to create intensity, diffusion, shape, and color (4.6).
- The need for a light plot (4.7).
- The importance of safety (4.8).

4.1 Types of Light: Incident and Reflected

Light exists in the form of waves that move at the speed of 186,284 miles per second. Variations in frequency of those waves account for what many living creatures perceive as differences in color. Visible light is part of a much larger electromagnetic spectrum that also includes X rays and all frequencies of the broadcast band. All light that comes to our eyes is one of two different forms of the same basic light energy. When it comes *directly* from a source, such as the sun or a lightbulb, it is called **incident light.** As important as this light is, it conveys little beyond the fact that we are looking at a car headlight or a neon sign, for example.

Our ability to see is largely the result of **reflected light** that has first come in contact with some material surface before it enters our field of vision. In this process it has been changed, and this now *reflected light* can tell us much about such things as an object's color and structure. As children, we constantly reinforced our developing visual sense by touching the objects in our immediate vicinity. We were, in effect, programming our computerlike brains so that we could "believe our eyes" and, looking out on the world, we began to *know* that things were hard, soft, red, curved, or maybe wet.

The reflected light from all of these diverse surfaces comes to our eyes in differing intensities depending upon the position of the incident light source as it relates to the physical structures that we are viewing. Our brain learns to translate variations of light and shadow into the concept of shape and texture. Take, for example, the instructor's desk in a classroom. The desktop dimensions are defined for us by the uniform intensity of the light reflected from all points of its hard, smooth surface. The light reflected from the side of the desk is of a different intensity, possibly in a shadow. This tells us that these side surfaces are at a different angle from the top and, indeed, are the sides of the desk. Other features, such as the drawer handles and the legs, are defined by the shadows that the light source "molds" around them.

Reflected light also tells us much about the *texture* of a surface. The even, shiny quality of light reflected from the desktop denotes a hard, uniform surface. Cloth is much more light absorbent. We can perceive the texture of heavy cloth material by the many tiny shadows created by the design of the weave.

Illumination for video production is an art that involves the proper use of lighting equipment to control the light that is reflected *from* the subject *into* the camera lens. It is the way in which we shape and control this reflected light that determines what the TV camera perceives as a picture, and the result creates somewhat of an illusion of three dimensions on the viewing surface of a picture tube.

4.2 General Lighting Objectives

When the **lighting director** (LD) designs the lighting plan for any type of video production, two interacting concerns must be addressed. On one hand, important considerations grow out of specific *artistic needs* of the program. On the other hand, the LD knows that those creative aspects of lighting must coordinate with the larger context of a plan for *general illumination* based on the technical needs of the camera system.

The lighting plan starts with the need for all performers to be lit in a way that allows their features and person to be adequately portrayed in all locations of the set. Is there even light on all background locations of the set? Are there adequate light levels for performers as they face into multiple camera directions from varying set locations? Are the performers' features clearly visible? Do colors, especially flesh tones, look realistic? In order to achieve good general illumination, the lighting director needs to measure the light for intensity and consistency, consider the contrast ratio of the scene, and make sure the color temperature is correct.

This photo of the set for the nationally syndicated "**Jeopardy!**" program actually shows only one of a number of different lighting effects that are used within various phases of the program. Every one of the lights shown in figure 4.32 is used during the program to illuminate the set as well as to enhance the mood and pace of the program.   *Courtesy of "Jeopardy."*

PLATE B

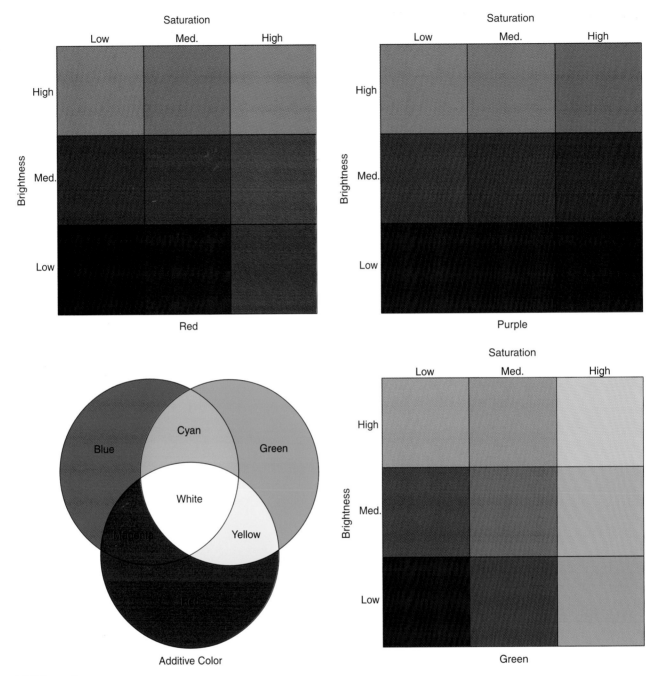

Additive color

Where any two of the three primary colors (red, green, blue) overlap, they form a secondary color—cyan (green-blue), magenta (blue-red), or yellow (red-green). Combinations of varying intensities of the three primary colors can produce all possible hues. When all three primary colors are combined in the specific proportions of 59 percent green, 30 percent red, and 11 percent blue, the result is a pure white.

The properties of color: hue, brightness, and saturation

Each of these three boxes illustrate nine variations of one color that can result when the factors of brightness and saturation are varied in different combinations. With computer controlled graphics units, two or more colors can be mixed together with these innumerable gradations of saturation and brightness to produce (theoretically) close to one million individual color combinations.

PLATE C

Which monitor is adjusted correctly?

The monitor looks as if it is adjusted correctly, but the vectorscope to the right shows that this color signal is out of adjustment. (The points on the green display are outide of the boxes etched on the overlay.) The phase of the color signal should first be adjusted (by a competent technician or engineer), and then the monitor should be adjusted so that it will reproduce the color signal *faithfully*.

In this case, the vectorscope shows that the signal is accurate, therefore the monitor is out of adjustment. This usually happens when the monitor is adjusted by someone trying to make a bad signal look better. The picture on the monitor should be corrected by a competent technician or engineer.

PLATE D

(a)

(b)

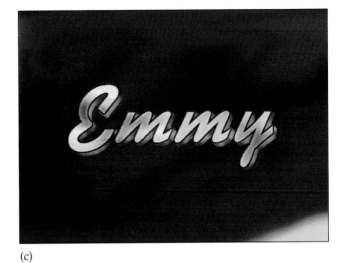

(c)

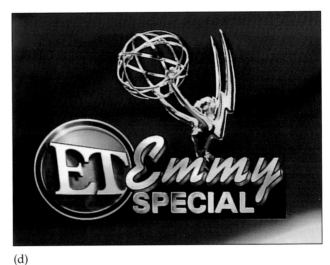

(d)

The process of animating this promotional graphic for the "Entertainment Tonight" program starts with the individual elements pictured here in examples (a) the basic ET logo, (b) the Emmy statue, and (c) the word "Emmy" (along with the additional word "special"). Each visual is taken from a storage disc or is specially designed on the day of production. When needed, each visual is then put on a line from the computer and fed to the switcher in the control room. A typical assembly would start with the live camera shot of anchor Mary Hart. Then, individually or grouped as with example (d), the visual elements come whizzing into the picture (along with sound effects) to complete the final graphic effect (e). *Courtesy of "Entertainment Tonight."*

(e)

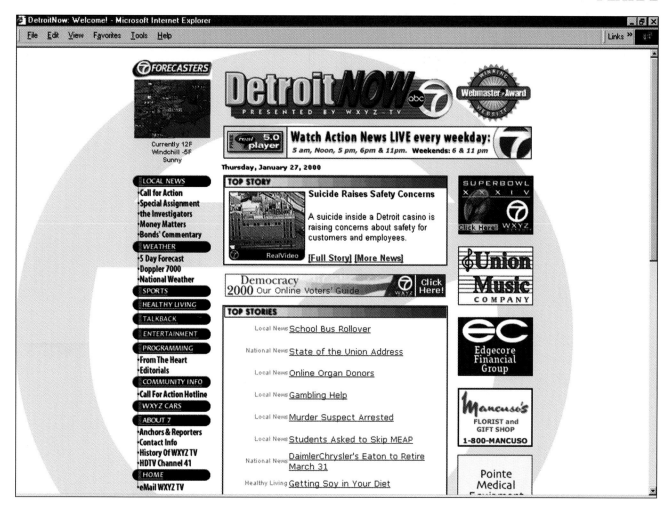

The World Wide Web (WWW) is increasingly being used by television stations to provide content. Here, WXYZ-TV in Detroit provides links to the top stories of the day, including video clips. Updated weather information is provided in the upper left corner of the screen, and a variety of other information is made available through links on the left side of the page.   *Courtesy of WXYZ-TV.*

Intensity and Consistency

At the most basic of levels, there must be enough light on a scene so that the camera can record a picture. This is not much of a problem with modern cameras because they can record in low light levels. In fact, cameras have been designed that can "see" at night better than human beings. But the presence of lighting enhances the quality of the camera's picture. Most cameras used in studios operate best if they have at least 150 **foot-candles** of light.[1] Foot-candles can be measured using a **light meter,** a meter that visually indicates the intensity of light coming from the direction in which the meter is pointed. Some light meters have an analog foot-candle scale with a needle that indicates the number of foot-candles being registered. Other light meters give a digital readout of the number of foot-candles. (See Figure 4.1.)

During the lighting setup time, the LD uses the light meter to make sure there are enough foot-candles for the camera to operate optimally. The LD also uses the light meter to check for balanced light within the set. For most productions, the amount of light at the left side of the set should be similar to that in the middle and at the right side. If this consistency is not maintained, the scene will look very different when the director switches from a camera capturing a straight-on angle to one that is pointing toward the right of the set. The lighting also needs to take into account what will be photographed. Lighting should look approximately the same when a light-skinned person is on camera as when a dark-skinned person is shown. Similarly, someone walking onto the set in a bright dress should not make the lighting look different. All surfaces absorb and reflect light, but generally the darker the surface the more light it absorbs, and the lighter the surface the more light it reflects.

The LD checks for intensity and consistency by measuring light two different ways. *Incident* (source) light is measured by holding the meter very near the camera subject and pointing it directly toward the light source. This incident-light measure tells how much light *arrives* at a given point. *Reflected* light is measured by pointing the light directly at the subject

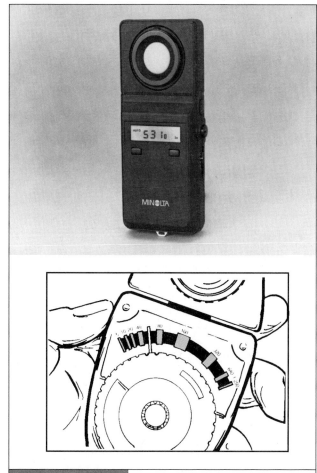

Figure 4.1

The photo above shows a digital readout of foot-candle levels. The illustration below shows an older type of meter, originally used for film photography, with a movable needle that points to various foot-candle readings on a scale.   *Photo courtesy of Minolta.*

from the perspective of the camera. The meter should be held close to the subject, but care must be taken to avoid casting any sort of a shadow on the subject. This reading indicates how much light is reflected *from* the surface areas *into* the camera lens. (See Figure 4.2).

As could be expected, the two methods of measuring light produce different intensity readings. Reflected light loses strength in the process of being reflected, and the reflecting ability varies considerably. The two different meter readings are generally used for different purposes. In the primary stages of setting up a lighting pattern, the LD measures incident lighting to look for more

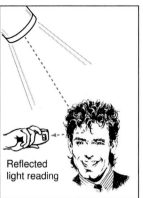

Incident
light reading

Reflected
light reading

Figure 4.2

Incident and reflected light readings. An incident light meter reading indicates the amount of light energy that is falling on a subject or larger surface from one general direction, possibly a single source. A reflected light reading indicates the amount of light energy being reflected from that subject or surface directly toward the camera lens.

general levels of intensity and consistency in area coverage as generated by the main source lights. The LD first adjusts the primary strengths of individual lighting instruments, and then again uses the meter from different points in the set to find *hot spots* where overlapping projection patterns have caused the intensity to exceed the average level. The members of the lighting crew can then correct the hot spots by moving lights or blocking off some of the light with various lighting accessories.

When dealing with the more subtle aspects of lighting, the LD works with the reflective qualities of the texture and color of a surface. While only reduced amounts of the original source light are reflected back to the cameras, this is the light that really matters. A light green knitted dress might reflect 30 to 40 percent of the illumination falling upon it, whereas a black knitted dress might reflect less than 10 percent. The measures of reflected light are used to fine-tune the lights and the elements of the set. One of the main considerations is contrast ratio.

Contrast Ratio

The human eye can accept a **contrast ratio** of up to 100 to 1. In other words, within your range of vision,

the brightest element can be 100 times brighter than the darkest element. The eye allows you to see both. A conservative but safe figure for the standard television camera would approach a ratio of 30 to 1. This means that the brightest area of a picture should not be more than 30 times as bright as the darkest area. High-definition cameras have a contrast ratio that is higher than standard definition but still not as good as the eye. This disparity between the eye and a video camera obviously means that some care must be taken in designing lighting that falls within the safe parameters of the camera.

Different elements of the set may produce large variations in the amount of reflected light bounced back to the camera. The reflected light readings tell the LD when the contrast ratio for a given camera has been exceeded. The contrast ratio is determined by dividing the brightest reflected light reading by the darkest reading. For example, if the brightest spot at which the camera aims is 600 foot-candles and the darkest spot in the picture is 20 foot-candles, the ratio is 30 to 1; the regular camera probably will not handle it too well. If, on the other hand, the brightest spot is 450 foot-candles and the darkest is 30 foot-candles, the contrast ratio is 15 to 1. Under most circumstances, this would be acceptable. Whenever the contrast ratio is too great, either the bright hot spots must be toned down or the darker areas must have more light.

As an example, take an evenly lit living room scene on a wide shot. A performer wearing a white raincoat enters and steps into a brightly lit area at the left of the shot. This sends much more light into the camera lens than was expected, and several rather drastic things immediately happen to the picture. The camera's **automatic gain control** (AGC) reacts to the introduction of the very bright area by decreasing the intensity of the rest of the picture. Without changing either the lighting or the camera controls, the right three-quarters of the picture will suddenly become much darker. The colors will have a muddy tone and the set details will be obscured. The raincoat will be an out-of-focus blur, and the person's face will be a dark spot. Stated in simple terms, the acceptable range of contrast between the brightest and darkest elements of the picture has been greatly exceeded. The light level that was previously sufficient for a picture has been distorted by the introduction of an overpowering amount of light. The best solution is to have the actor wear a different coat—a gray one or a green one. If the white coat is necessary to the story, a lighting plan can be devised that will minimize light to the performer's entrance area but still allow for a small light to cover the performer's face from the close-up camera angle.

An error commonly occurs as students are learning balanced lighting techniques. For example, consider a picture in which the faces appear to be slightly darker than the background. In an attempt to solve the problem, the novice LD adds more light to the set. If this light, aimed toward the dark faces, also falls on an already too brightly lit background, the problem has actually been made worse. As this additional light illuminates the background, the camera's automatic gain control reacts as described above and attempts to compensate for the generally brighter video, and that adjustment darkens the entire picture. The faces remain dark in relationship to the brighter background. The solution to the problem is to use equipment, described later in the chapter, that provides additional light on the faces while blocking the light falling on the background. Another part of the solution could be to change the angle from which the light falls upon the subjects. A higher angle would put light harmlessly on the floor.

Color Temperature

In order for colors to remain true throughout a scene, all lights should have the same **color temperature.** This is measured on a scale of **Kelvin** (K) degrees. What is being measured is neither heat nor brightness but the *frequency* of the light wave. One rule of thumb to remember is that the redder the light source, the lower the Kelvin temperature frequency; the bluer a source, the higher the Kelvin temperature. All light within one setting should be the same color temperature. A camera cannot adjust for differing temperatures, and color will not be true if the Kelvin varies widely from one light source to another.

Most studio lights register about 3,200 degrees Kelvin and have a slight red tint. If a light is connected through a dimmer board that allows for grad-

ual changes in applied voltage, the light-wave frequency and color temperature will decrease as the light voltage is decreased. Thus, a lighting element that produces a white light when operated at full intensity of 3,200 degrees K will gradually begin to produce an increasingly reddish tint as voltage is decreased. Increased voltage results in a bluish white tint. This distortion is not readily perceived by the naked eye, but the camera is very sensitive to any drop in color temperature over a few hundred degrees Kelvin. As a result, most lights are connected through a lighting patch bay, and only those used as part of a special effect fade-out are connected through the dimmer.

Color temperature is a much greater problem outdoors, where lighting cannot be as well controlled as it can in a studio. Outdoor light for many daylight situations registers about 5,000 degrees Kelvin and is quite blue. However, red sunrises and sunsets go down to about 2,000 degrees K, and color temperature is also affected by haze and clouds. If color temperature changes, video cameras must be adjusted by changing the built-in color temperature filter and/or by resetting the white balance. (See Chapter 5.) If this is not done (and sometimes even when it is), shots taped at one time of day may not edit together well with shots from another time of day.

4.3 Creative Lighting Objectives

As a creative or artistic factor in video production, lighting can be said to have four main purposes: (1) to define the shape and texture of physical form and, by extension, to create a sense of depth and perspective within the elements of the set or location; (2) to imitate the quality of light that is characteristic of a situation or setting in reality; (3) to establish and enhance the psychological mood of a performance or setting; and (4) to focus attention upon a single performer or aspect of the production and, thereby, to separate that subject from any feeling of relationship with setting or location.

While this last concept usually has a specialized application, the other three purposes should be thought of as principles that can be simultaneously applied within a given production situation. The same light that gives shape to a person's features can also provide mood and at the same time relate to the setting itself (for example, a beam of sunlight coming through a window and falling on a woman's face). At first glance, it might seem that some of these purposes apply only to dramatic productions. This is not necessarily true. These principles apply to all types of programs, from game shows to live-news remote transmissions.

Shape, Texture, and Perspective

When a light source is placed right next to a camera, the light waves reflected back into the lens are of a generally uniform quality. This effect is *flat lighting*, because the illumination has "filled" the hollows and curves that are the distinguishing features of the subject. When the light source is moved so that the beam comes from an angle, the resulting shadows "etch" the features so that the eye can perceive depth and texture. The camera system functions best when there is an exaggeration of light values within the video picture. The art of creating the illusion of depth on a flat video tube is largely a matter of accentuating the illumination patterns that influence our normal process of vision.

The experienced lighting director knows that often the manipulation of shadows, rather than direct illumination, most effectively adds form and texture to any object. Light coming from the side or below an object will throw shadows in certain shape-defining ways. Extreme side lighting (at right angles to the camera position) emphasizes textural quality by exaggerating shadows, making any object look more textured than it would otherwise appear.

The heightened sense of perspective necessary to the video picture is simply an application of this basic concept in the context of the entire set. Performers and foreground objects can be separated from the background when the angle and intensity of the light beam are adjusted to create a slight "highlight" effect.

Reality

Light operates on our conditioned responses in other equally important ways. We all have tuned in to the middle of a television play and watched a series of close-up shots. Either consciously or unconsciously, we are soon aware of being indoors or outdoors and of the time of day by the quality of light on the actor's face. It is probably outdoors and near noontime if the light is relatively bright and if there are definite shadows under the actor's eyebrows, nose, and chin. If the scene has been shot inside a studio, the *imitation of reality* is a product of the lighting.

Other specific shadow and lighting effects suggest certain kinds of realistic situations. Shadows of venetian blinds or prison bars cast on the rear wall of a set help to suggest a particular locale. Other *off-camera* lighting effects help to pinpoint a setting: A low-angle flickering light indicates a campfire or fireplace; a continually flashing red light indicates the presence of an emergency vehicle. Other effects help to carry forth the dramatic narrative: A shaft of light coming from under the door of a previously unoccupied room indicates the presence of an intruder; a flashlight probing around a darkened room helps reveal evidence of a burglary in progress.

Mood

Similarly, the psychological *mood* of a performance or production can be reinforced by the quality of light and its abundance or absence. Comedy is bright; therefore, bright **high-key lighting** is used to give an intense overall illumination with a fully lit background. Situation comedies, game shows, and big musical numbers in a variety show rely on this kind of lighting to establish a lighthearted mood. Conversely, tragedy or fear is communicated when the area surrounding an actor is dark or dimly lit. **Low-key lighting** refers to selective illumination that highlights only special elements of a scene. Usually the background is dark, and extreme lighting angles are used. Specific dramatic moods may be reinforced by special effects—a flashing neon sign outside a sparsely furnished hotel room suggests a seedy part of town; lightning flashes create an eerie mood; source light from a low angle gives a character a sinister, unnatural appearance.

Sometimes lighting will change within a show because the mood changes. An actor in a daytime soap opera may go through most of the day with

Figure 4.3

Sinister lighting effect. Lighting from unusual angles or sources can give unnatural or symbolic effects; for example, lighting from a low angle usually results in a foreboding, sinister appearance.

Figure 4.4

Typical cameo lighting: figure against a dark background.

fairly basic lighting, but for a certain shot, there may be special needs for that actor. For example, a particular scene could reveal that the character is sinister. For this revelation, a light could be placed at a low-angle mood giving the character a foreboding, unnatural appearance. (See Figure 4.3.) Such techniques are not limited to drama. Some of the most successful quiz programs use what appears as very general illumination of the host and participants, but in the final playoff rounds of competition, there is a dramatic change. Suddenly the background grows darker and the key lights on the participants are from a steeper angle that is almost directly above them. The host's light gets very intense. Most of the audience is not consciously aware of the changes but feel the increased tension, aided by a talented lighting director.

Focus of Attention

When a high contrast exists between the light on a subject and the light on the background area, the eye is drawn to the subject. The most obvious exam-

ple is the use of a **follow spot,** where the light follows a performer in a musical or variety show as he or she moves from one place to another. Another variation of this technique is **limbo lighting,** where the subject is placed "in limbo" against a softly lit cyclorama or some other nondescriptive, neutral background.

Another way to achieve focus of attention is with **cameo lighting**—the performer is lit, but the background is completely dark. (See Figure 4.4.) A **silhouette** effect—with the performers kept in darkness, but outlined against a brightly lit background—may be desired for a dance routine or other special situation. (See Figure 4.5.) A single shaft of light may be used to accent a contestant in the suspenseful climax of a game show. The host of a documentary may be accented with a strong back or side light. Subtle lighting highlights may be used in many other dramatic and nondramatic settings to control focus of attention.

So, above and beyond the necessity of using enough **base light** for basic illumination, the lighting director must also plan creative lighting to add shape, texture, and perspective; heighten the illusion of reality; create and enhance a specific mood; and focus attention.

Figure 4.5

Representative silhouette lighting: dark figures against a light background.

4.4 Lighting Instruments

The actual apparatus used to light a set generally consists of a lamp (lightbulb) and a housing in which the lamp is placed. Both of these are important in determining the characteristics of the light. Different lamps are used for various situations, and housings allow for lights to be **spotlights** or **floodlights.**

Lamps

One type of bulb that is used a great deal in television lighting is the **quartz lamp,** which is also referred to as a **quartz-halogen** or **tungsten-halogen lamp.** The bulb is made of quartz glass that is filled with halogen gas and has a tungsten filament. To some extent, the lamp restores itself as it burns. The halogen helps deposit the tungsten back onto the filament as it burns so that the light doesn't burn out as fast. Quartz lamps give off light that is 3,200 degrees Kelvin, and this color temperature is consistent for most of the life of the lamp.

Quartz lamps have largely replaced regular household-type incandescent bulbs that at one time were used for lighting. These, too, have a tungsten filament, but the filament is in a vacuum and does not regenerate. The color temperature, which is about 2,800 degrees K, begins to drop after only a few hours of use. Also, quartz lamps produce more light with a small bulb, making the instruments more portable, and they do not generate as much heat as regular incandescent bulbs. However, there are still some lights used in television that are similar in construction to regular household bulbs.

A newer type of lamp is the **high-speed fluorescent** (HSF). Traditionally, fluorescent lights, such as the ones used in offices and schools, have not been satisfactory as television lights. There are many different colors of fluorescent lights—some tend toward blue while others give off a yellow tint and others are more on the green side. There is little consistency in their color temperature, and most of them do not contain much red. As a result, people lighting for television have been well advised to turn off the fluorescent lights and use only quartz lights. However, the new HSF lights are a consistent 3,200 degrees K color temperature. They also consume very little energy because they operate through a chemical reaction that involves phosphors, and they last for about 10,000 hours as compared to 400 hours for quartz. At present they are more expensive than quartz lamps, but they are becoming more common for television lighting.

A bulb with a totally different color temperature is an **HMI** (short for hydrogen medium-arc-length iodide). This lamp has a color temperature of 5,500 degrees K, so it looks like outdoor light. Its main use, in fact, is to supplement light outside. However, it can also be used in a studio situation when a set is to look like it is outside—a patio, a street, or the like. Each HMI lighting instrument needs a ballast unit (a high-voltage power supply) to produce a consistent, flicker-free light. Figure 4.6 shows instruments equipped with several different types of lamps.

Generally lamps fall into one of two basic categories—spotlights and floodlights.

Spotlights

Spotlights have a controlled beam that is highly directional and can be shaped and focused to cover a rather narrow area. Its chief characteristic is the ability to throw a variable-sized spot of light on an area or performer. It is commonly referred to as a **Fresnel** (pronounced without the *s*), although each manufacturer

Figure 4.6

Lighting equipment with various types of lamps. *Left*, a quartz lamp; *middle*, HSF *right*, HMI. *(Left and middle) Photos courtesy of Lowel-Light Manufacturing. (Right) Photo courtesy of Mole-Richardson.*

will have a different name for it.[2] Although they are constructed in a number of different ways, the basic concept of a spotlight is that shown in Figure 4.7.

This type of lamp has a special structure of step lens rings to help dissipate the heat and direct the light. Another distinguishing feature is the movable assembly that allows the illuminating unit (bulb and reflector) to move back and forth between the front and rear of the instrument. With the bulb in the rear **"pinned"** position, the light rays focus in a narrow beam of high intensity, perhaps spreading no more than 10 degrees. As the bulb moves forward in the housing, the beam becomes **"spread"** and its intensity is diminished. In its full-forward spread position, the beam forms approximately a 60-degree angle.

The models of spotlights most generally used range from 500 watts to 10,000 watts. In a 2,000-watt instrument (commonly called a "junior"), a spotted (pinned) light produces an intensity of 600 foot-candles when measured at a distance of 25 feet. In the fully flooded (spread) position, the intensity of the same instrument drops to roughly 60 foot-candles, but the light now covers an area six times larger in circumference. Fresnel spots are also classified by the

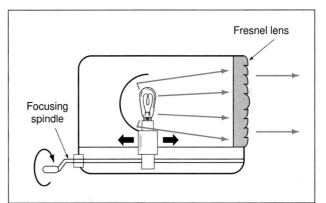

Figure 4.7

Spotlight construction. By turning the focusing handle or spindle, the bulb-reflector unit can be moved toward the lens *(right)* or back to the rear of the housing *(left)*. When in the forward position, the spotlight beam is "spread" to cover a relatively wide area. When moved to the rear of the housing, the beam is more narrowly focused, or "pinned," on a smaller area. Not all units use a spindle. Some use a lever attached to the lamp mechanism that moves it back and forth.

diameter of the lenses. The most common studio sizes would have lenses ranging from 10 to 16 inches, and smaller field models would feature 6- and 8-inch sizes.

There also are spotlights that do not have a lens on the front of them and, therefore, weigh less than the regular Fresnels. However, although these open-face housings allow the lamp to be moved back and forth, they do not have the same degree of beam control as the Fresnel.

Some spotlights are designed to be fully adjustable from the floor with a **light pole.** (See both photos of Figure 4.8.) To make adjustments, knobs located on either side of the yoke and on the lower assembly are engaged by a connector on the end of a matching pole. The light can be spotted and flooded, adjusted up and down, and moved sideways or back and forth without the crew member climbing a ladder. The same pole can adjust the four movable panels extending from the front of the instrument. These are called **barn doors** and are used to block off selected areas of the projecting light beam.

The Fresnel (and, to some extent, its open-face cousin) is the workhorse of studio lighting, but occasionally other types of spotlights are used. For example, when an intense directional beam is needed, the **ellipsoidal** spotlight (also called a **leko**) may be called into duty. It consists of a curved, fixed reflecting mirror at the back of the unit, a long tube, and a focusing lens. These elements enable it to project a beam that is well defined at its edge. The beam can be further shaped by movable metal shutters (also known as *cutters*) located inside the lamp housing behind the lens (see Figure 4.9). At this point, where all the reflected light rays are in sharp focus, there is also a place to insert a patterned metal design cutout. The shadow of this **cucalorus** or **cookie** or **kook** is then projected to add visual interest to large, plain background surfaces (see Figure 4.10). Another spotlight that is sometimes used is the **internal reflector** spotlight, which looks much like an auto headlight in that the lens, bulb, and reflector are built together as a single unit. This is commonly used as a portable light source for news and similar work done on location.

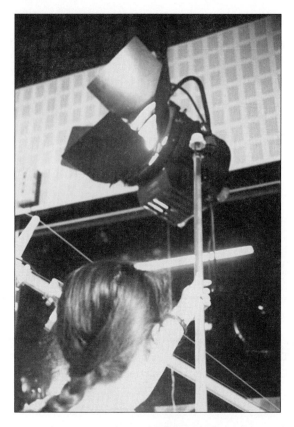

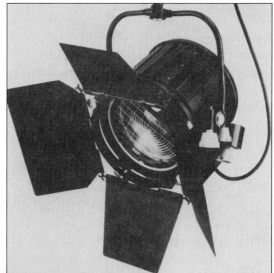

Figure 4.8

Fresnel light. Both of these Fresnel lamps are equipped to adjust focus as well as vertical and horizontal movement by means of a pole that fits into receptacles on the instrument. The four barn door beam controls can similarly be moved into required positions. *Photo courtesy of Strand Lighting.*

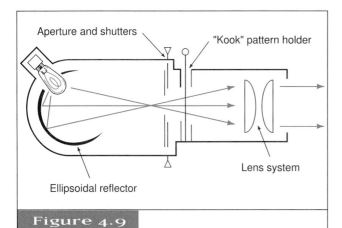

Aperture and shutters

"Kook" pattern holder

Lens system

Ellipsoidal reflector

Figure 4.9

Lens system of the ellipsoidal spotlight. Light rays are reflected from the fixed reflector and focused through the aperture. At this point, the shutters can be adjusted to shape the beam of light precisely, or cucalorus patterns may be inserted to project hard-edged shadow designs through the lens system.

Floodlights

Floodlights have a diffused beam and cast a soft light that is spread out over a wide area. The purpose of this light source is to soften and thereby control the shadows that are created by the angle of the focused spotlight. When a number of floodlights are used in a set, the effect is a soft, diffused light that eases the harshness of the shadows. To help achieve the effect of a large source area of light and the resultant easing of shadows, the floodlight does not use a lens. It uses a diffusing reflector that has the effect of spreading out the source. Sometimes the front of a floodlight is covered with a **scrim**—a soft, spun-glass filter or other translucent piece of material in a rigid frame that further diffuses the light. A 2,000-watt floodlight has a pattern of illumination that is more than twice the area of a 2,000-watt Fresnel spotlight in the maximum spread position.

The classic model for a floodlight is the one-half hollow globe structure known as a **scoop.** (See Figure 4.11.) Its large reflecting area is made of a light-diffusing material that spreads the illumination in a nonfocused scattered pattern. Floodlights built in a rectangular shape are known as **pans** or **broads.** (See Figure 4.12.) Some have controls that allow adjustment of the degree of spread. Their square shape

Figure 4.10

Top: ellipsoidal spotlight. *Bottom:* example of a shadow pattern cast by a "cookie" inserted in a leko (ellipsoidal) spotlight. *(Top) Photo courtesy of Strand Lighting.*

makes possible the additional use of barn doors. When a series of pans are constructed in a continuous side-by-side row, they are called **strip lights.** (See Figure 4.13.) They are used frequently with colored **gels** in lighting the background **cyclorama** (cyc) or other large set surfaces. Each individual lamp is typically 500 to 1,000 watts. Another type of floodlight is the **softlight.** (See Figure 4.14.) It is constructed with the bulb (or bulbs) positioned so that the light is reflected off the back of the lamp housing before leaving the housing; the reflection material diffuses the light intensity coming from the bulb.

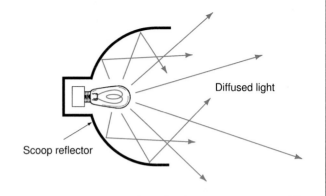

Figure 4.12

The *pan* shape of the reflector or the *broad* beam provided is the source of the name that describes this lighting instrument. *Left,* a floodlight that uses high speed fluorescent lamps; *right,* a 1,000-watt broad with a quartz bulb and barn doors. *(Left) Photo courtesy of Lowel-Light Manufacturing (Right) Photo courtesy of Colortran.*

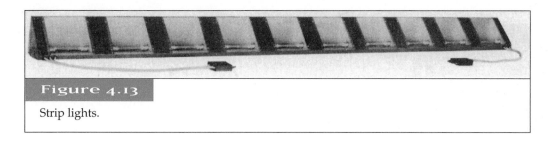

Figure 4.13

Strip lights.

Figure 4.14

Softlights. In this 8-kilowatt super-softlight, there is no direct light from the eight 1,000-watt quartz bulbs; all light is reflected by the large, curved surface.
Photo courtesy of Mole Richardson.

This brief review of lighting instruments barely suggests the scope and variety of available equipment. In the past decade, leading manufacturers have developed a whole new generation of highly efficient, lightweight, and portable lighting systems. This section has provided a practical background for an understanding of the principles on which all stage, film, and television lighting is based.[3]

4.5 Fundamental Lighting Concepts

As noted in section 4.3, creative lighting is largely a matter of careful control over the effects of light and shadow. The manipulation of these two factors permits the camera to create an illusion of depth on the viewing screen.

Three-Point Lighting

The specific techniques through which these effects are accomplished can be easily understood by examining the classic lighting setup. It is known as **three-point lighting,** because it involves the use of three different light sources—the **key light,** the **fill light,** and the **back light.** Each has a separate effect upon the subject being lit, because the three lights differ in relative angle or direction (or apparent source), level of intensity, and the degree to which they are either focused or diffused. Taken together, the cumulative effect is that of a balanced and an aesthetic unity—what Rembrandt called a "golden triangle" of light. Figure 4.15 illustrates how the three sources are used in a typical situation. The effect of three-point lighting is very natural, often occurring in our usual surroundings. By modifying one or another of its three sources, it can be made to achieve the *creative purposes* of form and texture, reality, mood, and focus of attention.

It is important, however, to keep in mind that the three-point lighting model was perfected as an ideal for film production where a *single* camera shoots the

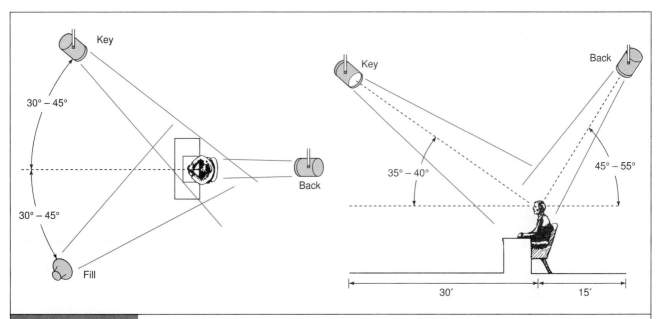

Figure 4.15

Three-point lighting. The key light and fill light should normally be placed approximately 30 to 45 degrees from a line drawn straight in front of the talent (with the fill being more directly in front of the talent). The backlight is always behind the talent at a steeper angle than the key or fill lights.

subject or subjects from only one angle. Each shot is separately set up and lit. The ways that this underlying concept must be modified to apply to multiple-camera, continuous-action video production are discussed throughout the rest of this section. (Single-camera video production, of course, can come closer to the filmic model of separate setups with balanced three-point lighting carefully plotted for each shot; see Chapter 13.)

Key Light

The most important illumination in any lighting plan is the *key light*. It is the apparent source of the light hitting the talent and provides the majority of the light that is reflected back into the camera lens. (See Figure 4.16.) Almost invariably, a spotlight is used for the key light; its strength and directional beam emphasize the contrast of light and shadow, defining the shape and texture of the subject. The use of the key light brings out the features of the face and illuminates that most dramatic feature, the eye itself.

While more extreme angles can produce special dramatic effects, the optimum result is achieved by placing the key off to one side of the subject's face,

Figure 4.16

Subject with key light only.

coming in at an angle between 30 and 35 degrees. (If the key light is placed directly in front of the talent, the result is a flat, washed-out appearance with no shadows and no sculpting, or molding of the face.)

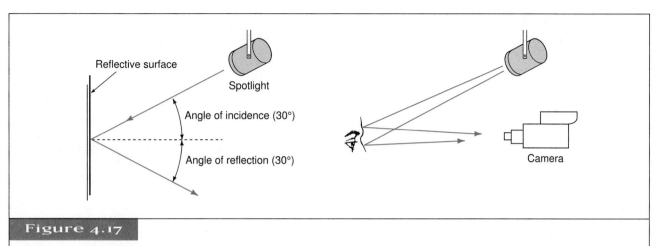

Figure 4.17

Angles of incidence and reflection. Basic laws of optics tell us that the angle at which the rays of light hit a flat reflective surface (angle of incidence) will equal the angle at which the reflected rays (angle of reflection) bounce away from the surface. Depending on the angle, a reflective surface such as metal or the talent's shiny forehead may send an unwanted glare or highlight back into the camera.

The height of the key will depend to some extent upon the talent's facial contours. It should be placed high enough to produce a slight shadow under the chin and nose, yet low enough to get the light directly into the eye socket itself. (If the talent has deep-set eyes and the key light is at too steep an angle, the result is simply two dark shadows under the eyebrows.) A good rule of thumb is that the key should normally be placed at a 35- to 40-degree angle above the subject's vision line.

In setting all lights—but especially the key—you must consider carefully the angle of light hitting the subject as it relates to the light intensity being reflected back into the camera lens. In terms of the basic laws of optics, *the angle of incidence equals the angle of reflection;* or reflected light bounces off a flat surface at the same angle as the incoming light hits the surface.

If you have a light source projecting a beam perfectly perpendicular to a flat surface, that beam would reflect directly back upon itself. However, if you raise the light source to create a 30-degree angle above the perpendicular, as in Figure 4.17, the reflected beam will bounce back downward at a corresponding angle of 30 degrees. If the subject being lit has a rough texture or an uneven surface, the reflected light will be diffused and this angle is not important. However, if you are lighting a smooth and relatively polished surface (such as vinyl or polished metal), this angle can become very critical.

Applying this principle to the way light is reflected from the subject's face, you can see how the relatively smooth (and sometimes oily) surfaces of the forehead and nose can create shiny, highly reflective "hot" spots as light is bounced back directly into the camera lens. This same effect may occur many times within a large set with various angles and planes. Similarly, productions using studio graphics or photographs mounted on cards may have trouble with reflected glare—unless a dull matte surface is used or the cards are properly angled to reflect the light away from the camera lens.

Fill Light

In order to "fill in" on the dark side of the face or object being lit, some sort of *fill light* is needed. It should come in at an angle on the side opposite from the key. Ordinarily, a floodlight (such as a scoop or broad) would be used, although a spotlight in its *spread* position can often be effective. In any case, a soft diffused light is desired. (See Figure 4.18.) Fill light is used simply to soften the shadows and give some illumination to the less illuminated side of the face or other object. Fill light should not be as strong or directional as key light; it should not compete in creating shadows or countering the shaping qualities of the key.

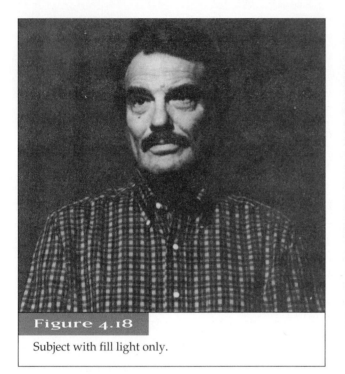

Figure 4.18

Subject with fill light only.

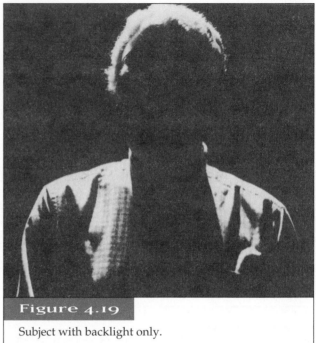

Figure 4.19

Subject with backlight only.

Backlight

As the name implies, *backlight* comes from behind and above the subject (not to be confused with *background light,* discussed below). A spotlight is virtually always used so that the light can be directed and focused like the key. The backlight falls upon the subject, and as a result, accentuates such features as hair, shoulders, and top surfaces of set elements. (See Figures 4.19 and 4.20.) This highlighting effect separates the talent from the background, adding to the illusion of depth within the total picture. Without adequate backlight, the subject appears flat and tends to blend in with the background, as in Figure 4.16. Backlight requirements vary with the background and some important items relating to the subject. Hair color and texture are especially crucial. For example, blonds require relatively little backlight. Their natural hair color separates them from the background. On the other hand, darker tightly curled hair generally needs extra backlight because it does not reflect light well. The effect of different material in a person's clothes must also be observed.

Auxiliary Light Sources

One of the most important additional illumination sources, often used in conjunction with three-point lighting, is the **set light** or **background light** (not to

Figure 4.20

Subject with balanced three-point lighting (key, fill, and backlight).

be confused with the *backlight*). This is the major source of lighting for the cyclorama or background set behind the performers. In addition to helping fill in the overall picture (basic illumination), background lighting can give form and texture to the setting, provide a sense of reality, or suggest mood (creative functions). Colored gels on a plain cyclorama can help establish mood in a production. Sometimes the background is hard to control because the background tends to catch the wash of a lot of other lights being used for other purposes. As mentioned earlier, there can suddenly be too much light if the lighting director has not kept an eye on the set as lights are being turned on.

In one function or another, most types of lighting instruments can be used appropriately for background lighting. Floodlights (scoops or strip lights) are often used for general illumination of a cyclorama or flat space. Spotlights can be used to highlight certain areas or present dramatic lighting effects (for example, strong diagonal slashes of light). And, of course, the ellipsoidal spot can be used with a variety of cucalorus patterns for various shadow effects.

Other special lighting effects depend upon careful background lighting. A good *silhouette* (see Figure 4.5) demands an evenly lit background, balanced from top to bottom as well as from side to side. A good *cameo* effect (see Figure 4.4), on the other hand, requires a complete lack of any light hitting the background; front lighting must be carefully controlled to make certain that no spill is reflected onto the set behind the talent.

Another auxiliary light often used on a set is the **kicker.** Its illumination comes from the side, usually over the camera left shoulder of the subject(s). It can work on the side of the face without really disturbing the basic three-point effect. It is often used to create facial sculpting when people will be turning their faces to talk to each other.

Actually, in any moderately complicated lighting setup, the illumination is coming from many directions and angles. In addition, the subjects—the persons being lit—will be moving within the set. The concept of key, back, and fill lights should be used as a guide, not as a rigid set of rules. Auxiliary lighting and special effects will be added as needed for certain creative purposes. The important consideration is that the lighting director be in total control of the *direction, intensity, quality* (harsh shadows or diffused), and *color* (if applicable) of light falling upon performers and set.

Multiple-Camera Lighting

As previously mentioned, the concept of three-point lighting was developed for the motion-picture single-camera technique—always concerned with lighting from the viewpoint of the camera. With this approach, every shot has its own lighting setup. When the subject and camera move, the lighting changes.

With television's multiple-camera formats and continuous-action productions, lighting directors have found it difficult to adhere to classic three-point lighting. In the talk-show format, for example, the host or hostess moves to people in the audience, and the cameras must shoot from many angles. The solution to this situation is to create an overall *wash* of illumination throughout the entire set. Many soft fill lights (fewer keys) are used from all possible camera angles. The result is called *"flat"* lighting, because the faces take on more of a flat look as differentiated from the *"shaped"* effect of shadows created by a strong key. It is a workable solution to a common lighting problem.

Some situation comedies shot with electronic multiple-camera techniques have had substantial success in overlaying the three-point lighting within a flat-lit set. Working together, the TV director and lighting director select points within the scene where the actors will remain in place for a period of time. In these spots, careful three-point lighting can be used for close-ups. When portions of the scene contain physical movement, the action is picked up by the cameras on wider shots, so the flat lighting will not matter as much. Close-ups are kept to a minimum in the areas lit by flat lighting. It is a compromise, but it works fairly well.

Daytime serials ("the soaps") that crank out an hour a day of multiple-camera production are hard-pressed to spend much time on subtle lighting, but using the previous technique, they manage to achieve an overall satisfactory lighting effect. Since productions of all types operate within tight budget constraints, lighting directors never have all the time and crew they need to do a perfect job. They simply do the best they can with what resources they have. But in all video production, three-point lighting—with its potential for texture, depth, modeling, perspective, and focus—remains the standard against which all lighting work is measured.

Two Lighting Approaches

To examine some multiple-camera lighting problems, as well as their solutions, let us look at the example of a four-person discussion program. The participants are seated in an L shape with the host on the camera-right side. This arrangement allows the host to keep eye contact with the three guests while leading the discussion.

If the three guests speak to the host or straight out to an audience area behind the camera 2 location, and the host addresses the viewers by means of camera 1, then we can use the "Plan A" lighting plot as shown in Figure 4.21. In this illustration, the key light is provided by the 5-kilowatt Fresnel spotlight that is spread to cover all four participants. Its angle creates slight shadows on the faces of the three guests. It should be tilted so that its light also falls on the cyclorama in the background. Fill light is provided by the two 4-kilowatt *softlights* from the camera left side. This is basically an application of the *three-point lighting* technique.

One possible problem may occur when guests 1 and 2 occasionally turn to their right to speak to guest 3 (on the camera left side)—they would have only fill light on their faces from the angle of camera 1. This problem can be solved by placing a spotlight *kicker* from over their right shoulders to provide a "modeling" effect from the camera 1 angle. To do its job properly, this controlled beam light should be hung somewhat lower than the two backlights. The host is covered by a pinned spot from a slightly different angle from the camera 1 shooting perspective. This gives the host's face some shape and definition. The host's fill light comes from the two *softlights*.

The backlights are located behind the talent as indicated on the lighting plot. Whenever possible, their intensity should be adjusted to take into account the different amounts of backlight needed, for example, by blonds as opposed to brunettes. Differences in light or dark clothing around the shoulder area may also require back light adjustments. Light falling on the cyclorama must be checked to be sure that its brightness and color are the same behind all camera

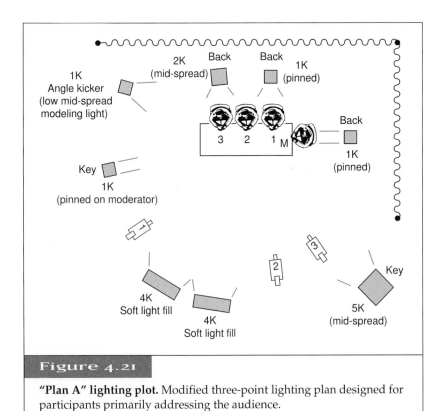

Figure 4.21

"Plan A" lighting plot. Modified three-point lighting plan designed for participants primarily addressing the audience.

shots. Placing additional scoops or broads to fill any dark spots on the cyc can solve problems.

However, if the guests for the most part will be constantly turning to speak to each other and to the host during the course of the discussion, then the "Plan B" lighting arrangement (see Figure 4.22) would be more appropriate. It utilizes a **cross-key** lighting technique, so named because the multiple key lights are aimed onto the set from different directions. Their beams *cross* each other as they light their respective subject areas.

The lighting must be done in this way, because both guests 1 and 2 will at times be facing to their extreme right or left as they talk to their fellow panelists and the host. Note that cameras 2 and 3 have been moved farther to the right and camera 1 more to the left in order to be shooting faces at less than a 30-degree angle from a straight-on position. A well-lit camera shot showing the eyes and other facial movements then tells us much about an individual.

It should be noted that Figures 4.21 and 4.22 are not exactly drawn to scale. Both the key and the fill lights would be half again as far away. The backlights would be placed about as they are drawn in relation to the guests. As mentioned earlier, all lights, and especially the *key lights,* should be sufficiently distant from the subjects and at a low enough angle to eliminate any possibility of dark areas around the eyes and unflattering shadows under the nose and chin.

Balanced Lighting Ratios

The first step a lighting director must take to create a multiple-camera lighting setup based on the three-point lighting pattern is to decide on the relative strengths of each light source. There are some basic guidelines that should be used in making preliminary plans. Figure 4.23 shows the suggested ratio of key, back, and fill lighting that can be applied in most basic lighting situations, at least during the preliminary stages. The foot-candle figures represent incident meter readings that would be made from the point where incident light strikes the subject.

During the lighting setup period, the lighting director and crew should follow a definite sequence of activity. Working from light Plan B, the LD would

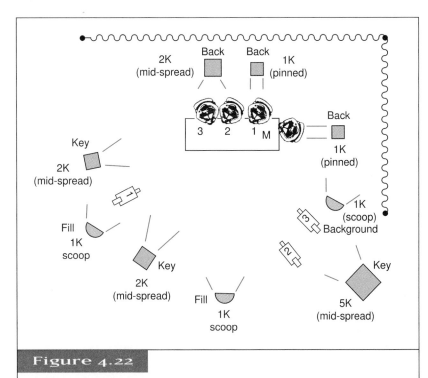

Figure 4.22

"Plan B" lighting plot. When the shape of a discussion is such that participants are turning side to side for discussion, cameras 1 and 3 must move to appropriate angles. At this point, cross-key lighting is used in "Plan B" so that faces are well lit from those side angles.

Light	Foot-candles	Relative Strength
Key	150 ftc.	Reference point of 1
Fill	75 ftc.	½ of key
Back	225–300 ftc.	1½ to 2 times key
Background	75–115 ftc.	½ to ¾ key

Figure 4.23

This suggested ratio among key, back, and fill as well as background incident light strengths is intended only as an initial structure to facilitate the setup process. It would need to be modified by later reflected light readings as well as constant checking through the camera.

first turn on the 5-kilowatt light and adjust it on all three guests, over the shoulder of the host, and on as much of the background as possible. An *incident* light reading from the position of the three guests at this point should be just under 200 foot-candles. (Remember, the dimmer is not primarily used to adjust brightness.) Spread and pin the pattern to lessen or increase the brightness. Then, the other two 2,000-watt lamps should be similarly adjusted. These three *key lights* should be adjusted to add up to about 200 foot-candles on all performers from all three camera directions. An all-too-common mistake among those doing projects for the first time is to turn on all of the lights at once and then try to adjust. The result is confusion.

Second, the *fill lights* should be turned on so that they both soften facial shadows and, at the same time, help out the background lighting. Check on camera to see if more background light is needed, making sure that intensity is the same behind all camera shots. The last lamps to be adjusted are the backlights. They will not add much to the accumulative general illumination of the set because of their downward angle, but they are important and must be set with the help of a camera.

As soon as the actual guests are present and can sit in their assigned positions, it is wise to check close-up shots on camera to see if the shots match. If there are problems, then take some *reflected* light readings from faces to see if natural skin tones are markedly different and adjust with the application of powder.

At this point, the LD should walk around the set and take a number of incident readings, both from guest positions as they face into all cameras and along the background of the set. Guest faces should be receiving about 200 foot-candles and the background wall should be at about 110 foot-candles, possibly more depending on its reflective texture. What you are looking for is a consistency of light.

Frugality in the use of lighting instruments is an important consideration. Good lighting technique is often as much a matter of knowing when to take out or soften lights as it is of knowing how to add lights to a set. The modeling and texturing effects of a few well-placed key lights are easily wiped out by adding too many lights from too many directions.

4.6 Lighting Setup Procedures

Having looked at some of the basic television lighting requirements and concepts, we are ready to consider the actual techniques and procedures involved in lighting a television setting. Several of these also involve practice and discipline in the execution of specific lighting functions in, for example, the precise preparation and use of lighting plans and plots and in careful observance of all safety precautions.

Mounting Lighting Instruments

Our first concern should be with the way the lights are actually mounted or supported. How are they to be positioned and held in place? Basically, there are two ways—by *hanging* them from above on the grid or by mounting them on a *floor stand*.

Hanging Mounts

Nearly every television studio is equipped with a lighting **grid** for mounting lights above the staging area. It comprises pipes and supporting mechanisms that place the lighting instruments in a position to produce a proper angle of illumination while leaving the studio floor uncluttered for camera and talent movement, microphone placement, and various set elements. The grid is a rigid permanent arrangement of pipes positioned several feet beneath the studio

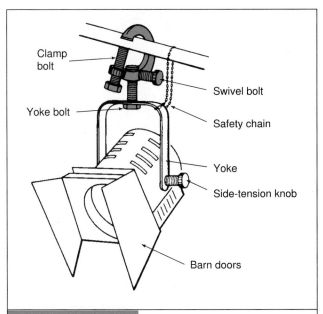

Clamp bolt

Yoke bolt

Swivel bolt

Safety chain

Yoke

Side-tension knob

Barn doors

Figure 4.24

The C-clamp is the most common type of lamp hanging device. It is held in place on the pipe by tightening the clamp bolt against the pipe. There are three additional control bolts. At the bottom of the clamp unit there is the important yoke bolt that connects the yoke to the light itself. This bolt (Y-bolt or yoke bolt) should never be loosened. Instead, the swivel bolt should be loosened to allow for left and right lateral movement of the lamp. The two side-tension knobs are used for the vertical movement. A steel safety chain is used as illustrated or sometimes connected directly to the lamp housing.

ceiling. Some studios have a **batten** system upon which the lights are actually suspended. It is movable in that it raises or lowers the pipes by a counterweight system so that lights can easily be worked on from the studio floor and then raised again to ceiling height. In some studios pneumatic-driven telescoping poles are suspended from rails attached to the grid.

Lighting fixtures are connected to the grid by a **C-clamp.** (See Figure 4.24.) The clamp is always used in conjunction with an additional steel **safety chain** that prevents the light from falling should there be any accidental disconnection of the clamp. Whenever possible, the hanging of lamps should be considered as a permanent placement. While lights can be moved when necessary, the effort is strenuous, and there is always a degree of danger involved, especially with students. With a well-designed permanent grid, the lighting director can save much time by planning the

best use of existing positions in the form of a **light plot,** shown in simple form in Figures 4.21 and 4.22.

With this plot, the actual work involves aiming the lamp, adjusting the light intensity, and shaping the beam by means of the barn doors. All of these efforts come under the title of **trimming.** With most equipment, trimming is done at the height of the grid, although some of this work can be done with a connecting pole mentioned earlier in the chapter. In most studios, trimming is undertaken with a movable *lighting ladder* that allows lighting personnel to climb up to various working positions in relation to the light, as shown in Figure 4.25. In other studios lighting technicians can walk on the grid or catwalk to move lights.

Floor Stands

In many kinds of studio arrangements, the suspended lights often have to be supplemented by lights mounted on floor stands. (See Figure 4.26.) Although too many floor stands tend to clutter the studio floor and get in the way of other production elements, they do represent a certain degree of flexibility and simplicity of setup. Sometimes there are positions where it is simply impossible to position a light except on a floor stand.

Floor stands for studio use are usually mounted on a heavy metal base for stability or weighted with sandbags. They come in a variety of weights and sizes capable of handling many different types of lighting instruments. Of course, for location productions (wherever supplemental lighting is needed), the portable floor stand is indispensable. You should take care to avoid tripping over cables and pulling over the light stands.

Lighting Control Factors

The video camera system is quite sensitive. Optimum performance is possible only when illumination is kept within prescribed limits. To achieve the artistic and technical purposes of lighting, the lighting director must work within four separate yet interrelated parameters:

1. The level of intensity.
2. The degree of focus or diffusion.
3. The shape of the projected beam.
4. The color quality.

Figure 4.25

High-tech it may not be, but this type of wooden ladder, with one alert person to stabilize it, provides a quick and efficient way to trim lights.

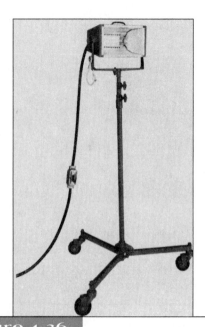

Figure 4.26

A light mounted on a floor stand.   *Photo courtesy of Mole Richardson.*

After the initial setup is completed, the lighting director, working with the director and camera operators, makes a continuing series of adjustments throughout the rehearsal period and prior to the final take. A number of mechanical and electronic controls are utilized during this process.

Intensity

We have already briefly described the way that the beam from a Fresnel lamp can be spread to lessen its intensity and, at the same time, cover a much wider area. Remember that the fully *spread* beam has roughly 1/10th the intensity of a completely *pinned* beam. But whether a beam is focused or diffused, another factor has important implications in terms of intensity. Although it is not easily apparent to the naked eye, variations in the distance between a source light and the subject create large differences in intensity.

The same **inverse square law,** which in Chapter 3 informed us about critical microphone-to-source distances, also applies to illumination. As shown in Figure 4.27, the strength from a light source is reduced to one-quarter of its previous strength as the source-to-subject distance is doubled (and, of course, the strength is multiplied by four as the distance is cut in half). It is actually a matter of an increasing surface being covered by the same amount of light energy. As a result, the power to illuminate diminishes. A light that produces 1,600 foot-candles at a distance of 10 feet is reduced to only 400 foot-candles at 20 feet as it covers four times the area.

In terms of a practical field-production example, let us assume that a *clip-on* spotlight attached to a camera working 10 feet from a subject produces a reading of 160 foot-candles (exactly 1/10th of the figure reading illustrated in Figure 4.27). Should the sub-

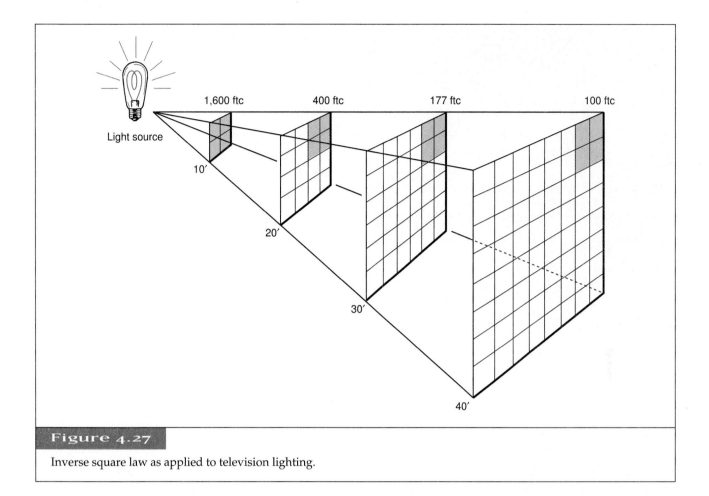

Figure 4.27

Inverse square law as applied to television lighting.

ject move away to a distance of 20 feet, the light level is now 40 foot-candles. Depending on the camera used, this may not be adequate for professional purposes, because the very process of zooming into the subject even further reduces the amount of light coming through the lens. On the other hand, in a studio situation where we are working with much stronger illumination and with the talent at greater distances from the lights, a change of even 10 feet in the source-to-subject distance should be noted but is not critical.

Located some distance from the actual lighting instruments—either in a corner of the studio or in a separate control room—is the patching and control equipment that, in any kind of sizable studio operation, is centered around a **patch bay** with a **dimmer board** nearby. (See Figure 4.28.) Although this equipment will vary in size and capacity, it all functions on the same general principles. The *patch bay* serves to connect numbered lights on the grid with similarly numbered cables for connection to switches in the control area, creating a **nondimmer circuit.** For rapid control of a group of lights, the cables for a number of lights can be brought through one **dimmer circuit** at the dimmer board. As mentioned earlier, the majority of lights would go through nondimmer circuits, because any lessening of power light causes a drop in color temperature that in turn produces a reddish tone to the light source.

Diffusion

Diffused light is created and controlled in several ways to keep it in its proper perspective in relation to the focused key light. The primary control factor is that of adjusting intensity through some of the methods described previously. Placement is also very important. The best diffused light is achieved by using several instruments placed at differing angles.

Several devices for diffusion are also important to the lighting director's toolbox. The most commonly used pieces of equipment for these purposes are

Figure 4.28

A patch bay. A patch bay is the connecting point between a power source, numbered switches, and the cables that run through the grid to all lighting instruments. It also may be used in conjunction with a dimmer board that can provide gradual increments of more or less power to selected lines. *Photo courtesy of KCET, Los Angeles.*

either attached to the front of the instrument or mounted in front of it. A *scrim* is a wire mesh or spun-glass filter, shaped to fit the front of the lighting instrument. (See Figure 4.29.) It works by scattering the beam and cutting back on intensity. Scrims are used to soften a spread Fresnel light or to soften the light from a scoop or broad. In a remote situation, lights are often pointed toward a shiny **umbrella** that captures and diffuses the light.

Shape

If lighting directors had to work with only the large raw beam projected by most instruments, their work would be difficult indeed. One of the main difficulties is controlling the overlap of multiple light sources. Fortunately, there are a number of shaping devices that are used to modify and block parts of the beam. These can produce high-intensity hot spots. The most common solution to this problem is achieved through the use of barn door shutters that, as mentioned earlier, are attached to the front of a spotlight. (See Figure 4.8.) Used in pairs or sets of four, these hinged plates can provide an adjustable edge to the beam. By

moving the shutters, both the height and width of the projected light can be limited. Most assemblies can be rotated to provide maximum adjustment. In a leko or ellipsoidal lamp, the movable shutters are inside the instrument (adjusted with outside handles) to provide an even greater definition to the projected pattern. (See Figure 4.10.)

Sometimes the lighting director needs to create a small area of reduced intensity *within* a projected beam. For this a **flag** is used. Flags are rectangles of varying size made either of metal or of frames covered with black cloth. They can be hung from the lighting grid or mounted on a floor stand in a position to block out light to a specific area. (See Figure 4.30.) One use, for example, is to cast a slight shadow on the forehead and on top of the head of a person with thinning hair who otherwise might appear almost bald under the bright lights of a close-up shot.

Occasionally, an added amount of light must be pinpointed at a particular area of the set. If barn doors cannot project quite as precise a pattern as needed, a **snoot** can be used to do the job. Inserted in the same frame designed to hold the barn doors, the snoot, a cir-

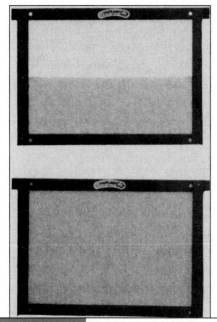

cle that ranges in diameter from 4 to 12 inches, can reduce the spotlight's beam to a smaller, clearly defined circle without increasing the intensity of the spot.

The *cucalorus* (*cookie* or *kook*) is a cutout design that, when placed in front of a spot, projects a pattern upon a cyclorama or large set surface. Ellipsoidal spotlights are especially good for projecting cookies. (See Figure 4.10).

Color

There are occasions when a set or other production location is simply too dull and drab for attractive pictures with sufficient color contrast. It may be that more "warmth" from red-brown earth tones is needed. Or possibly the "cool" effect of green and blue is desired. To solve this problem, variously colored *gels* are used to add color to the setting and occasionally to the performers' clothes and flesh tones. The gel is a thin transparent celluloid material and is available in a wide variety of colors. The gels can be cut to fit a specially designed holder that slides into the frame of a scoop (see Figure 4.31) or the same frame that is intended to hold the barn doors on a spotlight.

In using gels, the lighting director must work carefully with both the video control operator and the makeup artist. The effect of projecting three or four different colors onto a set can be subtle, but must be carefully controlled. Since the camera system tends to pick up and accentuate red, you should be especially cautious with its use. Because most normal makeup is in the reddish range, too much light through a red gel will greatly exaggerate flesh tones. A green gel, on the other hand, has an unflattering effect on most people—especially on those with darker complexions.

One of the most effective applications for gels is to use them with strip lights (see Figure 4.13) to color a cyclorama. A wide variety of color combinations and effects are possible. A continually changing dawn effect, for example, can be created with the background shifting from a deep violet, through various reds and pinks, to a light blue during the shooting of a scene.

Figure 4.31

Gel holder on a scoop. Frames that hold a gel filter in place are designed for all types of floods and spotlights. *Photo courtesy of Mole Richardson.*

4.7 Preproduction Planning

Newscasts, as well as talk programs and game shows, make very few changes in their lighting on a day-to-day basis. A new production or one with continuing changes in set, such as a soap opera, usually schedules its lighting period to run right up to the beginning of the main camera and sound production time. Woe be unto the lighting director whose work runs over into this period, causing a delay in its conclusion. In professional studios both large and small, the performers, engineering, crew, and equipment are scheduled very tightly. Any extension of studio time becomes prohibitively expensive. It is therefore incumbent upon the lighting director to be very sure that planning the lighting design is done with the utmost care. First, there must be a session with the director (and possibly the producer) in which the lighting needs are carefully detailed. Only after this is completed can the lighting director start the process of drawing up the *light plot* that will serve as the basis for both the setup period and operations during the camera production phase. With some additions and instructions, Fig-

ures 4.21 and 4.22 could both serve as the basis of a light plot for a simple discussion program.

Figure 4.32 shows the light plot for the set of the nationally syndicated TV program *Jeopardy!* (See the *Jeopardy!* set shown in color plate A.) It provides an insight into what is needed to achieve the numerous lighting changes and special effects seen during the show. When a new set was installed in the fall of 1996, lighting designer Jeffrey Engel was commissioned to create an entirely new lighting scheme to be implemented for each show by the regular LD, Vince Cilurzo. Those who know the program will recognize the podium for Alex Trebek in the center of the set. If you look carefully, you can find his keys and backlight. Contestant podiums 1, 2, and 3 are to his left (camera right). As indicated, two different sets of key lights are strategically located for these positions. For most of the program, contestants are lit by keys directly in front of them. (See corresponding numbers on lamps.) When the show reaches the point of *Final Jeopardy!*, the second trio of keys is used. When aimed correctly for the production, they strike the participants from a 30-degree angle, giving the faces a more sculpted look. Light on the background panels is also reduced and changed in color. These two factors help to create a sense of added tension.

It may not seem possible, but all of the remaining lights provide some function, either generally illuminating the set or providing the flashing lights at the show's conclusion. In this plot, lights are shown in their positions on each grid, but not exactly as they will be aimed. Those lights shown with a tail and check mark indicate that they are hung from a device that drops them three or four feet lower from the grid. Accompanying any light plot is always a key that indicates the type and strength of each light as well as the use of floor stands, grids, and other information. Several more pages of paperwork would accompany a plot as complicated as this one.

In the Sony Studio (Culver City, near Los Angeles), where the show is produced, each light is on a computer-controlled dimmer. Such computer-controlled lights can be observed in large stage productions, where the light projection patterns move in addition to changing color and focus. It all happens on the command of a computer program.

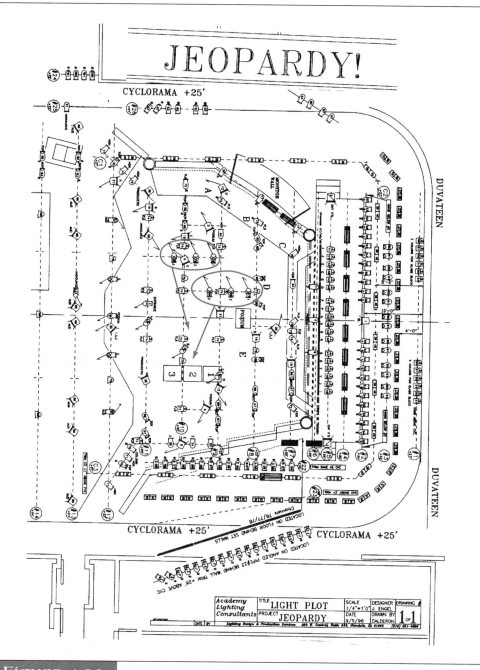

Figure 4.32

Light plot for the *Jeopardy!* television program. A relatively large number of lighting instruments are needed for a large-scale television program such as *Jeopardy!*, which features numerous lighting changes and special effects. As can be seen in color plate A, much of the effectiveness of the set is the result of the lighting design.

Of course, the style of the show changes occasionally, and with it the lighting. The lighting diagram shown here has been changed recently. Watch the show and see if you can determine what the differences are.

Safety is the responsibility of everybody connected with a television production. Any unsafe situation can be avoided by using common sense and observing basic precautions. Part of the *discipline* of television production is the habit and attitude of *thinking safety*. Every crew member, whether or not part of the lighting team, should be disciplined to think always in terms of avoiding or correcting hazardous conditions.

When working in a studio, you should always "think overhead." Are all lights, mounts, and other equipment securely fastened? When heavy equipment is moved or repositioned overhead, is everybody warned and the area below cleared out? In addition, crew members should "think electrically." Is all equipment turned off before moving or inspecting it? Is the circuit turned off before it is plugged into an instrument? Everyone should also "think hardware." Has the item of equipment been thoroughly checked out and is it ready for use? Has everything been connected? Tightened? Tested?

Whenever a lighting assistant is moving or trimming lights, at least one person should steady the ladder from below. Some universities do not allow students to climb ladders because of the safety factor. The person on the ladder should always carry a wrench (secured by a band or tie around the wrist to prevent dropping it on persons or equipment below) to tighten any lamps that may have become loose from excessive turning. When making any adjustment on any lighting instrument, the safety chain must always remain fastened, securing the light to the pipe or grid.

When changing the direction of a light, always loosen the thumb screw (swivel bolt) *first*. Do not mistake it for the bolt holding the lamp hanger to the clamp—loosening that bolt will detach the lamp from the lighting grid.

When moving a light (clamp, hanger, and housing), always make certain that no people or equipment is below the working area. Be certain the power to the lamp is off. Just because no light is being emitted does not mean no power is coming through the cord. Damaged lights, burned-out bulbs, and short circuits are all potential dangers. Again, be sure the power is off at the lamp's new location before plugging it into the grid outlet. When you are moving an instrument from one location to another, the safety chain is always the last item to be unfastened, and it is the first thing to be hooked up when the instrument is repositioned.

As indicated earlier, in professional studios lighting instruments are rarely moved. There is a deliberate oversupply of instruments on the grid, many more than are needed for any single production. If a light goes out during a production, the LD can replace its function very quickly, and the audience is usually unaware that any difficulty occurred. Moving a light is also unwise from a financial standpoint. Rough handling, whether it takes place during movement or even during adjustment, greatly cuts down on the usable life of the bulb and/or lighting element.

When focusing lights, never look directly into them. A light that measures 200 foot-candles at 30 feet may approach 100,000 foot-candles at the source. Studio lights are bright enough to permanently damage or even blind the naked eye.

Lights also create a dangerous amount of heat—a fact that should always be foremost in your mind as you are working in a studio. After being on for only a few minutes, most studio lamps are hot enough to cause serious burns. Most studio lamps have handles—use them! Lighting technicians should also be furnished with heavy-duty, heat-retardant gloves. Use them! Special caution must be used when adjusting barn doors, as they are directly in the path of the light source at only a few inches and absorb a large amount of heat.

Make sure never to touch the surface of a quartz bulb with your bare fingers (even when the bulb is cold). Always use gloves or some other cloth between your hand and the globe. A small amount of finger oil or acid on the face of the globe will interact chemically to weaken the glass envelope and even cause it to explode.

Discussion Questions

1. Assume a production situation where two people sit on a couch and talk and then one of the people moves to another area of a set and sings a song. What would be your suggestions for lighting this type of situation?

2. As a lighting director, what steps should you go through before you start lighting the set? What are the first several things you should do when you are actually lighting the set?

3. What safety precautions should you be aware of in your own studio?

Footnotes

1. One foot-candle (ftc) is the amount of light that falls upon a surface placed at a distance of one foot from an established theoretical source approximating the brightness of one candle. In many European countries light is measured in lumens or lux (approximately 10 lux = 1 foot-candle).

2. Augustin-Jean Fresnel was a 19th-century scientist who did important research into the nature of light and for whom the light was named.

3. In order to see the vast array of lighting instruments available, visit the Websites of some of the major lighting equipment companies—http://www.Strandlighting.com; http://www.Lowel.com; http://www.colortran.com; http://www.mole.com.

chapter 5

Cameras

Perhaps no other piece of equipment exemplifies video production like the video camera does. It is, in many ways, the symbol of video production, and most video work begins with raw images, captured and recorded onto tape or computer disk by the video camera.

A wide variety of cameras are available for video production, ranging in price from around $1,000 to hundreds of thousands of dollars. Some cameras are designed for use in a production studio, while others are designed to be used in field production environments. Many of these latter types are referred to as **camcorders** because they have an onboard videotape recorder. (See Figure 5.1.)

No matter what the price or designed purpose of a particular video camera, it performs the same function: transducing, or converting physical energy in the form of light waves into electrical energy in the form of video signals. This is, you should recall, essentially the same function the microphone performs with audio energy. However, unlike the relatively simple microphone, the video camera must have an entire support system of additional equipment, because the process of transducing video is much more complex then transducing sound. Depending upon the camera, its output will be either an analog or digital signal. Increasingly, video cameras are designed to output a digital signal, as this facilitates the growing use of computers and digital equipment in other areas of production.

What happens to the video signal after it leaves the camera will be discussed in later chapters, as this process varies according to the production situation. In studio productions, the output of one or more cameras will be routed through a **switcher** (Chapter 6) and then broadcast live or recorded onto either tape or computer media (Chapter 7). In field work, the signal is recorded directly onto tape or other media (Chapter 7), and then edited (Chapter 8).

(a)

(b)

Figure 5.1

Cameras can be designed for either field or studio use. The Panasonic AJ-D215 camcorder (*a*) is designed for field use and has a built-in DVCPRO tape unit. The Panasonic AK-HC880 high-definition camera (*b*) is designed for studio use.
Photos courtesy of Panasonic Broadcast and Television Systems Company.

This chapter introduces the basic function and operation of the video camera and its integral lens and mounting systems. Like any piece of production equipment, the video camera is a *tool*, and using that tool to its greatest functional and creative potential requires an understanding of both *disciplines* and *techniques*, including not only how to operate the tool but the underlying principles that make the tool work. As you read this chapter, you should firmly grasp the following topics:

- The video scanning process for both NTSC and ATSC (5.1).
- The role of hue, saturation, and luminance in creating video color (5.2).
- The color video system and how it works, including how the camera produces video signals (5.2).
- Lens characteristics and principles of lens operation (5.3).
- The theory and operation of zoom lenses (5.4).
- Camera unit controls and how they are used (5.5).
- Camera mounting equipment and how it is used to create shots (5.6).
- Basic fields of view (camera shots) (5.7).
- Basic principles of picture composition, including framing, headroom, angle of elevation, and balance (5.8).
- Production techniques of camera operation (5.9).

5.1 The Video Scanning Process

The video picture that you see on a television monitor is composed of a series of small, illuminating phosphors called **pixels** (short for "picture elements"). The "movement" of images on the screen is an illusion caused by a phenomenon known as **persistence of vision,** in which the human eye perceives smooth movement of an image when its position is changed rapidly on the television screen.

During the transducing process, a video camera produces a rapidly changing series of "still" images, each made up of thousands of pixels "drawn" electronically in a process called **scanning.** The speed at which the images change and the number of pixels that make up each image depend on the television standard being used. In the United States, there are two such standards: NTSC and ATSC.

NTSC Television

For more than 50 years, a single television standard—**NTSC**—was the only one used in the United States. Although color was added in the 1960s, the NTSC standard has been essentially the same since the 1940s. With the advent of **high-definition television** (see below), the NTSC standard is also referred to as **standard definition** (SDTV).[1]

In the NTSC system, each picture image is made up of more than 300,000 pixels, arranged into 525 rows of 640 pixels each. Of these 525 rows, however, only 480 are actually used to display picture information on the screen. Thus, the effective **resolution**—or fineness of detail that can be reproduced on the screen—of the NTSC video picture is 480 rows by 640 columns, which is usually stated as "640-by-480," giving the width of the picture first. This creates a 4-to-3 **aspect ratio,** meaning the NTSC television picture is four units wide for every three units high.

Each second of NTSC video is made up of 30 **frames,** which are individual static pictures. Each frame is itself created by an **interlace scanning** process, which actually creates half of the frame every 1/60th of a second. Each of these picture "halves" is called a **field.** This scanning method, which was necessary because of the technical limitations of equipment in the 1940s, creates a noticeable "flicker" on the screen. Figure 5.2 shows how interlace scanning works in the NTSC television system.

Although NTSC television signals can be converted to digital form, as will be discussed in Chapters 7 and 8, the standard is based on analog signal transmission.

ATSC Television

ATSC television, which is more commonly referred to as High-Definition Television (HDTV), is scheduled to replace NTSC television by the year 2006.[2] However, unlike NTSC, which provides a single standard format for scanning and picture resolution, ATSC actually encompasses *several* digital formats. One of the great uncertainties of HDTV, as discussed in the opening chapter, is how the lack of a *single* standard will affect the implementation of digital television.

Some ATSC formats use interlace scanning and others use **progressive scanning,** which creates an entire picture with each pass. This type of scanning, most often used on computer monitors, eliminates the flicker effect seen on NTSC television. ATSC also provides formats in various resolutions. In general, the more pixels you have to make up a picture, the greater detail you can display on the screen; thus more pixels equals higher resolution and (all else being equal) better picture quality. Figure 5.3 shows how progressive scanning works in the HDTV "720p" format.

ATSC also can use different aspect ratios. Some HDTV formats specify the standard 4:3 ratio used by NTSC, while others use a 16:9 ratio, which is closer to what you see on film when you go to a theater. Finally, HDTV provides for various **frame rates,** or number of frames per each second of video, ranging from 24 to 60.

An increasing number of cameras are being designed for use in ATSC production. Many of these cameras can work with more than one ATSC format, depending on the application. Some cameras can also provide either a digital or analog output.

(a)

(b)

(c)

Figure 5.2

The interlace scanning process works in the following manner: (1) each of the odd-numbered rows, from left to right and top to bottom, is scanned, creating the first field (*a*); (2) each of the even-numbered rows, left to right and top to bottom, is scanned, creating the complementary field (*b*). Each field scan takes 1/60th of a second; thus, a new frame is created every 1/30th of a second (*c*). Note: for clarity, the number of rows in these illustrations has been reduced.

Figure 5.4 shows a comparison of several ATSC formats.

5.2 Principles of Video Color

The video camera, as discussed in the opening of this chapter, essentially converts the light energy reflected off of objects into an electrical signal. To understand how this is accomplished, it is important to understand some principles of how colors are processed by a video camera and how humans perceive color.

Light enters a camera through the lens, which focuses it onto one or more **charge-coupled devices** (CCDs). The CCD, which is actually a computer chip, is the device that actually transduces the light energy into electrical energy.[3] A camera may have a single CCD chip or three CCD chips. On three-chip cameras, each CCD chip is designed to process the color infor-

Figure 5.3

The ATSC "720p" format uses progressive scanning. The entire picture area is scanned in a single pass. Note: for clarity, the number of rows in this illustration has been reduced.

mation for one of television's three **primary colors**—red, green, and blue. A device called a **beam splitter,** which is essentially a light prism, separates the incoming light into the three primary colors, directing each set of color information to the appropriate CCD. On single-chip cameras, one chip processes all color information. Three-chip cameras normally provide a much higher quality picture than single-chip cameras, but they are more expensive as well.

At the receiving end of the television system—the home TV set—the electrical energy of the video signal is converted back into light energy. The screen of most televisions (and computer monitors, for that matter) is a **cathode-ray tube** (CRT), a large and somewhat cumbersome set of electrical components

encased in glass. However, an increasing number of TV sets utilize **liquid crystal display** (LCD) screen technology. Among other advantages, liquid crystal displays allow for flatter television designs.

Video cameras and video display devices, like the human eye, are sensitive to three attributes of color: the color tint itself **(hue);** the vividness of that color **(saturation);** and its relative brightness **(luminance).**

Hue

Color plate B indicates the three primary colors and shows how any two of them can be combined (in the overlapping areas) to produce the three additional **complementary colors**—cyan (a turquoise formed from blue and green), magenta (blending red and blue), and yellow (the combination of red and green). These primary and complementary colors are the basic pure hues seen when a prism breaks up white light into its individual color components, or when we marvel at a rainbow, which essentially is millions of droplets of water acting as tiny prisms to create vivid primary and complementary colors.

When light waves of all three primary colors are added together in a proportion that relates to the color sensitivity of the human eye (59 percent green, 30 percent red, and 11 percent blue), the resulting effect is white. Sometimes thought of as the *absence* of color, white is actually *the presence of all colors.* The proportions are a bit off, but you can get the idea from color plate A. If you still have trouble accepting this on faith, prove it by looking carefully at the individual grains of sand

Horizontal Pixels	Vertical Pixels	Aspect Ratio	Scanning	Frame Rate
640	480	4:3	Interlace	30
640	480	4:3	Progressive	24, 30, or 60
704	480	16:9	Interlace	30
704	480	16:9	Progressive	24, 30, or 60
1280	720	16:9	Progressive	24, 30, or 60
1920	1080	16:9	Interlace	30
1920	1080	16:9	Progressive	24 or 30

Figure 5.4

Popular HDTV Formats. When referring to a particular format, a shorthand with the number of vertical pixels and a "p" or "i" for scanning method is often used. For example, the first format listed would be referred to as "480i," while the last format listed would be referred to as "1080p."

that make up a white sandy beach. The variety of colors that we are used to seeing in our daily lives result from the reflected combination of these primary colors.

As the proportions among the hues being combined are varied, an enormous range of colors becomes possible. For example, when red and green are added together, a range of pure hues from red to orange to yellow to green can be created. As the third primary color, blue, is added, a wide variety of browns, tans, mahoganies, beiges, ochers, maroons, sepias, and so forth are achieved. You may have experimented with this using a computer-graphics program that has the ability to mix ultrafine gradations of color and, as a result, can create literally millions of different hues.

Saturation

The intensity or vividness of a color is described in terms of its saturation. If we are dealing strictly with a red hue, the intensity of that red can range from a highly saturated vivid red, as shown in the lower right square of color plate B, to the less saturated pastel red shown in the upper right square. The pastel red is achieved by diluting the color with white. Another effect is achieved by diluting the vivid red with gray, producing more of a brown tone, as seen in the lower left corner.

As other hues are blended together, other color combinations result. Red and green hues combined in varying proportions with different amounts of white produce yellows. If increasing amounts of gray are used to dilute the saturation of the red and green factors in this yellow, a series of golden brown tones will result. Just as the saturation effect can be controlled on a scale leading to white, gray is on a scale of increasing darkness leading to black. Together, the hue and saturation portions of a video picture are termed the **chrominance** signal.

Luminance

The final color attribute is the luminance, or brightness of the color. As shown in color plate B, colors with low brightness are darker than their high brightness counterparts. The luminance of a color relates to, but must not be confused with, the increase and decrease of **video gain,** which increases (or decreases) the brightness of an *entire* picture through an amplifi-

cation of the video signal. You can also accomplish the same effect by adjusting the "brightness" control on your home TV set. When used to describe color, however, luminance refers to the brightness of an *individual* color as displayed on the screen.

5.3 Lens Characteristics

Possibly the most crucial element in the whole process of producing video pictures is the lens. The quality of the lens, to a large extent, can determine the quality of the picture produced by a particular camera—and, consequently, the quality of the picture seen on the home TV screen or studio monitor. A high-quality lens on a "cheap" camera can improve its output significantly, while a low-quality lens can substantially drag down the quality of even the finest camera.

From an operational standpoint, the **focal length** of a lens determines how "wide" or "narrow" the viewing range or **field of view** is, as will be discussed below.[4] Although **fixed-focal-length lenses** were common on cameras in the early days of television, now a **zoom lens** is found on nearly every video camera. Unlike a fixed-focal-length lens, which can provide only one range of view, a zoom lens is continuously variable along a range of focal lengths.

Although zoom-lens technology is constantly improving, a zoom lens is never quite as optically perfect as

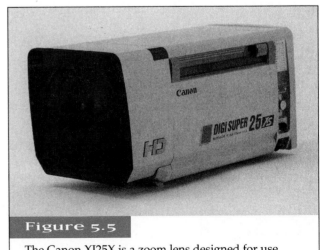

Figure 5.5

The Canon XJ25X is a zoom lens designed for use with either NTSC or ATSC television cameras. *Photo Courtesy of Canon, U.S.A., Inc.*

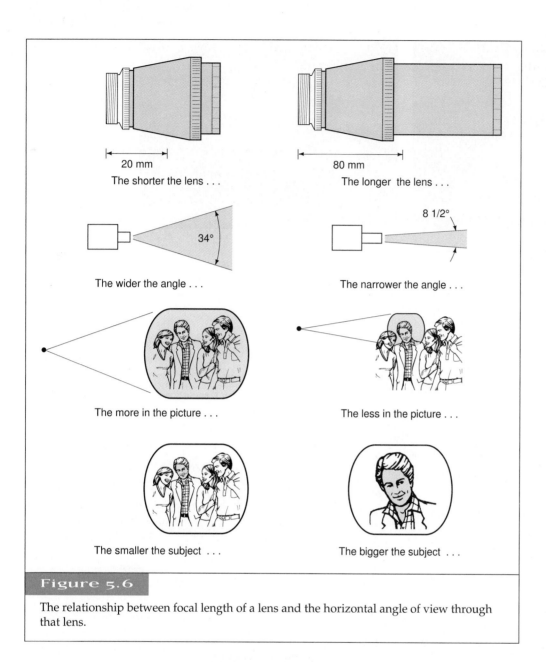

20 mm

The shorter the lens . . .

80 mm

The longer the lens . . .

34°

The wider the angle . . .

8 1/2°

The narrower the angle . . .

The more in the picture . . .

The less in the picture . . .

The smaller the subject . . .

The bigger the subject . . .

Figure 5.6

The relationship between focal length of a lens and the horizontal angle of view through that lens.

a fixed-focal-length lens designed for one specified viewing range. Still, these slight deficiencies are normally not noticeable in television use, although zoom lenses made for use in high-definition formats must be carefully designed to maintain high quality. (See Figure 5.5.)

Focal Length

Differing focal lengths are used primarily so that differing amounts of a scene can be included in the picture when shot from the same position. *The longer a lens is, the narrower its viewing angle will be, the less you will be able to fit into the picture, and therefore, the more magnified individual subjects will be.* Conversely, a short-focal-length lens will give you a wider viewing angle, thereby allowing you to fit more into the picture, but individual subjects will appear smaller. This law of lenses is illustrated in Figure 5.6. A **long lens,** or **telephoto lens,** therefore, can be used to obtain closer views of objects and can get a relatively close-up view of an object from a great distance. A short-focal-length lens is similar to a zoom lens that is zoomed *out,* while a long-focal-length lens is similar to a zoom lens that is zoomed *in.*

Figure 5.7

The picture on the left shows the shot of a 54mm high-magnification fixed-focal-length lens. Note the optical compression even though the children are nine feet apart. The picture on the right approximates a 9mm lens. The children are still nine feet apart, but the effect of the wide-angle lens shows the actual separation. To approximate the girl's position in the earlier picture, the camera was moved much closer to her for the second shot.

A long lens will *compress* distance. Two objects that are far apart from each other and at a great distance from the camera will be brought closer to the camera with a long lens and, consequently, will seemingly be brought closer to each other. A common example is the baseball shot of the pitcher and batter as seen with a long telephoto lens from center field, perhaps 400 feet away. Although the pitcher and batter are about 60 feet apart, the camera shot from the long lens makes it *look* as if the two players are much closer to each other. On the home screen, they may look as if they are only 10 or 15 feet apart. Figure 5.7 shows another example of the distance compression created by a long lens. On the other hand, a **short lens,** or **wide-angle lens,** will tend to increase distance and make things look farther away than they are.

Focus

A video image is in proper **focus** when the subject is clear and distinct, not fuzzy or blurred. On zoom lenses, the focus control is the slip ring located farthest toward the front of the lens. (See Figure 5.8.) When a camera is set up for studio use, this ring is usually adjusted by the use of a remote-control cable. The determining factor in setting proper focus is an object's distance from the camera lens. For example, if you focus on an object that is 4 feet from the camera

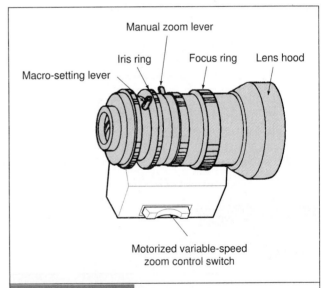

Figure 5.8

Portable camera zoom lens. In addition to the motorized variable-speed zoom control switch, adjustments on the lens include the macro lens setting, the iris (f-stop) setting, the manual zoom lever, and the focus ring.

and then the object moves 20 feet away from the camera, it is likely that you will have to refocus.

The distance between the nearest point at which objects are in focus and the farthest point at which objects are in focus is called **depth of field.** The depth of field in a given situation depends on a number of factors, which are discussed below.

To set the focus on a zoom lens, zoom in all the way to the tightest shot possible and then adjust the focus. This is called **front focus.** Following this procedure ensures that the object will remain in focus throughout the range of the zoom lens (assuming, of course, that the distance between the object and the camera does not change). If you find after setting focus that the object goes out of focus as you zoom out, check the lens's **macro flange,** which is normally located at the point that the lens attaches to the camera, to be sure that it is not set for **macro focus** (discussed in section 5.4). If this does not solve the problem, it is likely that there is something wrong with the lens.

The camera operator—whether in a studio or field situation—must be constantly diligent to ensure the proper focus is maintained. As cameras and objects move, there is a constantly changing distance relationship between the camera and its various subjects. Each change necessitates checking to be sure that the lens is properly focused.

The F-stop Aperture

All camera lenses have an adjustable **iris** that allows the amount of light coming into the camera to be controlled. When the iris is adjusted, it opens or closes the **aperture,** which is made up of a series of metal "blades" that adjust the size of the lens's light opening. The aperture does not, however, affect the size of the picture the lens will pick up. Some cameras are equipped with an **automatic iris,** in which the camera adjusts the aperture depending on the amount of light present. Still, there are many production situations where the camera operator will want to override the automatic iris control and adjust the iris manually for a variety of creative reasons.

The various sizes of aperture openings are identified by different **f-stop** numbers. The lower the f-stop number, the larger the lens opening, and the higher the f-stop number, the smaller the lens opening. (See Figure 5.9.) For instance, f-22 is typically the smallest aperture found on most television lenses. The widest opening could be f-2.8, depending upon the lens. In between, the numbers would range through 4, 5.6, 8, 11, and 16. The change from one stop to another represents a doubling or the cutting in half of the amount of

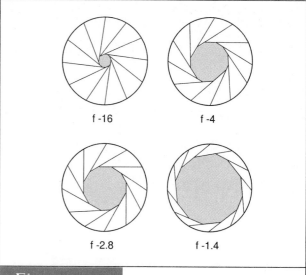

f -16   f -4

f -2.8   f -1.4

Figure 5.9

Diagrams of various f-stop openings. The basic rule to remember with iris changes is the higher the f-stop number, the smaller the opening. Each marked position on the lens represents one full f-stop, and each time the stop is changed one position, the light going into the camera is doubled or cut in half.

light being allowed into the camera. It is a precise measurement, hence the need for some decimal figures.

If working under very poor lighting conditions with no option for increasing the amount of light, for example, it might be advisable to open up to f-4. On the other hand, if working under extremely bright conditions (perhaps outdoors on a sunny day), you might want to "stop down" to f-11 or f-16. The term stop down, which actually means closing up the iris to a higher number, may take a little getting used to, but it's the accepted phrase.

One word of warning about f-stop adjustments should be stated at this point. Generally speaking, the camera operator should not routinely think of the f-stop as a means of compensating for bad lighting. Bad lighting or uneven lighting should be handled by correcting the lighting, not by adjusting the camera. Studio cameras in educational institutions are often set up in automatic iris control, and this setting should only be changed with the knowledge of a responsible engineer. Overriding the automatic iris control may make possible a desirable creative effect, but the changeover should be tested and planned in advance.

The depth of field of a lens can be increased by altering any one of three different variables:

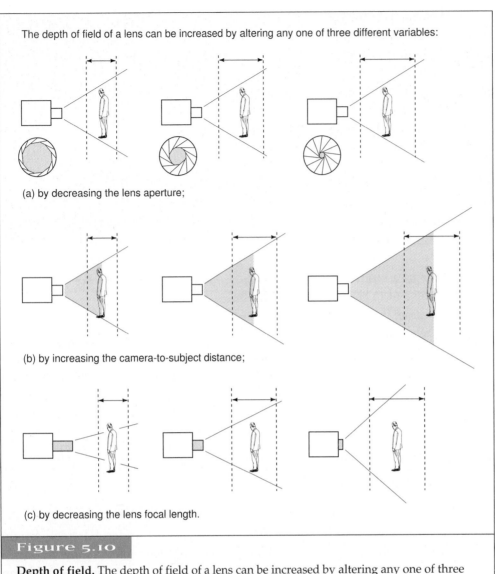

(a) by decreasing the lens aperture;

(b) by increasing the camera-to-subject distance;

(c) by decreasing the lens focal length.

Figure 5.10

Depth of field. The depth of field of a lens can be increased by altering any one of three different variables: (*a*) by decreasing the lens aperture, (*b*) by increasing the camera-to-subject distance, (*c*) by decreasing the lens focal length.

Depth of Field

As discussed, depth of field is the range of objects that are in proper focus in a given shot. Once the focus is set for a specific object, other objects closer to the camera will be out of focus, as will objects located farther away. Making sure that you can predict the location and range of the middle ground where objects are in focus is important in the production planning process.

Three different factors interrelate to determine the depth of field: the f-stop (the smaller the lens opening the greater the depth of field); the distance from the subject to the camera (the greater the camera-to-subject distance, the greater the depth of field); and the focal length of the lens (the shorter the lens, the greater the depth of field). Figure 5.10 illustrates these three variables.

The manipulation of depth of field is often used for artistic effect. In some situations, such as sporting events, you might want to have a very large depth of field so that rapidly moving action will stay in focus. In an interview situation, you might want to have narrower depth of field so that the element in focus (the person being interviewed) is separated from the background. Figure 5.11 shows another artistic effect

Figure 5.11

Using a narrow depth of field can help separate the focal point of a picture from the background.

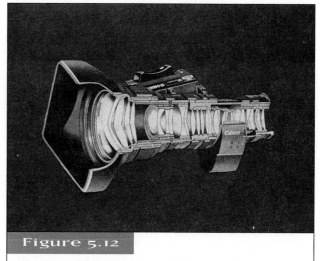

Figure 5.12

Cutaway illustration of movable lenses and gears in a 14-to-1 ratio zoom lens. *Photo courtesy of Canon, U.S.A., Inc.*

created by a narrow depth of field. The best way to increase the depth of field is simply to add light and to stop down the lens. This allows the shot to remain the same, which would not be the case if attempts were made to change the focal length with a zoom movement or to change the camera-to-subject distance. Similarly, depth of field can be decreased by reducing the amount of light on the scene (and opening up the lens) or by moving the camera farther away from the subject and zooming in.

Another artistic effect that relates to depth of field is called the **rack focus.** In this type of shot, the camera operator initially focuses on one object in the frame (with other objects blurred), then smoothly adjusts the focus so that *another* object in the frame comes into focus. For example, the camera may start on a tight close-up shot of a half-empty glass close to the camera with the background out of focus; the camera operator would then change to focus on a person lying on the sofa, while the foreground glass goes blurry. Such shots tend to be most dramatic when the depth of field is relatively narrow.

5.4 Production Use of the Zoom

The zoom lens allows camera operators and directors to achieve rapid and continuous adjustment of the focal length of the lens and, consequently, to control pre-

cisely the size and framing of shots. In addition to giving the director and camera operator a wide range of lens lengths that are immediately available, the zoom lens also facilitates very smooth on-the-air movement.

The variable-focal-length zoom lens is essentially an arrangement of gears and optical elements that allows the operator to shift these lens elements—moving them back and forth in relation to each other. (See Figure 5.12.) This achieves varying focal lengths by changing the theoretical center point of the lens. Zoom lenses vary greatly with price and manufacturer, but lenses designed for professional and industrial levels all share some of the same basic characteristics.

Lens Ratio

For most production situations, a 10-to-1 magnification ratio is common. On a typical lens this would result in focal lengths ranging from 10.5mm at the wide-angle position to 105mm at the zoomed-in position. Figure 5.13 provides some indication of the range of shots available with a 10-to-1 zoom ratio lens. Consumer camcorders are often equipped with a 6-to-1 zoom lens, providing a 9mm to 54mm range. For sporting events and other outdoor productions, professional cameras with zoom ratios of 30-to-1 and greater are not uncommon. The use of an **extender** increases the focal length of a lens, allowing it to zoom in even closer to distant objects. A 2X extender, for

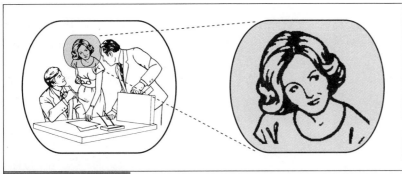

Figure 5.13

Range of a zoom lens. These two views represent the extreme focal lengths of a 10-to-1 zoom lens: *left,* zoomed "out" to the shortest focal length (widest angle); *right,* zoomed "in" to the longest focal length (narrowest angle).

example, doubles the focal length of the zoom lens at both the wide-angle and zoomed-in positions. Some extenders are placed between the zoom lens and the camera, while others are built into the zoom lens itself. On these latter types, the camera operator can select either normal or extended lens lengths.

Movement Control

Virtually all zoom lenses have a motor-driven zoom mechanism. Less expensive models may have only one or two speeds, which does not give much artistic control. Professional lenses usually have variable-speed controls. Generally, professional zoom lenses also will provide a manual zoom control lever that allows the operator to zoom without the aid of the motor. Most commonly, this manual control is used to perform a **snap zoom,** in which the lens is rapidly (in effect instantly) changed from one focal length to another. If you are using a camera that allows manual operation of the zoom control, it is important that you disengage the power zoom before moving the zoom lever. Serious damage can result if the manual lever is moved while the power zoom control is engaged.

This ability to obtain smooth, on-the-air zoom movement gives the director and camera operator a great deal of production flexibility. It is possible to tighten up a shot on the air, going smoothly from a wide shot to a medium shot to a close-up at variable speeds. The best zoom work usually goes unnoticed, because it does not call attention to itself.

Macro Lens

Under normal circumstances, most zoom lenses cannot focus on objects that are very close to the lens. For instance, it may not be possible to set focus on a small insect that is being held eight inches from the lens. However, on lenses equipped with a macro flange, it is possible to set focus on objects very close to the lens. By moving the macro lever attached to the macro flange (see Figure 5.8), you can take extreme close-ups of printed material or small objects at distances of two inches or less from the lens.

5.5 Camera Unit Controls

A number of controls on the camera unit itself can be set for optimum picture quality or to achieve an artistic effect. Not all of these controls, however, are found on all cameras, and they may not be on the cameras you use at your school. You should also be aware of your school's policy on changing these controls; some of them may be set only by an engineer or instructor.

Viewfinder Visual Indicators and Controls

Although the viewfinder has no effect on the signal that is actually produced by the camera, it does provide a great deal of information about how the camera unit's controls are set. The primary purpose of the viewfinder, of course, is to show how the shot is framed on a small (usually black-and-white) video monitor that shows the camera's output. Most cameras offer brightness and contrast controls so that the operator can adjust the picture shown on the viewfinder monitor. These controls, however, have no effect on the actual output of the camera.

Modern cameras also provide a great deal of other information to the camera operator through the viewfinder. By using small LED lights around the viewfinder monitor or by superimposing information over the picture on the viewfinder monitor, cameras provide information about the current settings of the controls. For example, visual indications in the viewfinder may show how filters, white balance, and gain controls are set (see below). The viewfinder also may provide visual warnings to the operator for such problems as a low battery or insufficient lighting.

Finally, **tally lights** on the front side of the viewfinder tell the talent/subject that the camera is currently "on the air" or, in field-production situations, that the tape is rolling.

Filters

Some professional cameras designed for both studio and field use have a built-in filter system to compensate for Kelvin temperature differences between indoor and outdoor lighting (see Chapter 4). Usually located between the lens and the beam splitter, this filter component is an integral part of the camera system. Typically, a camera has a rotating disk of filters for different lighting conditions: (1) tungsten studio lamps and sunrise and sunset; (2) bright outdoor light; and (3) clouds or rain. If the camera is kept in a studio, there is no need to ever change the filter setting; the studio position (which is actually no filter) is always the correct one.

If it is taken outside, then the filter disk should be changed to one of the outdoor filters. These are both orange to compensate for the more bluish outdoor light. The difference between the bright outdoor filter and the cloud filter is the amount of **neutral density** (ND) that is mixed with the orange filter. Neutral density filters are designed to limit brightness but do not adjust color. The ND #1 allows one-half the light

to pass through, while ND #2 and ND #3 allow one-quarter and one-eighth, respectively. The filter for bright light has more neutral density than the one for cloudy conditions.

Sometimes other filters are part of the filter disk or they are added to the front of the lens. For example, a **soft contrast filter** is used to create a fuzzy effect, and a **star filter** gives a star effect that radiates from bright spots on the screen.

White Balance

An important control on the camera is the one that establishes the correct color balance by electronically adjusting the red, green, and blue components of the signal so that pure white *looks* pure white. Since different types of lighting have different Kelvin temperatures; some types of light may produce a bluish or reddish tint if no compensation is made. **White balance** adjusts for different color temperature conditions.

Depending on the camera, there are several ways that proper white balance can be set and maintained. An increasing number of cameras have an **automatic white balance** control that continuously tracks lighting conditions and adjusts the white balance accordingly. On low-cost and older cameras, however, automatic white balance can produce less-than-optimal results.

Some cameras have one or more **preset white balance** settings that allow the user to select a preadjusted white balance setting for specific lighting conditions. On these cameras, the presets may be labeled with color temperature (e.g., 3,200 degrees Kelvin) or with lighting situation (e.g., indoor).

Perhaps the safest way to ensure proper white balance, however, is to set it yourself. To do this, set the camera to the **manual white balance** setting and position a pure white object in front of the camera lens. Then, press the appropriate button on the camera to set white balance. Normally, you will need to hold the button for a second or two, and the camera will give some sort of indication in the viewfinder that proper white balance is set. The disadvantage of using manual white balance, of course, is that you must constantly be aware of changes in lighting conditions and reset white balance as appropriate.

Video Output Level Selector

Many cameras have an **automatic gain control** (AGC) that automatically adjusts video levels to compensate for differing amounts of light. Other cameras have a **video output control** that allows the operator to adjust to some degree for low light levels. The "0 dB" position is established by the manufacturer as the standard level of video output for the camera under prescribed lighting conditions. The video output control increases the **decibels** so that the camera can function at lower light levels than at the 0 dB position. The term decibel (dB) has been borrowed and slightly altered from its audio derivation; however, as with audio, each 6-dB increase means that the amplified signal is doubled. This control should never be thought of as a way to make a poorly lit picture better. All it can do is make the poor picture look a little brighter. Increasing the automatic gain control in this way also usually makes the picture appear more grainy.

Other Controls

Some cameras have several additional controls that, while not necessarily complicated, are best suited to an individualized-study approach. Such items as the fade time control, the negative/positive selector, and the phase control selector should have clearly marked "0" or neutral positions. The beginning student should be made aware of these off positions and make sure that such controls are in the safe neutral position for normal camera operations.

5.6 Camera Mounting and Movement

Efficient use of the camera depends upon several primary factors that interact with one another during a production. The first of these is simply the *position* of the camera in relationship to a subject (or multiple subjects in wide-angle shots). The camera reveals the front, side, or top of the elements in the picture according to where it is placed. A second factor involves changing the *direction* in which the camera is aimed to reveal different subjects.

There also can be a continuing change in the *point of view* of the camera as it is moved to reveal different aspects of a subject or sequence of subjects. This movement also can involve changes in the *elevation* of the camera, especially for artistic effect. The effectiveness of these operations is very dependent upon the hardware that provides movement and support for the camera.

Camera Head Movement

Figure 5.14 shows the basic parts of a studio camera unit, including: (a) the video components of the camera itself; (b) the **mounting head** containing the equipment used for movement of the camera; and (c) the **camera mount** that controls floor movement of the entire unit.

Shot changes involving vertical and horizontal camera movement are fundamental to video production. When these kinds of movements are continuous on-the-air moves, they require a skilled operator and a suitable mounting head with which to execute them. A horizontal movement to the left or to the right is known as a **pan.** (See Figure 5.15.) When told to "pan right," the operator moves the camera lens in the direction of his or her right hand. This is the reverse of stage movements, which are given from the standpoint of the performer looking out toward an audience.

Up-and-down movements of the camera are called **tilts.** The lens end of the camera is moved up or down to view elements at different elevations of the set. (See Figure 5.16.) Both pans and tilts are accomplished by exerting pressure on the **pan handle** that projects from the right rear of the camera. Zoom and focus controls are usually located on this pan handle. In the mounting head area, there is a coupling device such as a cam or cradle assembly that is important to smoothness of motion, especially in a tilting action.

Camera Mounts

While both pans and tilts can be accomplished by simply moving the camera head, any change of camera position, whether done as an "on-the-air" movement or simply for the purposes of changing the framing of a shot, is accomplished through movement of the camera mount.

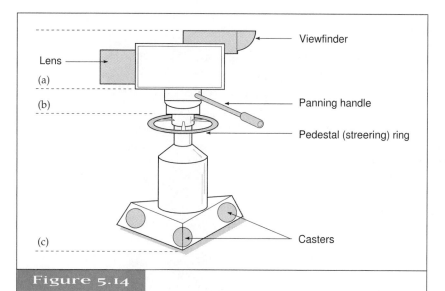

Lens —
(a)
(b)

Viewfinder
Panning handle
Pedestal (streering) ring

(c)
Casters

Figure 5.14

Three basic parts of the camera. (*a*) The video components of the camera itself, including the lens, viewfinder, and CCD; (*b*) the mounting head with the panning handle that controls camera movement; and (*c*) the camera mount that is the transport and support mechanism for the entire unit.

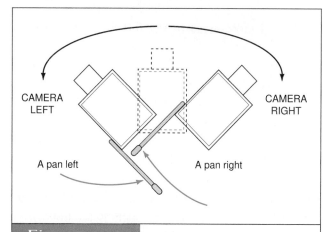

CAMERA
LEFT

CAMERA
RIGHT

A pan left

A pan right

Figure 5.15

Camera panning. To pan the camera in a given direction, the panning handle must be moved in the opposite direction. Thus, to execute a "pan left," the camera operator has to move the panning handle to the right.

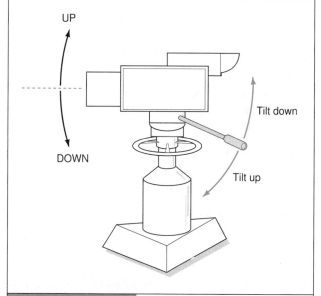

UP

DOWN

Tilt down

Tilt up

Figure 5.16

Camera tilting. In tilting the camera up or down, the camera head is pivoted through the use of the pan handle.

The simplest and least expensive camera mount is the **tripod.** When used in a studio environment, this three-legged stand is usually fastened to a dolly base consisting of three casters. The casters can either rotate freely, which facilitates quick and easy movement of the camera in all directions, or can be locked into a non-movable position, resulting in a steady camera unit.

The field model tripod, illustrated in Figure 5.17, has a crank-operated elevation adjustment that can be used to raise and lower the camera—although not smoothly enough to be used on the air. Many tripods

Figure 5.17

Camera mounted on a camera head assembly with an adjustable tripod. *Photo courtesy of Panasonic.*

Figure 5.18

A studio camera on a pedestal mount. *Photo courtesy of Panasonic.*

have no adjustment for height other than the laborious process of mechanically adjusting the spread of the tripod legs. Thus, there is no way to achieve any elevation change during an actual production. The tripod, however, is lightweight, and most models are readily collapsible. This makes the tripod a desirable camera mount for most remote productions.

The **pedestal mount** shown in Figure 5.18 has been the standard for studio production since the beginning of television. Its distinctive feature is the central pedestal that can be raised or lowered with the assistance of counterweights or air pressure. It also has a steering ring that controls all three casters in a synchronized manner to allow smooth on-the-air camera movements across the studio floor. This ease and steadiness in camera movement have made the studio pedestal a must in any big studio production.

When more pronounced changes of position and elevation are called for, they are accomplished through the use of specialized mounts, such as the motorized **crane** mount (shown in Figure 5.19) and the smaller **crab dolly.** With the crane, considerable camera movement over a wide range is possible, because there is a separate driver for the motorized base. Inherited from the film industry, the crane is the largest and most flexible type of camera mount and comes in a variety of sizes. The camera itself is mounted on a boom arm that can be moved vertically or laterally without moving the crane base. Depending upon the model, the length of the arm extension is 10 to 15 feet for studio models and much more for a few special field units. For everything from rock concerts to Olympic coverage, the moving crane shot has become an indispensable part of the visual language of television.

Figure 5.19

A large truck-mounted crane used for Olympic coverage. Such equipment is now commonplace for any large-scale outdoor concert, parade, or sporting event. *Photo courtesy of ABC Sports.*

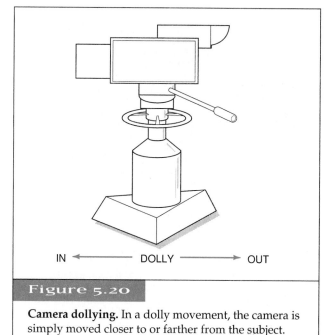

IN ← DOLLY → OUT

Figure 5.20

Camera dollying. In a dolly movement, the camera is simply moved closer to or farther from the subject.

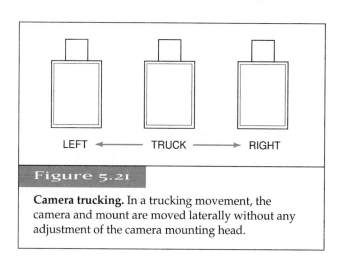

LEFT ← TRUCK → RIGHT

Figure 5.21

Camera trucking. In a trucking movement, the camera and mount are moved laterally without any adjustment of the camera mounting head.

Camera Mount Movements

One of the most obvious changes in picture framing is accomplished by moving the camera closer to or farther away from the subject. This is referred to as **dollying** the camera, and it produces a **dolly shot.** (See Figure 5.20.) While the zoom lens may have reduced the use of dolly-in and dolly-out shots, this movement still has its uses. As noted in Figure 5.7, there is a definite difference in the way the zoom lens in a wide-angle mode sees two subjects separated by 10 feet or so and the way those two subjects are seen with the lens in the high-magnification mode.

Lateral movement of the camera and its mount is known as **trucking.** A change of picture is accomplished as the camera trucks right or trucks left, because the camera moves sideways without panning to the right or left. (See Figure 5.21.) In the field, dollying and trucking movements normally cannot be attempted unless special tracks have been laid down to facilitate smooth, level movement. Usually, such movements are set up only for ambitious productions like high-budget dramatic programs or major sporting events.

A **follow shot** can use both the trucking and dollying techniques. In it a camera moves with the subject and maintains a constant distance from it, while the background is seen to move past in a constantly changing panoramic sequence. An **arc shot** is another variation of a trucking movement. The camera circles around the stationary subject to reveal different aspects of the subject. (See Figure 5.22.)

An older move that is still used involves studio camera pedestals that are designed to facilitate a slight change in camera height. In this case, the word "pedestal" is used as a command verb as the camera operator is asked to "pedestal up" or "pedestal

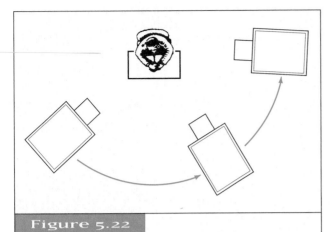

Figure 5.22

Camera arcing. This move is accomplished mainly by a maneuver of the camera mount as the camera arcs around, keeping the lens pointed at the subject. The move is much easier to make with a crab dolly than with a tripod or pedestal mount.

ment, except that much greater vertical distances can be covered. Another kind of motion is the **arm move.** With a large crane, the boom arm or crane can be moved left, right, up, or down or any continuing combination of these, while the base remains stationary. With both the crane and the crab mounts, the camera operator retains control over the angle and tilt of the camera throughout all these moves.

It should be noted that all these movements are difficult to use on-air when a zoom lens is at a position of high magnification (narrow angle). The slightest unsteadiness during the camera movement is exaggerated, because the long lens, while magnifying the subject, is also magnifying the shaky camera movement. To a lesser extent, the same problem is apparent with panning and tilting movements.

Handheld Cameras

For out-of-studio production work, the use of handheld cameras is very common. Shoulder-supported professional units and consumer-oriented palm-sized camcorders facilitate situations where the camera *operator* becomes, in effect, the camera mount.

down." (See Figure 5.23.) In larger studios where crane mounts or crab dollies are used, other effective movements are also possible. **Craning,** or **booming** (up or down), involves raising or lowering the crane or boom arm. The effect is similar to a pedestal move-

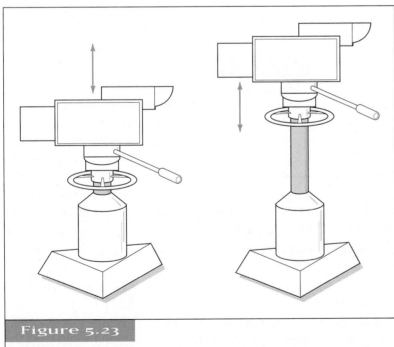

Figure 5.23

Camera pedestaling. In a pedestal movement, the entire camera and mounting head are moved straight up or down by a system of counterweights or compressed air.

Since no mount is used, the camera operator is not constrained in either time (by having to pick up and move a camera mount) or space (by having to shoot only from locations where a mount can be set up). The use of a handheld camera can provide greater flexibility and thus is considered indispensable for "reality-based" television, news, sporting events, and concerts.

However, it is important that the operator of a handheld camera be able to keep the camera *steady* and avoid shaky shots and jerky movements. Such skill usually comes from practice, not only in building arm and shoulder strength but in learning ways to "cheat," such as leaning against a wall to keep the camera steady. Sophisticated gyroscopically balanced systems also are used to steady handheld cameras for professional EFP programs or film shoots. These systems are just becoming available for smaller-scale and amateur productions. (See Figure 5.24.)

Robotic Camera Control

As a result of the rising costs of video production, the use of **robotic camera control** in news, public affairs, and sports programs is on the rise. In these systems, the zoom, focus, and camera mount movements of one or more cameras can be controlled by a single camera operator. Sophisticated camera moves (such as a simultaneous arc shot, pedestal up, and slow zoom in) can be programmed to execute automatically during a show.

5.7 Field of View

The camera operator should be familiar with the various terms designating the size of the shot desired, or the field of view. Generally most television shots can be related to several basic categories, as shown in Figure 5.25.

The Long Shot (LS)

The perspective of the **long shot** (LS), also referred to as the **wide shot** (WS), is far enough away from a person that the entire body and quite a bit of the surroundings are included. Often, the facial features of a performer are not exactly distinguishable at this dis-

Figure 5.24

Sophisticated balanced camera mounts such as the Glidecam V-8 help handheld camera operators get steady shots. *Photo courtesy of Glidecam Industries, Inc.*

tance. It is also known as an **establishing shot** when used in the beginning of a production (or segment), because it relates those people involved in a program not only to each other but also to the setting and circumstances of that program. In drama and in other applications, these wider shots are also necessary whenever people move from one part of the set to another. It can be used as a closing shot to signal a pulling back from the action—out of the drama—as it comes to a close.

Sometimes you might want to establish a panoramic scene or cover the sweep of action with a very wide shot. If characters are so far away that they are hardly identifiable as specific individuals, the shot can be labeled an **extreme long shot** (ELS or XLS).

The Medium Shot (MS)

These shot designations are to some degree relative to their use and the artistic concepts of the director or camera operator. What is a long shot for one dra-

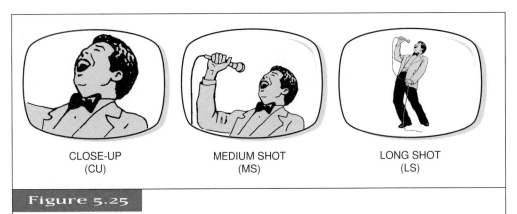

CLOSE-UP
(CU)

MEDIUM SHOT
(MS)

LONG SHOT
(LS)

Figure 5.25

Basic television shots. In addition to these basic shots, many other designations and modifications are possible, such as the "extreme long shot," the "medium long shot," the "medium close-up," and the "extreme close-up."

matic segment could be considered a **medium shot** in another situation. For the most part, however, a medium shot of a person includes most of the body or perhaps even two people. The medium shot (MS) is the basic shot in standard television production. It is used to convey much of the dialogue in drama and most of the action in talk shows, game shows, variety programs, and many other studio productions.

The Close-up (CU)

The **close-up** shot—with its sense of physical intimacy—can probe the individual and personal aspects of what a program is communicating. In many dramatic situations, the close-up is the only way to get insight into the emotional state of a person or performer. A close-up shot may, of course, be used to view objects as well as people. It may be a close-up of some item that has importance to the narrative of a drama. In a commercial, it may be the product that is examined in more detail.

The **extreme close-up** shot is most often used to intensify the emotion of a dramatic situation or musical performance. When these shots are used carefully, they can add the right artistic effect at the right moment. While the difference between the close-up and extreme close-up is open to interpretation, the essential distinction is that the *extreme close-up* normally calls attention to itself. While a close-up of a person's entire face will not normally call special attention to itself, for example, an extreme close-up of a tear rolling down that person's face will.

Alternating Fields of View

The process of alternating among long shots, medium shots, and close-up segments of a program is possibly the most important element in the communicative language of both film and television. This basic principle was discovered by pioneers such as Edwin Porter and D. W. Griffith during the early days of the motion picture. They realized that by moving the camera into a closer position, they could accomplish what is automatically done by the eye and the mind. While the scope of human vision is almost 180 degrees, we immediately isolate and particularize the focus of our attention to a single person or object when the brain is motivated by a stimulus such as motion or sound. Cutting from a wide-angle to a close-up camera shot is much the same process, except that the distance factor is greatly reduced by lens magnification. This process of alternating shots, as you will see, is accomplished through either video switching (Chapter 6) or editing (Chapter 8).

5.8 Picture Composition

Beyond understanding how cameras are operated and how different types of shots are identified, it is important to understand some of the aesthetic disciplines of shooting video. As we discuss the following elements of framing, headroom, lead room,

WRONG WRONG CORRECT

Figure 5.26

Correct headroom framing. Although it is largely a matter of subjective judgment and artistic "feel," it is important that the camera operator always be aware of the headroom on every shot. Too much headroom is as bad as too little.

depth composition, angle of elevation, balance, and movement, keep in mind that the various "rules" that have evolved as part of the grammar of the medium should be considered guidelines. As with any artistic effort, there is always room for a new approach if it communicates something to an audience. Once the rules have been mastered, they can be modified or even ignored as long as the creative person does so with a full understanding of the basic purposes of those guidelines.

Framing

Television directors have developed a simple terminology to describe the basic dimension of a shot to the camera operator. The scope of a shot is described in terms of that portion of the body that is to be cut off by the bottom edge of the picture. Thus a *full shot, thigh shot,* or *chest shot* quickly communicates the desired framing of the person or persons in the picture.

Equally useful are the terms *single, two-shot,* or *three-shot,* which describe the number of people to be included in the shot. Other descriptive labels have evolved to specify certain kinds of desired shots. For example, an *over-the-shoulder shot* (O/S) might be called for in a situation when two people are facing each other in a conversation (such as a dramatic scene or an interview program). This is a shot favoring one person (who generally is facing the camera) framed by the back of the head and shoulder of the person whose back is to the camera.

Headroom

An important discipline for all camera operators is to consistently maintain an appropriate amount of **headroom.** This term refers to the space between the top of a subject's head and the top of the frame. When this distance is not observed, the results can be somewhat distracting. (See Figure 5.26.)

It is especially important that headroom distance be uniform among all cameras on any production. A helpful guide for shot consistency is to place the eyes of subjects at the point of an imaginary line approximately one-third of the way down from the top of the picture. In close-up shots, the framing is best with the eyes slightly below the line; in wider shots, they should be slightly above the line. (See Figure 5.27.)

Lead Room

When speakers or performers directly address the camera, they generally are centered in the frame, unless a foreground object or over-the-shoulder visual effect is to be included in the frame. When a subject in a close-up shot is speaking to another with his or her head turned toward that person, the framing is much more attractive if there is an added amount of **lead room** (talk space) in the side of the frame to which the person has turned. (See Figure 5.28.) By the same token, a distracting, crowded effect is created if the framing is such that the face of the subject is placed too close to the frame edge. The concept of lead room applies even more strongly to moving subjects. If a person (or animal or object, for that matter) is moving

Figure 5.27

Correct headroom on different-sized shots. As a general rule—with many exceptions—the longer a shot is, the more headroom it should have.

BAD   BETTER   BEST

Figure 5.28

Proper lead room or "talk space." The camera operator should always intuitively give additional space in the direction that the talent is looking.

laterally across the screen, it is important to allow lead room in front. (See Figure 5.29.)

Depth Composition

The video message is transmitted by means of a two-D medium. To simulate some feeling of depth, the director has a number of options that involve lighting, camera work, the set, and the placement of performers. One method is to make sure that the performers are separated from the set in the background both by their physical positions and by the constructive use of lighting. In this situation, it is important to portray something familiar like the interior of a room or office to provide a feeling of scale or perspective. If a plain or abstract background is used, the viewer has no yardstick against which to gauge the distance from the subject to background.

Foreground objects can add significantly to the feeling of depth. By framing some nearby objects off to one side or along the bottom of the picture, the subject in the background is placed in greater relief. Care must be taken, though, not to force an unnatural effect for its own sake, as this will undoubtedly appear contrived to the viewer.

Whenever possible, depth composition can be achieved with the arrangement—or **blocking**—of talent. If several people appear in a scene, try to arrange them so that some are closer to the camera than others. In a two-shot, an over-the-shoulder shot as a rule is preferred to a flat two-shot of a double profile. (See Figure 5.30.)

A feeling of depth also can be achieved by careful use of angles. If a shot calls for someone to sit behind a desk, the camera can get a much more interesting shot by shooting the desk and subject from an angle.

BAD   CORRECT

Figure 5.29

Proper lead room for a moving subject. Whenever a subject is moving, the camera operator should visually anticipate the flow of movement, allowing the viewer to see where the subject is going.

Figure 5.30

Depth staging. The over-the-shoulder shot (*left*) generally presents a more dynamic, interesting, and aesthetically pleasing picture than the flat double-profile two-shot (*right*). By shooting the person behind the desk from an angle (*left*), a more inviting and vigorous effect can be achieved than with a formal head-on flat shot (*right*).

(Of course, the dramatic context might call for a formal head-on shot of a character such as a judge or stern employer.)

Angle of Elevation

For most conventional composition, the camera should shoot at an angle relatively level to the subject. Generally speaking, try to place the camera lens at eye level with the talent. This is fairly normal when the talent is standing. When seated, however, this means that you must move the camera down so the camera is as low as the talent. To achieve this level angle, most "talk sets" (news programs, interviews, discussion shows, talk shows) are staged on a raised platform or riser. If you cannot avoid shooting down into an interview or discussion set, the steep angle can be minimized somewhat by using a longer lens setting and dollying back away from the set. The farther back you can get, the less steep the angle will be.

There are times when, for dramatic effect, you will not want to shoot the talent at a level angle. To portray an actor as being overwhelmed, submissive, or downtrodden, you will shoot the actor from a higher elevation. Shooting from a high angle implies control and dominance over the individual. On the other hand, if you want to give a character power and authority, you should shoot that actor from a low angle. By placing the viewer in the lowered position, you endow the character with force and strength.

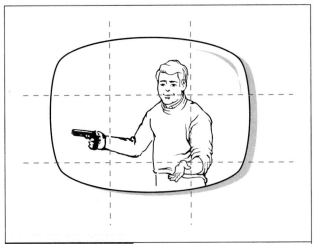

Figure 5.31

Asymmetrical balance and the rule of thirds. Note how the two main focal points—the face and the hand holding the gun—are located at the intersections of the thirds.

Figure 5.32

Poor shot composition. The sign looks like it is "growing" out of the person's head.

Balance

Many beginning camera operators try to achieve a pleasing composition by striving for **symmetrical balance.** They try to place the most important element directly in the center of the picture and/or try to balance picture components with equal elements equidistant from the center. This kind of mechanical or symmetrical balancing can lead to very stiff, dull, formal pictures.

A more dynamic kind of composition is **asymmetrical balance,** wherein a lightweight object some distance from the center of the picture can balance a heavier object closer to the center (similar to a seesaw with a light person at the end of the board balancing a heavier person seated close to the center).

Another way to avoid centralization of picture elements is to think in terms of the **rule of thirds.** Imagine the television screen divided horizontally and vertically into thirds. If major pictorial elements are placed at the points where the lines intersect, the result is a more pleasing balance than if perfect symmetry is achieved. (See Figure 5.31.)

Other Composition Problems

There are other compositional problems to avoid, some of which may arise when cameras are used

outside the studio. For example, you should be aware of the background when shooting a close-up or medium shot of talent; you should avoid framing the person so that it appears a sign, telephone pole, or plant is "growing" out of his or her head. (See Figure 5.32.)

You should also be sure that the camera is level when shooting. A misadjusted tripod (with one leg extended farther than the others, for example) will create a "tilted" camera. Consequently, the **horizon line** in your shots will not be flat, creating the impression that people and objects are about to "fall" out of frame. (See Figure 5.33.)

5.9 Production Techniques

Since cameras are used in such a wide variety of situations, it is difficult to generalize the operational procedures you should follow. Using a camera in a studio situation will be much different from using a camera in the field, for example, and production techniques for a quiz show will be much different from those used for a drama.

However, a few standard procedures will help you no matter what the production situation. The first of these is to become familiar with the camera's oper-

Figure 5.33

Tilted horizon. An improperly leveled camera mount can lead to shots in which the horizon line is not exactly horizontal, and thus people and objects appear to be "leaning."

ational controls as much as possible *before* the production begins. Of course, the only way to learn some things is through the "trial by fire" that comes with real production, but you should take the time to familiarize yourself generally with the camera and its mounting components beforehand. Practice using the motorized zoom control, try doing a few tilts and pans, and practice focusing, for example.

You should also develop the habit of checking the camera before the production starts to make sure it is in proper working order. Here, again, true expertise will come only with experience, but it is important to "put a camera through its paces" to make sure all of its components are functioning properly. A lot of this will come from simply going through the process of familiarizing yourself with the camera, but you should do other things as well, such as checking connectors and making sure the picture controls are properly adjusted.

When using a camcorder, or a camera connected to a separate recorder in the field, it is a good idea to record some "test" footage before the production begins. In this way, you will check to be sure that both the camera and recorder are operating properly.

It is also a good idea to practice specific camera moves you know you will have to do during a production. Before the show, you may be given a **shot**

sheet that lists the shots you will have to get during the production. If one of these, for instance, is a smooth zoom out and tilt up from the logo on the desk to the talent sitting at the desk, you can practice this move before the production begins.

Finally, once the production begins you should stay alert and ready. If you're working in a studio environment, it is likely you will wear headphones so that you can talk with the director and other personnel through the studio intercom system. Be ready for the director's commands and to provide feedback if the director asks for it. In some situations, such as live talk shows, the director may occasionally ask you to look for good audience or guest reaction shots, for example.

Many specific operational procedures will be established by the production facility. In your classes, for example, the instructor will establish operational procedures for the cameras and other equipment, including what controls you should *not* operate. Learning and properly following these procedures is itself an important production technique.

Discussion Questions

1. What is the difference between interlace and progressive scanning? In what types of equipment is each used?
2. How do the three aspects of color (hue, saturation, and brightness) combine to create specific colors?
3. What are the basic aspects of lens design, and how do they affect shots?
4. How do different camera mounts affect camera shots? What types of shots are possible with each type of camera mount?
5. Discuss the basic guidelines of picture composition. Why is each guideline relevant, and how does each serve to make a better picture?

Footnotes

1. In 1941, the Federal Communications Commission adopted the National Television System Committee (NTSC) television system with the format described in this chapter. Two other

systems, PAL and SECAM, are similar to the NTSC system and are used in other parts of the world.

2. ATSC stands for Advanced Television Systems Committee, a group created in 1982 to coordinate the development of a new digital television standard. In 1995, the group released "The Digital Television Standard," a report describing the HDTV system.

3. Throughout much of television history, the transducing devices in cameras were the pickup tubes, variations of the vacuum tubes used in old radios. Now, CCDs have replaced pickup tubes in all new video cameras, and you would be hard-pressed to find a "tube" camera still in use professionally.

4. Technically, the focal length of a lens is the measure from the optical center point of the lens (when it is focused at infinity) to a point where the image is in focus. Focal length is measured in either millimeters or inches (25.4 millimeters being equal to 1 inch).

chapter 6

Video Switchers

I t's no exaggeration to call the switcher the "heart" or "nerve center" of a modern video production facility. More than any other piece of equipment, the switcher is central to the creation of video programs of all types, and it is literally the connecting point for virtually all the other pieces of video equipment in a studio. Although switchers are also used in **postproduction editing** facilities, as you will see in Chapter 8, this chapter concentrates on the operation of the switcher in a studio production environment. The general operation of the switcher is the same in either situation.

The video switcher's functions are much like those of the audio console. First and foremost, it is an *editing* device that facilitates the time-ordered sequencing of inputs within a live or live-to-tape video production. To do this, the switcher serves a *channeling* or routing function as it selects a video source from all the available inputs, such as cameras, videotape machines, remote feeds, character generators, and computer-generated graphics. The switcher also functions as a *mixing* component that can combine two or more picture sources in a number of different ways. Through the use of **digital video effects** (DVE), a switcher can become a **special effects generator** (SEG), thus functioning as a *shaping* device that can alter the appearance of video inputs.

Despite the wide range of switcher types and levels of complexity, a few basic principles of design, function, and operation are common to all units. Once you understand these essential principles, you can more confidently approach the operation of the advanced switcher units found in professional production environments.

The *disciplines* of switchers include understanding how they are connected to other equipment and the basic concepts of their design. This understanding will make the *techniques* of switcher operation to achieve various effects much easier to grasp. This chapter covers the following topics:

- The basic configuration and design concepts of switchers (6.1).
- The types of buses found on switchers (6.2).
- The function of various buses found on switchers (6.2).
- Basic operating concepts of a typical switcher, including performing cuts, dissolves, wipes, and other effects (6.2–6.3).

- Advanced functions of switchers, including digital effects and the control of external equipment (6.4).
- Commands given by the director to the technical director operating the switcher (6.5).

6.1 Basic Principles of Video Switchers

Figure 6.1 shows a simplified block diagram of how a switcher might be connected in a typical studio. As you can see, several video sources are connected as inputs to the switcher—in this case there are three cameras, two videotape recorders, and a **character generator,** which is used to put words and graphics on screen. Usually all video sources in a studio will be run through the switcher, and in advanced settings these might include several cameras, tape machines, satellite feeds, and various graphic computers.

Two additional video inputs are usually connected to the switcher. **Color bars** provide a reference source for adjusting the technical quality of video

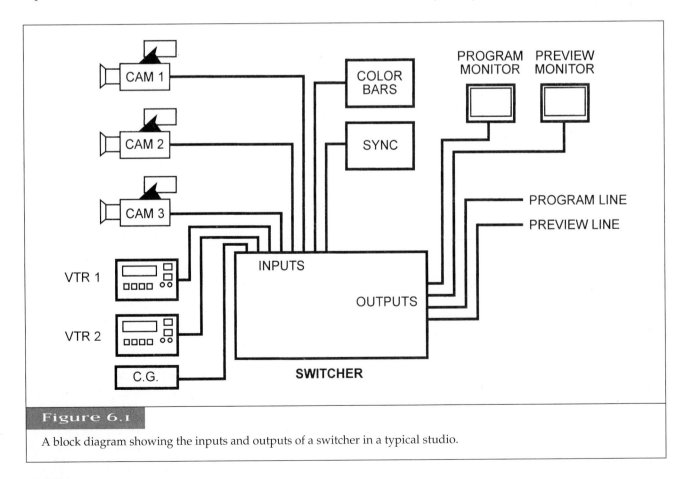

Figure 6.1

A block diagram showing the inputs and outputs of a switcher in a typical studio.

components, as will be discussed in Chapter 7. Some switchers generate their own color bars, while others facilitate the use of color bars from an external source. A **sync generator,** also discussed further in Chapter 7, provides a systemwide signal that keeps all video components synchronized as to when each picture frame begins. Without a sync signal, pictures will tend to jump or distort when transitions between video sources are attempted.

The switcher shown in Figure 6.1 has two outputs. The **program line** is the main output—the one that goes over the air or is recorded to tape. A **program monitor** allows studio personnel to see the video signal that is being put out by the switcher. The **preview line** is a separate output that is used to set up video effects before they are put on the air. For example, you might want to see what a graphic placed over a camera shot looks like before it is actually put on the air; a **preview monitor** allows you to do this. In more advanced facilities, a number of preview lines and monitors may be available to set up particular special effects.

Video monitors in the control room are essential to the proper use of the switcher as well as for camera operations. Even in a moderate-sized studio, there may be up to a dozen different monitors, each performing an important individual function. Each studio camera, character generator, and video recorder, for example, will have a small (7- to 10-inch) individual monitor. In a live broadcasting situation, an **air monitor** always shows the actual broadcast picture, which is received over the air from the transmitter or other source.[1]

Digital Switchers

Like nearly all components used in video production, switchers are increasingly using **digital** technology. For years, a number of advanced **analog** switchers have used digital technology to process some special effects. These switchers, however, still process input and output signals in analog form—the signal is converted to digital form only to create the special effect, then converted back to analog. Now a growing number of switchers have the capability to process digital signals all the way through from input to output. This increases the quality of effects and allows switchers to

directly process signals that come from digital equipment such as cameras, videotape players, and **video servers** (as discussed in Chapter 7). Fortunately, these new digital switchers still operate in the same basic manner as analog models.

Some digital switchers also are capable of processing **high-definition** signals in a number of formats. Beyond that, many are equipped to *simultaneously* output both **standard-definition** television's 4:3 **aspect ratio** and high-definition television's 16:9 aspect ratio. This capability is likely to come in handy for television stations and production companies as the industry gradually moves to high definition while simultaneously "phasing out" standard definition.

Several companies make switchers based on computers. Play's® Trinity™ system, shown in Figure 6.2, includes a digital switcher, DVE unit, nonlinear editing system, and graphics capabilities. It is operated using a mouse and computer keyboard, although you can see that the control screen is designed to look like a typical switcher.

Master Control and Routing Switchers

Less sophisticated switchers are found in the **master control** area of television stations, where they are used to select various video sources such as network feeds, commercial tapes, and studio output. Even simpler units, known as **routing switchers,** are used to distribute video sources within a studio. For example, a simple routing switcher may be used to select which video input is viewed on a particular studio monitor.

6.2 Basic Switcher Design

A video switcher, especially one as elaborate as the one shown in Figure 6.3, can be an intimidating-looking piece of equipment. There can be literally hundreds of buttons, dozens of knobs, several LED display readouts, and numerous other controls. It is well beyond the scope of this chapter to equip you to competently operate such an advanced switcher, but a number of design and operation principles are common to *all* switchers. Once you gain a basic

Figure 6.2

The interface of Play's® Trinity™ system is designed to look like a traditional switcher. Trinity NLE and Play are cool and thus trademarks of Plan Incorporated. *Courtesy of Play Incorporated.*

understanding of how switchers are designed and the essential elements of how they are operated, then practice on simpler switchers, you will eventually be prepared to tackle advanced units. At that point, the sea of buttons, knobs, and levers will make a lot more sense to you, and indeed will become familiar tools that you'll use routinely to achieve your production goals.

Buses

The main operational feature of any switcher is the rows of switches called **buses** or **banks**.[2] Each bus has one button for each video input, and additional but-

tons for other functions. Figure 6.4 shows a bus for the sample switcher shown in Figure 6.1. In addition to the video inputs, this sample bus also shows a **black** button used to select a fully synchronized black signal. Only one signal source per bus can be pressed down at a time. The buttons are mutually canceling—when one button is pushed, that action releases the previously depressed button. Therefore, each bus can have just one signal punched into it at any given moment.[3]

The number of buses, their functions, and their design vary from switcher to switcher. However, a few types of buses are common to most switchers.

Figure 6.3

Wayne Parsons, seen here working the Grass Valley 4000 digital switcher, is technical director of the nationally syndicated program *Entertainment Tonight*.

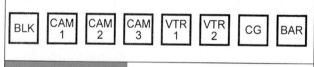

| BLK | CAM 1 | CAM 2 | CAM 3 | VTR 1 | VTR 2 | CG | BAR |

Figure 6.4

A bus as it might appear on the switcher illustrated in Figure 6.1.

The first of these is the **program bus,** which selects the video input that will be put out over the program line. If we were to consider the sample bus shown in Figure 6.4 as the switcher's program bus, we could select video outputs by pressing the appropriate button on the bus. For example, if we want to have camera 1's output go over the program line, we would press the "Cam 1" button. To change the shot to camera 2, we would press the "Cam 2" button. The "Cam 1" button would then deselect, and camera 2's output would be seen on the program line. Changing from one shot to another is called performing a **transition.** The simplest type of transition,

as illustrated above, is the **cut,** where one picture is instantaneously replaced by another.

Using the Preset Bus

To perform a transition other than a cut, we need to add one or more additional buses and have a method to gradually move between the buses. Figure 6.5 shows a new bus added to our sample switcher and a **fader bar** we use to transition from one bus selection to the other. The program bus still determines the video source that is going out over the program line, but now we use the **preset bus** to select the *next* video input. The preset bus also normally has its own video monitor, meaning that the operator can see (preview) the input selected on the preset bus before it is actually put on the air.

The use of two or more separate buses allows us to perform transitions such as **dissolves**—where one picture gradually fades into another—**wipes,** and advanced effects; the specific transition is determined by selecting the appropriate controls elsewhere on the

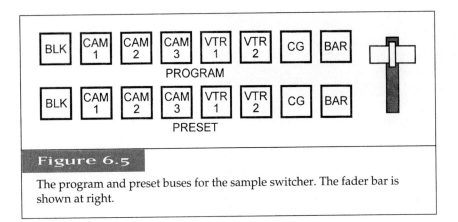

Figure 6.5

The program and preset buses for the sample switcher. The fader bar is shown at right.

switcher. Wipes and advanced effects will be discussed later in this chapter, but for now let's assume that we want to perform a dissolve.

The simplest type of dissolve is a **fade-in** from black signal to a video input, commonly used at the beginning of a program. For example, let's say we want to begin on black signal, then fade in to camera 1. We set up our buses as shown in Figure 6.6(a): We select "Black" on the program bus, "Cam 1" on the preset bus, and place the fader bar in the fully downward position. As set up in this manner, we will see black signal over the program line. When we move the fader bar upward, the input selected on the preset bus gradually fades in, eventually completely replacing the original signal on the program bus. At completion, as shown in Figure 6.6(b), "Cam 1" is selected on the program bus, and camera 1's signal is now seen on the program line. The speed at which we move the fader bar determines the speed of the dissolve between buses.

We can still perform cut transitions by simply depressing other buttons on the program bus. For example, we could cut to camera 2, then camera 3, then back to camera 1 by appropriately pressing the buttons on the program bus. If, in the middle of the program, we want to dissolve from camera 2 to camera 3, we simply press "Cam 3" on the preset bus ("Cam 2" will already be selected on the program bus, since it is currently on-air), then move the fader bar back down to perform the dissolve.

It is important to point out that on switchers that use preset buses, the *physical* position of the fader bar does not correspond to which bus is selected. For example, just because the fader bar is in the down posi-

tion, it does not mean that the preset bus selection is currently on-air. The program bus is *always* on-air, and moving the fader bar—whether down to up or up to down—always replaces the program bus input with the preset bus input. It also—as you can see in Figure 6.6(b)—replaces the preset bus selection with the previous selection on the program bus. Thus, the fader bar essentially "flip-flops" the program and preset bus selections.

In a manner similar to how we performed the fade-in from black, we can **fade out** to black at the end of the program. To do this, we would simply select "Black" on the preset bus, then move the fader bar to its opposite position. On our program monitor, we would see the picture gradually fade to black, the speed of the fade determined by how quickly we moved the fader bar.

If in the process of performing a dissolve between video inputs we simply stop the fader bar at its midpoint, we end up with a **superimposition,** or **super.** This is simply two pictures that are blended together. You have probably seen this effect in live musical performances, where, for instance, a close-up of a guitar player's hand is blended with a wider shot. We can "hold" the super as long as we wish by simply leaving the fader bar at midpoint.

Wipes

In making a transition between two consecutive pictures, there are times when neither the cut nor the dissolve is suitable. An example might be if you want to draw special attention to a picture or series of pictures. The wipe transition often accomplishes this perfectly—by letting the viewer see portions of both

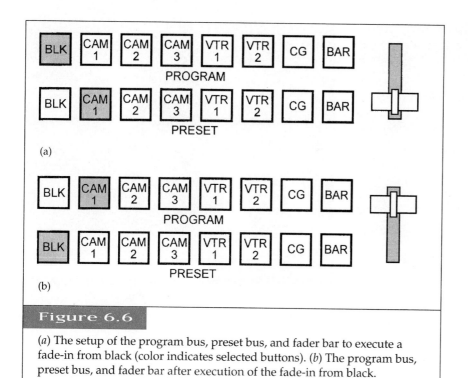

Figure 6.6

(*a*) The setup of the program bus, preset bus, and fader bar to execute a fade-in from black (color indicates selected buttons). (*b*) The program bus, preset bus, and fader bar after execution of the fade-in from black.

pictures as the separation line moves through the screen. Used excessively, the wipe calls attention to itself as a gimmick, but when used with discretion, it can become an important part of your visual vocabulary.

Many switchers have dozens of patterned wipe designs—ranging from the traditional vertical line moving horizontally across the screen (or the horizontal line moving vertically down the screen) to diagonals, diamonds, circles, and boxes, to the jagged shark-tooth effect, which is the cliché of the late-night horror-movie show. Most switchers also have at least some capability to create and manipulate the borders, or edges, that appear between wipe effects. These borders can be made different colors and thicknesses and also can be set as either "hard" (creating a sharp delineation between the border and the video) or "soft" (where the border fades into the video).

Wipe transitions are performed just like dissolves; it is, as noted in the previous section, simply a matter of selecting a wipe instead of a dissolve by pressing the appropriate button on the switcher, as will be discussed later.

Just as dissolves can be halted at midpoint to create superimpositions, wipes also can be halted at mid-

point to create a number of effects. One common application of a "suspended" wipe transition, the **split screen,** combines two pictures with either a horizontal or vertical (or occasionally diagonal) line separating the screen into two distinct areas—with a different picture (from separate cameras or other video sources) in each part of the screen, as shown in Figure 6.7. By positioning the fader bar, the relative sizes of the two pictures can be adjusted.

It also is possible to create a **corner insert,** which places the inserted camera picture in any quadrant of the screen, as shown in Figure 6.8. Again, the exact size and proportion of the corner insert can be adjusted by using the fader bar. Another useful special effect is the **spotlight,** which enables the operator to dim the entire screen except for one circle of light that can be shaped, changed in size, and positioned anywhere on the screen with a joystick.

Keys

We have already discussed how a suspended dissolve can create a superimposition that blends two separate video sources. A key effect also blends two or more

Figure 6.7

A split-screen effect between two cameras produced using a wipe halted at midpoint.

Figure 6.8

A corner insert effect produced using a wipe transition halted at midpoint.

sources but actually "cuts out" part of one source and replaces it with another source.[4] In this way, both sources are able to maintain their brightness level, unlike the superimposition that actually weakens the level of both sources. Keys are most often used to place lettering or graphics "over" a video signal; in reality, the switcher "cuts a hole" in the video signal and inserts the lettering (from a separate video source) into it. Figure 6.9 illustrates the difference between a super and a key.

This example is called a **self key** (also known as a **luminance key** or **internal key**) because the dominant brightness level of the lettering cuts its own electronic pattern in the background picture. However, in many such effects, a wipe pattern is used to create the outline shape, and a third source is used as an input to fill the hole with another picture. Another version of this three-source effect, known as an **auto key** or **external key,** uses one video source to establish the external shape of a letter or figure—in effect, stamping out an image much like a stencil might cut out a shape. The key effect then uses a third source to fill in the picture and color of the "stenciled-out" part of the design.

Keys can be created in a manner similar to dissolves and wipes. For example, you could select a "key" effect on one of the buses, then set up the appropriate video inputs. Some switchers have one or

more dedicated **key buses** that are used to select key backgrounds and overlays. Switchers equipped with **downstream keyers** actually perform the key effect *after* the signal has gone through all other effects, thus saving other buses for more advanced effects.

Chroma key is a process in which a specific color—rather than a graphic design or pattern—is used as the electronic key to cut out part of the picture. Any color can be designated to be used as the key; however, light blue or green is most often used because it is farthest from any skin tones. Wherever the foreground or key camera detects the designated **hue** (and **brightness**) in its picture, that video information is discarded and background picture signals are supplied from a second source such as a graphics unit, camera, or VTR.

Probably the most common example of this process is seen nightly on the local weathercast. The studio camera has a shot of the weathercaster standing in front of a light blue background (but not wearing any blue item of clothing), as shown in Figure 6.10(a). Through the switcher, this picture is combined with the computer-generated local or national weather map that includes cloud movement and other animated effects. As seen on the home set in Figure 6.10(b), the result gives the impression that the weathercaster is standing in front of a map. Much of the effect's success, of course, depends on the weathercaster's skill in

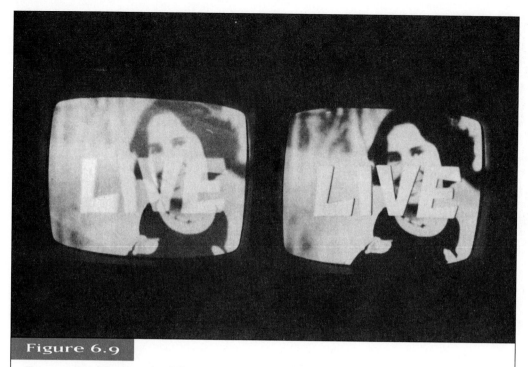

Figure 6.9

Two monitors illustrate the difference between a super and a key. The left-hand monitor shows white lettering from a character generator supered over the woman's face. The right-hand monitor shows the same lettering keyed over the woman's face.

pointing out specific areas on the blank wall through the use of monitors not seen by the audience.

Although the use of chroma key is widespread, it is not without potential difficulties. The electronic equipment has to be adjusted delicately; lighting of the color background of the key camera has to be perfectly even. Considerable attention must be given to selection of costumes and scenery. Slight problems in any of these areas lead to troubles such as "tearing" of the foreground image, an obvious border around the foreground figure, discoloration, or indistinct contours. Many of these drawbacks have been overcome by newer systems, such as Ultimatte,[5] which has supplanted or replaced chroma key in most major professional studios.

Mix and Preview Buses

Many switchers have additional buses, called **mix buses** or **mix/effects** (M/E) buses to facilitate dissolves, wipes, and other effects. Mix buses are actually sets of two buses on which transitions or effects can be set up in advance, then selected on the pro-

gram bus. The necessity of such buses becomes apparent when you think about the limitations of the sample program/preset bus switcher we have been using as an example. Using this switcher, there is no way to go directly from a shot on camera 3 to a corner insert effect or split-screen effect using cameras 1 and 2. Think about it—our only choice would be to start on camera 3, select camera 2 on the program bus, then quickly set up the corner effect on-air; we would have no way of setting up the effect before it went out on-air. Obviously, this is not the most professional way to do things.

Mix buses not only allow us to set up effects in advance, then seamlessly put them on the air, they also allow us to see what the effect will look like before it is put on the air. This is normally accomplished through the use of one or more preview lines, discussed at the beginning of this chapter. On these preview lines (connected to video monitors), we can see an effect without putting it on the air. Depending on the switcher, each mix bus may have its own preview line, or the preview function may be facilitated by

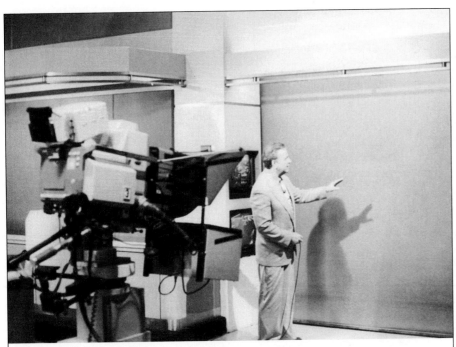

(a)

(b)

Figure 6.10

(*a*) Like most weathercasters, KABC-TV's Johnny Mountain actually works against a blank blue or green screen. The orientation of hand movements and visuals is done through the use of monitors to his left and right.
(*b*) The computer-generated map and other animated effects are chroma-keyed through the switcher to produce the visual effect seen on the televised picture.   *Photos courtesy of KABC-TV.*

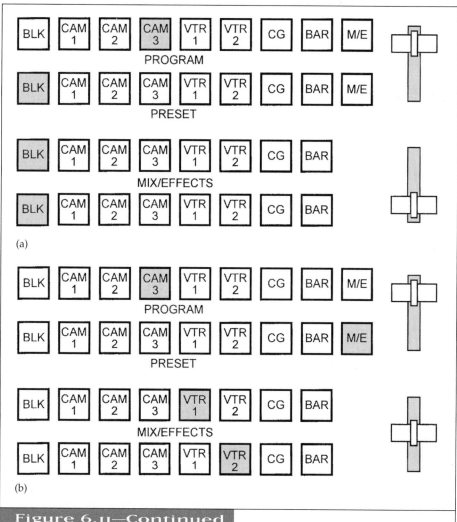

Figure 6.11—Continued

The use of a mix/effects bus to set up a split-screen effect. (*a*) A mix/effects bus has been added to the sample switcher, along with buttons to select the mix/effects bus on the program and preset buses. (*b*) Selecting the mix/effects bus on the preset bus allows the operator to see the effect on the preset monitor before it airs.

using a **preview bus** that allows us to select the input(s) we want to preview.

Let's add a mix bus to our sample switcher, as shown in Figure 6.11(a). Let's assume that camera 3 is on the air as shown, and we want to next go to a split-screen effect using cameras 1 and 2. First, we select the "M/E" (mix/effects) input on the preset bus; this allows us to see the effect we're creating over the preset monitor before it goes on the air. Now, we set up the effect on the mix bus by selecting camera 1 on the top bus of the mix bus, selecting camera 2 on the bottom bus, selecting a horizontal wipe transition, then using the mix bus fader bar to position the wipe

halfway across the screen as shown in Figure 6.11(b). (Remember, we can look at the preset monitor to set up this effect just the way we want it.)

When we're ready, we can put the effect on the air by pressing the "M/E" button on the program bus, cutting from camera 3 to the split-screen effect as shown in Figure 6.11(c). If we had wanted to dissolve to the split-screen effect, we could have done so by selecting a dissolve transition between the program and preset buses, then moving the main fader bar to its opposite position, as shown in Figure 6.11(d). By comparing the results in 6.11(c) and 6.11(d), you see that the end result is much the same, with the exception

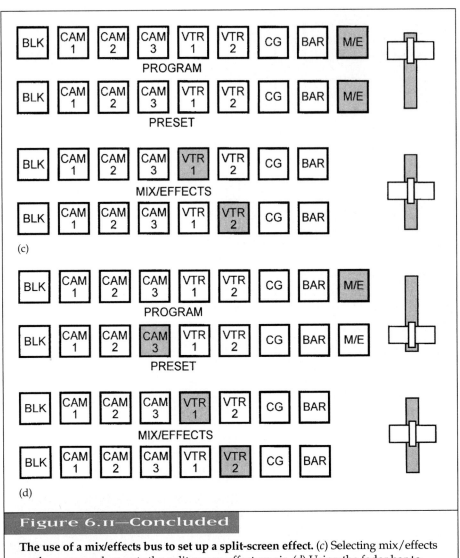

(c)

(d)

The use of a mix/effects bus to set up a split-screen effect. (*c*) Selecting mix/effects on the program bus puts the split screen effect on air. (*d*) Using the fader bar to dissolve to the split-screen effect.

that the fader bar is now in the opposite position and the program and preset buses have "flip-flopped" in Figure 6.11(d). There was no flip-flop in Figure 6.11(c) because we selected the M/E input directly on the program bus.

6.3 Operational Techniques of Video Switchers

Now that we have discussed some of the general principles of how video switchers are designed and operated, we can move on to some actual operational examples. To do this, we will use the Grass Valley Group Model (GVG) 110HD Production Switcher, shown in Figure 6.12, as an example. The GVG Model 110HD is based on the analog Model 100, which has been a workhorse of the video industry for many years. The 110HD, however, is fully digital and supports ATSC formats. Still, in nearly every functional sense, it is operated identically to the analog Model 100.

GVG 110HD Overview

A careful look at Figure 6.12 shows that the GVG 110HD uses a program and combined preset/preview bus design, similar to our sample switcher discussed in the last section. It also has a key bus, located above the program bus. The GVG 110HD can accept up to

eight video inputs in addition to black and color bars; you will notice that each bus, then, has a total of 10 buttons. To the immediate right of the three buses is the fader bar, along with several controls for selecting transition type. The downstream keyer controls wrap around the fader bar, above it and to the right. In the middle of the switcher above the key bus are controls for performing other types of key effects, as well as controls for creating background colors.

The wipe controls are located in the upper left corner of the switcher, including a joystick to position "spotlight" and other wipes. Finally, at the upper right of the switcher are the auto transition controls, which allow the operator to set the switcher to perform automatic transitions of a desired length.

Performing Dissolves

Let's follow an example of a simple dissolve from camera 1 to camera 2 on the GVG 110HD. We would first go to the transition section shown at the right-hand side of Figure 6.13 and press the "mix" button

Figure 6.13

Operating buses of the GVG switcher. The "transition control section" is composed of the individual buttons on each bank for input selection and the fader arm for dissolves and effects. *Photography provided by Grass Valley Group.*

just above transition type, because with a dissolve we will be mixing two signals together. We also press the background ("bkgd") button above the next transition section of the effects transition group of controls. (We will look at this in more detail later.) Next, with the fader lever in the upper position, we press the camera 1 button on the upper program bank and the camera 2 button on the lower preset bank. The camera 1 button on the program bank will glow brightly with what is called *high tally*; this reinforces what our program monitor tells us—that we are feeding a camera 1 signal on the program line. The camera 2 button on the preset bank glows with a softer intensity called a *low tally*; this indicates that camera 2 is selected to be the next camera on the air.

Fader Movement

As we begin to move the fader downward, we will see a green arrow glow at the place where the fader arm will be when we have completed the dissolve to camera 2. (This reinforcement of the direction of our lever move is important in more complex operations.) As we continue the fader movement downward, both the camera 1 and the camera 2 buttons glow brightly as both cameras are seen briefly on the program monitor (a momentary superimposition) during the dissolve.

As the dissolve is completed and the fader lever makes contact at the lower position, we have put camera 2 on the air, and we see camera 2 on the program line monitor. The upper program bank now shows its camera 2 button glowing brightly (high tally); on the lower preset bank, the camera 1 button (the camera from which we have just dissolved) is now glowing dimly (low tally).

Automatic Transitions

If we had wanted a dissolve lasting exactly two seconds, we could have used the automatic transition feature of the GVG 110HD and not used the fader levers at all. We would start out by having the program and preset buses set up exactly as in the beginning of the previous example, with the fader bar in the upper position. (Remember, we could just as well have started with it in the lower position.) We would then have used the auto transition rate controls at the upper right-hand corner of the unit. (See Figure 6.14.) Keeping in mind that there are 30 frames in each second of NTSC video, we would use the controls to set the transition rate to 60 frames.

In this same group of controls, we would use the "select" button to move the red indicator light to the

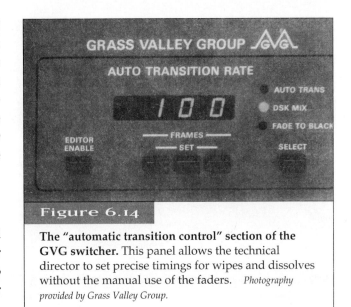

Figure 6.14

The "automatic transition control" section of the GVG switcher. This panel allows the technical director to set precise timings for wipes and dissolves without the manual use of the faders. *Photography provided by Grass Valley Group.*

"auto trans" position. The mix button for the "transition type" and the "bkgd" button for the next transition are still pressed. (See Figure 6.13.) By pressing the "auto trans" button, we achieve a perfect two-second dissolve from camera 1 to camera 2. The fader bar is not moved, although it can be used to override the automatic dissolve at any time.

For an instantaneous cut between cameras 1 and 2, we would only have had to press the "cut" button (right next to the auto trans button) instead of the auto trans button itself.

Execution of the Wipe Transition

As you know, the method of handling the patterned wipe transition is not too difficult once you understand the basics of the dissolve transition. On the GVG 110HD, we first need to push the "wipe" button for transition type next to the fader bar (see Figure 6.13), canceling the "mix" transition button. On the pattern control section of the switcher (see Figure 6.15), the "select" button (under the pattern with a confirming red light) determines the basic shape of the wipe. Keep in mind that the new video from the preset camera will appear in the *white* area of the pattern shown on the button. With the center circle wipe (the fourth wipe from the left in the bottom row of patterns), the new picture will emerge on the screen

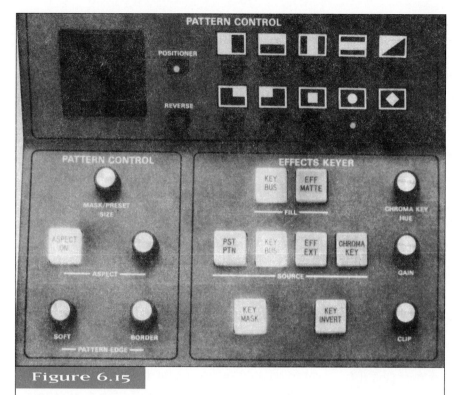

Figure 6.15

The "pattern control" section of the GVG switcher. The pattern control buttons allow the switcher operator to select specific patterns for wipes and inserts. It also has controls that can further position and shape the patterns.
Photography provided by Grass Valley Group.

as a circle in the middle of the picture; its image will be widened by the movement of the fader bar.

Selecting the "reverse" button causes the *black* area of the pattern to represent the new camera. Other controls allow for changes in position and shape of the circle or other selected design. You also can adjust the appearance of the edge of the wipe and the width of the border between the two video source pictures. The auto transition feature discussed previously can be used for the execution of wipes as well as for dissolves.

Keyed Special Effects with Two and Three Sources

Let's say that we are going to use a key over camera 1 at the beginning of a program. To do this, we press *black* ("B") on the program bus, camera 1 on the preset bank, and button 5 (for titles from the character generator) on the key bus (refer back to Figure 6.13). In this case, camera 1 is the preset background, and the character generator will be the key source. The fader arm can be in either the upper or lower position to start.

The two next transition buttons in the effects transition area allow us to select the source bus or buses used in the next transition or effect. In this case, we press both the "bkgd" (background) and "key" buttons, because when we come up from black, we are going to fade to a key consisting of two images—the preset background from camera 1 and, keyed over it, the lettering originating from the character generator on the key bus 5 position.

In the effects keyer section (see Figure 6.15), we must press both "key bus" buttons, because the key bus will be both the source and the fill of the effect. (If we were preparing a three-source key, we would punch up different sources for the source and for the fill.)

Once the selections have been punched up on the preset background bank (camera 1) and on the key bus bank (the character generator), the preview monitor will display the key effect of those two sources. Because the difference in brightness between the lettering and the background is always a matter of delicate balance, a look at the preview monitor will now tell us just what adjustments must be made. The "clip" knob sets the brightness threshold for the key source video that allows the letters to "cut" the electronic hole, and the "gain" knob sets the sharpness of the key effect itself. After viewing the result of these adjustments, we are ready to fade up on our key effect by moving the fader bar to its opposite position. The key effect is brought up on the line, and we see the results on the program monitor.

6.4 Advanced Switcher Functions

Like most other components used in video production, switchers are becoming increasingly sophisticated, with additional capabilities and automated control. Still, the basic operating functions remain the same, as discussed in the first two sections of this chapter.

Digital Effects

Digital effects, either through the use of a separate digital video effects unit or—on some switchers—built-in DVE effects, allow the switcher to perform more sophisticated transitions and other effects. One of the digital switcher effects most often seen is **continuous image compression** that enables the switcher operator to compress the full-frame picture down to the size of a tiny circle, square, or other shape (at any speed, to any size) and—with a joystick—to place the shrunken image anywhere on the screen. **Image expansion** allows the operator to take any segment of the video frame and enlarge it. Another effect is **image stretching,** where any portion of the picture can be expanded or compressed in any direction; ratios can be altered, and graphics can be shaped to fit the picture. One of the common uses of these effects is the creation of a spinning "cube" on which each side is a different video image.

Other DVE transitional devices include the **video split,** which literally takes a picture and pulls it apart in the middle to make room for a new frame; the **push-off,** which "shoves" a whole frame off the screen sideways while replacing it with another image (as opposed to the wipe, which does not move the two stationary frames involved in the transition); and the **page turn,** in which one video image "peels off" the screen like the page of a book to reveal a second image underneath.

Digital effects also can improve upon many functions that can be performed—albeit awkwardly—without DVE. For example, let's revisit the corner insert effect created in Figure 6.8, which has been repeated in Figure 6.16(a). This effect, as originally performed on a switcher without DVE capability, requires the two cameras to frame their shots as shown in Figure 6.16(b). This is rather awkward—especially for camera 2—but it is necessary because the switcher cannot actually "squeeze" the individual camera shot into the corner. Rather, since it uses a suspended wipe, it is simply showing a selected portion of the existing shot from camera 2—no actual changing of the video input can take place. A switcher equipped with a DVE, however, *could* actually "squeeze" a normally framed shot into a corner of the screen, as shown in Figure 6.16(c). Thus, the operator of camera 2 could frame his or her shot normally, as shown in Figure 6.16(d). This would make it easier to cut from the shot on camera 2 to the effect shown in Figure 6.16(c). Or the switcher operator could set up a "live" DVE effect that would actually squeeze the full-frame shot from camera 2 into the corner in real time.

Advanced Control

High-end switchers can be set up to actually *control* other studio equipment. For example, some switchers have the ability to not only take the video output from a tape machine but actually to *play* the tape machine. Similarly, switchers can control external DVE units by triggering when and how the DVE effect is executed and also can manipulate character generators and other graphics equipment.

Advanced switchers also allow the user to automate complex switching functions and switcher setup, saving the settings to computer disk and then

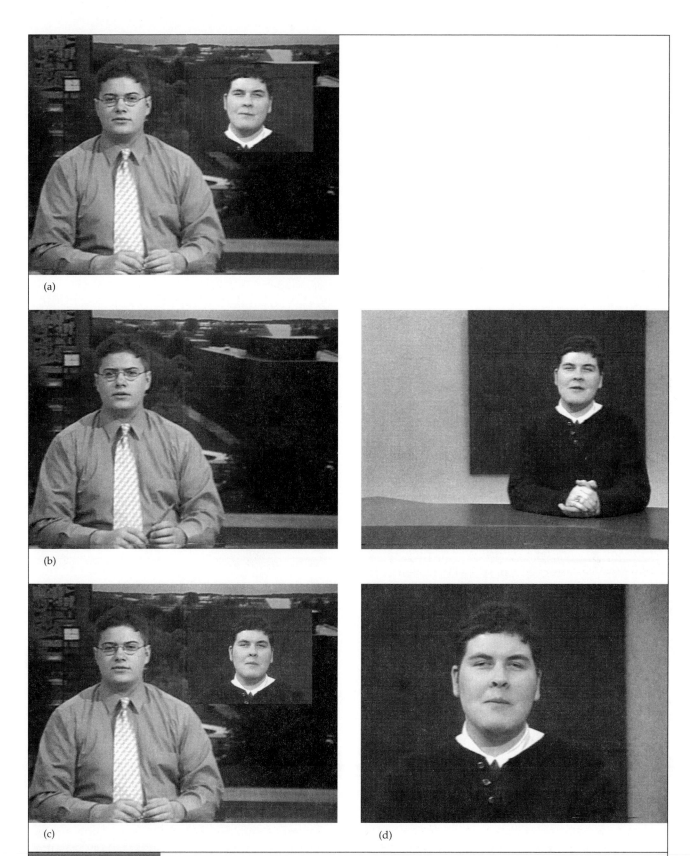

Figure 6.16

(*a*) The corner insert effect originally shown in Figure 6.8. (*b*) The individual camera shots required to produce the corner insert effect on a switcher without DVE capability (camera 1 on the left, camera 2 on the right). (*c*) The corner insert effect produced using DVE. (*d*) The camera 2 shot for creating the corner effect using DVE

recalling them. In this way, an operator can program complex switching functions and then have them execute with the touch of a single button. With proper planning, this allows very complex switching operations to be performed in real time during a live broadcast with much less chance of error.

6.5 Video Production Commands

In discussing audio production techniques (see Chapter 3), we stressed the difference between commands of *preparation* and commands of *execution.* Nowhere is this distinction more important than in giving commands to the **technical director,** the person who operates the switcher in a studio environment.[6] The preparation and execution of the various transitions and effects involve different amounts of switcher operation time. A straight take is ready instantly, but a dissolve to a chroma key effect requires a number of operations, done in a precise order. The commands of preparation must allow for sufficient lead time. Such commands, given over the intercom system, allow camera, VTR, and graphics operators time for their own preparations.

One helpful rule is that the command of preparation for any straight take is "ready." The preparation for any dissolve, super, fade, or special transition or effect that involves getting something set or prepared on another bus uses the command "prepare." (A few directors prefer to use the command "set up.") Although some directors use the term "standby" as a preparation for both takes and dissolves, this can be confusing to the crew. The use of correct terminology immediately lets the technical director know whether to simply get ready to push a button on the same bus or to prepare or set up another camera or effect on another bus. The command sequence for a direct take from camera 1 to camera 2 is stated by the director as follows:

(Preparation): "Ready camera 2" (or simply "Ready 2").

(Execution): "Take 2."

The word "ready" lets the technical director know only to place a finger on the camera 2 button on the program bus.

No matter how rushed the director may be or how fast-paced the program, the director should never skimp on the commands of preparation. If occasionally the director does not have time to give full commands, some abbreviation could be used:

(Preparation): "Ready 2."

(Execution): "Take it" (or simply "Take").

If time is so short that even this much preparation is impossible (for example, shooting a game show, fast-paced panel discussion, or football game), the command of preparation still must be given priority:

(Preparation): "Two."

(Execution): "Take."

When such abbreviated commands are used successfully, it is usually in a situation where the director and the crew have worked together for an extended period of time. Even so, most directors will return to the safer, more complete commands when time allows.

A dissolve requires a different-sounding command of preparation to allow the technical director time to prepare for a more complex series of actions. Assuming you already have camera 1 on the program line, the correct commands for a dissolve would be:

(Preparation): "Prepare a dissolve to 2" (or "Prepare 2" or "Set up 2").

(Execution): "Dissolve to 2."

For a super, the actions are the same, so the commands are much the same:

(Preparation): "Prepare to super 2 over 1" (or) "Set up 2" (implying that camera 1 stays on the air).

(Execution): "Super camera 2 over 1" (or just "Super 2").

We depart slightly from the basic pattern whenever two cameras are to be taken together in a super or key. While these effects involve a movement of the control levers to set them up, the movement is not one of program execution. As previously outlined, the command of execution is "take"—calling only for the technical director to press the line mix output button or take bar. For this reason, the voice procedure in this case should be as follows:

(Preparation): "Ready to take 2 and 3 in super."

(Execution): "Take super" (or "Take 2 and 3").

The repetition of camera numbers in the command is optional, but it does reinforce the intent of the command.

Much of the discipline necessary for keeping a program under control comes from this pattern of preparation followed by execution. The technical director must be able to depend on this sequence. The pattern is broken when a complicated effect that must be set up in advance is called for. A complicated key, for example, might need to be preset several shots before its use. In this situation, after the command of preparation that acknowledges the time delay in execution, there may be several intervening commands. Then a new command of preparation is issued before the execution command for the key. The command of preparation must be given far enough in advance so that the technical director has a chance to do the preset at a time most convenient during the ongoing program. The director keeps an eye on the preview monitor to see when the key is ready. The commands might be as follows:

(Advance preparation): "We're about to wrap, so preview your key of camera 2 and credits on the CG."

(Ongoing shots in the program continue): "Ready 1, take 1 . . . etc."

(Immediate preparation): "Now set up a dissolve to the key of credits over camera 2."

(Execution of the key): "Dissolve to the credits."

Similarly, any command to preview and adjust—say, a corner wipe or an insert—in the coverage of a live event may be given well in advance of its eventual use on the air. There may be several intervening ad-libbed shots. This can be thought of as a non-time-specific command. For example:

(Advance preparation): "Preview a top-left corner insert, camera 3, of runner off first base, within camera 2."

(Intervening shots ad-libbed): "Ready 4, take 4, . . . etc."

(Adjustment of preparation): "Tighten the framing on camera 3 insert."

(Intervening shots ad-libbed): "Ready 1, take 1, . . . etc."

(Immediate preparation): "OK. Now, ready to take corner insert."

(Execution of the effect): "Take effect."

One final note: Fades to and from black are handled in a manner very similar to the dissolve. Because a sync black picture has such a definite connotation of separation and/or conclusion, many directors reserve the term "fade" for use as a command only to dissolve to or from black. This serves as a safeguard to protect against any inadvertent dissolve to full-screen black.

As switchers have become more complex, the numerous visual options available to the director have placed many demands upon the technical director. The director is obligated to use the clearest of command language, which in turn must be based upon an operational understanding of what is involved in achieving execution of those commands. Beyond common courtesy, there is a very practical aspect to this. Ill-timed and poorly stated commands simply cannot be executed within the time framework that the director may have in mind. Such a disparity can have serious side effects, especially with live programming.

Discussion Questions

1. Evaluate the switcher in your school's studio. Is it a special-effects-generating switcher? Does it have a downstream keyer? How many inputs does it have? What kinds of effects can it perform?
2. Why has the key replaced the superimposition in most video production situations? Can you think of a program in which you've seen a superimposition?
3. How does the use of buses on switchers help simplify operation? Can you think of a more logical way to lay out a switcher?
4. Explain the difference between a split-screen effect created on a non-DVE switcher and a similar effect using a special-effects-generating switcher. Do you think a viewer at home would notice the difference?

Footnotes

1. The video monitors used in studio environments are distinguished from regular television receivers in that these monitors are usually high-quality units with the ability to reproduce fine detail. They receive a direct unmodulated video signal, as opposed to a modulated radio frequency signal. Thus, there is no audio and no channel selection capability.

2. Technically speaking, the line and its connectors that run under each row of buttons are termed the bus, and the row of buttons is called the bank; however, in common usage, the two terms are interchangeable.

3. On most switchers, a selected button does not *stay* depressed but simply lights up to show it is selected. So the way to tell which button is selected on a bus is not to look for a button that is physically pressed down but to look for the button that is lighted.

4. Occasionally the word *matte* is associated with the key process. The term was derived from the traditional film technique that printed or "matted" inserts within the larger film frame.

5. Ultimatte is a trademark of the Ultimatte Corporation.

6. The term "technical director" is derived from professional situations where the person given that title has a much larger engineering responsibility to supervise the entire technical staff and to operate the switcher only at the latter part of the production effort. There are circumstances when a person may function only as the switcher operator and is usually then known as the "switcher."

chapter 7

Video Recording and Playback

When Ampex introduced the first commercial videotape recorder in 1956, it sparked a revolution in television production. That same year, when CBS first used videotape for the delayed rebroadcast of its newscast to the western states, the industry immediately saw the possibilities that tape could provide for the *distribution* and *storage* of program material. For the next four decades, tape would provide the primary medium for not only moving and storing video information but for editing as well.

Now the television industry is on the verge of another revolution in distribution and storage, and this one holds the possibility of bringing even greater changes than those brought by tape. "Video storage will forever be recast in both purpose and principle," one industry observer has noted, leading to "the potential elimination of videotape usage as we know it today."[1] This new revolution, holding such potential to change the way television is produced and used, is being brought by the increasing **digitization** of video and audio information, and the subsequent use of computers to distribute and store this information.

You have already seen how digital technology is finding its way into video production components including cameras, switchers, and DVE units. In most of these cases, though, the video starts out in analog form, is converted to digital, and then output in analog form once again. Such digital "islands" have become increasingly common in analog production facilities over the past two decades. However, the true fundamental change is coming as video information is converted to digital once (as it is **transduced** by the camera) and then *remains in digital form* as it is distributed throughout a production facility or television station and stored for later retrieval. As this happens, video will be stored exclusively on **video servers**, powerful computers with large storage capacity, and through the use of **networks**, any number of people in a production facility will be able to simultaneously access and manipulate this information.

But the day when every station and production facility has gone all digital and "tapeless" is still a ways off, if for no other reason than that storing video on tape is still more cost-effective than storing it on computer. For that reason, this chapter will concentrate on the function and operation of **videotape recorders** (VTRs), which are likely to be prevalent for at least the near future. It is important to note that digital signals can be recorded on tape, and digital tape formats have become more common and versatile in the past decade. However, this chapter will begin with a discussion of some technical aspects of video (in analog and digital form) and their impact on how video is stored and distributed. This chapter also includes an introduction to video server technology, including the unique attributes of video in digital form.

There are both important *disciplines* and *techniques* to the operation of video storage and distribution equipment. The *disciplines* include an understanding of how video is recorded, digitized, and distributed, while *techniques* include specific operating and maintenance procedures. This chapter includes the following topics:

- Different types of signals used for video distribution (7.1).
- The special attributes of video that affect its storage and distribution (7.1).
- The structure of analog video flow, including control components and monitoring equipment (7.2).
- The basic design and operation of digital video servers (7.3).
- Principles of videotape recording, and the function of various videotape tracks (7.4).
- The basic layout and operation of typical videotape recorder operational controls (7.5).
- Basic procedures for operating and maintaining videotape equipment (7.6).

7.1 The Video Signal

In Chapter 5, the three color components (**hue, saturation,** and **luminance**) that make up a video signal were discussed. There are a number of different ways to distribute a video signal, based on different ways of handling these individual color components.

The original method of distributing video signals, standardized by the National Television System Committee (NTSC), uses a **composite** signal. This system combines the **chrominance** (which, you should remember, includes hue and saturation information) and the luminance (brightness) information into one signal. This method's chief advantage is that all the video information can be carried as a single signal, yet it also suffers quality degradation because of interference between the chrominance and luminance information.

In a **component** system the chrominance and luminance information are kept separated and distributed as distinct signals. While maintaining a higher quality signal because there is no interference between chrominance and luminance information, a component system requires the distribution of at least two separate signals. Many component systems, in fact, use *two* chrominance signals and the luminance signal, requiring three separate signals.[2] Each signal must be carried on a separate wire, although these wires may be molded together into a single cable unit with individual connectors on each end.

Both analog and digital signals can be distributed in either composite or component format. Specific videotape formats, as you will see in section 7.4, are designed to use either composite or component signals. Because of the higher quality offered by component systems, however, most high-end videotape formats use component systems. Such component videotape systems also keep the luminance and chrominance signals separated on the tape as well.

Increasingly, videotape machines are being designed to handle *multiple* distribution systems to maintain compatibility with other pieces of video equipment. For example, a component videotape machine also has connectors for inputting and outputting composite video signals. A peek at the back panel of the Panasonic AJ-D580 videotape recorder shows a wide variety of both analog and digital inputs and outputs. (See Figure 7.1.)

Another method of distributing video should also be acknowledged, although it is normally not used for

The rear connection deck of a Panasonic AJ-D580 (D-5) VCR shows the connections necessary to receive, record, convert, and output a wide range of digital and analog signal combinations, including those using the multiple-pin connectors that match disk units and digital formats. *Photo courtesy of Panasonic.*

carrying video information within production facilities or television stations. When converted to a **radio frequency** (RF) signal, the video and audio signal are combined onto a **carrier wave** that can then transmit the signal through the air. This is how television stations broadcast signals, and also how cable television signals enter the home. Videotape recorders, especially units designed for consumer use, usually offer an RF output so that you can watch (and listen to) a tape by plugging it into the VHF antenna jack of a television set tuned to channel 3 or 4. However, because it combines all video information along with audio information, it causes much greater signal degradation than either component or composite distribution.

Special Attributes of the Video Signal

Although video signals can be stored and distributed through wires in a manner similar to audio signals, word-processing files, or even electricity, it is important to point out some unique attributes of the video signal. These attributes, as you will see in the following sections, have a substantial impact on how video storage and distribution systems must be designed and operated.

The first factor is that the video signal—whether in analog or digital form—contains a tremendous amount of information. You know, for instance, that there are more than 300,000 individual pieces of information corresponding to the **pixel** information on an NTSC television screen. The amount of information contained in an ATSC signal is even greater—perhaps two million or more pixels. This means that storing a video signal—in analog or digital form—requires a lot of space.

The second factor relates to the first in that the video signal is *constantly changing*—meaning that *new* information must be moved quickly. The NTSC television signal creates an entirely new frame of information 30 times a second, so it is essential that information is able to flow quickly. The term used to designate the ability of a system to carry an amount of information is **bandwidth,** and it is—metaphorically speaking—equivalent to the size of a pipe. A large-diameter pipe, for example, can carry more (water, oil, sludge) than a small pipe, and thus a large-bandwidth system can carry more information than a small-bandwidth system.

Finally, the video signal requires great precision in order to operate properly. An NTSC videotape recorder, for example, must *precisely* record 30 frames of video per second; even a slight deviance can create a picture that will be unusable. While an audiocassette can be played in a machine that runs at the wrong speed (the music will just sound too fast or too slow), a videotape player that runs at the wrong speed is practically useless. Thus, methods of storing and distributing video signals—NTSC or ATSC—must operate precisely and accurately.

It is imperative that the scanning sequence in the camera and other video components be precisely synchronized at every stage of a video signal's journey through the switcher to all other recording and editing equipment in a production facility, as well as to the home receiving set. A series of specialized pulses—generated independently of the color and luminance portion of the video signal—are used for this purpose. The **vertical sync pulse** coordinates the start of each new frame or field, while the **horizontal sync pulse** coordinates the scanning of individual lines within a frame or field. The timing and frequency of these pulses depends on what type of signal (NTSC or one of several ATSC formats) is being used, but the point is that all components in a video system must be synchronized to one another.

All of these factors are relevant whether we are discussing analog or digital video signals, although bandwidth and storage concerns have become especially crucial to the digital storage of video. Still, if you think that video storage and bandwidth concerns have only become a factor in the digital age, consider that the technology to record *audio* on tape existed for several decades before the advent of the first *videotape recorder.* The reasons for this lag time were the ones just discussed.

Generational Losses in Videotape

Whenever a copy of an analog videotape is made, the quality of that copy is not as good as the original. The reason for this loss of quality is that it is impossible to make an *exact* copy of an analog video signal on tape. For instance, if you start with an original recording—called a **master**—and make a copy (also called a **dub**) of it, the copy will not look quite as good as the master, although it may take a trained eye to see the difference. If you then make a copy of that copy, the resulting tape will look even worse. Each copy made in this manner is called a **generation,** and the quality of each succeeding generation is diminished. The amount of generational loss depends on the videotape format (home VHS tapes deteriorate noticeably after only a single generation, for example), but in general you should be sure not to work with copies of videotapes when it isn't necessary.

The advent of digital tape formats has greatly lessened generational losses caused by videotape copying. While other factors eventually degrade the quality of digital tape copies, in theory it is possible to copy many generations while maintaining the quality of the original.

7.2 Analog Video Signal Flow

Until very recently, video has been distributed nearly exclusively in analog form and—in the United States—in NTSC format. The islands of digital equipment, discussed in the opening section of this chapter, are largely self-contained—video still enters and exits these devices in analog form. Although digital distribution of video signals is rapidly replacing analog, it is still important to understand the basic connections and equipment used in analog signal flow.

Figure 6.1 in the switcher chapter showed a block diagram of the video switcher as the connecting point for video sources in a typical studio. Figure 7.2 is a modified version of that block diagram, showing some other important components in the flow of video signals. As the signal travels through the components shown, it may be necessary to amplify the video signal

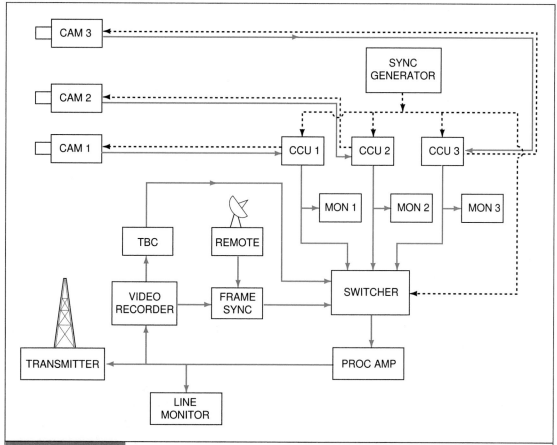

Figure 7.2

Simplified diagram of the video signal flow. A portion of the synchronizing ("sync") pulse (dotted line) is sent out from the sync generator to each camera control unit (CCU) and on to each camera, keeping all cameras in perfect synchronization. The complete sync pulse is also sent to the switcher. Simultaneously, the picture information (solid line) flows from each camera to the CCU, where the video signal can be shaped and altered. The signal is then channeled into the switcher, with the picture information also being displayed on the video monitor for each camera. (In the diagram, from the CCU on through the rest of the system, the solid line represents the complete video signal—color and brightness plus sync pulse; the dotted line is omitted for simplicity's sake.) From the switcher, the composite signal can be sent through a process amplifier, to the line monitor, to a video recorder, and/or to the transmitter after audio is added. A video recorder can also be used, of course, as a picture source, sending its recorded program material through the time-base corrector (TBC) and on to the switcher or to the transmitter. Remote sources (satellite feeds, microwave links) can also serve as inputs to the switcher, flowing through the frame synchronizer that conforms the sync pulse with the other composite signals.

or simultaneously send a signal to several locations. Although not shown in the diagram, **distribution amplifiers** (DAs) perform these functions.

It is also usually necessary at several points in the signal flow to actually *see* the video signal being produced. In any regular studio production, the camera operators, like videotape and audio operators, must have television monitors to provide informational feedback needed to control their equipment. In the video control room, numerous monitors are crucial for various personnel to perform their duties.

Control Components

Because of the complexity of the video signal, several unique components are required along the analog video flow chain. These components are designed to keep video signals synchronized and to lessen interference.

Synchronizing Generator

To coordinate the functioning of all components in the video system, the **sync generator** creates a series of timing pulses that lock all elements of the video signal together at every production stage: switching, recording, editing, transmission, and reception. This **synchronizing pulse** (often shortened to "sync pulse") can be compared to the sprocket holes that keep motion-picture film moving precisely through a camera or projector. When "locked" to the sync pulse, all video outputs are precisely coordinated, meaning that new frames of video begin at exactly the same moment, no matter what the source, as discussed previously. Since the sync generator provides the reference point for all other pieces of video equipment in a studio or other production facility, it is said to provide "studio sync" or "house sync."

Process Amplifier

The **process amplifier** (often shortened to simply "proc amp") takes the video signal—color, brightness, and synchronizing information—from the switcher and then stabilizes the levels, amplifies the signal, and removes unwanted elements, or **noise** (interference).

Time-Base Corrector

The synchronizing pulses from videotape recorders often deteriorate slightly or become altered during the processes of recording and playback. The **time-base corrector** (TBC) takes these signals, encodes them into a digital form, and then reconstructs an enhanced synchronizing signal for playback and editing purposes. In effect, the TBC "repairs" synchronizing pulses.

Frame Synchronizer

The **frame synchronizer** is used to synchronize particular video sources to the sync generator. Most often, the frame synchronizer is used to synchronize video sources that come from outside the production facility, such as satellite feeds. It takes these signals, compares their sync pulses with studio sync, and adjusts the differences between the two. In effect, the frame synchronizer digitally "holds" each frame of video briefly, then outputs it at the proper time to match studio sync.

Color Bar Generator

This component sends a standardized pattern of vertical colored bars through the switcher. This monitor display is used to calibrate the color values and adjustments on all cameras, video recorders, and monitors. The **color bars** are also recorded at the beginning of a video recording so that the playback machine can be matched to the color levels set at the time of the recording.

Diagnostic Components

In many cases, it is not enough to merely look at a video signal on a television monitor. To be sure that the signal is properly adjusted at various points in the signal flow, it is necessary to use a **waveform monitor** and **vectorscope**, which are sometimes combined into one unit. In many cases, this adjustment will involve internal calibration of a component (such as a switcher) so that it outputs a properly adjusted video signal. This type of calibration, usually done by a studio engineer, is probably done only at certain intervals (a period of weeks or months, perhaps). However, time-base corrector units usually have external controls that allow more convenient adjustment of video signals being output by tape machines or other sources, and cameras used in a studio have a **camera control unit** (CCU) for adjusting their output. Such devices are normally adjusted on a daily basis, if not more often.

While the art (or, perhaps more accurately, *science*) of properly adjusting an NTSC video signal using a waveform monitor and vectorscope is best learned through hands-on practice with direct instruction, this section will briefly describe what these monitoring devices actually *monitor* and how to adjust the video signal to its optimal level.

The initial adjustment of any piece of video equipment usually uses color bars as the video output. A camera's CCU can be set to output color bars, or a tape with color bars recorded on it can be played in a VTR. The waveform monitor shows the black and white (luminance) information in a video signal, while a vectorscope shows the color (chrominance) information. Figure 7.3(a) shows color bars output on a

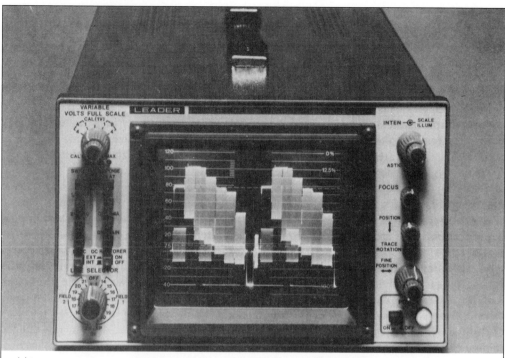

(a)

(b)

Figure 7.3

The waveform monitor (*a*) is used for analyzing and adjusting the luminance portion of an analog picture. The vertical bars indicate differing ranges of color brightness. The display on the vectorscope (*b*) provides information on the status of both the hue and saturation levels of an analog color signal. Positioning of the light spots within the boxes indicates correct adjustment of the three primary and three complementary colors. *Photos Courtesy of Tektronix.*

waveform monitor, while Figure 7.3(b) shows color bars on a vectorscope.

The left-hand side of the waveform monitor shows a scale of **IRE units,** which measure the brightness of the picture.[3] The marking at 7.5 IRE units is used to indicate the **black level,** also called **setup** or **pedestal** of the video signal. In Figure 7.3(a), you can see that the black level (indicated by the brighter horizontal line running through the last three bars) is set at 7.5. Setting black level too high will cause blacks to appear washed out, while setting it below 7.5 makes a signal unsuitable for NTSC broadcast. After setting the black level, the video, or brightness, control of the video component can be used to set the brightness to 100 IRE units maximum.

The vectorscope is then used to make sure the component is properly color calibrated. To do this, you adjust the hue and saturation controls until the six bright dots indicating the six colors on the color bar signal (the primary colors red, blue, and green and the complementary colors yellow, cyan, and magenta) are aligned to the small "boxes" on the vectorscope screen. This process is shown in color plate C as well.

Both the waveform monitor and vectorscope can be used to adjust video signals when they are not showing color bars. For example, you could use the waveform monitor to properly set the iris level for a studio camera.

7.3 Digital Video and Servers

Once converted into digital form, video signals become simply computer data files, or **bitstreams.** These bitstreams can then be stored, distributed, and manipulated just like any other piece of computer data, be it a word-processing file, an e-mail message, or a digitized sound. However, given video's high bandwidth and storage requirements, components for digital video work are normally specifically designed for handling video data. While you can play rather jumpy, grainy moving "video" on a regular PC computer over the **Internet,** storing and distributing *high-quality* video requires substantially more powerful and capable equipment. As an example, a two-gigabyte hard disk (which is larger than the hard disk found on many PCs in operation today) can only store somewhere between one and two *minutes* of high-quality digital video.

Perhaps the main advantage of an all-digital system is that digital distribution of video signals can be completely **transparent,** meaning that there is no loss of signal quality as the bitstream travels from point to point. In fact, the quality of the signal is determined at its point of origin (as the analog visual information is converted to digital data by a camera, for instance), and then can maintain that pure quality throughout the storage, distribution, and production processes. Analog signals, on the other hand, are subject to quality degradation whenever they are stored or distributed.

The use of digital bitstreams thus eliminates the need for much of the analog equipment described in the last section, although some is still used. For instance, a waveform monitor may still be used although, as shown in Figure 7.4, the readout looks very different. Since the signal is completely digital, it is possible to automate many signal-monitoring and diagnostic functions.

Converting between Analog and Digital

Some video sources, such as graphics created on a computer, can start out in digital form and remain in digital form for storage and distribution. However, a great many other sources of video—most notably the images shot by a video camera—start out in analog form and must then be *converted* to digital. The process of converting from analog to digital requires **sampling** and **quantization.**

Sampling refers to the process of literally sampling the analog signal and converting its value to digital form, as discussed in regard to audio in Chapter 3. The higher the sampling rate (or the more frequently the analog signal is sampled), the more accurately the digital output will reflect the original analog signal. In component video systems with two chrominance signals, the sampling rate is normally stated as a ratio, such as 4:2:2. This means that for every four times the luminance signal is sampled, each chrominance signal is sampled twice. On a 4:1:1 system, each chrominance signal is sampled only once

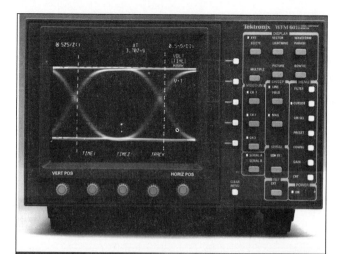

Figure 7.4

These two waveform monitor displays are among several that are used to show the status of a digital video signal.

The digital video bitstream is just that: a stream of digital bits, each of which has the value of either 0 or 1. This bitstream is converted to and from a coherent video image through the use of a **codec** (short for "coder/decoder").

Compression

To ease the demands on digital equipment, video data is usually made more compact through the use of **compression.** Compression literally analyzes the video information and "compacts" it, leaving out information that is not needed. Compression systems are termed **lossless** if they do not lessen picture quality, or **lossy** if they do. In practice, all useful compression systems cause some degradation of picture quality, although it may not be noticeable to most viewers.

Several compression systems are in use, each using a different method of compacting the video signal. Motion-JPEG was the first popular compression scheme, and MPEG-1 was popular for video designed to be distributed on CD-ROM.[5] Increasingly, companies are designing equipment that uses one of several MPEG-2 compression systems, and this is the compression system that will be used for ATSC as well. The inexpensive DV compression format has also gained popularity through its use in the Digital-S, DVCAM, and DVCPRO tape formats. The term **compression ratio** refers to the size of the original signal as compared to the compressed signal. The higher the compression ratio, the more information that is discarded.

Servers and Networks

Once the video is in digital form, a video server acts as little more than a sophisticated storage and retrieval device for the digital bitstreams. (See Figure 7.5.) Most servers consist of two parts: a record/play unit with a computer interface that allows the operator to access and manipulate video information and an array of disk drives used to actually store the data. One popular method of providing the storage and speed capacity required to work with digital video is **RAID** (Redundant Array of Independent Disks). RAID uses a group of hard disks wired and controlled as if they were one large, very fast hard disk.

Servers vary in price, speed, and capability. Some servers are designed specifically for use with one

for four samples of the luminance signal. Figure 7.12 shows sampling ratios for various digital tape formats. The higher the sampling rate, the higher the quality of the digital signal produced. All else being equal, then, 4:2:2 sampling yields better results than 4:1:1. However, greater sampling rates also require greater bandwidth and larger storage capacity.

Quantization is how many **bits** the digital signal is forced into. A bit (short for "binary digit") is an individual digital pulse that can have a value of either 0 or 1. The greater the number of bits, the higher the quality. The two most common quantizations for digital video are 8-bit and 10-bit, with 10-bit allowing higher quality pictures. Here again, the higher quantization level leads to greater bandwidth and storage demands.[4]

Figure 7.5

A video server unit. *Photo Courtesy of Grass Valley Group.*

compression system, while others can use a variety of types. More expensive systems also have the capability to simultaneously input and output multiple bitstreams, meaning that video can be going into and coming out of the system at the same time.

Servers can be connected together (and to other video components) using a network system. Such systems allow servers to share digital bitstreams and to move digital data from place to place within a production facility or across long distances.

7.4 Principles of Videotape Recording

The development of video recording was based on the technology that had already been used for sound. Namely, sound energy can be made to align particles of iron oxide on a tape through the action of a magnetic **recording head** passing in contact along the tape. As shown in Figure 7.6, these alignment patterns (which are invisible to the naked eye) are actually an electromagnetic "memory" of the original waveform. When the tape is moved past the magnetic head in **playback** mode, this action reproduces the original frequencies and amplitudes that were recorded, and the resulting signal can be amplified and transduced into sound.

This simple configuration, however, in which a single stationary head records information laterally along the tape, would not be able to handle the massive amount of information required to reproduce a video signal. For such a system to work, it would have to either use *very wide* tape or move the tape *extremely quickly* past the head, neither of which would be feasible.

Helical-Scan Videotape Recording

An alternative—and decidedly more practical—way to record and play back video information on tape is to use a **helical scan** system. In this system, two or more playback/record heads are mounted on a tilted drum, as shown in Figure 7.7. During recording or playback, this drum spins rapidly, allowing the heads to move at an angle to the tape. As the tape is drawn past the spinning heads, they record (or play back) information in successive parallel slanted tracks across the tape, as shown in Figure 7.8. For this reason, helical scan is often referred to as **slant-track recording.**

To make helical scan systems work, the tape must be partially wrapped around the spinning head drum. The configuration used in VHS tape recorders, as shown in Figure 7.9, is typical of other systems. When the tape is inserted into the machine, movable roller posts pull the tape out from the cassette and wind it around the head drum. As the tape records (or plays back), it follows the path created by the roller posts. This allows the tape heads to maintain contact with the surface of the tape for a longer period of time as the tape moves past, creating longer recording tracks.

Videotape Track Functions

There is, of course, more information on a videotape than just the recorded video information. Audio information must also be recorded, and there must be a way to make sure that the recorder maintains proper speed and synchronization. This additional information often is recorded on **longitudinal tracks** that run parallel to the tape edges (similar to the sound recording example discussed at the beginning of this section). The heads that record and play back this

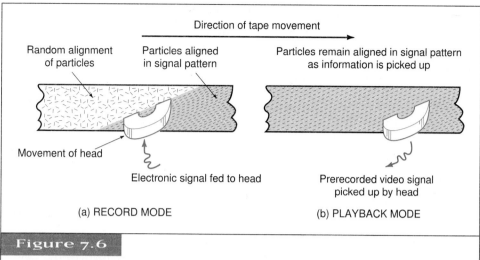

Direction of tape movement

Random alignment of particles

Particles aligned in signal pattern

Particles remain aligned in signal pattern as information is picked up

Movement of head

Electronic signal fed to head

Prerecorded video signal picked up by head

(a) RECORD MODE

(b) PLAYBACK MODE

Figure 7.6

Video recording and playback heads. (*a*) Record Mode. The electronic video signals sent to the record head activate the magnetized head to align the iron oxide particles on the tape to retain a permanent (until erased) pattern of the recorded electronic video signal. (*b*) Playback Mode. The prerecorded video signals on the videotape generate a small amount of electrical current in the playback head that duplicates the original video signal.

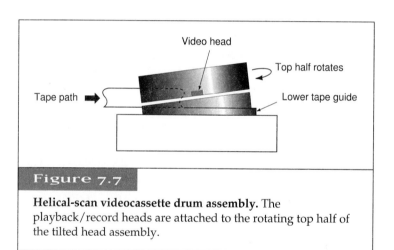

Video head

Top half rotates

Tape path

Lower tape guide

Figure 7.7

Helical-scan videocassette drum assembly. The playback/record heads are attached to the rotating top half of the tilted head assembly.

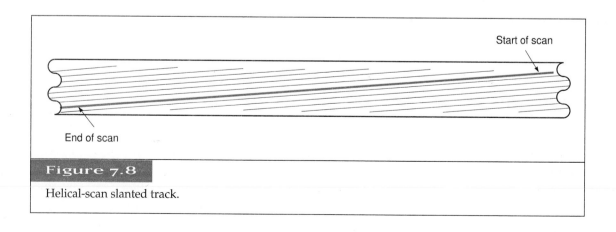

Start of scan

End of scan

Figure 7.8

Helical-scan slanted track.

information remain stationary as the tape is drawn past them, as shown in Figure 7.9.

Many different tape formats are in use, and these formats use many different track configurations. In fact, the only generalizations that can be made about *all* videotape formats are that they use helical scan tracks to record video information and that they have one or more additional tracks available for audio and other information. While it is beyond the scope of this chapter to show the track configurations of all tape formats, it is certainly necessary to understand generally how video and other information is recorded on tape. For that reason, this section will look at two tape formats—Betacam and DVCPRO—that are representative of analog and digital formats respectively.[6]

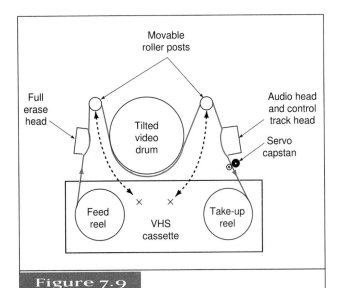

Figure 7.9

The VHS "M" wrap system of transporting tape past the head drum after it has been pulled from the cassette. The "M" refers to the shape of the tape's path, as shown.

Betacam Tracks

Figure 7.10 shows the track configuration of the Betacam tape format. Starting from the "top" of the tape, you can see two longitudinal audio tracks, on which audio information is recorded just as it is on an audiocassette recorder. Most analog tape formats provide at least two channels of audio, recorded onto separate longitudinal tracks. On some formats, however, audio is recorded along with the video information on helical tracks in a process called **audio frequency modulation** (AFM). The downside to AFM, however, is that it does not allow the audio information to be edited without disturbing the video information. AFM was used on the original 8mm tape format and also is used to record hi-fi stereo audio on VHS.

The portion of the videotape that carries the series of slanted tracks is known as the **video track.** As with every tape format, the video information takes up the majority of the space on the tape, usually roughly 80 percent of the tape area. It is here that the information dealing with the picture signal, color, and brightness is carried. Since Betacam is a composite system, it records separate luminance and chrominance tracks as shown.

Earlier sections have described how various video components are synchronized by means of synchronization pulses. When video information is recorded, these synchronization pulses are recorded onto the **control track** of the tape. During the playback of recorded videotape programs, the machine reads the signals and uses them to regulate the speed of the tape and the video head wheel to maintain proper synchronization. It does this by feeding the synchronization information to the **servo capstan,** the device that actually pulls the tape through the machine (as shown in Figure 7.9).

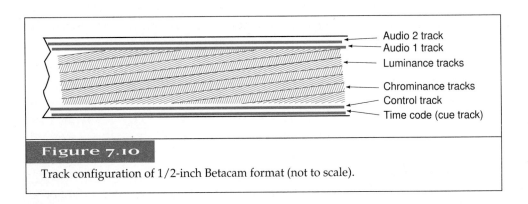

Figure 7.10

Track configuration of 1/2-inch Betacam format (not to scale).

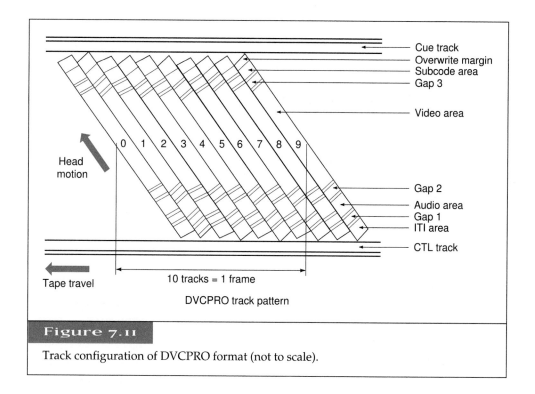

Cue track
Overwrite margin
Subcode area
Gap 3

Video area

Head motion

0 1 2 3 4 5 6 7 8 9

Gap 2
Audio area
Gap 1
ITI area

CTL track

Tape travel

10 tracks = 1 frame

DVCPRO track pattern

Figure 7.11

Track configuration of DVCPRO format (not to scale).

The final track on a Betacam tape is the **cue track,** the name of which is derived from a time when it was used for verbal editing cues. Today, it is most often used to record **time code,** which is discussed below.

DVCPRO Tracks

The DVCPRO system, as shown in Figure 7.11, is typical of digital formats in that the audio and video information is interspersed in the helical tracks. As shown, 10 such tracks make up one frame of video. It is also important to point out that even though the DVCPRO tape is shown much larger than the Betacam tape for the purpose of clarity, in reality DVCPRO tape is about half as wide as Betacam tape. (See Figure 7.12.)

Digital audio is recorded onto DVCPRO tape by the use of **pulse code modulation** (PCM), which samples the analog audio signal and records it in digital form. Unlike AFM, PCM audio is separate from the video, so it can be edited easily. DVCPRO can be configured to record either two or four channels of PCM audio. However, because it is not possible to "scan" the PCM audio when a DVCPRO tape machine is in "search" mode, audio information can be duplicated on the longitudinal cue track.

The **subcode** areas of the tape are used to record time code information, while the **insert track information** area provides signals used for automated functions, editing, and audio dubbing. The gap and overwrite areas are used to keep the different types of information separate. The control track performs the same function as in the Betacam system.

Time Code

Time code provides an accurate *address system* that assigns each frame of video a unique numeric designation. Developed by the Society of Television and Motion Picture Engineers (SMPTE), time code assigns each frame of video an eight-digit address in the format hours: minutes: seconds: frames, as shown in Figure 7.13.

Time code consists of electronic signal pulses recorded onto the tape using a **time code generator.** There are two ways to record time code on tape. The first method records the time code pulses in the **vertical interval** sections of the tape, which are essentially the spaces between frames. Called **vertical interval time code** (VITC), this type of time code must be recorded at the same time as the video information.

Format	Date Introduced	Analog/Digital	Tape Width	Component/Composite	Sampling Rate
U-Matic	1971	Analog	3/4-inch	Composite	N/A
VHS	1976	Analog	1/2-inch	Composite	N/A
Type C	1978	Analog	1-inch	Composite	N/A
Betacam SP	1986	Analog	1/2-inch	Component	N/A
D-1	1986	Digital	19 mm	Component	4:2:2
M-II	1986	Analog	1/2-inch	Component	N/A
S-VHS	1987	Analog	1/2-inch	Component	N/A
D-2	1988	Digital	19 mm	Composite	N/A
Hi-8	1989	Analog	8 mm	Component	N/A
D-3	1991	Digital	1/2-inch	Composite	N/A
D-5	1992	Digital	1/2-inch	Component	4:2:2
D-6	1993	Digital	1/2-inch	Component	4:2:2
Digital Betacam/SX	1993	Digital	1/2-inch	Component	4:2:2
Digital-S (D-9)	1995	Digital	1/2-inch	Component	4:2:2
DVCAM	1995	Digital	1/4-inch	Component	4:1:1
DVCPRO (D-7)	1995	Digital	1/4-inch	Component	4:1:1*

* 4:2:2 for DVCPRO50 and DVCPROHD versions

Figure 7.12

Popular videotape formats.

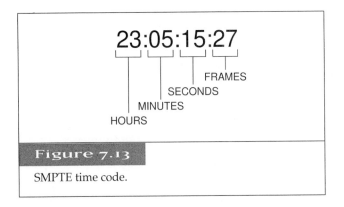

Figure 7.13

SMPTE time code.

The second type of time code, **longitudinal time code (LTC)**, is recorded onto an unused audio channel or cue track of the tape. The advantage of LTC is that it can be added *after* the video has already been recorded, a process often called **striping.**

Most high-end video equipment has time code generators and **time code readers** built in. For instance, high-end cameras can record time code as they record video; this time code can then be read by playback and recording equipment. The time code generator is normally set to **record run** mode, which means the time code "clock" runs only while the camera is recording. For example, if you stop the camera at time code 00:05:35:15, then begin recording again 20 minutes later, the time code will resume at 00:05:35:16. In **free run** mode, the time code continues to increment even if the camera is not recording. In this mode, if the camera stops recording at time code 00:05:35:15, then resumes recording exactly 20 minutes later, the time code on tape will pick up at 00:25:35:15. Free-run time code is often used to set the time code to the time of day, allowing the footage to be identified by the precise time it was shot.

Time code also can be set to either **drop-frame** or **non-drop-frame** mode. In drop-frame mode, the time code periodically "skips" a frame number to compensate for the fact that NTSC color video runs at 29.97 frames per second and not exactly 30 frames per second. This allows the time code to be time-accurate, meaning that one hour of time-coded video is exactly one hour long. Non-drop frame does not skip frame numbers, and thus one hour of non-drop-frame time code video is actually one hour plus 3.6 seconds long. In time-critical applications, drop-frame time code is usually the preferred type, for obvious reasons.

If you're using a camera that cannot record time code but your editing equipment can read it, you can add longitudinal time code after shooting. You could also dub the tape and add vertical interval time code, but this would, of course, cause a loss of generational quality.

Time code also can be used in nontape applications. Most video server and nonlinear editing systems, for example, can assign time code identifications to frames of video in computer memory.

7.5 Video Recorder Operation and Controls

The setup and operation of any videotape machine involves the use of components that generally fall under three headings: connectors, control mechanisms, and visual indicators. The arrangement, appearance, and even terminology may vary with the manufacturer, but once you know what to look for, these basic components can be identified on any video recorder.

First, since videotape machines work in conjunction with other electronic units (cameras, microphones, other recorders, speakers, monitors, editing equipment, etc.), as a primary step, you must be able to make these hookups accurately and quickly. Second, you must learn how to manipulate the collection of knobs, switches, levers, and push buttons that are used to start, stop, or change the basic audio and video functions of record, playback, and editing. Third, you must be able to monitor and understand those things that tell whether the machine is operating the way you want it to—informational feedback provided by items such as monitors, lights, and meters.

Connections

In a studio where equipment and its related cables are permanently in place, the connection process takes place primarily at the patch bays, where labeled receptacles indicate the sources and termination points of feeds. Often the camera, VCR, and other pieces of equipment are semipermanently connected, so you, as an operator, do not need to deal with the connections unless you do not obtain proper picture and sound.

However, much of the small format video for educational and industrial purposes—and much of the semi-EFP production for training purposes—involves a temporary "lash-up" of video recorders, cameras, mics, monitors, and associated gear in out-of-studio field locations. Whether in the studio or in the field, the operational linking of components will be most efficiently accomplished when three interacting factors are kept in mind:

1. The nature and purpose of all signal feeds.
2. The direction and pathway of all signal flow.
3. The structure of the connective hardware.

If you know what your signal is supposed to do, it is easier to know where it should be going and how you are going to connect it to get it there.

Signal Flow

The first thing to keep in mind when making any connection is simply whether you are dealing with an *input* or an *output*. Does the receptacle into which you are putting one end of a cable represent the signal output of a component? If so, with that connection made, the other end of the cable obviously becomes the new output of the signal—and as a result goes into an input receptacle to continue the movement of the signal. It must be emphasized that incorrect connections not only cause operational delay but also can cause serious damage to equipment.

Signal Levels

One of the main principles involved in the connection process is understanding the different compositions and strengths of signals that you must deal with in making those hookups. In addition to differentiating audio from video feeds, you must realize that some lines, such as RF signals, carry both audio and video.

The basic concept of amplification differences was introduced when discussing audio in Chapter 3. The same principle applies to the way in which the video recorder handles audio and video. The recorder has a provision for the input of an external microphone ("mic in"). This low-level signal is then amplified to **line level** within the machine before being recorded

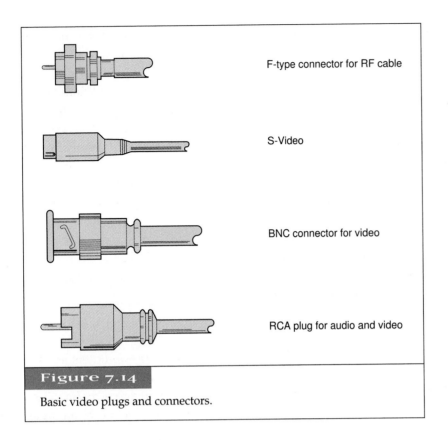

Figure 7.14

Basic video plugs and connectors.

on tape. However, previously amplified signals (an audio recorder, for example) are to be plugged only into "line" audio inputs. If these are plugged into a "mic" input, you will get a distortion from the double amplification.

Connecting Hardware

Connective hardware for audio and video equipment involves a wide variety of receptacles and matching plugs. For example, line video may utilize a BNC, S-Video, or RCA plug. Audio is usually handled by a phone plug, Sony miniplug, or RCA plug. With low-impedance mic lines, a three-pin XLR connector is quite common. Figure 7.14 shows the most commonly used video-connecting hardware. The F-type connector (which may be either a "push-on" or screw-type) is used to make RF connections of both video and audio. It is, in fact, the connector you most likely use for the cable TV service in your home. Both the RCA plug and the BNC connector are used to connect video, although the former is usually used only in low-end applications. In a professional environment, you are more likely to use a BNC connector. The

S-Video is a four-connector plug that provides separate luminance and chrominance signals. Of course, digitized video also can be connected using a wide variety of computer cabling as well.

Because of all the differences in plugs and receptacles, the connecting process is greatly aided with a good supply of adapter plugs. It should also be noted that a variety of cables are available with different connectors at the two ends. These cables often make convenient adapters. With a variety of these on hand, you can quickly connect a number of components from different manufacturers with some degree of confidence. Caution and common sense, of course, should always be exercised when making such connections.

Controls

Regardless of the age or simplicity of design, the transport (tape movement) functions on all video recorders will have 8 to 10 basic controls. Normal-speed playback is accomplished by activating the control labeled "play." On many machines the recording mode is initiated by pressing "play" simultaneously with the "record" button; on other machines, just pressing "record" starts that function.

The "pause" control stops either the record or playback function and halts the movement of the tape. When pausing in record mode, you will continue to see and hear whatever signal was being shown on the tape machine's monitor. When pausing in playback mode, you will see a "freeze-frame" picture. Pressing the "pause" button again will cause the previous function to resume.[7] You should be cautious about leaving a videotape recorder in "pause" mode for long periods of time, however, as it can cause wear on the tape and **head clogs,** in which small particles from the tape become lodged in the head and prevent proper recording and playback. The "stop" button differs from pause in that it actually releases tension on the tape, preventing damage to the tape or heads.

To get the tape quickly from one point to another, fast-forward and rewind controls are used. This is usually referred to as **search** mode. On some units, these two modes will produce a somewhat recognizable picture for visual search purposes. Many VTRs also will have variable-speed controls that facilitate slow or sped-up motion, either forward or backward. A **jog/shuttle knob** allows you to either rapidly search through a tape forward or backward or actually move the tape manually frame by frame by spinning the knob.

The "audio dub" (audio edit) control puts the audio record head into the record mode without activating the video record heads, making possible short audio-only edits or the addition of a whole new audio track.

Tracking and Skew

The path of the tape around the video drum is crucial to the playback of a proper picture. Bands of picture distortion sometimes result when a tape recorded on one machine is played back on another with a slightly different horizontal alignment. This problem can usually be corrected by an adjustment of the **tracking control.** The normal operating setting as determined by the factory is located at the top point (12 o'clock position) on the dial. The slight "click" you feel when passing this point is known as a *detent* position. After

any tracking adjustment is made, the knob should be returned to this position for each new recording or playback.

Most professional units have an additional control for the tape transport called **skew.** When the top third of the picture appears to bend to the left or the right, it is usually caused by an incorrect amount of tension on the tape as it passes around the video drum. This is adjusted by means of the skew control knob. Keep in mind that this is a problem on the playback machine, not on the machine on which you are editing or dubbing. As with the tracking control, the knob should always be returned to the detent position before that same machine is used for a subsequent recording or playback.

Selector Switches

As discussed previously, most video recorders are designed to function with a variety of different types of inputs such as a camera, the tuner in a receiver/monitor, or a studio line feed. There must, therefore, be an **input selector switch** that differentiates between the various levels and/or sync sources of these inputs. The advice of a studio technician may be needed to determine proper switch positions. Whereas a camera signal from the studio switcher would feed through the line input, a single camera might use some other selector position.

On some machines, there is another switch that separately controls the use of internal or external sync sources. The internal sync position allows the recorder to strip off any incoming sync signal and use the synchronization pulse from the machine itself during the recording process.

The **remote/local switch** determines whether the machine responds to controls on the front panel of the machine or to an external controller. When in "remote" position, you can activate the machine's functions (playback, search, record, etc.) from an external editing controller or computer. When in "local" position, the machine will respond only to front-panel commands.

Recording Tabs

One important control element is not located on the videotape machine but on the tape itself. Most formats provide a **recording tab** designed to prevent

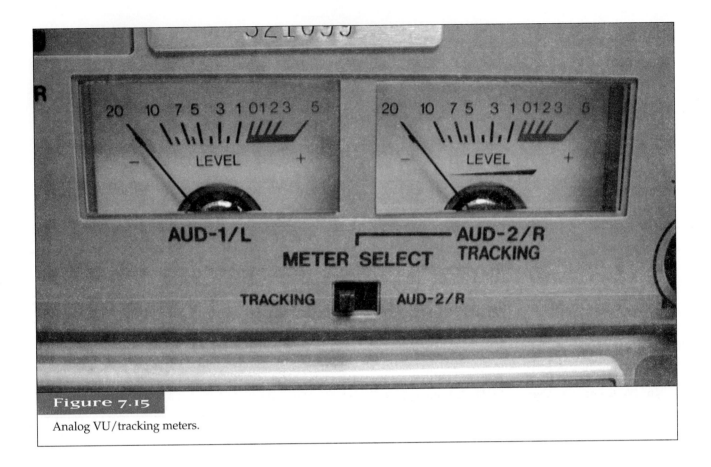

Figure 7.15

Analog VU/tracking meters.

accidental erasure of a tape. When the tab is either broken off (in the case of a VHS tape) or switched to record-inhibit position, a VTR will not record on the tape. A sensor located inside the machine determines the position (or absence) of the record tab when the tape is put in the machine. You should become familiar with the location of the record tabs for the tape format you use in your classes.

Visual Indicators and Meters

Although they vary from machine to machine, there are a number of controls that group together in operational units and directly relate to a visual readout, starting with the light that indicates when the power on/off switch is activated.

The **VU meters** are used to monitor the level of audio signals being played or recorded. Before recording, you should use an audio reference tone to set the audio level to 0 dB. On many machines, you must first put the unit into "record pause" mode (by pressing the play, record, and pause buttons simulta-

neously) before the VU meters will register incoming audio. During recording and playback, you should monitor the audio level on the VU meters and adjust levels if necessary.

On many machines, the VU meters also are used to monitor tracking. To show tracking level on the VU meter, you usually move a "meter select" switch to the "tracking" position. After adjusting the tracking, you can return the meter to audio monitoring by moving the switch back to "audio."

VU meters can be either analog or LED. Analog units have moving "needles" that indicate the setting of audio or tracking, as shown in Figure 7.15. LED units indicate readout with rows of small LED lights, as shown in Figure 7.16.

Automatic Gain Control

Most portable recorders have an **automatic gain control** (AGC) option for audio. When this is switched on, the AGC serves as a limiter that keeps incoming audio feeds within a range that does not exceed the capabilities of the recorder. However, the AGC will

The JVC Component Digital S BR-D85U features LED VU meters. *Photo courtesy of JVC.*

often automatically boost the "noise" of the line signal when there is momentarily no other incoming signal (a pause in the voice or music source), thereby recording an amplified hiss. The AGC selector switch allows you to defeat this feature.

Most machines reflect their recording and editing functions with additional video control switches and indicators. A **video control** knob adjusts the level of incoming video, and a related AGC off-on switch allows for automatic gain control of the video signal. These are usually grouped with the video VU meter.

Warning Indicators

An increasing number of portable recorders include warning lights and status indicators that provide several types of important feedback to the operator. Sometimes these are on the body of the camcorder, and sometimes indications appear in the camera viewfinder. On some machines, a *pause mode* light serves as a reminder that the heads are continuing to scan the tape. There are also lights that indicate the condition of the battery, the presence of moisture that is dangerous to the circuitry ("auto off"), a tape sup-

ply warning light that lets you know you are coming to the end of your videotape, and a *servo lamp* that warns of improper tape transport.

Counters and Location Indicators

Virtually all recorders have some sort of counter or other component that allows an operator to locate predetermined points on a recorded tape. On consumer models and lower-end industrial units, there is usually only a three- or four-digit readout that counts the revolutions of the take-up reel. Since the circumference of the tape on each reel changes as the reels unwind and wind, the operator must keep in mind that a given number of revolutions will indicate different amounts of tape footage, depending upon how far you are into the program. The "real time" counters found on higher-end consumer and professional VTRs are far more useful.

On most consumer-level VCRs, there is a zero-point reset button that, on rewind, brings the tape back to the zero point and comes to an automatic stop. A somewhat more complex memory control permits the quick location of a series of selected points with the tape in the fast-forward mode.

7.6 Video Recorder Performance and Maintenance

The key to successful operation of the videotape recorder—whether for a student instructional project or the operation of the latest digital/component unit—is *familiarity* and *practice*. Instructions and specific controls will, of course, vary significantly from machine to machine. Become familiar with the ones you have access to. Make certain you have taken full advantage of the instructions and directions for the particular models with which you will be working. Especially, follow the recommended care and maintenance instructions. This is particularly important for routine cleaning of the video heads. And then practice. Become familiar with the recorder. Under the guidance of a trained technician or instructor, work with the machine; experiment with it; find out what it will and will not do. Only then can you have the confidence and discipline to handle any video-recording and playback assignment given to you.

A major part of your professional discipline will be care and respect for all production equipment—and the video recorder is one of the most expensive and delicate machines you will handle. Everyone will benefit if you follow a few common rules of preventative maintenance.

1. Videotape recorders require a constantly renewed supply of clean, cool, dry air. Heat, moisture, and cigarette smoke are damaging to all electronic equipment, especially VTRs. Never place books, cassette cases, or papers on top of the recorder; doing so seriously inhibits the flow of air. Liquid containers should be kept away from video recorders.

2. Place a dust cover on the machine when it is not in use, but only after the unit has had time to cool off.

3. When a video recorder is moved, be extremely careful not to bump or jar the unit. Delicate components are easily damaged by slight shocks. Do not attempt to operate a recorder immediately after it has been moved from a cold to a warm environment.

4. Videotape should not be left in the recorder when the unit is not in use. Tapes should be rewound and properly stored in a cool, dry place.

5. Keep the recorder and tapes at a distance from other equipment that may be generating strong magnetic fields, as these can erase the information on the tapes.

6. Do not tinker with various controls and functions without a clear purpose and idea of what you are doing. Maintenance personnel who are unaware of the misadjustments may spend hours trying to find and correct the resulting problems.

7. As the videotape operator, always allow yourself time to think carefully through all connecting and patching procedures as well as the basic disciplines of machine operation. The time spent always pays off later in time saved.

Discussion Questions

1. Describe some of the different methods of distributing video signals. What are the quality advantages or shortcomings of each method?

2. Describe some of the control and monitoring components used in analog video flows. How are these components used (or not used) in a digital environment?

3. How is video digitized, and what are some factors that determine the quality of a digitized video signal?

4. Name and describe the various tracks recorded onto videotape. What is the function of each track?

5. How are visual indicators used to monitor the operation of videotape machines?

6. Given the advantages of digital video storage systems such as video servers, what do you think is the future of tape systems?

Footnotes

1. Karl Paulsen, *Video and Media Servers: Technology and Application* (Boston: Focal Press, 1998), p. 1.

2. Another type of component signal, RGB, separates the red, blue, and green color information of video signals, using three separate wires. RGB signals are sometimes used on computer systems.

3. IRE stands for Institute of Radio Engineers, a group that originally set this standard. IRE has since become Institute of Electrical and Electronics Engineers (IEEE).

4. Interestingly, the human eye is much more forgiving that the human ear when it comes to quantizing an analog signal. While 8-bit quantization (and certainly 10-bit) can produce a visually "flawless" picture, to produce the same perceived quality level of audio it takes at least 16 bits, and perhaps as many as 24.

5. JPEG stands for Joint Photographic Experts Group; MPEG stands for Motion Picture Experts Group.

6. For a more complete overview of the recording tracks on analog and digital formats, see Steven E. Browne, *Videotape Editing: A Postproduction Primer* (Boston: Focal Press, 1989), and Arch Luther and Andrew Inglis, *Video Engineering* (New York: McGraw-Hill, 1999).

7. On some machines, you must press the "play" button to resume playback or recording.

chapter 8

Video Editing

Reduced to its most basic definition, video editing is the process of combining video elements from various sources into a coherent whole. For example, you may have one videotape that has footage of the mayor waving to a crowd and then walking into his office and another that has an interview with the mayor in which he talks about his bid for reelection. Through editing, you can combine these two video sources into one, discarding any footage you don't need.

Using a switcher in a studio production situation, as discussed in Chapter 6, can be thought of as a form of *real-time* editing. Here, too, you are selecting various sources of video (cameras, satellite feeds, graphics, etc.) at appropriate times to create a coherent production. **Postproduction editing,** however, is usually a more deliberative process in which much more time is taken in selecting and combining various sources of video. As its name implies, postproduction editing takes place *after* the video material has been gathered. A postproduction editor may take many hours to create a finished product that is only a few minutes in length.

The *disciplines* of video editing include thorough planning before the editing even begins and attention to aesthetic considerations. The *techniques* of video editing, while differing according to the equipment being used, still involve general practices that will be addressed in this chapter as it covers:

- The difference between linear and nonlinear editing, including the advantages and disadvantages of each type (8.1).
- The variety of situations in which editing is used (8.2).
- The difference between off-line and on-line editing (8.2).
- The need for creating a log and making decisions about editing *before* entering the editing suite (8.3).
- The process of nonlinear editing, including digitizing, editing, managing files, and outputting (8.4).

- The difference between cuts-only and multiple-source linear editing (8.5).
- The difference between assemble and insert editing (8.5).
- The process involved in undertaking linear editing (8.5).
- The importance of understanding editing aesthetics, including continuity and ethical considerations (8.6).

Although it is commonly referred to as "video editing," it is important to point out that audio can be edited during the postproduction process as well. For example, the raw material of a video editing session might include music on audiocassettes or CDs or even "live" audio recorded with microphones during the edit session. Other sources of video and graphic elements such as **character generators, paintboxes,** or **digital video effects** units also can be used.

8.1 Comparing Nonlinear and Linear Editing

Two basic editing processes can be used in postproduction editing. **Linear editing** has been around for many years and uses videotape both as the source of most of the footage to be used and as the recording medium. Linear editing is, in essence, the process of recording from one tape onto another. **Nonlinear editing** has become common in the last decade, its growth fueled by the advent of faster computers and digital video. In nonlinear editing, video footage is digitally recorded onto a random access medium (such as a hard drive), then edited using a computer. Tape—if incorporated at all—is used only to gather the initial video footage and then to record the finished editing project. All editing functions, such as selecting shots and putting them together, are performed using a computer.

Advantages of Nonlinear Editing

The main advantage of nonlinear editing is in its ability to overcome some of the temporal limitations of linear editing. While you can truly appreciate the full scope of nonlinear's superiority only if you have spent many years working with linear equipment, a simple example can illustrate the most basic advantage of nonlinear editing.

Suppose you have edited together a series of shots as shown in Figure 8.1(a), which illustrates the shots in a timeline form. You have a five-second shot of the outside of the zoo, a six-second shot of chim-

panzees, a five-second shot of a giraffe, a seven-second shot of elephants, and finally a six-second shot of penguins. Now, suppose that after you have finished editing this piece you realize that you forgot to put in a six-second shot of people buying tickets and entering the zoo, which needs to go *between* the first and second shots.

If you are using tape-based linear editing, there is no easy way to add the shot and preserve all of your existing shots. If you just record the shot of people buying tickets after the initial shot, you will lose the shot of the chimpanzees, as shown in Figure 8.1(b). There is no way to "stretch" the tape and make a six-second opening so that you can put in the new shot and retain all of the shots that come after. Your only choice is to put in the new shot, then reedit the four shots that need to come after it, as shown in Figure 8.1(c). Editing the four shots likely will not take you a long time, but what if there were tens or even hundreds of shots after the new shot? You would have to reedit them all if you wanted to insert the new shot.

If you are using nonlinear editing, on the other hand, the solution is simple. The computer allows you to simply "drop in" the new shot and it then automatically "pushes," or **ripples,** all of the following shots in order to make room, as shown in Figure 8.1(d). There is no need to reedit any of the other shots; nonlinear editing allows you to easily "add time" to the middle of a presentation, just as a word-processing program allows you to add a new sentence in the middle of a paragraph.

Another advantage of nonlinear is that it allows you to experiment and easily revert back to the original if the experiment doesn't work. An **undo** feature on most nonlinear systems allows the user to simply

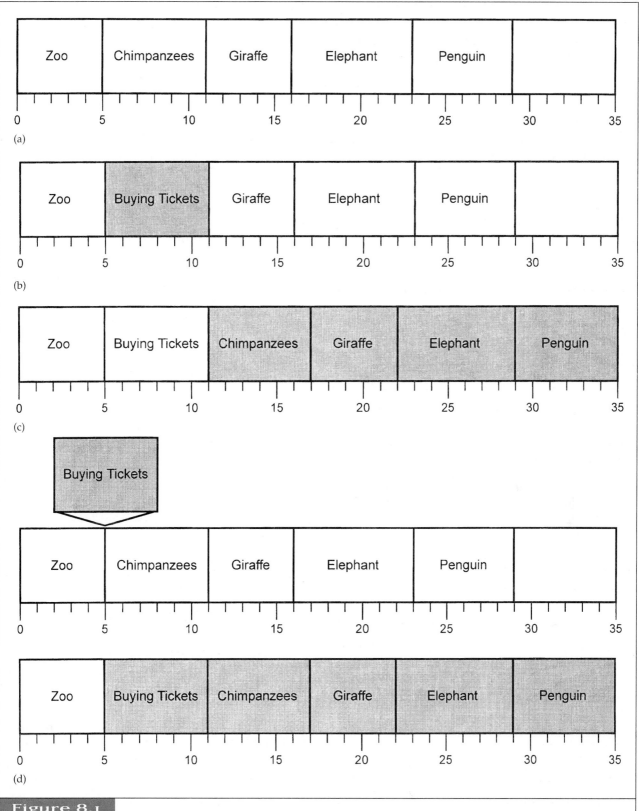

Figure 8.1

(*a*) A sample edited program. (*b*) Edited program after adding a new shot using linear editing. (*c*) Program after reediting shots that follow the new shot. (*d*) Added shot using nonlinear editing.

"take back" the last operation or series of operations. For example, you could try adding shots of different animals to the zoo presentation, and if you didn't like the effect, you could return to the original with a few clicks of the mouse. Using linear editing, you would have to reedit any of the shots that you had disturbed.

Nonlinear editing also allows simple and cost-effective use of **transitions** such as dissolves, wipes, and digital video effects as discussed in Chapter 6. These advanced transitions and effects are possible in linear editing, but not with the ease available in nonlinear.

Disadvantages of Nonlinear Editing

The most significant disadvantage of nonlinear editing is that the video footage has to be **digitized**—converted into digital form and stored on the computer's hard drive—before it can be edited. This can be a significant consideration, especially in settings such as news production, where story turnover is high and time constraints are tight. Although a number of technological solutions are on the horizon for this problem, as will be discussed in section 8.4, at present most video is shot on videotape, then fed into a computer.

Another concern is image quality, especially when considering possible upgrades to high-definition ATSC formats. Although the quality of high-end nonlinear editing systems rivals the best tape-based systems, lesser nonlinear setups that rely on video **compression** may not be able to make the transition to **high-definition** television. Nonlinear editing systems using uncompressed video cost $150,000 and more, thus erasing many of the initial cost advantages over tape-based systems. Also, the quality of some of the transitions and other video effects on some of the lesser nonlinear systems is not as high as they are on traditional linear systems. These disadvantages, however, are likely to become less of an issue as nonlinear technology continues to develop.

8.2 Types of Editing

As discussed, video editing differs from studio production switching in that it is largely a postproduction process. There are, however, several different types of situations in which video editing is used, each calling for a specific technique.

Editing Situations

Editing can be used in conjunction with studio-based production. The daytime "soaps" and some prime-time situation comedies are shot using a multiple-camera technique. Scenes are videotaped as the director calls the shots as if it were a live production. Later, slight errors such as a poorly lit close-up or a flubbed line are corrected by editing in **pickup shots** that are reshot at the end of the scene. Correcting and improving shots and sound from the "live" studio-based production in this way is called **sweetening.**

Editing is also used in single-camera production situations such as dramas, commercials, rock videos, and documentaries. In these projects, camera footage usually includes multiple takes of individual segments, often shot out of sequence and at different locations. The editing process, then, essentially starts from scratch, assembling the program from these diverse video elements. This type of editing—on a much less sophisticated scale—is also used in news-gathering situations, as a videojournalist shoots the various parts of a news story (such as interviews, reporter stand-ups, and footage), then edits them together into a coherent story called a **package.** These packages, which are edited onto tape or a video server, are then used as part of the live production of the nightly newscast. The newscast itself is produced in a manner similar to studio-based productions described above, and the taped packages are rolled during the show. For example, the news anchor will say, "Joe Smith has the story about the mayor's visit to France," and then the director will instruct the tape operator to roll the taped package of the mayor's visit. Shows like *Entertainment Tonight* and *60 Minutes* use the same technique.

Off-line and On-line Editing

Apart from the types of editing situations just discussed, there are two basic modes of editing: **off-line** and **on-line.** When working in off-line mode, the intent is to produce a **rough cut** that is a basic representation of what the finished product will look like. In

Title Class Project 1 TC: Non-Drop Frame								
001	Footage1	V A1	C		01:05:15:00	01:05:25:00	00:00:10:00	00:00:20:00
002	Interview1	V A1	C		05:10:10:28	05:10:42:28	00:00:20:15	00:00:52:15
002	Interview1	V A1	D	015	05:10:10:13	05:10:10:28	00:00:20:00	00:00:20:15
003	Footage1	V A1	C		01:10:10:15	01:10:20:20	00:00:52:15	00:01:02:20

Figure 8.2

A sample portion of a printed edit decision list. At the top, you see the title of the project, and the time code mode (in this case, non-drop frame). From left to right, the columns are: (1) the event number, (2) the tape that the footage comes from; (3) the edit mode (all of the edits shown are video and audio channel 1); (4) the transition type (C=cut, D=dissolve); (5) the length of the transition (shown only in event 2); (6) the begin time on the playback deck; (7) the end time on the playback deck; (8) the begin time on the record deck; and (9) the end time on the record deck.

off-line editing, the editor works with individual edits to make sure that each segment ending leads comfortably to the next, that the timing is right, and that all of the elements of the program are put together properly. Once the editor and others involved in the program are satisfied that everything is "just right," the program is edited again in on-line mode, usually with higher-quality equipment. At the completion of on-line editing, an edited **master** will have been created, which is then used to actually air the program.

The transition from off-line to on-line mode is greatly facilitated by the creation of an **edit decision list** (EDL). As shown in Figure 8.2, the EDL keeps a record of each edit, including what tape the shot came from, where the shot is on the tape, and how long the edited shot is. It also shows transitions and which video and audio channels were edited. Once created in off-line mode, using either a computer-controlled edit controller (see section 8.5) or a nonlinear editor, the EDL can be fed into the on-line system, allowing the editor to automate the production of the completed product. It should be noted that in order to use EDLs to duplicate edits across different systems, all tapes must have **time code,** which was discussed in Chapter 7.

The process of starting with off-line editing, then duplicating the edits in on-line mode, is not used in all situations. In news-gathering situations, for example, off-line editing is seldom used: A videojournalist shoots his or her footage, then edits it once to put on the air. High-end television-production houses and television stations, however, normally have both off- and on-line edit suites. In some situations, such as the

production of a videotape that will not be broadcast, the completed product might be created in the off-line suite. Normally it is significantly less expensive for a client to purchase editing time in an off-line suite than it is in an on-line suite.

A variety of types of editing equipment might make up off- and on-line edit suites. Both linear and nonlinear systems can be used in either application. A common trend, however, has been to replace tape-based off-line suites with nonlinear editors, allowing the faster production of an EDL that can then be transferred to the on-line suite and edited with linear equipment. Nonlinear equipment is increasingly being found in on-line situations as well.

8.3 Editing Preparation

The process of editing preparation should begin long before you sit down at a video editor to put together a program. Taking time to properly *prepare* for the editing process will pay off once the actual editing begins, and the extra time you spend in the preediting phase is likely to be more than made up for by the time you will save during editing. And, since editing time— either off-line or on-line, linear or nonlinear—is expensive, there are financial rewards for good preparation as well. In fact, you should begin preparing for editing before the first shot is recorded, and each step in the production process should be taken with the editing process in mind.

Whether it is to be edited using linear or nonlinear equipment, most footage to be used in editing is initially shot or recorded onto videotape. Although an increasing number of products, such as Avid's CamCutter and Ikegami's EditCam, record directly onto computer disk, tape is still by far the most cost-effective method of acquiring and storing video. This cost advantage is likely to last for some time as well.

For that reason, the remainder of this chapter will assume that video footage is being acquired using tape. Although there are a wide variety of tape formats as discussed in Chapter 7, the basic process of gathering video to edit is the same no matter what format is being used. Of course, it is usually best to shoot your video using a format that is compatible with your editing system; otherwise, you will have to make a copy of your tape in the proper tape format, and thus lose some quality from the original.

Shooting

The old adage, "Shoot to edit" is an excellent admonition to keep in mind. To this end, you should follow not only the aesthetic rules discussed in Chapter 5 but also the directing methods discussed in Chapter 12. All tapes should be clearly and logically labeled to facilitate later use. Since many field tapes are less than an hour long, it is also frequently a good idea to set the time code hour to a different number for each tape. For example, the first tape could begin with time code 01:00:00:00, the second with 02:00:00:00, and so on. This can help speed the review and editing process, because the editor will immediately know that any shot with a time code reading of 02 hours must be on tape 2.

Review

Once all of the footage has been shot, you should critically and systematically examine the material. During the review phase, you should assemble a **shot log** that lists all of the shots on each tape. To facilitate review (and keep the original tapes from being damaged), you might make a VHS dub of all of the footage using a **time code burn-in,** as shown in Figure 8.3. This will allow you to see the time code points for all shots on a regular VHS recorder.

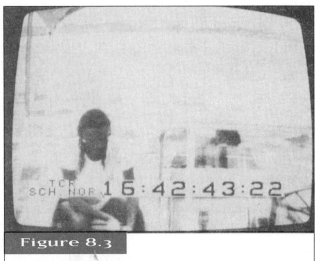

Figure 8.3

A dubbed VHS tape with time code burn-in shows the time code addressing from the original tapes.

Decision Making

As part of the review process, you also will begin to make decisions about how the footage will be edited. This includes picking shots and deciding which takes of particular scenes will be used in the finished product. Although some final shot selection decisions will have to wait until editing actually begins, during the review and decision-making phases you will begin to assemble a preliminary edit decision list by hand, noting which shots will be used along with time code points. Selecting the shots to be used is especially important when using nonlinear editing, as this will determine which portions of the tape will have to be digitized, as will be discussed in the next section.

8.4 Nonlinear Editing

An ever-growing number of nonlinear editing systems available from a variety of manufacturers are designed for many different applications. Companies such as Avid, Media 100, and Blossom each offers several systems, ranging from low-end "prosumer" editors to high-end solutions designed for broadcast and film use (see Figure 8.4). Most use either a Windows-based or Macintosh computer outfitted with specialized software, video input and output cards, and large hard drives. Adobe's Premiere is a software

Figure 8.4

The Avid Media Composer® 1000XL nonlinear editing system. Shown here are the system's two computer display screens in front of an NTSC monitor showing the editor's output. *Photo Courtesy of Avid Technology, Inc.*

Raw Material— Importing and Digitizing

Before any editing can take place on a nonlinear system, the raw material that will make up the completed presentation must be **imported,** or brought into, the computer. The bulk of this material is likely to be video footage, although graphics, animations, and audio files also can be imported. As noted, most video footage is still gathered on tape, although with time an increasing percentage of video footage will be shot on nonlinear media such as hard disks.

The process of importing video footage into the computer is called digitizing. This is normally done by connecting the video and audio outputs of a video-tape machine to the inputs of the nonlinear editing system. This type of connection usually transfers the video in analog form, even if you are using a digital tape format, but some systems, such as Sony's DVCAM machines, have an IEE-1394 connector that can allow direct feeding of a digital signal into the computer. Originally developed by Apple Computer, the IEE-1394 data-transfer format, also called Firewire, is used by a number of companies. Several versions of the Serial Digital Interface (SDI) also allow digital video to be transferred directly from tape machines to nonlinear editing systems.

Most nonlinear systems allow the user to select from a wide range of digitizing quality options. Depending on the application, the editor can choose an appropriate level of quality; the higher the quality, the more hard-disk space that will be required to store it. The editor can also choose whether to digitize only the video portion of the tape or both video and audio. To begin the digitizing process, the editor cues the tape to the first piece of video to be digitized; a cable connection between the videotape machine and the editor allows the editor to control the videotape machine using the computer.

Digitizing an entire videotape would normally be a waste of time and hard-disk space, especially if that tape includes a lot of material that will not be used in the final product. For that reason, only portions of the videotape—selected during the editing preparation process—are digitized. (See Figure 8.5.) These selected portions—digitized individually—become video **clips** inside the computer. To select a section of

program that allows a user with appropriate input and output hardware to edit video on a Macintosh, Windows 95/98, or Windows NT computer.

The basic variables among nonlinear systems have to do with speed, quality of output, formats of video graphics and audio accepted, digitizing options, storage capacity, and sophistication and quality of special effects. Not surprisingly, the more features, speed, and quality you desire, the more you will have to pay for a nonlinear system. Adobe Premiere and a low-end video capture card might cost about $1,500 (plus computer), while a high-end system can cost hundreds of thousands of dollars.

Since such a wide variety of systems are available, and each system has its own particular operating methods, this section will discuss nonlinear editing in general terms, concentrating on common techniques using a Media 100 editing system as an example. Operating features that are significantly different on other systems, such as Avid editors, are discussed in endnotes. The only effective way to learn to use any nonlinear editing system is to study the manual and devote many hours to hands-on practice.

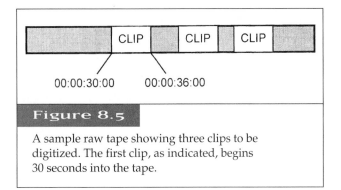

Figure 8.5

A sample raw tape showing three clips to be digitized. The first clip, as indicated, begins 30 seconds into the tape.

00:00:30:00   00:00:36:00

tape to be digitized, the editor designates an **in point** and **out point** on the tape, representing the beginning and end of the clip respectively. In Figure 8.5, for example, the in point of the first clip would be 00:00:30:00 and the out point would be 00:00:36:00.

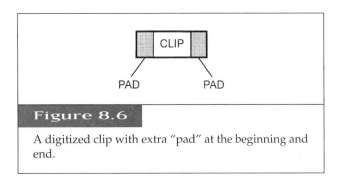

Figure 8.6

A digitized clip with extra "pad" at the beginning and end.

PAD   PAD

After these points are selected, the editor clicks a "digitize" or "record" button, and the computer cues the tape, plays it, and digitizes the selected clip, usually with extra **pad** space before and after the clip, as shown in Figure 8.6. Once digitized, the clip will appear as an icon inside a window called a **bin,** which is a storage area for clips. (See Figure 8.7.)

Video can be digitized without time code, but having time code on the tape can help automate the digitizing process. Using the **batch digitize** mode, an editor can simply play a tape from the beginning, then select in and out points for multiple clips "on the fly." When all of the in and out points have been set, the computer will go back and digitize all of the clips. Batch digitizing also allows an editor to initially digitize clips at low quality to save disk space, edit a program together, then redigitize all of the clips at higher quality once the editing is completed.

Although batch digitizing can greatly speed things up, you can see that digitizing is a rather slow and labor-intensive process. The process, however, is likely to be continually improved as new technologies develop. For example, some digital tape formats allow video to be digitized at four times normal speed, meaning 20 minutes of video could be digitized in 5 minutes. Other systems allow multiple streams of video to be digitized at one time, storing

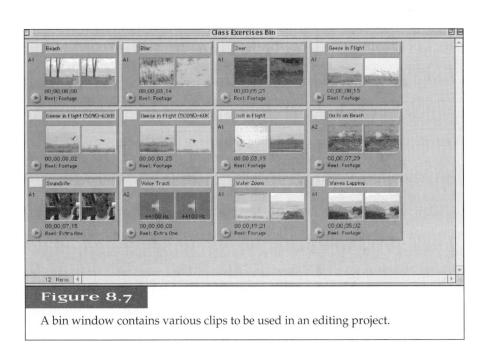

Figure 8.7

A bin window contains various clips to be used in an editing project.

the data on a centralized server and then making the information available to individual editing systems over a network. For the time being, however, digitizing is a process that, in most situations, takes place manually and in real time.

Editing—Clips and Programs

Once all of the video clips, audio clips, and other media have been brought into the nonlinear editing system, the editor has remarkable power to manipulate and assemble these individual elements.

One or more bins may be created to hold the clips, and clips can be easily copied and pasted among bins by dragging them with the mouse. The use of multiple bins allows an editor to organize an editing project either according to individual media (audio, video, and graphics) or according to parts of a program. Special effects, such as a specific wipe or digital video effect, can be stored as clips in a bin as well.

By double-clicking the mouse on an individual clip in a bin, the clip will be displayed in an editing window, which allows the editor to make changes to the clip. The length of a clip can be changed by dragging in- or out-point locators to a specific location, or by pressing a key on the keyboard. In this way, individual clips can be precisely edited (you can set the clip to end just as the actor closes the door, for example). An important advantage of nonlinear, however, is that even if a clip is shortened, it can be restored later to its original length. The editor also can apply

special effects such as color correction or slow motion to a clip. In these cases, depending on the sophistication of the nonlinear system, the effects may be instantly applied or may have to be slowly "computed" in a process called **rendering.**

Although individual clips can be prepared and "edited" in the bin window, to put clips together the editor must create a **program line.** This is easily done by selecting a menu item on the screen. The program line is the timeline on which the various media elements will be placed. To begin editing, the editor simply drags a clip from a bin onto the program line, then drags and places subsequent clips in the same manner.[1] Clips that contain video and audio will appear in the appropriate channels on the program line; a clip that is audio only will only appear in an audio channel. Figure 8.8 shows an edited project consisting of three video shots with sound and a voice track in the second audio channel.

Once placed in the program line, shots can be manipulated by dragging them with the mouse. Clicking near the edge of a clip can expand or contract it; clicking the left side of the clip changes the in point, while clicking the right side changes the out point. Adjacent clips will automatically "move" to make room for changes made to another clip. Similarly, as discussed in the opening of this chapter, time can be added to the middle of a program, and the subsequent portions of the program will automatically ripple to make room. As the editor puts together the presentation on the program line, he or she can view it by selecting a "play" command. The developing program on the program line is saved separately from the clips and

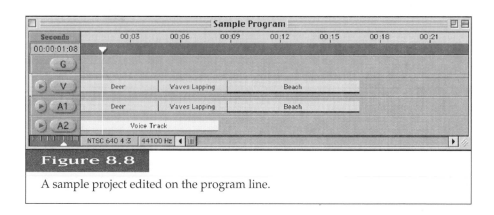

Figure 8.8

A sample project edited on the program line.

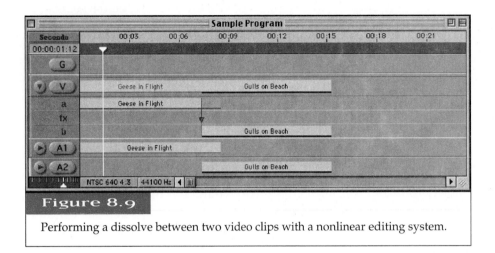

Figure 8.9

Performing a dissolve between two video clips with a nonlinear editing system.

bins, so the editor can create many versions of a program from the same clips.[2]

To perform a transition other than a cut, the editor overlaps video clips in two separate video channels, as shown in Figure 8.9.[3] Then, he or she selects a transition type (such as a dissolve, wipe, or DVE effect) and sets a duration for the transition. Depending on the type of transition and the sophistication of the nonlinear system, the transition may have to render or may be immediately viewable. Graphics can be placed over video by putting them in the program line's graphics channel. Audio portions of the program can be manipulated by the editor in a manner similar to video clips. The audio level can be set numerically or by dragging a line that represents the audio level.

File Management

Since the central element of a nonlinear editing system is a computer, considerations relating to managing data files are an extremely important aspect of the editing process. By far, the largest files will be the data files for the digitized video and audio clips, likely occupying many megabytes or even gigabytes of storage space. Since storage space is likely to be at a premium—especially in academic settings—it is possible you will have to move your data files off the machine during the times you're not editing. This can be accomplished by transferring the files over a network to a central server computer (which, unless you have

Figure 8.10

An Iomega Jaz removable disk can be used to transfer data files between computers.

a very fast network, can be a time-consuming process) or by copying them onto removable media such as **Jaz disks** (Figure 8.10). Jaz disks can hold up to two gigabytes of data and allow you to transfer files among any machines that are equipped with Jaz disk drives.

It is also important to make sure your data are backed up, or copied to another location. If you have a project that you've devoted many hours to and you experience a hard disk crash or other mishap, you can lose all of your work. For that reason, you should save your data files frequently and be sure to make regular backups.

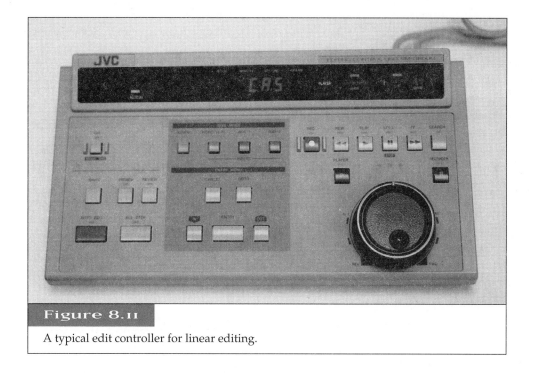

Figure 8.11

A typical edit controller for linear editing.

The editing system also will make files for your assembled program and bins. These files are actually "pointers" to the larger data files, and although much smaller in size, they are equally important, and should be saved and backed up regularly as well. Your nonlinear editing system's manual can give you more information about identifying and managing these important files.

Output

A "finished" nonlinear editing presentation initially exists only as a series of digital data bits inside the computer's memory. Depending on the application, the finished presentation can be dubbed onto tape, recorded onto a CD-ROM, DVD disk, or other medium, or sent across a network onto a **video server.** If the nonlinear editing was conducted as an off-line session, the most important output might be the computer-generated edit decision list, which then will be transferred to the on-line editing system.

Dubs to tape are made by simply playing the completed program with a tape machine attached to the nonlinear system's outputs. Some systems can be set up to automatically create and play back color bars, audio tones, black signal, and slates before making the actual dub of the program. "Recordings" to a

video server or other digital media are usually made by copying the finished data files.

8.5 Linear Editing

Although there are many different configurations of linear editing systems, they all consist of at least three elements: a playback tape machine, a record tape machine, and an **edit controller** that operates the two tape machines in synchronization. (See Figure 8.11.) The edit controller allows the editor to perform typical videotape recorder functions such as playback, record, fast forward, rewind, and search on each machine that is part of the editing system. The editor also uses the edit controller to set in and out points that designate the beginning and end of edits and to select the type of edit to be performed.

Once an edit has been prepared, the controller then synchronizes the playback and record machines and carries out the edit on the record machine. It synchronizes the machines by performing a **preroll,** which backs up each machine a few seconds before the edit point, then plays back the machines in unison to be sure they are running at exactly the same speed when the edit begins. At the conclusion of an edit, the edit controller stops all machines and normally recues them to the end of the edit.

Edit controllers vary widely in sophistication and capability. Most have digital time readouts that allow the editor to cue tapes and determine the length of edits. On non-time-code systems, these counters numerically display **control track** pulses, while on time-code systems they display the actual time code addresses. More sophisticated edit controllers also can control switchers, DVE units, and other devices, while computer-based edit controllers can "remember" edits through the use of an edit decision list.

Linear Editing Configurations

The most basic editing system, consisting of a playback machine, a record machine, and an edit controller, is called a **cuts-only** system. As its name implies, this type of system is capable only of editing cut transitions between shots.

To perform other types of transitions, you must use an **A/B roll** or **multiple-source** editing system. This type of system uses more than one playback machine, then allows the editor to perform transitions between footage on the playback machines. It is important to understand, however, that the record machine is still capable only of performing a cut edit; dissolves, wipes, and other transitions are achieved by actually rerecording a portion of the previous edit, then transitioning to the new edit, as shown in Figure 8.12. The transition is done either by the edit controller or by a switcher or DVE unit connected to the edit controller.

Normally, then, it is not possible to perform any transition other than a cut using a single playback machine. An exception, however, is possible using a recording deck that has a **preread** function. Several digital formats have preread capability, in which the recorder actually plays back the footage on its tape while simultaneously adding footage from the playback machine. This allows dissolves and other transitions to be performed, as well as sophisticated **layering** of video images, in which multiple sources of video are placed "on top" of one another.

As noted, several peripheral pieces of equipment may also be included in an editing system. The most

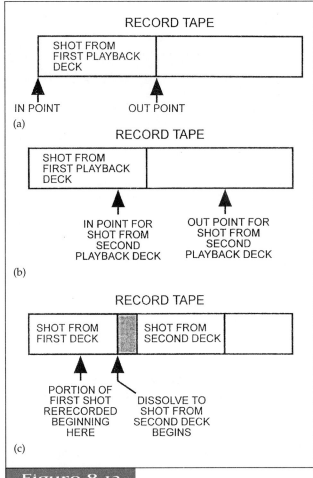

Figure 8.12

Even though some linear editing systems can create transitions such as dissolves and wipes, the record machine can only actually create a cut transition. A dissolve is created by (a) recording the first shot from the first playback deck, then (b) selecting the shot that will be dissolved to on the second playback deck. The system will then actually (c) rerecord the end of the first shot, then perform the dissolve at the desired location.

basic of these is one or more video monitors that allow the editor to view the footage on the various tape machines. Similarly, audio monitors are used to listen to audio sources. In a multiple-source system, a switcher, DVE unit, and graphics unit may be used to create more sophisticated editing effects, and each of these components may have its own video monitor. An audio mixer may be used to more precisely control the level and equalization of audio sources, which may include CD players, cart machines, and cassette tape players.

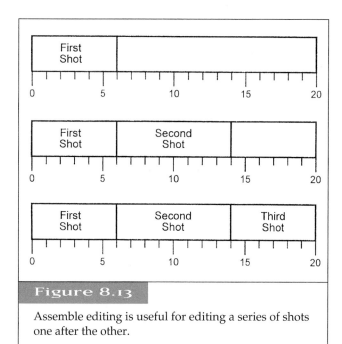

Figure 8.13

Assemble editing is useful for editing a series of shots one after the other.

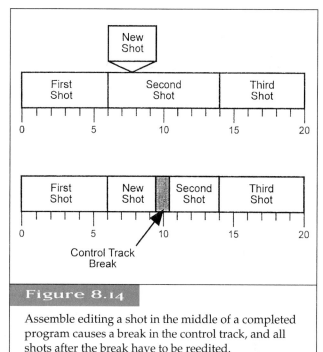

Figure 8.14

Assemble editing a shot in the middle of a completed program causes a break in the control track, and all shots after the break have to be reedited.

A final variable among editing systems is tape format. Most prosumer and professional formats offer a number of different editing configurations, from cuts-only to sophisticated multiple-source systems. Normally, all the machines in an editing system are the same format, although in **interformat** editing systems there may be a mixture of formats. For example, an edit system may record onto Digital Betacam, but allow both Digital Betacam and DVCPRO source tapes.

Types of Tape Edits

Audio or video information can be recorded onto tape during an edit session in two basic ways. The first of these, called **assemble editing,** records all tape elements (video, all audio channels, and control track), essentially wiping out any previous material recorded on the tape. Assemble editing is useful for simple editing functions, such as placing a series of shots one after the other, as shown in Figure 8.13. However, since it records *all* tape elements, it cannot be used to edit a shot in the middle of a presentation because it will cause a break in the control track, as shown in Figure 8.14. Obviously, assemble editing cannot be used to change an individual element (video or audio channel 1, for example) in a presentation.

More advanced editing functions require the use of **insert editing,** which allows the editor to select individual elements (video and/or specific audio channels) to record. Since it does not disturb the control track, insert editing can be used in the middle of an edited presentation. Insert editing gives the editor much more capability than assemble editing, and for that reason it is the kind of editing most often used. However, before you can perform insert editing, you have to have the control track already on the record tape. If you want to begin insert editing on a blank tape, you must first **black** the tape by recording the control track (and usually a black sync signal) onto it. If you have already used assemble editing to lay shots on the tape, you can then go back and use insert editing to change individual shots.

Linear Editing Techniques

Despite the wide diversity of edit controllers and tape machines, the basic techniques of tape-based editing remain the same. This section will use a simple editing example to illustrate some of these techniques.

Suppose that you have a raw tape with various footage on it. You want to rearrange this footage into

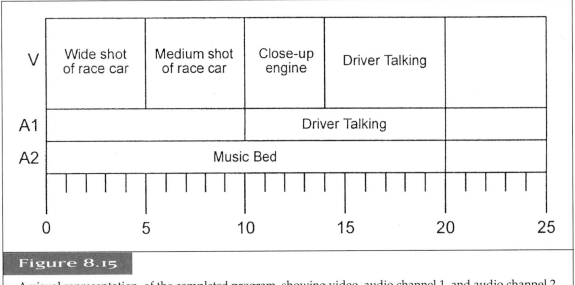

Figure 8.15

A visual representation of the completed program, showing video, audio channel 1, and audio channel 2 tracks in timeline form.

the completed form shown on the edit master tape in Figure 8.15. The finished program begins with a five-second wide shot of the race car, then a five-second medium shot of the race car. Next, there is a 10-second interview clip in which the driver talks about the race car; the first 4 seconds of the interview clip are covered with a close-up shot of the car's engine (in other words, we hear the driver talking for 4 seconds before we *see* him). Throughout the entire program, we have a music bed.

There are several ways to complete this program, but for our example we will build its basic structure using assemble editing, then complete it using insert editing. The first step is to perform a **cold edit** at the very beginning of the edit master tape. This is accomplished by simply pressing the "record" and "play" buttons on the recorder and letting the tape record black sync signal for at least 10 seconds. The reason for doing this is that we need to have space for the edit controller to preroll the first edit. If we simply tried to do an edit at the very beginning of the edit master tape, the recorder would "run into" the beginning of the tape while attempting to preroll and the edit controller would abort the edit. The 10-second black recording at the beginning of the tape will provide sufficient space for the preroll (which is normally set to between 3 and 7 seconds, depending on the edit controller).

Now, we are ready to begin building the program. First, we will use the edit controller to cue the edit master tape to 10 seconds; then we will press the "set in" button on the edit controller to tell the machine that we want the first shot to begin at that point.[4] Next, we use the edit controller to cue the raw tape to the wide shot of the car. Again, we will use the "set in" button to set the beginning of the shot on the raw tape. Finally, we will tell the edit controller that we want to perform an assemble edit by selecting "assemble" under edit type.

We are now ready to perform the first edit. In this case, it will be an **open-ended edit** because we have not set an out point to designate the end of the edit. When we press the "edit" button on the edit controller, it will preroll both the player and recorder to five seconds before their respective in points, and stop the machines momentarily.[5] Then, it will roll both machines in unison, and when we reach the in point of the record tape we will see the shot of the race car appear on the record monitor. When we have at least five seconds of the shot recorded, we will press the "all stop" button to stop both machines; the edit controller will then recue both machines to the point when we pushed the "all stop" button.[6] We are now ready to recue the machines, set in points, and do our next edit.

After similarly assemble-editing the next two shots, we end up with a program as illustrated in Fig-

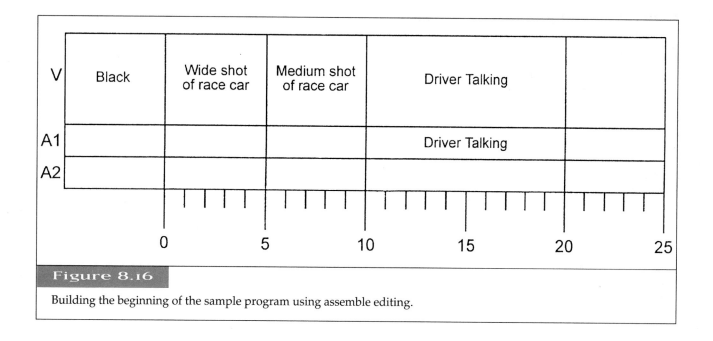

V	Black	Wide shot of race car	Medium shot of race car	Driver Talking	
A1				Driver Talking	
A2					

0   5   10   15   20   25

Figure 8.16

Building the beginning of the sample program using assemble editing.

ure 8.16. Now, we need to make two insert edits to complete the project. The first of these will be a video-only edit for approximately the first four seconds of the soundbite. We want the shot of the engine to end after the driver says, "This car has the most powerful engine of any car on the track." We will use the edit controller to cue the recorder to the beginning of the soundbite, cue the player to the shot of the engine, and set in points on both machines. Since we want the engine shot to end after the driver says "any car on the track," we will use the edit controller's shuttle/search knob to cue the record tape to just after the word "track," then set an out point on the recorder. This tells the edit controller to end the edit at this point. Out points can be set on either the record machine or the playback machine, depending on the situation. In this instance, the critical ending point (the word "track") is on the recorder, so we set the out point on the recorder. Finally, we will select only "video" under edit type, as we do not want to record any audio.

We are now ready to perform the edit, but in this situation we may want to "test" the edit to make sure it works as planned. Edit controllers allow us to do this through the use of a **preview** function, which rolls the machines through the edit-preparation process, then shows what the edit will look like without actually recording it. When we press the "preview" button on the edit controller, both machines will preroll, then play. If we watch and listen to the record monitor, we will see the engine shot inserted, but the machine will not actually perform the edit. If there is something wrong with the edit (if the engine shot ends on the word "car," for example), we can reset the in or out points. We can do this by just recueing the recorder to the proper location, then pressing "set out" again, or by **trimming** the existing edit. Trimming increments an existing in or out point frame by frame, normally by pressing a "+" or "−" button on the edit controller. If we press the "+" button 10 times, for example, the out point will be moved 10 frames later. Once we are satisfied with what we see, we will perform the edit by pressing the "edit" button. If we wish, we can look at an edit just completed by using the **review** function. We will complete the project by doing an Audio Channel 2 insert edit to add the music track under the entire program.

This is the basic process of linear editing: cueing tapes, setting in and out points, and designating the type of edit. More advanced controllers allow greater usability and functionality, such as the ability to set in and out points numerically on a keypad, or to perform transition effects on multiple-source systems.

8.6 Editing Aesthetics

A finished television program, be it a live talk show, a sitcom, a game show, a documentary, or a news program, should create for the viewer an uninterrupted sense of visual and aural progression. This consistent and unobtrusive "flow" is called **continuity,** and it is a function of several aesthetic considerations. In fact, many television professionals say the best edits are the ones the home viewer doesn't even *notice.*

Continuity allows you to create a sense of uninterrupted flow not only in "real-time" productions such as talk shows and live sports programs but in programs where time and/or space are fluid. For example, a documentary may contain footage shot over a period of days, months, or even years, and in several different locations. In a television drama, we may want to create the impression that the actor puts on his jacket, leaves his house, gets in his car, and drives away as one continuous action, despite the fact the scene was in reality shot in several different "takes" over a period of several hours. In that same drama, we may at another time want to smoothly travel to another time or place—10 years ago or a city located hundreds of miles away. Skillful editing can make all of these actions unobtrusive and *believable* to the viewer.

Regardless of how you are editing, whether linear, nonlinear, or in real time using a switcher, achieving continuity is as much a function of the shots you have available as how they are put together. Indeed, the degree of continuity you are able to achieve is often determined in the preproduction and editing-preparation stages of a project. This is, once again, another reason that *planning* is so important in television production.

Of course, continuity considerations are often violated for special effect, especially in music videos and commercials, where smooth flow is abandoned for attention-grabbing, disjointed editing. Here, too, however, it is important that the loss of continuity serves a creative purpose and is appropriate to the production in question. It is usually not appropriate, for example, to violate continuity in a documentary or a live studio production. Still, television production is a creative endeavor, so principles of continuity should be considered guidelines and not necessarily rules.

When to Edit— Information and Action

In general, you should change from one shot to another only when there is a specific *reason* for doing so. Broadly, these reasons fit into two categories: **cutting for information** or **cutting on action.** Cutting for information means that the second shot reveals information that the first shot did not. For example, we may cut from the medium shot of the show host holding the book to a close-up of the book so that the viewer can see the title of the book or the detail of the artwork on the book's cover. (See Figure 8.17.) During a discussion show, we would want to cut from the shot of the host to a shot of a particular guest when that guest starts talking. If what the guest says elicits an enthusiastic round of applause from the audience, we might want to cut to a wide shot of the audience.

In is important to *not* make a video edit if that edit does not reveal any significant information. For example, cutting from the medium shot in Figure 8.18(a) to the slightly tighter medium shot from a similar angle in Figure 8.18(b) serves no real purpose. We are not giving the viewer any new information of significance, so it is best not to make the cut.

Interestingly, it is likely that the transition to ATSC—especially in its highest definition formats—will make frequent cutting among shots less critical to visual storytelling. HDTV's increased picture resolution means that you can show all the detail of an NTSC close-up shot (and more) in an HDTV medium or wide shot. For example, consider a baseball game in which the pitcher is preparing to pitch to a batter as a runner leads off from first base. In an NTSC production, the director would have to cut among at least three cameras to follow the action: a camera to show a medium shot of the runner on first base, a camera to show a close-up of the pitcher watching the runner and preparing to pitch, and a camera to show a wide shot of the pitcher and batter as the ball is delivered to home plate. These three different camera shots are needed because NTSC television's lower resolution does not allow great detail to be seen in medium and

(a)

(b)

Figure 8.17

Editing for information. Start with the medium shot (*a*), and when the host holds up the book, cut to a close-up of the book's cover (*b*).

(a)

(b)

Figure 8.18

If no significant new information will be revealed by an edit, it should not be made. The shot shown in (*b*), for example, reveals no information not already shown in (*a*).

wide shots. The camera showing the runner on first could zoom out to show the pitcher as well, but there would be no way to see the concentration on the pitcher's face or the movement of his eyes from home plate, to the runner on first, and back to home plate.

With HDTV's greater resolution, however, a camera could get a shot of both the runner and the pitcher while maintaining enough picture detail to see the emotion on the pitcher's and the runner's faces. Thus, there would be no need to cut to the extra shot. In fact, an HDTV camera positioned near the third-base dugout could shoot the runner, pitcher, and batter in one wide shot while maintaining nearly all the detail we would see in three NTSC shots.

(a)

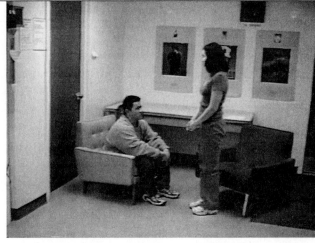

(b)

Figure 8.19

Cutting on action from shot (*a*) to shot (*b*) as the actress rises from her chair.

Cutting on action is an edit that is triggered by an action of a subject in the picture. For example, if the actress is about to rise from her chair, we could cut from a medium shot of her to a wider shot, as shown in Figure 8.19. Similarly, if we are on a medium shot of a police officer questioning a witness to a crime and a gunshot rings out, the police officer is likely to spring to attention and perhaps draw his gun. This would be an appropriate place to cut to a tighter shot of the police officer as he turns his head in the direction of the gunshot, then perhaps cut to a wide shot of a suspect scurrying away down the alley.

It is important to note that the action not only triggers the edit, it also provides the temporal *point* for the edit. The edit, then, should be either just before the action, during the action, or just after the action is completed. The choice among the three possibilities depends on the effect you are trying to achieve; however, for the action to act as a logical motivation for a shot change, that shot change must be made *in very close temporal proximity* to the action. Cutting to the second shot in Figure 8.19 two seconds before that actress actually gets up, for example, destroys the logical sense of making the cut created by the action.

Pacing refers to the overall speed at which shot changes are made in a production. A fast-paced production, for example, will have a lot of edits, and individual shots will be on the screen for only a short pe-

riod of time. There is no "right" number of edits to make in a production, nor is there a set time between edits; the most important thing is that the pacing is appropriate to the particular production, and that the individual edits themselves are motivated by logical information and action cues. A music video, for example, is likely to have a much faster pace than a documentary. It also is important not to simply edit formulaically, such as changing pictures every three seconds. This can give an impersonal, automated feel to a presentation. Instead, edits should be made at appropriate points—the end of a sentence on the narration track in a documentary, for example, or on the beats of the music.

Jump Cuts

One of the goals of continuity in editing is creating the notion in the mind of the viewer that he or she is watching action occurring in "real time," even if it is not. Perhaps the most glaring violation of continuity is the **jump cut,** in which a person or object changes in two successive shots. For example, if you edit a shot of a person typing at a computer immediately after a shot of that same person standing, as in Figure 8.20(a), you have created a jump cut. Such an edit creates confusion for the viewer, as it is physically impossible for a person to instantly go from standing to sitting at a computer.

A jump cut also can occur in less glaring forms. For example, if you cut from a shot of a man sitting on a

Figure 8.20

(*a*) A jump cut; (*b*) using a cutaway shot prevents jump cuts; (*c*) changing angle or type of shot can also prevent jump cuts.

chair with his left leg crossed over his right leg to another shot in which his *right leg* is now crossed over his *left leg,* this is in effect a jump cut. Similarly, it is a jump cut if a person's clothes change from one shot to the next or if an object sitting on a table is gone in the next shot. Many of these types of problems can be so minor that they go unnoticed; still, every effort should be made to avoid them. If you watch movies or television dramas very closely, you can usually see a number of minor (and sometimes major) jump cuts like these.

As you might guess, jump cuts such as those just described are a much greater problem in postproduc-

tion editing than in live editing. Laws of physics prohibit someone from changing position from one shot to the next in a live production. Still, many people consider it a jump cut when an edit such as the one in Figure 8.18 is made. The person has not changed position, but the effect is so jarring that in actuality it seems as if the camera itself has "jumped."

Jump cuts can be avoided by using **cutaway** shots, in which a shot that does not include the person or object in question is inserted between the two shots. In the computer example, you could put a shot of the person to whom the subject is speaking between the two shots, as shown in Figure 8.20(b). Jump cuts also can be avoided by changing angles or shot type. You could in this way effectively cut from the shot of the person standing to a close-up of the person's hands on the computer keyboard to the medium shot of the person at the computer, as shown in Figure 8.20(c). Even though the first edit is technically a jump cut, the dramatic effect created by cutting to the close-up shot masks the violation of continuity for the viewer.

Another way to avoid jump cuts is to allow subjects to leave or enter the frame. In the above example, if we started by showing a shot of the person walking and allowed him to walk *out of the frame,* we could then cut to the shot of him sitting at the computer. Since the person actually leaves the picture (if only for a brief moment), our next shot will not create a jump cut. Similarly, if we cut from a shot of the person standing away from the computer, then cut to a shot of the computer and allow the person to walk *into* the picture, sit down and start typing, we have not created a jump cut.

Screen Direction

Another continuity consideration is **screen direction,** the direction in which a person (or object) is facing or moving. When you are showing a conversation between two people, for example, you should make sure that each person maintains his or her same screen direction in all shots, and that the two people are looking in opposite directions. As shown in Figure 8.21, this maintains the effect that the two people are actually talking *to* each other. In editing shots in this sequence, you would make sure that the man was *always facing right* and the woman was *always facing left.* Putting in a shot in which the woman was facing right would create confusion for the viewer.

Similarly, if you are shooting shots of a car, once you've established that the car is moving in a particular direction (left to right, for example), you should only edit shots in which the car is moving in that same direction. Editing from a shot in which the car moves left to right to one in which it moves right to left creates a jarring effect and violates continuity. If you must edit together shots in which the car changes direction, you can insert a **neutral shot**—or head-on shot—between the two shots, as shown in Figure 8.22.

Figure 8.21

Maintaining consistent screen direction for two people. The last shot shows the disorienting effect of violating consistency of screen direction.

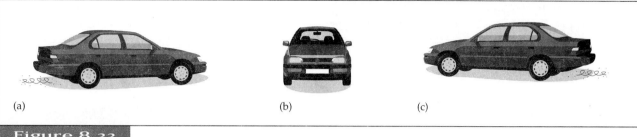

(a)   (b)   (c)

Figure 8.22

A neutral shot (*b*) can be used between two opposing direction shots (*a*) and (*c*).

Transitions

The majority of edits are simply cuts, where one picture is instantaneously replaced by another on screen. The reason for this widespread use is that the cut is the only transition effect that does not normally call attention to itself (unless it is a jump cut or other continuity violation). However, other transitions can and should be used in appropriate situations. The dissolve is most often used to indicate the passage of time, such as dissolving from a World War II photograph of a soldier to a contemporary shot of the same person. Dissolves also can be used to visually *connect* two images; changing from a shot of the soldier riding on a train to a shot of his wife back home holding his picture connects the two images more forcefully than a cut.

A fade to or from black indicates a strong separation. It is usually used to end a particular sequence or go to a commercial.

Wipes and special effects such as page turns call even greater attention to themselves, and thus should not be used when subtle transitions are needed. These transitions can be used to create interest and action in a presentation, however, and are often used (and many would say used *too much*) in commercials. In general, if you do not have a specific creative reason for using a dissolve, wipe, or special effect, you should just use a cut.

Ethics of Editing

The ability to edit sound and pictures gives the editor tremendous power to shape what the audience sees. Editing can be used to distort reality (such as by in-stantly transporting the viewer through space or time), create illusions, and—at its most extreme—create alternative realities (such as computer-generated animations). However, this tremendous power carries with it an *ethical responsibility* not to mislead the audience in inappropriate ways.

This ethical responsibility is most important when producing nonfiction programs, such as news, news features, and documentaries. While a viewer expects and accepts the distortion of reality in entertainment programming, a viewer does not expect distortion in programs that claim to present reality. Common techniques used in the production of entertainment programming such as staging events, giving cues to actors, and editing to create illusions *should not* be used in nonfiction programs. Such programs should be a reflection of reality, and—as much as possible—the production and editing process should not interfere with or distort this reality.

It also is unethical to use editing to create false impressions in nonfiction programming. This includes editing soundbites so that the person seems to say something he or she really didn't. It also includes editing together shots that do not belong together to create an inaccurate impression (such as following a soundbite from a politician with raucous applause from the audience when the audience didn't respond that way).

The evolving new technologies of video editing still give the producers of nonfiction programs tremendous new capabilities and artistic possibilities. It is important to remember, however, that these capabilities should not be used to mislead the audience.

1. Envision an editing project you might do for this class, such as a 30-second commercial or a two-minute news story. Would it be easier to complete this project using linear or nonlinear editing? Why?
2. If you were to begin shooting a video project tomorrow, what things would you do in the preediting stages to help facilitate the editing process?
3. If your school uses nonlinear editing systems, locate some of the video data files on the computer. How does their size compare to other types of computer files such as word-processing files or graphics files?
4. If your school uses linear editing systems, how would you describe them? Are they cuts only or A/B roll? Do the machines use preread?

5. Record a half hour of MTV and then discuss how rules of editing aesthetics are violated in programs, music videos, and commercials. Do these violations serve a creative purpose? If so, how?

Footnotes

1. On Avid systems, clips are not dragged to the timeline itself but rather to a "record" window that then places the clip on the program timeline.
2. On Avid systems, these functions are usually performed in the record window, with the result of the finished operations then showing on the program timeline.
3. On Avid systems, the clips need not overlap to perform a transition.
4. Depending on the editing system, edit point set buttons may be called "edit in," "in point," or "in" as well.
5. Depending on the editing system, this button may be called "perform," "auto edit," or "edit start."
6. Depending on the editing system, this button may be called "edit stop" or "stop."

chapter 9

Graphics and Sets

Graphics and sets are the two major pictorial elements that are a part of television production. Graphics include lettering and artwork, normally displayed on screen to supplement the images captured on camera. A news anchor's name, for example, can be shown on a graphic with simple lettering. More advanced graphics might include the map of a war zone, a chart showing how tax money is spent, or even a moving graphic of a working piston engine or blood flowing through arteries. A wide variety of set designs are also possible, from the simplicity of a single folding chair and a curtain for background to an entire re-creation of a classroom, corporate office, or apartment.

The *disciplines* of using pictorial elements include understanding and applying appropriate design functions. It is also important to have a clear understanding of *what* you want to convey to the viewer and *how* you will do it. The *techniques* of graphics include understanding your particular graphics system as well as a more general knowledge of the types of equipment and graphics effects available. Some of the techniques needed for sets require the skill of a carpenter or painter, but others are simple tasks that anyone can master with a little practice. This chapter covers graphics and sets by emphasizing the following topics:

- The informational and emotional aspects of pictorial elements (9.1).
- Design factors common to both sets and graphics (9.1).
- Different types of functions that are performed by graphics equipment (9.2).
- Techniques for using noncomputer-generated graphics (9.3).
- Aesthetic considerations in using television graphics (9.4).
- The possibilities available through virtual sets (9.5–9.6).
- Basic construction principles related to real sets (9.7).

- How sets and furniture are assembled and set up in a studio (9.7).
- The value of a floor plan (9.7).
- The difference between set dressings and props (9.7).
- The best ways to store sets (9.7).

9.1 Pictorial Design Factors

One of the major reasons for using graphics and sets is to convey a wide range of *information* to the viewer without disrupting the overall flow of a program. During a baseball game, for example, a graphic in the upper-left corner constantly shows the current status of the game (score, team batting, number of balls, strikes, and outs, and runners on base), while supplemental graphics show information about particular players. Networks such as CNBC (see Figure 9.1) use a lower-screen **crawl** to show continually updated stock prices as anchors read news stories and conduct interviews.

Sets, too, convey information to the viewer, although in a less direct way. A well-designed set made to represent the inside of a church tells the viewer that the scene is happening inside a church yet does not call attention to itself. In the same way, the set for a news program should provide an inviting, pleasant, and functional background without distracting from the message provided by the news anchors.

Beyond informational functions, graphics and sets also play *emotional* or *psychological* functions. Many subtle messages can be conveyed by the total production design, and the pictorial elements—graphics, sets, props, and furniture—combine to give an "image" or "feel" to the program. In a news program, do you want the image of an advanced technological communications center or of a working newsroom? In a religious program, do you want the image of a traditional church service or of an avant-garde contemporary movement? In a variety program, do you want the image of a conventional stage presentation or the electronic collage of a music video?

The emotional function of design also includes creating and maintaining a style or **continuity** for the program. This style should carry through to all the

Figure 9.1

Graphics are used on networks such as CNBC to present a wide variety of information at the same time.   *Photo courtesy of CNBC.*

pictorial elements used in the production; each pictorial element should look like it *belongs* with every other element. In some cases, for instance, a station has a news bureau in another city, and thus part of the newscast originates from the set located there. These "satellite" sets should match the main set, exhibiting similar style cues such as color and decoration. Maintaining this type of consistency is especially important in designing graphic elements. Thus, every pictorial design should serve both an *informational* function and an *emotional* function. The set should not only tell us what time of day it is but also give us a hint as to what is going to happen this day. The graphic should not only give us information but also emphasize how important the information is.

Although graphics and sets will be discussed separately throughout most of the chapter, it is useful to first discuss some design factors common to all types of pictorial elements. These factors include (1) balance and mass, (2) lines and angles, and (3) tone and color.

Balance and Mass

The concept of balance was introduced in Chapter 5 in connection with camera work. **Asymmetrical balance** is generally preferred over formal **symmetrical balance** in pictorial design as it is in camera work. The use of asymmetrical balance tends to create a more interesting and visually appealing design. The larger a mass, the nearer it must be to the center of the scene in order to preserve a sense of balance with a smaller mass. (See Figure 9.2.) In addition, the placement of mass within a scenic element tends to affect the stability of the picture. A heavy mass in the bottom part of the picture implies firmness, solidarity, support, and importance. A heavier mass in the top part of the picture projects instability, suspense, and impermanence. (See Figure 9.3.) These considerations of balance and placement have strong implications for the design of sets and graphics as well as for camera composition. A graphic title with lettering in the bottom of the frame projects a solid, strong opening. A scenic unit with heavy ornamentation near the top implies a feeling of uneasiness and suspense.

Lines and Angles

The use of dominant lines is one of the strongest elements available to the scenic designer. Straight lines suggest firmness, rigidity, directness, and strength. Curved or rounded lines imply softness, elegance, and movement. The direction of the dominant lines in a picture carries strong connotations. Horizontal lines represent serenity, inactivity, and openness; vertical lines are dignified, important, and strong; diagonals

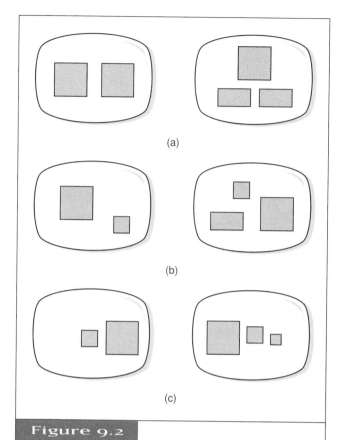

Figure 9.2

Symmetrical and asymmetrical balance.
(*a*) Symmetrical balance usually results in a rigidity and precision that is usually not desired, except for certain formal settings. (*b*) Asymmetrical balance usually is more interesting and dynamic, resulting in a more fluid and creative mood that is just as well balanced aesthetically. (*c*) An unbalanced picture can result, however, if care is not taken to position the asymmetrical elements with respect to their weight and mass. Temporarily, this may be desired.

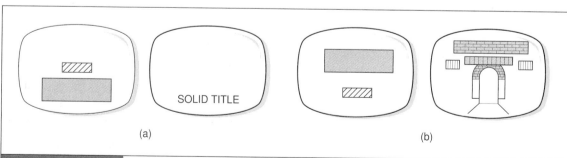

Figure 9.3

Location of mass in the picture. (*a*) Heavy weight in the bottom of the frame tends to give an impression of stability and security. (*b*) If the top of the picture contains more mass than the bottom, the result is a feeling of uneasiness and suspense.

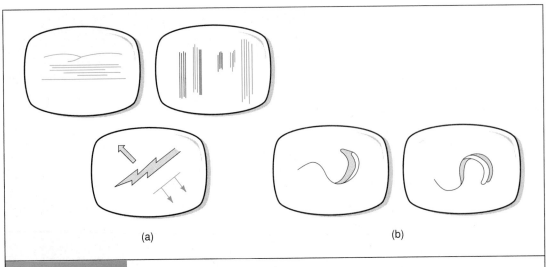

Figure 9.4

The effect of straight and curved lines. (*a*) Horizontal lines are restful, inactive, stable. Vertical lines suggest solemnity, dignity, dominance. Diagonal lines represent action, movement, impermanence. (*b*) Curved lines generally imply change, beauty, grace, flowing movement. With an upward open curve there is a feeling of freedom and openness. A downward open curve has more of a feeling of pressure and restriction.

Figure 9.5

Tone and balance. (*a*) A darker tone tends to imply more mass; thus the darker tone will overbalance the lighter mass (*left*). A smaller dark mass can be used to balance a lighter mass that is larger (*right*). (*b*) A darker tone or darker color at the top of the picture or scenic element will tend to imply a top-heavy feeling of depression (*left*). The lighter tone or brighter color at the top gives a feeling of more solidarity and normalcy (*right*).

imply action, imbalance, instability, and insecurity. (See Figure 9.4.)

Tone and Color

The predominant color tones determine, to a great extent, the overall emotional image of a production. Light tones result in a delicate, cheerful, happy, trivial feeling, whereas dark tones result in a feeling that is heavy, somber, serious, or forceful. Tone also affects balance. A dark tone carries more mass, weighs more, and can be used to balance a larger mass that is light in color or tone. The position of various tones or blocks of dark and light mass in a picture also affects its stability and emotional quality. A dark mass at the top of a picture tends to induce a heavy, unnatural feeling of entrapment and depression; heavier tones in the bottom of a picture give it more of a stable base. (See Figure 9.5.)

As mentioned in Chapter 5, color is usually discussed in terms of three characteristics: **Hue** is the actual color base itself (red, green, purple, orange, and so forth); **saturation** refers to the strength or intensity of a color, how far removed it is from a neutral or gray shade; and **luminance** (brightness) indicates where the color would fall on a scale from light (white) to dark (black). The considerations mentioned for tone apply to color; for example, highly saturated colors (a vivid red) appear heavier—for purposes of balance—than unsaturated colors (a grayish red). Various hues are also subjectively classified as *warm* (yellows and reds) or *cool* (blues and greens). Warm colors appear to be "heavier" than cool colors. Much of the secret of achieving good color balance is the art of mixing various hues that are compatible, balancing highly saturated colors with grayer shades and selecting the right brightness of a particular hue (for example, baby blue rather than navy blue).

All these elements of design—balance, line, tone—should be kept in mind as you look specifically at the elements of graphic composition and set design.

9.2 Computer-Generated Graphics

Many years ago most TV graphics consisted of "title cards" made by applying rub-on or stick-on letters to sheets of cardboard that were then placed in front of the camera. If a chart or graph was needed, an artist drew it by hand, sometimes aided by a compass and protractor. Those days are long gone; now, nearly all television graphics are created with computers.

Computer equipment for creating and manipulating graphics performs three basic functions: character generation, graphics generation, and electronic storage. In the past these functions were often performed by three separate machines, but today it is far more likely that one multipurpose graphics system will perform all these functions. However, to understand how computerized graphic equipment works, it is useful to examine each function separately.

Character Generation

If you have used a word-processing or desktop-publishing program on a computer, you are familiar with the basic concept of a **character generator** (CG).

Figure 9.6

Chyron's iNFiNiT!® Graphics system can function as a character generator and—with add-on equipment—can perform animations as well.   *Photo courtesy of Chyron Corporation. All rights reserved.*

CG units (see Figure 9.6) allow the user to type words that can be output as a television signal.

Using a dedicated CG unit or the CG portion of a multipurpose graphics system, you can perform functions such as copying and pasting, and you can choose from a wide variety of sizes and lettering styles, or **fonts.** Character generators also can produce many special effects such as boldface, italics, drop shadow, outline, and multicolor lettering. Most can even add graphic elements like lines, boxes, or even a station's logo to the screen. Character generators normally operate with a "screen" or "page" metaphor—information is typed in and saved as various screens or pages for later recall. With the push of a button, the operator can move to the next page, go back to the last page, or even skip to a completely new page. In a television newscast, for instance, the anchor's name might be on one page and the name of a reporter on another page. During the show, the CG operator can easily move from page to page.

(a)

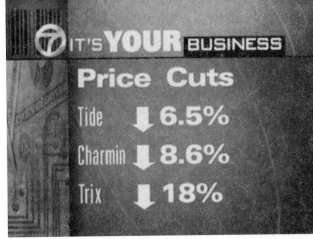
(b)

Figure 9.7

Graphics can be keyed over a portion of the frame or used as full screens. (*a*) Key of the anchor's name and station logo over a shot of the anchor reading a tease. (*b*) Full-screen graphic showing consumer information.   *Photos courtesy of WXYZ-TV, Detroit.*

Graphic information from a CG unit can be designed to be **keyed** with a switcher over other video information (as discussed in Chapter 6) or to be displayed **full screen,** as shown in Figure 9.7. Character generators also can perform special effects with text material: **Rolling** moves the text up or down the screen, an effect often used for closing credits; **crawling** moves the text horizontally across the screen in a single line. In Figure 9.1, you can see multiple crawls at the bottom of the screen.

Graphics Generation

More sophisticated graphics such as pictures, maps, and diagrams can be created using either a dedicated graphics generator (often called a **paintbox**) or a multipurpose graphics system. Most paintboxes also have lettering capabilities, although many do not provide easy access to text-editing functions like CG units. Paintboxes allow the operator to "paint" and "draw" on an electronic "canvas," and the result can be output as a television signal. To input information, the operator can use the keyboard or mouse, or a **graphics tablet** that allows the operator to actually "draw" electronically on a pad using a **digitizing pen.** (See Figure 9.8.)

Graphic artists may produce artwork from scratch or they may start with an existing frame of video.

Plate D shows how existing video can be used to create a sophisticated graphic. The paintbox can perform many functions, including resizing, rotating, and changing colors. Paintboxes also can create **animations,** or graphics that appear to move. In reality, the illusion of movement is created by using several frames, each one slightly different from the last. You have probably seen an example of this type of animation on your local television station's weathercast, where you can see clouds move across a map. Advanced paintbox systems can capture multiple frames of video, then be used to "paint" effects onto the video. For example, you could capture a shot of a car driving down the street, then use the paintbox to change the color of the car.

Like character generators, graphic generators can save their information to computer disk for later retrieval. Special effects such as animations can be preprogrammed so that they will play at the touch of a button.

Electronic Storage

In Chapter 7, several methods of storing video information were discussed. These same methods can be used to store graphics information as well. In addition, through use of **electronic still store** (ESS), graphic artists can "capture" individual frames of video, store

Figure 9.8

A graphics tablet and digitizing pen are basic tools for the electronic artist.

them, and index them for easy retrieval. For example, you might capture a video frame of each member of a basketball team using an ESS unit. You could then assign a specific number to each frame, and then by typing a number into the ESS unit's keypad you could instantly call up the desired frame. You also can add graphic and textual elements to frames and save the combined product. Many television stations use ESS units to store over-the-shoulder graphics for their newscasts. (See Figure 9.9.) These graphics are indexed by number ("1000" for the automobile accident graphic, "1001" for the city council graphic, for instance) and can be easily called up and reused as appropriate. ESS units store frames in digital form on computer disk. Obviously, video servers are increasingly performing these same types of storage and indexing functions.

Proprietary versus PC-Based Systems

A variety of systems are available for creating television graphics. Some are **proprietary systems,** meaning that they have been designed "from the ground up" to perform a specific function. Other

Figure 9.9

Over-the-shoulder graphics, such as this one indicating "Your World Tonight," can be stored, indexed, and recalled using an Electronic Still Store (ESS) unit.   *Photo Courtesy WXYZ-TV, Detroit.*

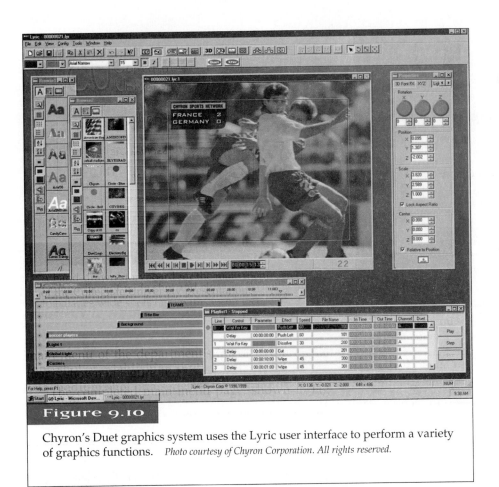

systems are PC-based, using a normal—or slightly modified—personal computer as a starting point. By adding specialized software and hardware, PCs can be made to function as character generators, graphics generators, still-store units, or combinations of the three. PC-based systems are often more cost-effective for operations with low budgets, and have the additional advantage that they can be used for other functions such as word processing or bookkeeping. Chyron's Duet system, for example, is an integrated CG, DVE, and still-store unit based on a PC running the Windows NT operating system. (See Figure 9.10.) Designed to be adaptable to various ATSC formats, the Duet can also run software designed by other companies.

NTSC and ATSC Aspect Ratios

As discussed in Chapter 5, different television systems have different **aspect ratios,** the ratio of width to height. In the NTSC format, the aspect ratio is 4 : 3, while in most ATSC formats the ratio is 16 : 9. (You might want to refer to Figure 5.4 to see the aspect ratios of various ATSC formats.) Graphics that are created for use on television, of course, must conform to the format's aspect ratio.

Graphics computers designed for use with only NTSC automatically produce graphics in the proper ratio, while graphics computers that are compatible with ATSC can be set to the appropriate aspect ratio. During the transition from NTSC to ATSC, however, producing graphics will be an additional challenge because they will have to look good in *both* formats. This leads to what some people jokingly call the "pect rat" problem, as shown in Figure 9.11, when graphics designed for one aspect ratio are viewed in a different aspect ratio. The best advice is to design your graphics for the ratio in which they will most often be viewed; there is really no solution to the problems created by multiple aspect ratios.

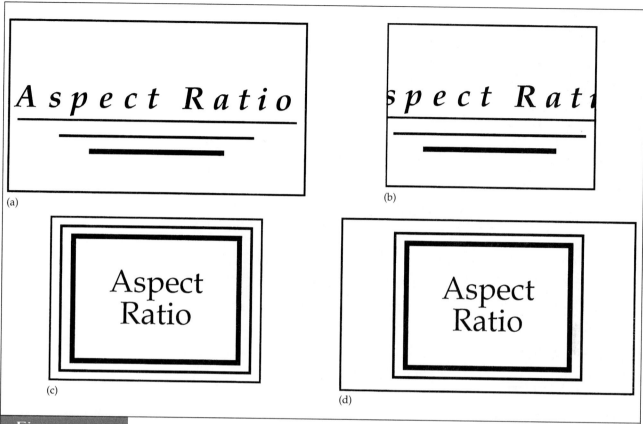

(a)

(b)

(c)

(d)

Figure 9.11

When graphics designed for one aspect ratio are viewed in a different aspect ratio, problems can result. Illustration (*a*) shows a graphic produced for use in 16 : 9, while (*b*) shows that graphic viewed on a 4 : 3 television screen (only the text "pect rat" will be visible). Similarly, a graphic produced for a 4 : 3 aspect ratio will have extra space on the vertical edges of the screen, as shown in (*c*) and (*d*).

9.3 Other Graphics

Sometimes it is necessary to use graphics that are not created by a computer—an award-winning photograph, a map of the world that you want to show in its entirety and then zoom in on Egypt, a page from an old manuscript. These types of graphics must be shot using a camera, but there are several things you can do to be sure that it will look good on TV.

Using Out-of-Aspect Graphics

To the extent possible, you should prepare the material with the same aspect ratio as the television format you're working in. If you are starting from scratch, you can make sure you create the proper aspect ratio, but if you are using something like an old manuscript page, it likely is not going to be the proper aspect ratio.

However, you can still use an "improperly" shaped graphic on television by employing one or more of the following techniques: showing only part of the graphic; tilting the camera from the top to bottom or panning from the left to right side of it; or mounting it on a larger board that is the proper aspect ratio and showing borders around it.

Keystoning and Essential Area

No matter how you shoot a graphic, you should be sure that the shooting angle is exactly perpendicular to the surface of the graphic. As shown in Figure 9.12, if the angle is not perpendicular, the result will be **keystoning,** in which the appearance of the original graphic will be distorted. Of course, you can

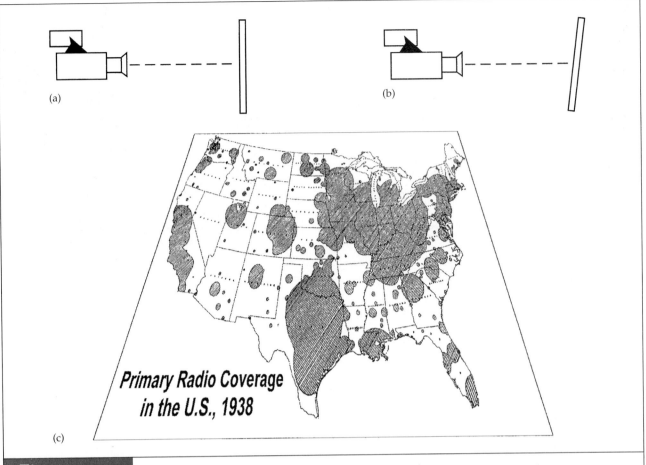

Figure 9.12

When shooting graphics on camera, always be sure the shooting angle is perpendicular to the surface of the graphic (*a*). If the angle is not perpendicular, as shown in (*b*), the resulting image will be distorted in a keystone effect (*c*).

intentionally shoot off-angle if you wish to achieve keystoning for creative effect, but normally you should avoid this type of image distortion.

It is also important to keep in mind **essential area** when shooting graphics on camera. From the time you look at a graphic through the camera's viewfinder to the time it reaches the home viewer's set, up to 30 percent of the picture area around the outer edge of the screen may be lost. These losses occur due to alignment differences in studio monitors and television sets, the transmission of the picture from the television tower to the home set, and other electronic factors. Because of this, you should always keep crucial graphic information within the essential area, which is the area left after cropping 25 to 30 percent from around the edges of the screen, as shown in Figure 9.13. Many graphics computers automatically

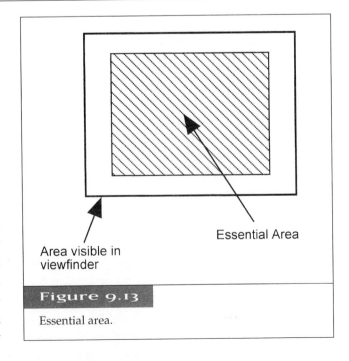

Figure 9.13

Essential area.

Serif

Non-Serif

Figure 9.14

These two text examples show the difference between serif and non-serif type. Serifs are the small protrusions on the ends of letters, as indicated by the circled portion of the letter *f*.

keep graphics within the essential area, and a number of cameras and studio monitors have markings on the screen to show the essential—or "safe"—area. By keeping all of your important graphic information within the essential area of the screen, you can be sure that it will not be cut off on the home viewer's set.

9.4 Graphic Aesthetics

Regardless whether graphics are computer generated or physical, they should be pleasing to the eye and easy to read on a television screen. Several factors are important for attaining this objective. They include the symbol size, simplicity and style, and color contrast.

Symbol Size

Given the ease of creating clean, crisp lettering with a computer graphics generator, the temptation is to flood the screen with information. But you must always remember the ultimate destination of the graphic information: not the high-quality monitor directly in front of you in the control room but rather the smaller, lower-quality television set found in a majority of homes.

As a rule of thumb, then, lettering on NTSC television should be *no smaller than ⅟₁₅th of the screen height*. If no line is less than ⅟₁₅th of the height of the critical area (and assuming some space is left between each

line of letters), this would mean that normally *no more than seven lines of information* should be included on a computer page or a graphic card. Of course, artistic considerations—balance and arrangement of mass— might dictate that much less material be used. In high-definition formats, more information can be included on the screen without sacrificing legibility.

Simplicity and Style

If there is one primary rule about the preparation of TV graphics, electronic or physical, it is simply this: *Keep it simple*—all lettering, all design elements, all artwork. The NTSC screen is too small and the scanning lines are too blurry to permit any fine detail work, but even with high-definition television, graphics do not stay on the screen long, so they must be simple enough for the viewer to grasp quickly.

This is particularly true with lettering styles. Letters should be bold, thick, and well defined, with a sharp, firm contour. As illustrated in Figure 9.14, some styles of lettering have **serifs,** small extensions on the tips of letters. In printed text, these extensions help guide the eye from one letter to the next and one word to the next, helping ease eyestrain. But because of NTSC television's scanning process and lower resolution, serifs often flicker or disappear on screen. Consequently, you should avoid lettering styles with serifs or make sure the serifs show up properly on the screen.

Any other artwork on a graphic card with lettering should also be kept simple. If it is too detailed, the audience will not get a chance to comprehend it; if it is too confusing and domineering, the audience will be distracted from the lettering.

All nonverbal graphics—pictures, cartoons, drawings, slides—must also be kept as simple as possible. Drawings or photographs showing a certain component or step in a process must show only what is absolutely necessary. One of the main problems in trying to use visuals prepared for other media (for example, charts from a book or photos from a magazine) is that they invariably contain too much detail. They are designed for a medium without the pressing temporal limitations of television. Usually they are visuals designed to convey as much information as possible in a single picture; they are designed for detailed study and comparison. Television, by contrast, may have to use three or four graphics sequentially to impart the same information. Do not try to crowd everything into one picture.

This admonition is particularly true with maps. Usually maps prepared for nontelevision applications cannot be used on television. Such maps normally contain more information (such as tiny roads, city names, and mileage markers) that cannot be deciphered on the television screen. When creating maps for television, use only outlines of countries or natural geographical bodies and a few key labels or key locations. (See Figure 9.15.)

Keeping simplicity is often particularly difficult with computer graphics because there are so many temptations. But just because you have 16 million colors, 40 fonts, and 125 wipe patterns, don't feel you have to use them all. If you are just trying to capture the viewer's attention, you can flaunt a few special effects, but if you are trying to convey information, remember that often less is better.

Color Contrast

A third factor that can help determine the readability of a graphic is color contrast. Working with color graphics, it is important to use hues that contrast and complement each other without actually clashing. (See color plate B.) Artistic judgment and experience will help determine which hues go well together.

Figure 9.15

Maps designed for use on television must be simple, presenting only the minimum amount of information necessary to convey the message, in this case the location of two landfill sites.   *Photo courtesy of WXYZ-TV, Detroit.*

With most basic computer graphics generators, thousands or even millions of colors are possible. Take time to experiment with your system and see what combinations of hues, saturation, and brightness work best for your purpose.

Video engineers like to have just a little white and a little black in a picture for reference points. Thus, a good graphic would be one that has two or three shades of brightness plus a little white and black for sparkle and interest. Avoid graphics that are all black and white or that consist entirely of high-contrast colors.

One problem to be avoided is the use of colors of the same brightness or saturation in preparing graphics. Two different hues (say, red and blue) will contrast best if you also consider differing levels of saturation and brightness. A dark brownish red will contrast better against a brilliant royal blue than against a dark navy blue.

In fact, contrasting saturations of the same hue (for example, a vivid chartreuse and a grayish olive green) provide considerable contrast. And even contrasting brightness or lightness of the same hue and saturation (for example, a light pink and a dark rose) provides essential contrast and legibility.

Working with graphics can be very rewarding. Computers have made the process fairly simple and fast, but the main responsibility, the creation of something that is aesthetically pleasing, is a discipline that still rests in the hands and minds of human beings.

A virtual set. The table is real but all the other set elements are computer-generated. *Photo courtesy of Orad.*

9.5 Basics of Sets

Most studio productions need some sort of set. For some programs, such as sitcoms, the set is essential to create a locale and give actors some of the needed elements for interaction. For others, such as dance programs, the set adds interest to the background and foreground and establishes a tone. For a news program the set creates interest but also has functional elements that allow videotape to appear beside the anchors and storm patterns to be seen behind the weathercaster.

Although most sets are made from real materials, such as metal, plastic, or wood, there is an increasing tendency toward **virtual sets** that are "built" in a computer and do not actually exist. Sometimes a set may be partially virtual and partially real.

9.6 Virtual Sets

When a virtual set is used, the performers are shot against a blank background and the set is inserted electronically. The procedure resembles the **chroma keying** already discussed in Chapter 6, but it is more sophisticated and complex. A virtual set can be three-dimensional, with articles placed in front of and behind the actors. Its perspective changes as the camera moves so that set pieces look natural and consistent from any angle.

A wide variety of basic sets are available as software programs from a number of companies that have entered the virtual set business.[1] Many of these sets can be customized (colors changed, logos added) by using techniques similar to those used for graphics or other computer applications. Some of the software requires that the production be shot against a blue screen. As the show is being taped or aired, the blue drops out and the computer-generated set replaces it. For other systems, the action takes place in front of a portable gray screen. The blue comes from a ring of blue lights that attach around the camera lens and project onto the screen. The color bounces back directly into the camera

lens at a carefully controlled angle that allows for a clean keying effect. Each camera is equipped with a tracking mechanism that communicates positional data to the virtual set computer program in order to generate the correct set position. A computer interface controls switching from one camera to another.

Sometimes only part of a set is virtual. For example, the walls of a set may be real, but the ceiling is added virtually for the few shots where the camera shoots with an upward angle. Virtual elements are often used for advertised products—a sign for Coke that isn't really there but appears on the TV set. (See Figure 9.16.)

The virtual set concept is fairly new but is catching on quickly. As more and more facilities convert to **digital** technologies, virtual sets will be integrated more naturally.

9.7 Traditional Sets

The real sets that are made of plastic, wood, metal, and other materials are still the most common. They need to be light, portable, and storable. Constructing, assembling, and storing them is a study in and of itself. It requires carpentry, metalworking, and artistic skills beyond the scope of this book. (See Figures 9.17 and 9.18.) All we can do is touch on some of the basic elements involved in making and obtaining scenery

Figure 9.17

This large scene shop undertakes work for a large number of entertainment companies and events. It includes woodworking, metalworking, painting, sculpturing, prop construction, etc. *Photo courtesy of Lexington Scenery and Props, Sun Valley, CA.*

units, setting them up in a studio, and storing them for repeated use.[2]

Constructing and Obtaining Scenic Elements

One of the most basic set units is the **flat.** It is a cross-braced wood or metal frame faced with either canvas (which is lightweight but too flimsy for repeated heavy use) or thin pressed board or plywood (which will take more abuse, although it is heavier to work with). The layout for a standard flat is shown in Figure 9.19. Flats can be made in any size, but common heights are 10 feet for larger studios with very high ceilings and 8 feet for smaller studios with lower ceilings. Widths also vary, although they are seldom broader than five feet (the width that one person can comfortably handle with arms outstretched). Often the fronts of flats are painted to look like whatever is needed for the production—a storefront, a child's bedroom, a garden. (See Figure 9.20.)

In addition to standard flats, studios use other rigid but lightweight materials, such as foam (see Figure 9.21) and corrugated feather board, to construct scenic elements. Construction of other set pieces (stairways, platforms, and so forth) is more complicated, requiring heavy bracing and sturdy framing for the amount of abuse and wear they will be subjected to. (See Figure 9.22.) Some flats must also be of sturdy construction. For example, a flat with a door through which people are going to enter and exit must be quite strong so that it looks realistic and doesn't wobble (or fall down) when someone slams it.

Figure 9.18

This is a computer-operated machine that takes dimensions for sets that are designed with a computer program and then sets dimensions to cut material (wood, metal, foam) to the appropriate size needed for the set piece. *Photo courtesy of Lexington Scenery and Props, Sun Valley, CA.*

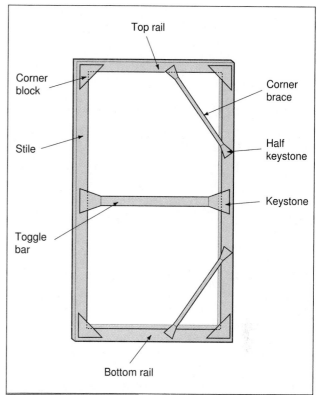

Figure 9.19

Construction of an ordinary flat. Standard construction of a simple flat consists of a frame made of 1″ × 3″ pine with ¼″ plywood for the corner blocks and keystones. The front of the frame is typically covered with canvas or with plywood (or pressed hardboard). If a solid wooden front covering is used, then the corner braces will not be needed.

Sets constructed for low-definition NTSC television have been able to be rather shoddy looking. Scratches or chipped paint or fake books looked fine because the camera did not pick up imperfections. However, this is changing for high-definition television. The sharper resolution of the picture means that sets must be constructed to more accurately depict details.

Large scenery pieces are often difficult to build in a university setting unless the college has a large scene shop used for stage productions. However, it is possible to obtain used scenery pieces from local stations, especially news sets, since stations change those frequently.

Cloth Backgrounds

Most studios use cloth backdrops, either **cycloramas** (cycs) or drapes. Cycs are made of canvas, duck, or gauze (depending on the desired texture and reflectance quality desired) and are generally designed to be stretched taught over piping and weighted down. They give a smooth limbo background or they can be painted to fit a particular need. A neutral gray is preferable. Seams should be vertical, not horizontal. (See Figure 9.23.)

Drapes, which are usually of a heavier material and often darker, can be either pulled taut or pleated, depending upon the desired effect. Darker, low-reflectance drapes are effective backing for **cameo lighting.** Drapes are usually used in smaller widths than a cyc and can ordinarily be easily rigged or hung for specific applications. A cyc, on the other hand, is often permanently mounted, covering two or even three walls of a studio.

Furniture

Most of the time a set will also consist of furniture—the chairs for talk-show guests, the podium for a game-show host, the porch swing for a drama. Sometimes these elements need to be specially constructed, but often they can be bought at used-furniture stores

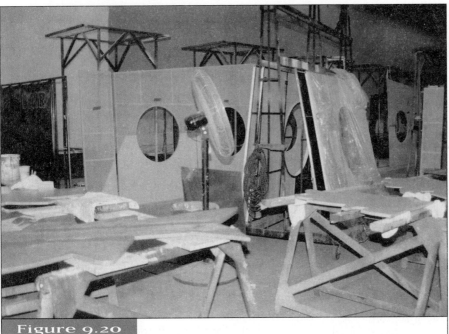

Figure 9.20

Flats that have been painted and are sitting on racks to dry. Note that very little of the flat touches the rack. *Photo courtesy of Lexington Scenery and Props, Sun Valley, CA.*

or borrowed from someone's apartment. Several types of furniture create problems on TV, however. One is the *swinging swivel chair,* in which guests vent their nervous energy by rotating back and forth. Another is the *precarious perch,* in which talent must sit uncomfortably on top of a high, hard stool. And a third is the *talent swallower,* overstuffed chairs and sofas that are so plush and soft that the person sinks down so far the director is left with nothing but a shot of the knees.

Set Dressings and Props

You must also take set dressings and props into account when designing and constructing sets. A **prop** is something that is actually used during the production—the toy the clown gives to a child, the vase someone throws in anger, the book someone reads from. **Set dressings** are not actually used but add to the interest or atmosphere of the production—toys that indicate that children live in the house, a vase of wilted flowers, books that litter the sofa. Again, you may need to construct some of these from scratch while others are readily available—sometimes set dressings and props can be rented from a furniture store. And, again, they need to be in better shape for HDTV than for standard TV.

All set elements must be considered well ahead of the production date. This is similar to the preproduction discipline needed for other aspects of production. How long will it take to build and paint the flats? Will the furniture clash with the artwork hung on the walls? Are the colors of the game show set bright enough? What types of magazines would the lead character be likely to have on the coffee table? Who is responsible for bringing each prop?

The Floor Plan

One of the best ways to ensure that all the elements are taken into account is to draw a **floor plan** ahead of time. (See Figure 9.24.) As with many other aspects of production, computer programs can aid and assist with floor plans and other elements of set design. **Production designers** and **art directors** often use these computer programs to plan the overall look of the set as well as the placing of specific flats, furniture, set dressings, and props. Some programs allow them to

A scenery element being carved from foam.
Photo courtesy of Lexington Scenery and Props, Sun Valley, CA.

scale; otherwise the director's shooting angles, the talent's movement, and the lighting design will all be off. A floor plan should be prepared with as much detail and precision as possible.

Assembling and Setting Up Scenic Elements

Set pieces are usually constructed and gathered somewhere away from the studio, such as a nearby scene shop. Studios are usually heavily scheduled with productions and cannot be used for the time-consuming job of set construction. At a specified time, shortly before production, everything needed for the set must be brought into the studio and assembled for use. This is a time-consuming process, so anything that can be thought through ahead of time should be. This is where a floor plan comes in particularly handy. How far will the sofa be from the chair? What will be the angle of the desk?

Many of the set pieces used in studios are solid and freestanding, so they simply need to be put into place. Others, however, particularly flats, need to be braced in some way so they do not fall over. One of the most common braces is a **jack,** which is a hinged triangle usually made of wood. When the flat is in place, the jack is swung out behind the flat at a right angle and held in place with stage weights or **sandbags.** (See Figure 9.25.) Sometimes flats or other set pieces must be joined together. This is usually done with power tools that can be used to shoot staples or removable nails through one piece of scenery and into another.

If props need to be in a precise place, their location is often marked in some way (a piece of tape on the floor, an inconspicuous chalk mark on a sofa). In that way they can quickly be placed in their proper position after they have been used and moved during a rehearsal.

The whole assembly process must take into account other aspects of the production such as camera movements, mic placement, lighting, and talent movement. Readying everything for production involves cooperation from many crew members.

Camera Movement

No matter what the set looks like, there must be provision for adequate camera movement. Several cameras will have to have free access from different

"enter" a set and look at it from a number of different angles. Programs also keep track of the supplies needed to construct set pieces, the cost, and what is finished and yet to be completed.

A good floor plan allows the director to make the most economical use of all studio and staging space. The director can plan how best to take advantage, for example, of the *cornerset*—a two-walled setting positioned in a corner of the studio—that provides good set backing for many types of productions (better than a flat backdrop), while allowing great depth and freedom of camera movement (more so than a three-walled set does).

A typical studio staging floor plan includes the placement of all flats and other set pieces and the exact location of all stage props and furniture. It is important that all flats and furniture be drawn to exact

(a)

(b)

Figure 9.22

Two approaches to designing part of an airplane to be used as a set piece. The first (*a*) shows a metal frame to be used to construct the fuselage. The second (*b*) is a section of an airplane fuselage that shows construction that is typical of specialized set pieces.   *Photo (a) courtesy of Lexington Scenery and Props, Sun Valley, CA. Photo (b) courtesy of Universal Studios, Universal City, CA.*

Canvas backdrop painted to serve as a street-front scene. *Photo courtesy of Universal Studios, Universal City, CA.*

angles in the setting. This usually poses no problems with settings that have few set units and very little furniture. A talk show with a desk and several chairs set against a cyc is easy for cameras to move around in. What creates problems are elaborate realistic settings with windows and doors and a great deal of furniture. For this reason, sets are usually constructed as just two-walled or three-walled sets. The open wall (the missing side of the set) is used for camera access. In three-walled sets, the walls do not have to be set at exactly 90 degrees; they can be left open at oblique angles so that the camera can have even more access. In some sets (occasionally a four-walled set may have to be used), it is possible to position cameras behind the

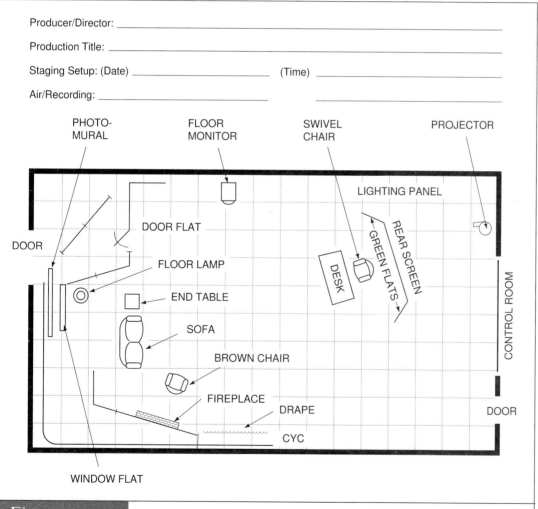

Producer/Director: _____

Production Title: _____

Staging Setup: (Date) _____ (Time) _____

Air/Recording: _____

PHOTO-MURAL   FLOOR MONITOR   SWIVEL CHAIR   PROJECTOR

LIGHTING PANEL

DOOR FLAT

DOOR

GREEN FLATS / REAR SCREEN

DESK

FLOOR LAMP

END TABLE

CONTROL ROOM

SOFA

BROWN CHAIR

FIREPLACE   DRAPE   DOOR

CYC

WINDOW FLAT

Figure 9.24

Sample staging floor plan. In this floor plan, the squares on the floor correspond to three-foot tiles actually laid on the studio floor. In other floor plans, a lighting grid or pipe battens might be superimposed over the studio layout.

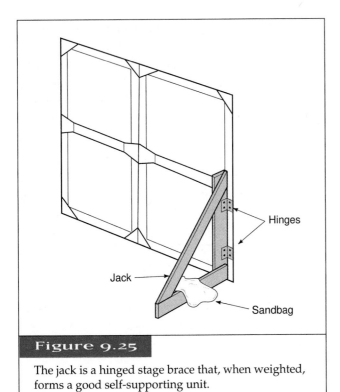

Figure 9.25

The jack is a hinged stage brace that, when weighted, forms a good self-supporting unit.

Figure 9.26

Backlighting problems with scenic flat. In this kind of situation, either the backlight will have to be mounted higher, the light will have to be repositioned closer to the flat, the flat will have to be moved back (closer to the backlight), or the talent will have to move forward, farther away from the flat.

flats or other scenic elements and shoot through a window, a doorway, a hole in the bookcase or fireplace, or other camouflaged openings.

Microphone Placement

The setting also has to have provision for adequate microphone placement and movement. Although the wireless microphone is increasingly used in studio dramas—soap operas and situation comedies—the beginning audio operator must learn how to cope with staging concerns involved with wired microphones. Many productions use some sort of **boom, giraffe,** or **fishpole.** These mic holders can create shadow problems on the set.

If the lighting has not been carefully worked out with the precise boom placement in mind, there will be a strong possibility of unwanted shadows from the horizontal boom or fishpole. This could be more of a problem in a setting with a plain background than in a busy set that may make a shadow less noticeable. In most cases, however, either the mic boom or the lighting instrument will have to be repositioned somewhat or the light will have to be barn-doored off the boom.

Lighting Instruments

Other lighting problems can be caused by certain kinds of setting arrangements. Occasionally, pillars or other foreground set pieces may be blocking crucial front lighting from a certain angle. Sometimes a strong **key light** may throw a very distracting shadow on a close-up shot of some small object; or if the talent is lighted too closely to the set (flat or cyc), the key light may throw too much illumination on the set. One of the most common problems, however, is the blocking of the **backlight** by a flat. If the flat is too high for the studio (a 10-foot flat might be high if the studio has a low ceiling), if the flat is out too far into the studio from the backlight, or if the talent is standing too close to the flat, it is going to be difficult to hit the talent with the backlight (See Figure 9.26.)

In this case, something—the backlight, the flat, or the talent—will have to be moved.

To minimize the problems between sets and lighting and make for ease of operation for both the staging and lighting crews, large set pieces such as flats are put up before lighting begins. However, furniture and set decorations are not put into place. This allows the lighting people to light according to the general placement of the sets without having to maneuver their ladders around pieces of furniture. Once the lighting ladders are put away, the set is dressed. Some minor lighting changes may then be made, but these adjustments can usually be made from the floor or with the aid of one small stepladder.

Talent Movement

Finally, the setting has to take into consideration all anticipated movement by the talent. How much action is required? Will several people be moving in the same direction simultaneously? How much space is needed for certain movement (a dance step or tumbling demonstration)? Is the set large enough to accommodate all the talent moves without the cameras being in danger of shooting off the set? Is there plenty of room for all entrances and exits? Will the talent be forced to maneuver so close to the set walls that part of their lighting will be cut off? Or, if the performers work too close to the set, will they cast unwanted shadows on the flat or cyc?

Storage of Scenic Elements

In many small stations and educational institutions, scenery storage can be a serious problem. There is never enough room to house everything that is needed, and scenery storage always seems to be one area that suffers the most. This can be a particularly critical problem because so many of the flats and special set pieces can be reused over and over in a variety of ways—with different set dressings—in a number of configurations. Yet they have to be stored somewhere and catalogued for easy retrieval.

Flats and other narrow units are usually stored in racks, which are simple frames designed to hold a number of flats in an upright position. Each rack can be designed and labeled to hold similarly matched scenic units (for example, living-room flats, office flats, green-speckled flats, log-cabin flats, and so forth).

Props and other small items can be stored on deep shelves in the storage area. Again, it is important that each shelf and/or cubicle be clearly labeled: "telephones," "dishes," "bottles," and so on. Even furniture and other large stage props can be stored in multitiered shelves. Large overstuffed chairs, sofas, and heavy tables can be stored on the floor level; medium-sized chairs and tables can be stored on another level (four to five feet off the floor); and lightweight chairs and stools and small appliances can be stored on a third level (perhaps seven to eight feet above the floor).

As would be expected, **high-definition** TV has made the care of sets and props more crucial than in the past. Minor imperfections such as scratches or tears are more noticeable than on regular-definition TV, so proper storage is one way to ensure realistic-looking scenery.

Discussion Questions

1. What types of computer graphics systems does your school have? Do you have CG/paintbox/still-store capability? Are these capabilities achieved by one machine or more? What kinds of graphics effects discussed in this chapter could you do in your school's studio?

2. You are producing a historical documentary, and the local museum has a very fragile 500-year-old book that you need to shoot. The museum will not let you remove the book from the museum, and it can be very gently handled only by a museum employee wearing gloves. What plans can you make to get shots of the individual pages in the book, which include maps, scientific drawings, and ornate text?

3. Come up with a list of virtual sets that it would be wise for your school to have. Why did you select these particular sets? How could you modify them so you could use them more often?

4. Think through a basic talk show. What background set pieces would you want? Furniture? Set dressing?

Footnotes

1. Some of the companies offering virtual set software are: Photron USA in San Jose, CA (http://www.photron.com); Orad in New York City (http://www.orad.com.il); Accom in Menlo Park, CA (http://www.accom.com); Computrend in Anaheim, CA (http://www.computrend.com); Videocam Corp. in Miami, Florida (videocam@bellsouth.net); Prism Media Products in Rockaway, NJ (http://www.prismMPI.com); and Polhemus in Colchester, VT (http://www.polhemus.com).

2. For a full discussion of scenery construction and use, consult any good theater stagecraft text or manual, such as Paul Carter, *Backstage Handbook* (Louisville, Ken.: Broadway Press, 1994); or Jay Michael Gillette, *Theatrical Design and Production* (Mountain View, Cal.: Mayfield Publishing Co., 1987).

chapter 10

Interactive Media

Computers have become a fact of life in television production. In previous chapters, you have seen how computers have had an impact on the way television professionals work in areas such as audio production, video storage, video editing, and graphics.

But while computerized videotape editors and character generators merely change the techniques of conventional production work, the marriage of computer technology and traditional media also is creating new ways to communicate. The convergence of computers, digital technology, video, and audio is at the heart of the so-called *New Media*.

Like many of the buzzwords of the computer age, establishing a precise definition of what the New Media are is difficult. In general, New Media are characterized by **user interaction** and **dynamic content,** meaning that the consumer of the media is not passive but rather actively controls the media and selects the content he or she wishes to experience. New Media are also referred to as *multimedia, hypermedia,* or *interactive media,* and while there may be subtle differences in the precise definitions of these terms, for clarity this chapter will use the term "interactive media."

You have probably seen examples of interactive media. Many museums and other public attractions now have interactive kiosks that enable visitors to find information by selecting options on a video screen. Home computer users can purchase interactive encyclopedias on CD-ROM disks that allow them to not only read words and view photos as they would in a printed encyclopedia but also see moving video and hear sounds. (See Figure 10.1.) Using a computer connected to the **Internet,** a user can access a variety of information sources around the world, complete with video and sound. There are many other examples, as you will see in this chapter.

The important thing to remember as you read this chapter is that interactive media production represents not only a convergence of media but a convergence of skills. Many of the same principles, for instance, that guide the production of graphics for an evening television newscast still apply to producing graphics for interactive media

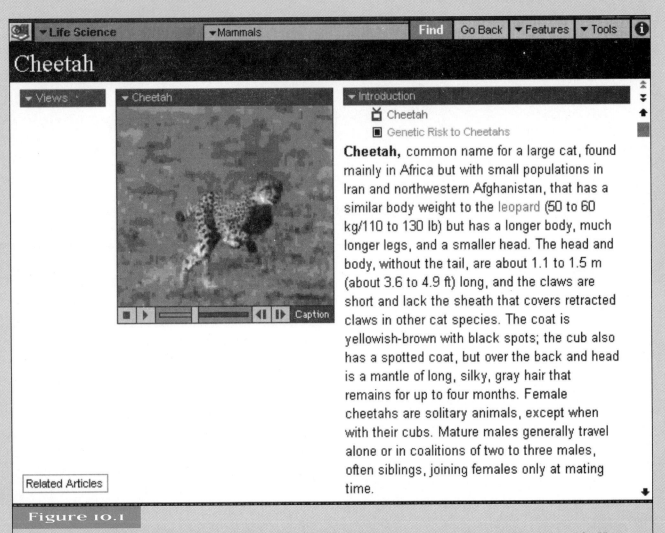

Figure 10.1

Interactive encyclopedias, such as Microsoft Encarta, allow users to experience a variety of media interactively. Here, users can read about cheetahs and see a video clip of a cheetah running. *Encarta is a trademark of Microsoft Corporation. Screen shot reprinted with permission from Microsoft Corporation.*

presentations; and the same fundamentals of audio, lighting, camera work, and editing that make for an effective documentary or sitcom also make for an effective interactive media production. The advent of computers doesn't mean you can forget traditional audio and video production principles; in fact, they become even more important.

The *disciplines* and *techniques*, then, of interactive media build upon those you have learned in other areas of video production. However, there are also disciplines and techniques unique to interactive media production, which will be covered in this chapter. Its topics include:

- The role of interactivity and dynamic content in interactive media presentations (10.1).
- The elements that make up interactive media presentations, such as text, graphics, audio, video, and links (10.2).
- The difference between stand-alone and World Wide Web–based interactive media (10.3).
- The variety of groups who produce interactive media (10.3).
- The hardware requirements for interactive media in terms of computers, storage, digitizing cards, input devices, monitors, video cards, and other peripherals (10.4).
- The software used to produce interactive media (10.4).
- The planning and production processes of interactive media production (10.5).

Most traditional media are **linear,** meaning that their content has a specific beginning, middle, and end. Such media are also static: Their content cannot be changed by the consumer of the media. For instance, when you watch an episode of your favorite sitcom, you normally begin watching at the start of the program and watch until the end, and you cannot affect the content of the program. Certainly, you *could* record the program on videotape and then skip around to various parts, but this would be a tedious process and the result probably wouldn't make much sense. And even then, you would not be able to actually change the show's content.

Interactive media, on the other hand, are characterized by their **nonlinear** design and dynamic content. Nonlinear means that the presentation does not have to proceed in a predetermined order. You have already seen this term used in the chapter on videotape editing, and its meaning in this context is similar. But while nonlinear videotape editing affects the production *process,* nonlinear media refers to the finished product. This is where the concept of interactivity comes in: interactive media presentations are normally designed to allow the consumer to "navigate" through them. The consumer does not merely passively take in the media content but rather actively controls how it is presented. The same presentation, in fact, may be experienced by different people in different ways; it can change according to each consumer's wishes. For that reason, consumers of interactive media are usually referred to as *users,* because that term implies actively employing something—putting it to use—rather than the passivity connoted by terms such as "viewer" or "listener."

To see how these concepts work, let's examine in more detail a hypothetical interactive presentation. The owner of a shopping center wants to provide an automated way for shoppers to find out three kinds of information: (1) the location of particular stores; (2) the shopping center's hours of operation; and (3) what items stores have on sale each week. Imagine that the owner has hired you to create a kiosk to dispense this information.

Your first instinct might be to produce a linear, tape-based presentation. You could shoot videotape footage of products that are on sale, use a graphic to show a map of the shopping center, and compose text on a character generator to indicate its hours. You could then edit this information, along with a narrator's voice, onto videotape, producing a presentation that might run 10 minutes. Illustrated as a timeline, the program might look like Figure 10.2. Your informational kiosk, then, would consist of a television monitor and a continuously looping videotape that would play the 10-minute program over and over.

But it is unlikely that such a presentation would meet the needs of shoppers. Most of them are probably looking for just one of the three categories of information given on the tape, and if they happen to arrive at the kiosk just after that information has been given, they will have to wait 10 minutes to see it again. In a busy shopping environment, it would be inconvenient for shoppers to stand around that long waiting for the information.

A more effective approach would be to design an interactive presentation. You could still use many of the same elements—graphics to show locations of stores and hours, video footage of sale items, and a narrator's voice—but you would make them part of an interactive presentation. Using a **multimedia authoring program** you could assemble the graphics, sound, and video so that they could be accessed in a nonlinear fashion, allowing the shopper to instantaneously "jump" to the information he or she needs. Figure 10.3 shows a graphical representation of how the program would work. Rather than having to wait through unwanted information to get to the desired information, the user can choose which part of the presentation to access and immediately access it. As shown in the illustration, the user selects which part of the presentation he or she wishes to see.

Later in the chapter, you will see how to facilitate this type of user control, but for now it is helpful to understand the concepts of **screens** and **menus.** In an interactive presentation, different portions are often referred to as screens; in World Wide Web–based systems, these screens are usually called **Web pages.** The example in Figure 10.3, for instance, has four screens. Each screen may contain various information and types of media. For example, the "Sale Items" screen

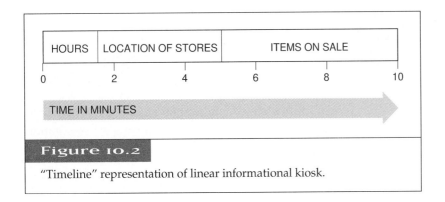

Figure 10.2

"Timeline" representation of linear informational kiosk.

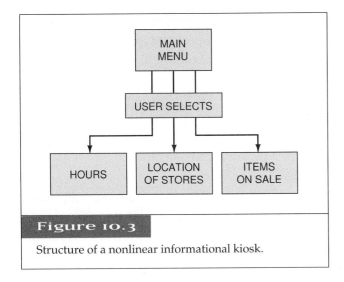

Figure 10.3

Structure of a nonlinear informational kiosk.

would contain text and pictures. Menus are screens that allow the user to make choices. The **main menu,** also called the **home page** on Internet-based presentations, is usually the first screen that the user sees, and from this menu he or she makes a selection. In the example, while the kiosk is not in use, the main menu will be displayed on the monitor. When a user selects an item from the menu, the presentation then displays the selected screen. The user can then return to the main menu to access other information if desired. The presentation would be programmed to return to the main screen after a certain length of time if no further selections are made. Thus, a shopper might approach the kiosk to find out how much shopping time he had left. He would select "Hours" from the main menu and then read the information. Since he needs no further information, he would probably simply leave the kiosk and continue shopping. After a certain amount

of time—say 30 seconds—the presentation will automatically return to the main menu so that it will be ready for the next user.

Varying levels of interactivity can be built into presentations. The example just cited has a fairly low level of interactivity: The user simply chooses from among three sets of "canned" information. To increase interactivity, we could ask for more input from the user and make the presentation more dynamic. For example, the user could use a keyboard to type a question like, "What stores have jeans on sale?" The presentation would respond by immediately moving to the part that shows what stores are having sales on jeans. Media presentations that respond to specific user requests in this manner are called **adaptive presentations.** Such higher levels of interactivity lead to more dynamic content, as users can tailor the presentation to their personal interests. Incorporating such increased interactivity, as you might imagine, also adds complexity to the production process.

10.2 Elements of Interactive Media

Computers are central to interactive presentations. In some cases, the computer may be well disguised; the user of the interactive presentation may not even realize he or she is operating one. But a computer is necessary to bring together the various media that make up the presentation and to allow the user to navigate through it.

For a computer to bring together different types of media, those media must be in **digital** form, meaning that they are represented electronically by a series of "on" and "off" signals, as discussed in previous chapters. Once digitized, audio and video signals become merely "data" as far as the computer is concerned. A properly equipped computer can thus bring together digital video, audio, words, pictures, and any other elements that are in digital form.

Computers can store digital information on a variety of storage media, from the traditional 3.5-inch floppy disk to CD-ROMs, hard drives, and optical drives. They also deliver those data from the storage area to the place where they are needed. In the case of a stand-alone computer kiosk, this involves simply moving the data through the computer to the monitor, but in cases where more than one computer are hooked together, or **networked,** the data must move a much greater distance. Network connections are said to have a certain **bandwidth,** which measures how much data they can carry. Finally, the computer is nearly constantly manipulating—or changing—the digital data. This manipulation is performed chiefly by the computer's **central processing unit** (CPU), an electronic chip that is, in effect, the computer's "brain." Any time digital data are changed in any way, displayed on the screen, or moved from one location to another, the computer's CPU is put to work. Because some of the elements of interactive media—especially digital video—are highly complex in digital form, powerful computers are required to produce and run interactive presentations. To be suitable for interactive media work, a computer must have sufficient capabilities to store, move, and manipulate digital media information. More information on specific requirements will be presented later in this chapter.

Text

Text is normally displayed on the computer's monitor, although the computer may have the ability to print text on paper as well. Text may consist of labels ("Main Menu"), instructions ("Click here to continue"), or substantive content. Long text passages may be displayed in a *scroll box* that allows the user to move up and down through it. The user can normally control how long text is displayed on the screen, thus allowing the presentation to be adjusted for different reading speeds.

Graphics

Graphics are usually displayed on the computer's monitor, although they, too, can be printed. Graphics may consist of original artwork composed with a computer program such as Adobe Illustrator, or they may be digital copies of existing artwork. Using a **scanner** and software such as Adobe PhotoShop, photographs and other printed material may be digitized and then manipulated. Individual video frames can also be digitized into graphics using **video capture** hardware and software. Users may be given control over how graphics are displayed. For example, they may be able to zoom in on static graphics in order to see more detail.

Animations, as first discussed in Chapter 9, are created by assembling individual graphics to create the illusion of movement. Much like video creates the illusion of movement by displaying a series of static "frames" in rapid succession, a computer can rapidly display a series of static graphics to create a similar effect. Animations can be used to demonstrate movement. For example, an animation showing how electrons move around the nucleus of an atom might be used in an educational science presentation. Presentations may be designed so that users can control when and how quickly animations play and may allow them to "pause" animations.

Audio

Audio is normally played through the computer's sound system. It can be made a part of interactive presentations either in conjunction with video clips or as a separate element. Digitized audio might consist of voice, music, or sound effects. Using an appropriate audio card (a circuit board and components that plug into the computer) and software, an audio signal can be digitized.

Users may have the ability to control when an audio clip plays and to "pause" the clip if they wish. They also may be given control over how loudly audio plays over the computer's speakers.

Through the use of **MIDI** (Musical Instrument Digital Interface), a computer can control certain musical instruments—such as electronic keyboards and drum machines—making them play particular notes, as discussed in Chapter 3. Some sound cards have built-in MIDI synthesizers that can mimic various musical instruments.

Video

Video is normally displayed on the computer's monitor, although in some applications—especially those using videodisks—it may be displayed on a separate monitor. Using a video capture card and software, video is digitized and compressed, as discussed in Chapters 7 and 8. The size and bandwidth of digitized video also can be cut down by using lower resolutions, fewer colors, or slower frame rates. Resolution, which is a measure of the video frame's size, is normally indicated in **pixels.** Common resolutions include 320 pixels wide by 200 pixels high and 640 pixels wide by 400 pixels high. You may also digitize the signal using fewer colors, although digitized video with fewer than 256 colors tends to look cartoonlike. Finally, you might digitize the video with fewer than the standard 30 frames per second. Each of these techniques lowers the quality of the image, however, and should be used only in situations where the highest quality video is not required.

Users may be given control over video clips in terms of when they play and may be able to "pause" or "rewind" the clip just like an animation. Users also may be able to choose whether the video fills the entire screen or only a portion of it.

Links

As you have seen throughout this chapter, a recurring characteristic of interactive media is user control. This control is facilitated through the use of **links,** which connect one part of the presentation to another. Virtually any part of an interactive presentation can be a link. When the link is activated, it triggers a designated action. This action may be as simple as emitting a short "beep" sound or as elaborate as playing a full-motion video clip with sound. For instance, a presentation may include a line of text, "Click here to see the video clip," which is designated as a link to a video clip. Thus, when the user clicks the mouse on that line of text, the video clip plays. Links may be used to move the user to a new location in the presentation, allowing him or her to quickly "jump" to a new screen. Text designated as a link is often called **hypertext.**

Pictures also may be defined as links. When the user clicks on the picture with the mouse, something happens. Different parts of a picture may be defined as different links. For instance, an interactive presentation may display a picture of the solar system on the screen. When the user clicks different parts, different things happen; a click on Mars might display additional information about Mars and a more detailed picture of the planet. Clicking the sun may cause the picture to animate, showing how the planets revolve around the sun. Graphics used in this manner also are called **image maps.**

The most common type of link is the **button,** which is a small graphic made to look like a button on an appliance. Buttons may be labeled with text ("Continue" or "Stop," for example), or they may have small pictures that define their function (a red hexagon to represent "Stop," for example). Video clips are often accompanied by a series of buttons that mimic the functions on a VCR, as shown in Figure 10.4. Thus, users can "pause," "play," "rewind," or "stop" a clip by pressing the appropriate button.

There are several ways to activate links. Most commonly, they are activated by clicking a mouse, typing on a keyboard, or touching the screen. In some presentations, the user may be able to talk into a microphone; the computer will then interpret what is said and make an appropriate response. The user may, for example, say "Go back" to make the presentation return to a previous location.

10.3 Types of Interactive Media

Interactive media are continuously expanding into new areas as computer technologies evolve and as new ways of combining interactive control and multiple media develop. The interactive media frontier is an exciting one for users, producers, and companies that develop interactive programs. Goldman Sachs, a Wall Street investment firm, has coined the term "Communacopia" for the seemingly

Buttons that allow users to control video clips in interactive presentations can be designed to look like the familiar controls found on a VCR.

endless variety of new ways to combine and use media.

Some forms of interactive media, such as **video on demand,** which allows subscribers of cable or satellite services to order movies and other programming at the exact time they want it, involve very little actual "authoring" of content. Instead, the challenges of providing video on demand are technical considerations of delivering an existing product. At the other end of the spectrum, **virtual reality,** which simulates activities such as flying a jet plane, hang gliding, or walking through dungeons and mazes, requires specialized equipment and a massive amount of programming. This chapter focuses on interactive media presentations that lie in between those two. The emphasis here is on presentations that involve original content and that can be produced using relatively

modest computer equipment. Those types of presentations fall into two broad categories: stand-alone systems and World Wide Web–based systems.

Stand-alone Computer Systems

Personal computer technology has developed to such a point that even modest home systems can be used to create and view interactive material. PCs—whether IBM or Macintosh—also lie at the heart of the majority of interactive kiosks and presentations used in business, education, and medicine. With a few required add-ons that will be discussed later in this chapter, most modern PCs are able to handle fairly elaborate interactive programming.

Nearly all interactive presentations designed for home use are distributed on CD-ROM disks. These disks normally contain data files for video clips and other content, as well as a program that facilitates interactive control. This program allows the user to navigate through the material contained on the disk. CD-ROMs come in many varieties, with literally thousands of titles. Among the most popular are interactive encyclopedias, as mentioned at the beginning of the chapter. Other CD-ROMs concentrate on home maintenance, auto repair, military history, golf, and many other topics. Some allow users to play elaborate interactive games, with digitized video images taking the place of the cartoonlike graphics of early computer games. Many educational CD-ROMs are available for students of all ages. CD-ROMs also have become a popular marketing tool, and many companies now distribute advertising and other information on them. Interactive kiosks, which are becoming a mainstay at shopping centers, museums, and theme parks, normally run on PCs. Such kiosks are programmed to provide very specific information to users. Some videotape rental chains, for example, have installed interactive units to help customers find information about movies they want to rent. These units allow movie enthusiasts to search for information on particular movies, actors, or directors, and even view short video clips of selected films. At the Rock and Roll Hall of Fame and Museum in Cleveland, music enthusiasts can hear music clips and find information about their favorite artists at interactive media stations. (See Figure 10.5.)

Figure 10.5

Interactive media exhibits at the Rock and Roll Hall of Fame and Museum, designed by The Burdick Group of San Francisco, allow guests to interact with music and video clips. This exhibit is titled "The 500 Songs That Shaped Rock and Roll." *Photograph by Timothy Hursley.*

World Wide Web—Based Systems

Networks can span entire communities, states, and even countries. The Internet, which is a massive network of computers around the world, allows users to access information on a seemingly endless variety of topics. You have no doubt heard the Internet referred to as "the Information Superhighway" for its vast informational resources. However, the Internet also has been criticized for its lack of organization, and it is often hard for even experienced users to find what they're looking for.

The advent of the **World Wide Web** (WWW) has helped to make the Internet's information more accessible and appealing. Through the use of **hypertext markup language** (HTML), a computer language that allows the creation of interactive presentations using text, pictures, sound, and video, the World Wide Web provides a standard format for Internet users. By using a **browser** program such as Netscape

Navigator or Microsoft Internet Explorer, a user can access information from computers located around the world. Browsers also allow users to interact with this information: By clicking on a particular picture or piece of text, for instance, the user can move to a new location or access different information. A browser is programmed to read HTML **scripts,** which look a lot like a normal text file. The scripts contain instructions to display text, pictures, and other media as well as links, as shown in Figure 10.6.

HTML itself is a relatively limited language for providing high levels of interaction, and the fact that information must travel over a network limits the amount of data that can reasonably be contained in a presentation. Add-ons to HTML, such as Sun's Java and Macromedia's ShockWave and Flash, allow for more significant interaction. Various **streaming video** systems allow moving video to be displayed on Web pages. Still, it must be understood that Internet-based systems where content is stored on an off-site computer and accessed via HTML are normally not able to match stand-alone systems in terms of speed and interactivity.

World Wide Web technology can also be used on smaller networks. Many organizations now run what are called **intranets,** which are essentially smaller, self-contained versions of the Internet. Intranet users can utilize HTML and browsers to access information from other computers on the network.

Who's Producing Interactive Media?

You have seen that the term interactive media encompasses a variety of applications and techniques. Not surprisingly, interactive presentations are produced by a wide range of groups. Software companies—both giants such as Microsoft and smaller companies—produce interactive media, and many schools, businesses, and institutions produce in-house presentations. Hundreds of small companies, often called boutiques, which specialize in producing interactive media, have sprung up around the country. Also, companies that have in the past concentrated on traditional media—like video-production houses and television studios—are now getting into interactive

media. There are also opportunities to start small interactive media businesses with relatively modest investments, much like the desktop publishing businesses of the late 1980s and early 1990s. Interactive media producers may work as part of a large team of videographers, editors, graphic designers, and others, or they may work alone, solely responsible for producing all aspects of a project from start to finish.

The number of corporations interested in interactive media continues to grow, boding well for future opportunities in interactive production. We are seeing joint ventures between telephone companies and cable providers, television networks and software makers, and many others. A key goal of all of these alliances is profiting from interactive media. It is likely that at least some of these much hyped alliances will fail and that some of the highly touted promises of the new media will never materialize. But interactive media, especially using World Wide Web systems over the Internet, have already staked out a significant place in the industry, and it is likely that that stake will continue to grow. And production professionals who can combine a solid foundation of production technique with an understanding of computers, interactivity, and nonlinear production will be in increasing demand.

10.4 Tools of Interactive Media

Because interactive media are so closely tied to computers, they require both hardware, the actual pieces of equipment, and software, the programs that allow for the creative use of the interactivity.

Hardware

Computer hardware is constantly changing. Components that were "state of the art" a short time ago may now be obsolete. Constant innovation is increasing the capabilities of every component, from the CPU to the mouse. The following is a general guide to components used in interactive work. For a particular application, you may not need all of these components, but you should be familiar with what they do.

```
1  <HTML>
2  <TITLE> Sample HTML Page </TITLE>
3  <H1> Welcome to the Lighthouse </H1>
4  <BR>
5  <H3> Click <a href="directions.html"> here </a> for directions
   to the lighthouse.
6  <a HREF="tour.html"><IMG SRC="lighthouse.gif"> </A>
7  <BR>
8  Click on the lighthouse to take a tour.
9  </HTML>
```

N. Netscape - [Sample HTML Page]   _ 🗗 ✕

File Edit View Go Bookmarks Options Directory   Help

Welcome to the Lighthouse

Click here for directions to the lighthouse.

Click on the lighthouse to take a tour.

file:///E|/DOCS/Burrows Television Text/HTML Test/tour.html

Figure 10.6

Here is an example of a simple HTML script (*top*) and how it looks when viewed with a browser program (*bottom.*) The numbers in the box to the left of the script are not actually part of the script; they are shown to explain what each line in the program does. Line (1) identifies the file as an HTML script. Line (2) is the title of the page and appears in the title bar of the browser. Line (3) uses heading level 1 for the line of text indicated. HTML allows different levels of headings, differing in size and type style. Line (4) inserts a line break command, which makes subsequent text start on a new line. Line (5) uses heading level 3 for the line of text indicated. The portion <a HREF="directions.html"> designates what follows as a link. In this case, when the user activates the link it will move to a new page called "directions.html." The </a>command designates the end of the link. Thus, the word "here" is designated as a link to the file "directions.html." Line (6) places the picture of the lighthouse on the screen with the section <IMG SRC="lighthouse.gif">. The portion <a HREF="tour.html"> designates the lighthouse picture as a link to the file "tour.html." Thus, if the user clicks on the lighthouse picture, he or she will be taken to the tour section. Line (7) inserts a line break. Line (8) places the indicated text. Line (9) indicates the end of the HTML script. In this case the script's "directions.html" and "tour.html" would need to be written separately.

Computer

Both IBM-compatible-PC and Macintosh computers are suitable for interactive media work. More expensive workstations, such as those made by Silicon Graphics and others, are also well-suited to authoring. Ideally, a PC should have a Pentium-class processor, and a Macintosh should have a PowerPC-class processor. A processor's power also is determined by its speed, usually measured in megahertz (MHz). Thus, a 500 MHz Pentium III is faster than a 450 MHz Pentium III. While there are many variables in processor model and speed, Pentium processors are normally at least twice as fast as 486 and lesser model IBM PCs, and PowerPC Macintoshes enjoy similar advantages over Macintoshes with 680x0-series processors. No matter what processor is used, 64 megabytes of system memory is the minimum for work involving digital video, and 128 megabytes or more may be required.

Storage

There is an ever growing range of options for storing digital data, some of which were discussed in Chapter 7. Hard drives remain the fastest storage media, and they are available in increasing capacities. Removable drives are becoming more popular, although most are slower than hard drives. The storage medium of choice for distributing interactive media remains the CD-ROM, although the new *digital versatile disk* (DVD), which can hold seven times as much data, is becoming the next standard. All of these storage media are **random access,** meaning that any portion of the stored data can be accessed nearly instantaneously.

Tape, on the other hand, is not random access. As you know, if you need to access a particular piece of information stored on a tape, you may have to go through the time-consuming process of rewinding or fast-forwarding. For this reason, the increasing number of affordable digital videotape formats has had little impact on interactive media production.

Audio and Video Digitizing Cards

Audio cards that can digitize stereo audio are pretty much standard equipment on most PCs sold today. A wide variety of video cards are also available, with differences in terms of frame rates, compression formats, and resolution. Both audio and video cards come with software packages that allow digitization, although for advanced applications it may be necessary to purchase more specialized software.

Input Devices

The mouse and the keyboard are the two most common input devices for home PCs. For kiosks, a touch screen, which fits over the computer's monitor and responds when a user touches it, is widely used. (See Figure 10.7.) Touch screens are preferred on presentations designed for public places because they are easy to use and cannot be tampered with as easily as a mouse or keyboard.

Monitor and Video Card

Monitors are available in various sizes, ranging from 14 inches to 20 inches and more. Naturally, a larger monitor allows more information to be displayed on the screen. Video display cards, which allow data to be displayed on the monitor, vary in terms of speed, memory, number of colors, and resolution.

Other Peripherals

Scanners allow printed material to be digitized, and are available in handheld and flatbed styles. Photographic slides can be scanned with a slide scanner. For some interactive applications, you may want to use a printer to give the user hard copies of information. There are many varieties available with different features, including the ability to print in color.

Software

Because the general types of interactive media are stand-alone and World Wide Web based, it stands to reason that software programs fall into these categories, too.

Stand-alone Authoring Programs

A variety of programs are available for stand-alone authoring. Macromedia's Director allows you to combine various media into interactive presentations.

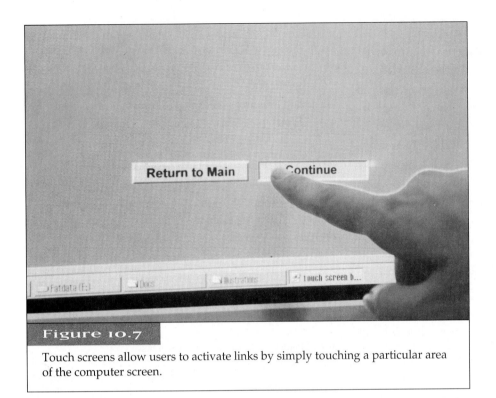

Figure 10.7

Touch screens allow users to activate links by simply touching a particular area of the computer screen.

(See Figure 10.8.) Presentations produced with these programs can be viewed on other computers. Thus, while you need to have the authoring program installed on your computer to produce the presentation, the finished product will run on machines that do not have the authoring program installed on them.

Web-Based Authoring

Since HTML is a text-based computer language, you can write HTML programs using a word processor. However, a growing number of programs are available that make it much easier to assemble HTML presentations without manually writing code. (See Figure 10.9.) For viewing HTML presentations, you will need a browser.

Other Programs

Since both stand-alone and Web-based authoring programs are designed chiefly to assemble various media, you may need other programs to prepare your media. For instance, programs like Adobe's Photo-Shop can be used to manipulate digitized pictures and produce original artwork. You might also use a

word-processing program such as Microsoft Word or Corel WordPerfect to key in long text passages, then bring the information into your presentation.

10.5 Interactive Media Production

Throughout this chapter, we have emphasized how interactive media represent not only a convergence of media but a convergence of skills. The concepts that apply to writing, editing video and audio, shot composition, and graphic design for "traditional" media still apply to interactive media. A poorly lighted interview, for instance, will look just as bad as part of an interactive presentation as it would as part of a documentary or news broadcast. Interactive production does introduce many new and exciting technologies, but it is important to remember that these "bells and whistles" do not change sound production techniques and disciplines.

Since a number of programs are available for putting together interactive media presentations that differ significantly in operation, it would not be prac-

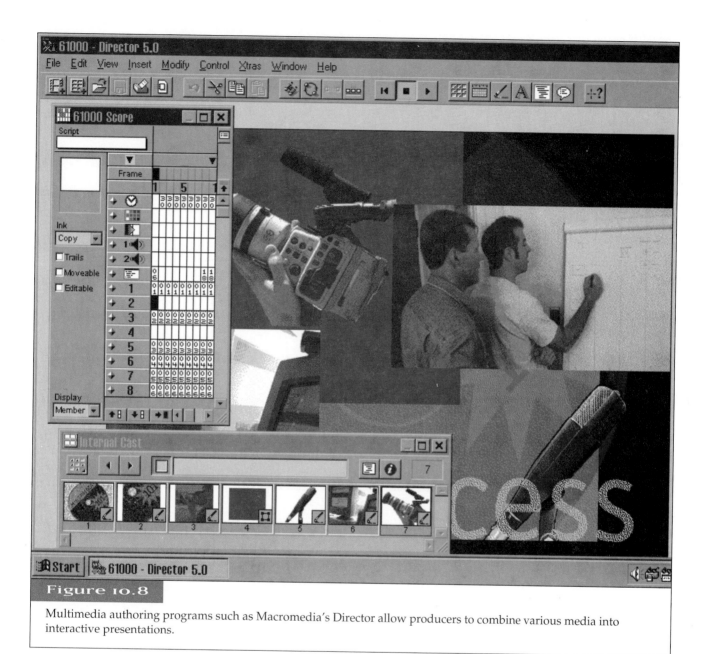

Figure 10.8

Multimedia authoring programs such as Macromedia's Director allow producers to combine various media into interactive presentations.

tical to give you a step-by-step guide to producing an interactive presentation. Instead, the remainder of this chapter will discuss the overall processes of interactive production, using a hypothetical example at the end to illustrate key points. The best ways to learn to use a particular system are to carefully read the manuals that come with the software, practice the tutorials that are provided, or work with someone who has experience with the program. Unfortunately, the learning curve on many authoring programs is very steep, and you may find yourself quite frustrated at times. As with most

pursuits, however, once you survive the initial difficulty you will soon find yourself moving rapidly toward mastery of the program and the process.

Interactive Media Planning

As with any type of production, you will need to do thorough preparatory work before you even begin the physical production process. Your interactive production should be well planned, meaning that you have a

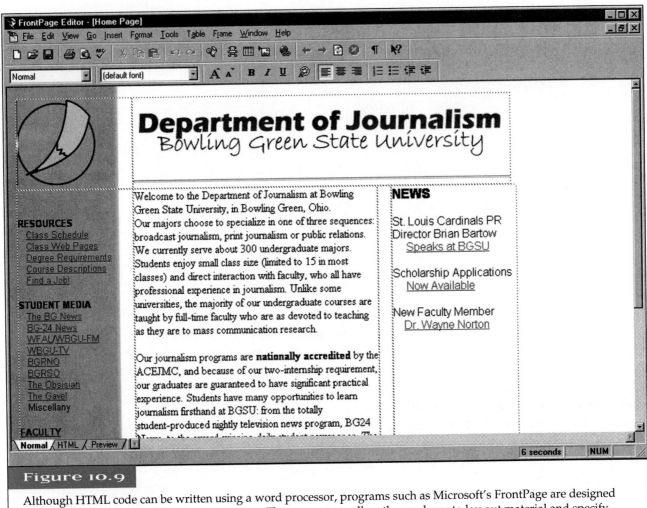

Figure 10.9

Although HTML code can be written using a word processor, programs such as Microsoft's FrontPage are designed specifically for authoring HTML presentations. These programs allow the producer to lay out material and specify links on the screen; the program will automatically create the HTML script to make the presentation run.

clear sense of what it is designed to do (sales, training, entertainment, etc.) and who the target audience is. Your presentation should have a defined set of objectives, outlining the specific information you want it to convey. You then have to determine what types of media are best suited to these objectives and audience. Would moving video work best in a particular situation, or would animations be better? How much text information is needed to make a particular point clear?

It is important to remember that you do not have to use every medium in every interactive presentation. It is possible, for example, that you can meet your objectives without using video or animations. Don't include extraneous media just for the sake of doing it; this will only make unnecessary work, con-

fuse the user, and bog down equipment. Having said that, keep in mind that few presentations can be effective without at least some text and graphics.

In both the preproduction and production processes, you also will need to keep in mind considerations related to *environment* and *resources*. Environmental considerations have to do with where the presentation will be used. Will it end up as a kiosk in the middle of a busy shopping center, or will it be a CD-ROM that individuals will use on their home PCs? Your final product should be appropriate for the environment in which it will be used. Resource considerations involve the equipment the presentation will be used on. You know, for example, that full-motion video requires tremendous processing, storage, and transmission resources and thus taxes less-powerful computer systems. A highly interactive, beautifully designed presentation loaded with moving video and animations that runs great on a Pentium III–based computer may hopelessly bog down a lesser machine. Remember, too, that if you are working on an HTML-based presentation, the data will have to travel over a network connection. That fact, combined with HTML's more limited interactive capability, means that Web-based presentations tend to be less elaborate.

Very early in the preproduction process, you also need to consider the level of interactivity of your presentation. The level of interactivity, as mentioned earlier, determines how much input you will require from the user and how much power the user has to control the presentation. The presentation may require very little user interaction, or it may depend on nearly constant user input. There are no hard-and-fast rules for determining an appropriate level of interactivity; it depends on the situation. In general, however, interactivity should be designed to give the user a feeling of control without burdening him or her with a lot of unnecessary work. In some situations, such as training presentations, it is better to design in a higher level of interactivity in order to make the user feel involved in the learning process. Remember the objectives of your presentation, and design in a level of interactivity appropriate to achieving those objectives.

The level of interactivity has a direct influence on the flow of the presentation. As you know, the power of interactive media is its ability to be used in a non-linear fashion. The simplest type of interactive presentation, however, as illustrated in Figure 10.10 is essentially a linear presentation that requires user input to move from item to item. The presentation is designed only to flow from element A to B to C to D. While the user may be able to move "backward" to previous parts of the presentation, there is no provision for branching to different locations. This type of design, while interactive, is still linear.

A more effective presentation can be created by using a model that is both interactive and nonlinear. The model illustrated in Figure 10.11 is quite similar to the shopping-center kiosk example cited earlier. In this example, the user is presented with a series of choices that allow him or her to select particular parts of the presentation. The user may decide to ignore the

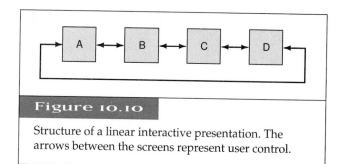

Figure 10.10

Structure of a linear interactive presentation. The arrows between the screens represent user control.

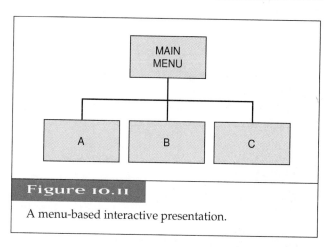

Figure 10.11

A menu-based interactive presentation.

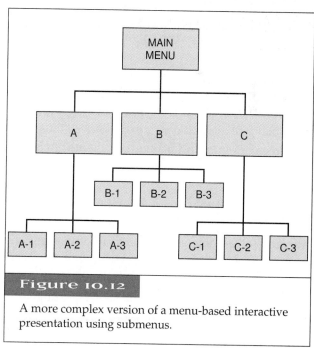

Figure 10.12

A more complex version of a menu-based interactive presentation using submenus.

information in one branch, for example, and proceed directly to another. This model allows the user to move more efficiently to a particular piece of information. Menu-based designs may also use submenus, as illustrated in Figure 10.12, to facilitate even more user

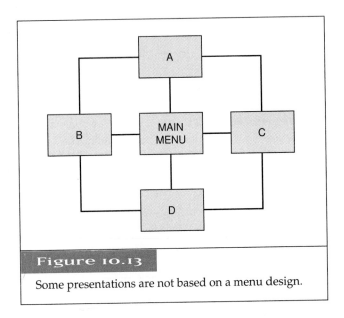

Figure 10.13

Some presentations are not based on a menu design.

Interactive Media Production

Once you have your presentation thoroughly planned out, you will then begin gathering the information and various media that will be a part of it. Text will need to be written, video shot and digitized, animations produced, graphics and audio digitized, and so on. Once these are gathered, you are ready to put them together using an appropriate authoring program.

If you have thoroughly planned your presentation, putting it together should be relatively easy. Work from your presentation map, scripts, and storyboards to produce what you have planned out. Your presentation should have an overall look that remains consistent throughout. This means that your selection of fonts, colors, and backgrounds should convey a sense of unity. Graphic elements such as buttons or logos should be consistently designed as well.

Your presentation's main menu or home page is in many ways its most important element. The opening page should be attractive and should clearly indicate what the presentation is designed to do. In this sense, it should provide orientation for the user, preparing him or her for the presentation. It also should provide links to the main parts of the presentation.

Throughout the presentation, links should be clearly labeled, letting the user know what will happen before he or she activates them. Vague links such as "Click Here" should be avoided. Links should provide feedback when the user activates them, either through an audible "beep" or some other sound, or by briefly changing color on the screen. Throughout the presentation, links should help guide users by giving them a clear sense of where they are in the presentation and what their choices are. In many Internet-based presentations, designers make available a **site map** that gives the user a graphical outline of the pages in the presentation.

These principles should give you a good idea of the basic concepts of interactive media production. You will need to tailor these concepts to your particular hardware, software, and objectives. An ever growing number of reference sources are available that discuss topics such as the operation of particular programs and design issues in greater detail. Remem-

control. Other presentations may have a less structured design that does not rely on a menu paradigm, as shown in Figure 10.13.

It is important to make your presentation's structure as simple as possible while still meeting its objectives. This relates directly to designing in an appropriate level of interactivity, as you don't want to send the user through 15 menu levels when 3 will do. You also want to avoid allowing the user to get "lost" in a presentation that is too complicated or confusing. Links that will allow the user to go back to the previous screen or return to a main menu should always be available. You should not send users down dead ends.

You will probably find it helpful to make a "map" of your presentation similar to the ones in Figures 10.10 through 10.13. Doing so will help you visualize both the user input and flow of the presentation. Once you have established these parameters, you will need to address issues such as treatments, storyboarding, and budgeting (see Chapter 11 for more information). Storyboards should be made for each screen in your presentation, showing a hand-drawn representation of how it is to be designed and indicating links, if any. When you are finished, you should have an individual storyboard for each block on your map. Some specially designed scriptwriting programs can help you plan out links and an overall structure to your presentation.

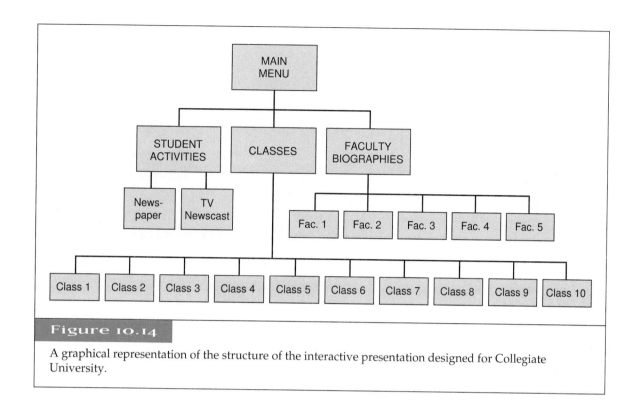

Figure 10.14

A graphical representation of the structure of the interactive presentation designed for Collegiate University.

ber, too, that you must apply what you have learned in other areas of television production as well.

10.6 An Interactive Media Production Example

Assume that you have been asked by the chairperson of the communications department at your school, Collegiate University, to produce an interactive presentation for the department. The chairperson wants to use this presentation as a way to interest high school students in the department. Prospective students will access this presentation over the Internet using World Wide Web browsers. The chairperson wants to provide information about student activities, classes, and biographies of the department's faculty. After a series of planning meetings with the chairperson, you agree that you will use the following media:

Text: brief description of the department, student newspaper, student TV newscast, classes, and faculty biographies.

Graphics: picture of the department's building, picture of students working on newspaper, picture of each faculty member, Collegiate University logo.

Video/Sound: brief (approximately 15-second) clip of student TV newscast.

This mix of media seems appropriate to accomplishing the assigned task. Since the presentation will be accessed by a wide range of students (likely with a wide range of computer equipment) over a network, the presentation will not include a lot of video.

You then decide on a relatively simple design: a main menu and three submenus, as shown in Figure 10.14. The three submenus correspond to the three main objectives cited by the chairperson: student activities, classes, and faculty biographies. From the main menu, users can choose one of these three areas to explore. The submenus then branch further. The student activities submenu has 2 branches: the student newspaper and the student TV newscast; the classes submenu has 10 branches, one for each class offered by the department; the faculty biography submenu has 5 branches, one for each faculty member. On each page of the presentation, a link to return to the main menu will be provided. A sample storyboard for the

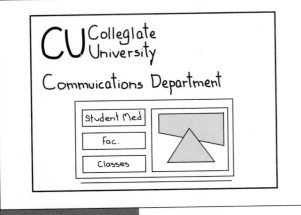

Figure 10.15

A hand-drawn storyboard for the main menu screen of the Collegiate University presentation.

Figure 10.16

The main menu screen from the Collegiate University presentation.

main menu of the department's interactive presentation is shown in Figure 10.15.

The completed main menu page, shown in Figure 10.16, illustrates the principles of consistency and clarity discussed in the previous section. The design elements shown on this page, such as the font styles, button styles, and layout, would be carried over to the rest of the presentation. The main screen describes what the presentation is designed to do, is attractively designed with a picture, and has links that are clearly marked.

Discussion Questions

1. Work through a mock planning process of designing a Web site similar to the one discussed in section 10.6 for *your* school. Who will the site be designed for? What information will it contain? What types of media will you use?

2. Surf the Internet and find a few examples of what you think are well-designed home pages. Share them with your classmates and discuss what you think makes them good.

3. Surf the Internet and find some examples of *poor* page design. Share these examples with your classmates and discuss what makes them bad. How would you improve them?

4. Find a stand-alone interactive presentation in your community. Use it, then map out its design. Is it linear, menu-based, or some other type of design? How would you improve on the presentation's design?

chapter 11

Producing

A s mentioned in Chapter 2, section 2.1, producing involves bringing everything together for a successful production. The *discipline* of thorough preproduction planning in this process cannot be emphasized strongly enough. The success of every production is determined, to a very great extent, by the way that problems are solved—before they occur. The *techniques* needed for producing involve a great deal of organizational ability and attention to detail. Successful producers develop a feel for the type of material that has the potential for success. They also develop a good instinct for people, which allows them to hire the appropriate cast and crew members who will bring the project to fruition.

Many of the disciplines and techniques of producing come through experience, but, as a starting point, a producer should have a good grasp of the material covered in this chapter, which includes:

- The different types of producers (executive, line, associate) and how their jobs differ (11.1).
- Why producers sometimes opt to be hyphenates and what their duties involve under those circumstances (11.1).
- How to construct a treatment and/or proposal (11.2).
- The different forms of scripts (film-style, two-column, rundown, outline, storyboard) and how and when to use each (11.2).
- How to build a budget and then adhere to it (11.3).
- The process of casting and selecting a crew (11.4).
- Various forms and letters that relate to organizing the production and making sure that copyright laws are not violated (11.5).
- Methods for preparing schedules for different types of shoots (11.6).
- The need for evaluating a production once it is finished (11.7).

11.1 Types of Producers

The nature and scope of a project may determine how many people are involved in producing. A public-access cable talk show may have one "guiding light" who produces, writes, and hosts the show and handles the expenses out of his or her own pocket. A network situation comedy series may have one or more executive producers, one or more producers, a line producer, and a number of assistant and associate producers.

Executive Producers

Executive producers are people who oversee a number of different productions. For example, a production company (such as Carsey-Werner, owned by Marcy Carsey and Tom Werner) may have several network series in production, in syndication, and in development. Each series has a hands-on **producer,** who does the day-to-day work, but the owners of the company, who made the deals with the networks and who are in the process of making other deals, make decisions regarding the overall scope and direction of the series—hence the term executive producer. In a similar vein, if the network itself produces its own programs, it has staff executive producers who oversee several projects. Your instructor probably serves as executive producer for your class projects.

Line Producers

Some productions, primarily movies, have a **line producer.** This is a person representing the producer who is on the set each day, mainly making sure that all is progressing properly so that the movie will be finished on budget and in time for its scheduled airing.

Associate Producers

Many productions have **associate** or **assistant producers**—people who help producers who would otherwise have too much to do. For example, a game show may have one assistant producer whose job is to acquire free prizes for contestants, while another assistant producer is in charge of screening potential contestants. Whether someone is an assistant or associate producer is not related as much to what job they are in charge of as to their level of experience and skill; an associate producer is paid more than an assistant producer.

Hyphenates

Sometimes people are **hyphenates.** They take on multiple roles such as producer-director, producer-writer, or even producer-writer-director.

There are advantages and disadvantages to handling a number of different roles. Most people evolve into becoming hyphenates because they want *creative control.* A writer who has been displeased with how a director has interpreted his or her script will decide to become the director for the next script. Directors who feel that cost-conscious producers unnecessarily curtail them may want to make their own decisions about how to prioritize spending. Producers who work hard to develop a project and raise the funding may want to ensure that their vision is carried out during the production phase.

Although being a hyphenate can lead to greater creative control, it is also more work. Given the time pressures of most TV productions, one person can become exhausted trying to polish a script, find Civil War–era guns, and plan camera angles all at one time. Also, few people have all the aptitudes necessary to undertake multiple jobs. Someone who is highly skilled in getting the best performance possible from actors may not be equally skilled in handling financial statements. Multiple inputs, undertaken *harmoniously,* can also enrich a production. One person, given too much responsibility, can flounder—or become an egomaniac. Often the reasoned judgment that comes from bouncing ideas off others can lead to a richer end product.

Regardless of how the producing chores are divided, however, somewhere along the way they will involve idea generation, budgets, personnel, production paperwork, schedules, and evaluation.

11.2 Idea Generation

An idea for a TV show can come from anywhere— a story in a newspaper, a dream, a casual conversation, an order from a boss, research on the Internet.

TREATMENT

"THE CAMPUS"

"The Campus" is a high energy series aimed at teens and young adults. It takes place on a college campus and features the adventures, problems, and experiences of four roommates.

Mark, a sophomore, is good looking and athletic. He is on the basketball team and seems destined to become one of its stars. He attracts coeds easily, but deep down he is uneasy with them. He comes from a wealthy family and seems to "have it all." However, he has trouble knuckling down and studying and is constantly on the verge of academic problems that will disqualify him from basketball. He's such a nice guy, however, that his friends try to come to his rescue and figure out ways for him to get through his classes.

Frank, on the other hand, has an easy time in classes, but always seems to have hard luck in social situations. He says the wrong things, wears the wrong clothes, spills his soft drink on a girl he is trying to win over, and generally falls prey to social indiscretions. He and Mark do not get along very well.

Juan tries to smooth the waters between Mark and Frank. He's not as bright as Frank or as athletic as Mark, but he's well rounded and a good mediator. He is on a scholarship and does not have much spending money. Mark sometimes tries to buy his allegiance by giving him material things, but Juan does not respond well to that. He works most evenings so does not have much time for social life.

George is the jokster of the group. In trying to make light of situations, he often utters what turns out to be prophetic philosophy. He likes to play practical jokes on people, especially Mark's girl friends, but he does not mean any harm. He is not particularly good looking, but he is a likable person.

In the first episode of the series, all four arrive back on campus for their sophomore year. Frank, Juan, and George had planned to room with each other and had thought their fourth roommate would be someone they had all befriended in their freshman year. However, that person has dropped out of school and Mark has been assigned to their room. He is unhappy about the situation. He thought he would be in special housing for athletes, but there had not been room for him.

Frank and Mark clash immediately and Frank goes to the housing authority to try to get Mark removed from the room. However, he is unsuccessful. Juan, realizing they will probably all have to live together, talks separately to both Mark and

1

Figure 11.1

The first page of a treatment that might be prepared by an independent production company to give to a network executive.

Getting from the idea to an actual production is a tedious road full of potholes, but in most instances it starts with a written explanation of the idea in the form of a treatment or proposal.

To be successful, even the simplest productions need something committed to paper to serve as a guideline. That something is referred to as a **script.**[1] The producer uses the script to organize the elements needed for the program and often to sell the idea of a series or program to someone who will pay the production costs. As with most other elements of TV production, scripts vary both in form and complexity.

Treatments and Proposals

Most drama and comedy series start with a **treatment.** (See Figure 11.1.) This is several pages, written in regular prose form, that tell the overall premise of the series, describe the main characters, outline the basic plots for several of the episodes, and highlight the strong points of the idea. In some cases a producer (or executive producer) from an outside production company (with a track record of success) makes an appointment to see the appropriate network executives for a **pitch** meeting. This is a session that lasts about half an hour during which the producer tries to convince the network executives that they should buy the series idea. Often they do this by comparing their idea to something that is already popular. (The show will have six *Friends* in a *Dawson Creek* type of setting.) The producer presents the information in the treatment orally and sometimes leaves the written treatment behind for the executives to study. If the network executives like the idea, they will commission (pay for) one or more complete program scripts. If they like the scripts, they will order a **pilot,** a produced program that is to be one of the series. If they like the pilot and decide to schedule the series on a regular basis, they will give the go-ahead for more scripts and productions. Throughout this whole process, the production company producer negotiates with the network regarding both creative and financial elements.

In other instances, ideas come from people within the network. In these cases a treatment is still needed but the pitch meeting and pilot process are more informal. One-shot dramas, such as made-for-TV movies, often have a treatment as a starting point, but, obviously, these outline the idea for the single movie, not several episodes.

Many other types of programs that are not fiction oriented also start with an idea that is written on paper. Sometimes these are called treatments, but more often they are referred to as **proposals.** Magazine, talk, documentary, and game shows that are planned for **syndication,** cable TV, or local broadcast often evolve from proposals. So do programs intended for educational or corporate outlets. Proposals define the purpose of the project, list the goals and objectives, indicate the demographics and psychographics of the target audience, and outline some of the planned segments.

A newscast script proceeds very differently. If a network or station has decided to present the news, no one needs to spell out specific ideas with a treatment or proposal—the ideas come from the news of the day. Parts of the newscast script are written during the course of a day (or several hours) as the producer and news director decide what is the most important news. Reporters and writers put together individual stories and transitions between stories that are eventually read by newscasters. Usually each element of the newscast is on a separate piece of paper so stories can be juggled easily as news breaks—even during the newscast itself.

Varying Script Forms

Because programs and circumstances differ, script forms also differ.[2] The type of script needed for a drama would be overkill for a talk show. A music video that is highly postproduced can use a script with less structure than a news script that must give accurate mistake-proof guidance for a live broadcast. A multimedia game that is interactive needs a different type of script than a TV game show that is not interactive. Although many different script forms have evolved over the years, the main ones that you, as a television student, are likely to encounter are film-style scripts, two-column scripts, rundowns, outlines, and storyboards.

Film-Style Scripts

As might be evident from their name, **film-style scripts** (see Figure 11.2) are the type that have been used for years to produce theatrical movies. The main characteristic of this script is that each scene is *separated* from the next so that each can be considered individually. Materials produced from film-style scripts are usually shot in a number of different locations with all the scenes from one location being shot on the same day or succeeding days. A script that highlights times of day, locations, and whether these locations are inside (interior—INT) or outside (exterior—EXT) can help a producer with preproduction planning. The producer uses the descriptive paragraphs to determine what will be needed in the way of props and set pieces.

Also, the director shoots each scene a number of times using only one camera. For example, the first time the camera might film a two-shot of a man and woman arguing. The second time the scene is shot, the camera would record a close-up of the woman delivering her lines and reacting to the man's lines. The third time through, the close-up would be of the man. Then, during editing, the various shots are cut together. The script form, by showing each distinct scene, helps the director figure out what to shoot. The

```
INT. - ELEGANT RESTAURANT - NIGHT

Joan and Philip, both dressed in stylish clothes, sit at a table.
Philip has leaned forward and is talking softly to Joan.  She is
leaning back and appears to be somewhat distant.

                    PHILIP
          I really want to come back, Joan. I miss the
          children and I'm tired of living out of a suit-
          case.

                    JOAN
                 (sarcastically)
          That's tender.

                    PHILIP
                 (exasperated)
          Now what did I do wrong?

                    JOAN
          You're just acting like your same old selfish
          self.  Everything revolves around you.  No
          consideration for me.  Not even any sign of
          love.

                    PHILIP
          But, of course, I care about you.  I don't need
          to tell you that.

                    JOAN
          That's a matter of opinion.

                    PHILIP
          Now you're being like your old sensitive self.
          I just don't get it.

                    JOAN
          That's right, Philip.  You just don't get it.

Joan gets up from the table angrily and walks away.  She realizes
she has forgotten her purse, returns for it, glares at Philip and
walks toward the door.  Philip looks hurt and confused.

EXT. - CITY STREET - NIGHT

Christopher is seen driving his car, weaving in and out of
traffic.  He pulls over to the curb and blinks his lights off and
on.  A large dark figure carring a briefcase emerges from the
shadows, opens the car door, throws the briefcase in the car, and
receeds back into the shadows.  Christopher drives off.

INT. - PHILIP'S OFFICE - DAY

Philip is going through a stack of papers, but he seems to be
having trouble concentrating.  Mildred comes in the door with a
stack of phone messages.
```

Figure 11.2

An example of a page of a film-style script. Note the separation of the scenes and the indentation of the dialogue.

dialogue is indented, keeping it separate from the writer's descriptive material about the scene. This gives the director room for notes and helps the actors pinpoint their lines.

Film-style scripts are very complete. They include all the words that will be spoken by the actors, describe all the primary action that will take place, and indicate basic moods and emotions. Of course, sometimes the words are altered by the actors or director, and the interpretation and execution of actions and emotion are the province of the director (hence, the occasional conflict about *creative control*).

Just about anything that is shot single-camera can use a film-style script, but it is most often associated with dramatic productions.

Two-Column Scripts

The film-style script is not appropriate for multicamera productions that are shot live or live-on-tape. The descriptions would get in the way and location does

```
                        NIGHTLY NEWS

            VIDEO                          AUDIO
TAPE: OPENING CREDITS          SOUND ON TAPE.  Runs :30.

                               Ends with drum beat.


TWO-SHOT - STEVE AND SHARON    STEVE: I'm Steve Anderson.

                               SHARON: And I'm Sharon

                               Hendricks here with the latest

                               news.


STEVE                          STEVE: Fire fighters are still

                               at the scene of a three-alarm

                               fire on Market Street that

                               destroyed two buildings

                               earlier today.  Fred White has

                               this report.


TAPE: FIRE REPORT              SOT: Runs 2:56. Ends with

                               "could have been a lot worse."


SHARON                         SHARON: The Japanese are still

                               trying to assess if any damage

                               was caused by this morning's

                               earthquake. The quake was

GRAPHICS: MAP OVER SHOULDER    centered two hundred miles

                               from Tokyo and registered

                               7 point 1.  Two strong

                               after shocks have been felt.
```

Figure 11.3

A sample page from a two-column news script. Note how the video and audio items line up with each other.

not change. More appropriate is the **two-column script** (see Figure 11.3) that pairs the video elements on the left-hand side with audio elements on the right-hand side. The producer can find all the materials that will need to be gathered together, especially since elements such as music and insert tapes are capitalized.

The director, who must act quickly, can easily see what visual images should be on the screen as the talk progresses and can set up cameras for what will be coming next. Usually the left-hand margin of a two-column script is fairly wide so that the director can make notes.

There are many variations on two-column scripts, depending on the type of program for which they are used. Some include every word of dialogue. Editorials and commercials, for example, need to be precise—no ad-libbing allowed. Dramas, such as soap operas, that are shot in-studio with multiple cameras can also use fully scripted, two-column scripts. Other programs, such as magazine shows and newscasts, include all the words to be spoken by the anchors but include just

```
                    RUNDOWN SHEET

                    "PROFILES" - NO. 37

                                          SEGMENT   TOTAL
SEGMENT   SOURCE         ITEM              TIME      TIME

   1      VCR            Opening Credits.       :25     :25

   2      Cam 2          Host welcomes Jane
          Host mic       Collins from Personnel.  :20     :45

   3      Cam 1,2,3      Host and Jane discuss purpose
          Studio mics    of the department, how it
          Graphics for   interfaces with each employee,
            guest ID     and its organzation.
                         ENDS: We can see this on a
                         chart.                   3:00    3:45

   4      Graphics of    Jane discusses the chart of
            chart        the department's organiza-
          Studio mics    tion.                    1:00    4:45

   5      Cam 1,2,3      Host and Jane discuss com-
          Studio mics    pany benefits.
                         ENDS: Let's look at the tape
                         your department produced
                         about this.              1:30    6:15

   6      VCR            Tape about benefits.
                         ENDS: Music and copyright
                         credit.                  5:35   11:50

   7      Cam 1,2,3      Host and Jane discuss how
          Studio mics    employees get additional
                         information.             2:10   14:00

   8      Cam 2          Host thanks Jane and closes
          Studio mics    program.                  :30   14:30

   9      VCR            Closing credits           :30   15:00
```

Figure 11.4

This is a rundown for one of a series of 15-minute programs that might be produced as a corporate video to highlight the job functions of people within the company. Note that exact wording cues are written in some places so that the director can move smoothly from one element to another.

basic information about edited field reports that are to be rolled in so that the director can bring them in and take them out without any flubs. Still others, such as talk shows and game shows, indicate the general topics to be discussed or questions to be asked, because the answers, of course, can not be scripted ahead of time.

Rundowns

Rather than using a two-column script, some talk and game shows (and other programs for which little can be scripted ahead of time) use **rundowns**. (See Figure 11.4.) These list the various segments that will be included in the program and are most often used for routine programs that are produced on a daily or weekly basis, such as *Today* and *Meet the Press*.

Specific information is given for each segment. This information may vary from one form of program to another, but generally it includes the source for that segment (videotape roll-in, studio cameras, graphics, remote feed), what the segment contains, and how long the segment should run. If a program has a set length, such as one hour, the total running time may be indicated so that the director can tell if the overall program is running short or long. Cues in and out of segments help the director prepare for transitions.

```
                    MUSIC VIDEO FOR
                "I LOOK SO GOOD IN YELLOW'
                         BRIAN

The video will consist of four different set-ups:
     1. Brian, dressed in a variety of yellow clothes, lip
syncing in a nightclub setting.
     2. A chorus of children dressed in yellow singing the "Oo la
la la la la" refrain.
     3. Brian, dressed in a yellow shirt and lip syncing, walking
a dog dressed in a yellow dog jacket.
     4. The three back-up singers in a department store trying on
ugly colored shirts and finally finding yellow ones they like.

We will build two sets in the studio, one for the nightclub scene
and the other for the children's chorus.  The nightclub scene
will have a 1940s look to it and will consist of a sequined
curtain and a floor stand microphone.  The audience will not be
shown.  An intense spotlight will highlight Brian's yellow
clothing.

The children's chorus (about twenty 8 to 10 year olds) will be on
risers against background flats that are painted with geometric
shapes in primary colors.

The dog walking scene will be shot on a street that has many
trees and colorful flowers that will show in the background.

The scene with the back-up singers will be shot in the men's
clothing store late at night when the store is closed.

As the track begins, we see Brian in the nightclub scene dressed
in yellow pants and a black shirt.  As the first verse
progresses, he adds (in jump cut fashion) additional yellow
clothing--a shirt, shoes, a jacket, and finally a large floppy
hat.

At the first "Oo la la" chorus, we cut to a long shot of the
children singing.

Next, Brian is seen walking the dog.  At first the dog is not
seen, but it is obvious from the leash and the way Brian is being
pulled that a dog is present.  When the next "Oo la la" section
comes, the dog and its yellow jacket will be revealed.  Both the
children and Brian will be heard for this "Oo la la," but the
children will not be seen.

The video returns to the nightclub lip syncing until the words "I
hardly know anyone who wears yellow shirts" at which point the
back-up singers are seen rummaging through shirts on a "sale"
counter in the men's clothing store.

                          page 1
```

Figure 11.5

An outline for a music video. Both general and specific ideas are given and the various set and remote locations are enumerated.

Producers use the rundowns to make sure all the guests are confirmed and ready to appear in the proper order. Usually these programs are directed by the same person day after day, so the director has a routine and is mainly concerned with knowing about anything unusual that is incorporated within a particular segment.

Sometimes rundowns include fully scripted material that can be written ahead of time. When they do, they look somewhat akin to a two-column script in that they include a column for video and another for audio. The line can blur between a *detailed rundown* and a *nonspecific two-column list,* but how to categorize the script is not nearly as important as whether or not it is useful for the talent, producer, and director.

Outlines

The line also sometimes blurs between rundowns and outlines. **Outlines** list the various elements of a program but usually in less specific terms than rundowns. They are often used for pieces such as music videos (see Figure 11.5) that are shot and then edited. Because of this, they can include some of the type of detail found in film-style scripts. The producer and director both have time to digest the information, and the shooting itself is usually undertaken with one camera from a variety of angles.

Documentaries often lend themselves to outlines. They can indicate general items, issues, or circumstances to be investigated, but the real conclusions and findings cannot be planned until the material has been shot.

Outlines do need to indicate to the producer the props, sets, locations, and other production elements that will be needed to ensure a successful shoot. They must give the director a general idea of what to shoot, but they allow plenty of room for improvisation.

Storyboards

Storyboards (see Figure 11.6) show pictures of each visual element and describe the actions and/or indicate the dialogue below each picture. They are usually used for short productions such as commercials or music videos, and they are a basic element of an interactive media script (see Chapter 10). A drama could certainly be storyboarded, but it would involve a great deal of tedious artwork and pages and pages of paper. Sometimes directors will storyboard complicated scenes of a drama to better visualize them, but the storyboard, as a script form, is usually associated with short productions.

In general, directors like to work from storyboards because they are so *visual*.[3] Although a director may superimpose his or her own ideas over the storyboard script, it gives a good starting point. Producers have to examine storyboards very closely to make sure all the props and other elements needed for production will be ready.

The type of script you choose to use—film-style, two-column, rundown, outline, storyboard—will depend on the type of program you are undertaking and the type of material you feel most comfortable with. Scripts are primarily a blueprint for production. People who try to produce without a script are asking for trouble in the same way that builders would be asking for disaster if they tried to construct a house without following a basic blueprint.

11.3 Budgets

Students often do not give much thought to budgets, because their monetary needs are small. The college provides the equipment; cast and crew members come from the class and do not need to be paid; props can be borrowed from dorm rooms or willing relatives. But in the "real world" of TV production, budgets are *very important*. A producer who goes over budget is not likely to stay employed.

Graduating students who understand the procedures of budgeting are likely to be looked upon as more *valuable* than graduates who have mastered only creative or technical talents. For that reason, it behooves you to practice budgeting by figuring out what it would cost you to produce your class projects if you were doing them in the outside world.

Costs of Productions

TV production expenses are usually divided into **above-the-line** and **below-the-line.** The above-the-line costs are creative in nature and include the pay given to talent, producers, directors, and writers. Below-the-line costs are more technical in form and include the salaries of the crew, the cost of the staging area and equipment, and the money needed for supplies such as scenery and makeup.

Costs vary greatly depending on many factors: whether the crew is union or nonunion; the recognition value and reputation of the talent; the length of the production; the number of complicated effects needed; the part of the country or world in which the production is taking place; and whether the equipment and facilities used belong to the production company or are rented from other companies.

Pay Rates

Most major production companies, networks, and some local stations are unionized and agree to pay at least the minimum cast and crew wages stipulated by the various **unions** that represent the technical people—International Brotherhood of Electrical Workers (IBEW), International Alliance of Theatrical Stage Employees and Moving Picture Machine Operators (IATSE), and others—and the **guilds** that represent the creative people—Screen Actors Guild (SAG), Directors Guild of America (DGA), American Federation of Radio and Television Actors (AFRTA), Writers Guild of America (WGA), and the like. Every several years the unions and the producing organizations negotiate these rates. Over time, the contracts have

Figure 11.6

A storyboard for a commercial. This enables the director to visualize all the action and how it juxtaposes with the words. The accuracy of this visualization is much more important than any artistic considerations. There are computer programs available to help with the construction of a storyboard.

```
                SELECTED TELEVISION INDUSTRY PAY RATES

 Directors
    If the program length is      the director is paid a minimum
                                         of appproximately
      0 to 15 minutes                         $4,000
     16 to 30 minutes                          6,000
     31 to 60 minutes                         10,000

 Producers
    Producers are usually paid about the same as directors

 Writers
    If the program length is      the writer's minimum is a
                                     total of approximately
      0 to 15 minutes                         $4,000
     16 to 30 minutes                          7,000
     31 to 60 minutes                         11,000

 Performers
    These types of performers     receive approximately this
                                        amount of pay
      Principal performers                $570 per day
      Stunt performers                     570 per day
      Singers                              625 per day
      General ability extra                 75 per day
      Special ability extra                 85 per day

 Technical and Crafts People
    Technical director . . . . . . . . . . .  $45 per hour
    Lighting director. . . . . . . . . . . .   40 per hour
    Camera operator. . . . . . . . . . . . .   35 per hour
    Audio operator . . . . . . . . . . . . .   35 per hour
    Audio assistant/Boom operator . . . . .    30 per hour
    Tape editor. . . . . . . . . . . . . . .   45 per hour
    Other technical personnel (graphics, . .   35 per hour
       VCR, teleprompter operators, etc.)
    Assistant director/Script supervisor . .   35 per hour
    Floor director . . . . . . . . . . . . .   30 per hour
    Stage hands. . . . . . . . . . . . . . .   25 per hour
    Electricians . . . . . . . . . . . . . .   25 per hour
    Scenic artist. . . . . . . . . . . . . .   30 per hour
    Set decorator. . . . . . . . . . . . . .   30 per hour
    Set painter. . . . . . . . . . . . . . .   25 per hour
    Propmaster . . . . . . . . . . . . . . .   30 per hour
    Costume designer . . . . . . . . . . . .   30 per hour
    Costumer . . . . . . . . . . . . . . . .   25 per hour
    Make-up artist . . . . . . . . . . . . .   30 per hour
    Hair stylist . . . . . . . . . . . . . .   25 per hour
```

Figure 11.7

Selected TV industry pay rates. These are approximate rounded-off figures of pay for various union positions for people working for a network. Note that some of these people are hired by the day, project, or hour. In reality, union provisions are much more complicated, taking into account such factors as how long a person has been in the union, how many hours or days they work total, overtime pay, meal breaks, and working conditions. These figures are intended simply to help students approximate their production costs if they hired union people.

become quite complicated, but Figure 11.7 shows some of the major pay provisions for performers, directors, producers, writers, and technical and crafts people that should help students practice budgeting their own productions.[4]

Shoots that are nonunion can pay whatever people are willing to work for, but the unions and guilds fine their own members if they work for anyone for less than union rates. Of course, people who are highly prized within the industry can demand much

```
                    FACILITIES RATE CARD

Studio and Control Room Rental              $500 per hour

(Includes a 35' by 35' studio with cyc, lighting grid and lights,
3 industrial grade CCD cameras with teleprompters, and up to 5
microphones; and a 12' by 20' control room with an 8-in 4-out
audio mixer, switcher with 2 effects buses, graphics generator,
and 1 play and 1 record VTR.)

Additional Equipment

     Extra microphones . . . . . . . . . . . $ 3 each per hour
     Extra cameras . . . . . . . . . . . . .  50 each per hour
     S-VHS VCR . . . . . . . . . . . . . . .  20 per hour
     Hi-8 VCR . . . . . . . . . . . . . . . . 20 per hour
     Betacam VCR . . . . . . . . . . . . . .  80 per hour
     Digital VTR . . . . . . . . . . . . . .  80 per hour
     Editing . . . . . . . . . . . . . . . .  80 per hour

Set Pieces

     Easels . . . . . . . . . . . . . . . . . 10 each per hour
     Plain flats . . . . . . . . . . . . . .  15 each per hour
     Chairs . . . . . . . . . . . . . . . . .  5 each per hour
     Tables . . . . . . . . . . . . . . . . .  5 each per hour
     Risers . . . . . . . . . . . . . . . . . 10 each per hour
     Piano . . . . . . . . . . . . . . . . .  20 per hour
```

Figure 11.8

A facilities and equipment rate card. Studio rental fees and the cost for renting individual pieces of equipment vary greatly depending on the size of the studio, the quantity and sophistication of the equipment, and the part of the country where the rental is taking place. These figures are based on a facility and equipment similar to that found on many college campuses.

higher pay than that stipulated by the union and guild minimums.

The trend within the television industry is to hire **freelance** cast and crew by the hour, day, or project as indicated in Figure 11.7. However, sometimes people are hired on a more permanent basis, usually referred to as **staff** positions. A local station, for example, would hire a news producer to work with the local news day after day, year after year. That same station might have a staff director who directs a public-service show one day and a children's program the next. Similarly five or six staff camera people might handle most local production—news, public affairs, children's programs—supplemented occasionally by freelance camera operators. Staff people usually receive less per hour than freelance people, but they are assured of steady employment, while their freelance counterparts must be constantly seeking new jobs.

Facilities and Equipment

Facilities and equipment are also major costs associated with production. If something is produced **in house**—that is, within a production facility that has its own studio and equipment—the cost could be considered to be next to nothing, because everything that is needed is already in place. However, the facility must be maintained and the equipment must eventually be replaced, so even a local public-affairs show produced at a local station is usually "billed" (on paper only) for use of the facilities.

When a producer rents an outside facility, costs are real and can be easily budgeted. Most organizations that rent studios and/or equipment have a **rate card** listing the cost for a fully equipped studio or for the various pieces of equipment that the client might wish to use. The rate card shown in Figure 11.8 lists the costs for a studio with three cameras and other commonly used production equipment as well as the rates for additional equipment. Once again, students can use these numbers to practice budget construction, keeping in mind that these numbers can vary greatly depending on the city in which the production is taking place.

Supplies are figured at what they actually cost. If the production calls for a wig, the producer (or assistant producer) must actually locate an appropriate wig and find out how much it costs. One supply that is necessary for all taped programs is videotape stock. The actual cost of the stock depends on which tape format is being used.

Constructing and Adhering to the Budget

Once all the information regarding costs has been gathered, the producer must actually construct the budget. It is laid out with the above-the-line costs separated from the below-the-line costs. Figure 11.9 shows a worksheet that can be used for a typical TV production budget. Computer spreadsheets are particularly helpful for budgeting.[5] Using them, producers can determine what costs would be under various circumstances—with three cameras versus four cameras; hiring two different audio operators versus paying one audio operator overtime; with and without the scene that requires renting a helicopter.

The Role of the Unit Manager

The people working with or for the producer who deal the most with budgets are the **unit manager** and/or **production manager.** Sometimes these titles are used interchangeably or the person is referred to as a unit production manager, but in common practice a person who works for a *production facility* is called a *unit manager* and a person who works for an *independent production company* is called a *production manager.* For example, a unit manager might work for a network that produces some of its own shows and rents out its facilities and crew members to others (corporations, advertisers, or production companies). The unit manager would be in charge of drawing up and adhering to the rate card and scheduling the facilities for use by both in-house producers and outside clients. This person has the responsibility for seeing that the production costs do not exceed the contracted amount paid (on paper or for real).

Production managers are usually associated with a *particular project* rather than a particular facility. They determine what costs will be incurred by the project in terms of people, facilities, supplies, and other requirements. Working closely with producers, they draw up the budgets. Then, during production and postproduction, they keep track of all expenses to make sure the budget is not being exceeded.

Budget Overruns

If a budget is being overrun, the producer is the one who must solve the problem. At times the producer can raise additional money to cover the shortfall; sometimes the producer can convince the director to work faster; other times some element of a program must be cut so that money can be saved.

Budgeting is a difficult process. Costs must not be exaggerated or people will not be willing to undertake the production. But sufficient money must be provided so that the program is successful. As money becomes tighter, *more care* must be given to drawing up and adhering to the budget.

11.4 Personnel

In addition to seeing that the script and budget are generated, another major duty of the producer is hiring the various people needed for the production. The most important person the producer hires is the director. Sometimes once the producer hires the director, he or she steps out of the hiring process, and the director hires the rest of the cast and crew. Of course, if the producer, director, and crew members are all on staff at a production facility, no actual hiring takes place, but the producer may lobby to have the most appropriate (and skilled) of the directors and crew members assigned to the project.

Casting

If the project is a drama or sitcom, **casting** is very crucial and producers often want to be involved. The usual procedure is that the producer and/or director draws up a list of the characters needed, along with their physical and psychological traits. (Often this is

```
                        BUDGET WORKSHEET

Production Name_____

Producer_____

Director_____

Date(s) of Production_____

DESCRIPTION            ESTIMATE        ACTUAL        NOTES

ABOVE-THE-LINE
Producer
_____
Director
_____
Writer
_____
Principal Performers
_____
Bit Performers
_____
Off-Camera Announcers
_____
Extras
_____
Musicians
_____
Other
_____

_____


TOTAL ABOVE-THE-LINE   _____     _____


BELOW-THE-LINE
Crew
Technical Director
_____
Lighting Director
_____
Camera Operators
_____
Audio Operator
_____
Audio Assistant
_____
Tape Editor
_____
Graphics Operator
_____
VCR Operator
_____
Teleprompter Operator
_____
Assistant Director
_____
Floor Director
_____
Stage Hands
_____
Electricians
_____
```

Figure 11.9

A budget worksheet. This worksheet should help you determine what the costs will be for your production. Use the space under each person or item to indicate how you arrived at your estimate. For example, 3 camera operators for 4 hours at $35 each = $420.

PERFORMANCE RELEASE

In consideration of my appearing on the TV program

____

(title)

and for no subsequent remuneration, I do hereby on behalf of myself, my heirs, executors, and administrators authorize

____

(producer)

to use live or recorded on tape, film, or otherwise my name, voice, likeness, and performance for television distribution throughout the world and for audiovisual and general education purposes in perpetuity.

I further agree on behalf of myself and others as above stated that my name, likeness, and biography may be used for promotion purposes and other uses. Further, I agree to indemnify, defend, and hold the producer harmless for any and all claims, suits, or liabilities arising from my appearance and the use of any of my materials, name, likeness, or biography.

Conditions:

Signature____

Printed Name____

Street Address____

City and Zip Code____

Phone Number____

Date____

Figure 11.10

A sample performance release. All people who appear on a television program who have not signed official contracts should be asked to sign a form such as this.

taken from the treatment or script.) This list is given to various **agents,** who then select actresses and actors they represent and send them to an audition where they read lines of the script. Then the director, producer, and others who have a vital interest in the production select the cast members. Sometimes specialized **casting agencies** are hired for productions with large casts, such as made-for-TV movies. The director may be involved with hiring the principal actors, but the casting agency alone fills the minor parts.

Although dramas present the greatest challenges for finding talent, other forms of shows also involve hiring or selecting talent. For example, great care goes into selecting contestants for game shows. The number of people wishing to try their luck on these shows far exceeds the number needed, so producers (or associate producers) look for people who are lively or unusual and who will perform well when the TV cameras are on. Talk-show producers try to line up people who are well known (or eccentric) and who will interact well with the host or hostess. Public-affairs producers look for people with something to say who can present their points in a dynamic (or at least not boring) manner.

Actors who appear on dramas or sitcoms sign *contracts* that stipulate how much they will be paid and what their general obligations and working conditions are. Nonprofessionals should also be asked to sign **performance releases** (see Figure 11.10) so that

```
          COMMUNICATIONS 350 - STUDIO PRODUCTION

                          GROUP 2

                          PROPS

  ITEM                WHO IS BRINGING IT              NOTES

  umbrella            Jorge M.

  world globe         Susan T.            will get from library

  purse               Kim S.

  waddling duck       Chris B.            bring it a week early
                                          to test it on camera

  lamp                Maria G.            get permission form
                                          signed by dorm coun-
                                          selor
```

Figure 11.11

A list of props as a student producer might prepare it for a class production.

they cannot come back at a later time and ask for money or other privileges. One student producer learned this lesson the hard way. He had a sword swallower appear on his student production and neglected to get the proper release form signed. Later he showed the production on a cable-TV public-access channel, and someone called the sword swallower to say she had seen him. The sword swallower, thinking the student was making huge amounts of money distributing the tape, sued for $100,000 in retroactive pay and residuals. Although the student managed to avoid paying the sword swallower, he had to hire and pay a lawyer to fight the suit. That student producer will never again forget to get each person to sign a release.

Crew Selection

The producer for any show will definitely hire the production manager and assistant producers, if needed. She or he may also be involved with selecting camera operators, scenic designers, makeup people, and the like. One of the most important considerations is gathering a group of people who work together harmoniously. Frequently, producers and directors have worked with people in the past whom they want to work with again because they have a common understanding of the TV production

process. This makes it hard for new people to break into the business, but it usually ensures a successful production.

If talent or crew must be brought in from a great distance, if the production lasts for many hours, or if any of the shooting is done at a remote location, then the producer must make arrangements for *transportation, lodging,* and *meals.* Creature comforts are definitely the domain of the producer.

11.5 Production Paperwork

Because one of the duties of the producer is to make sure all elements of the program are in the right place at the right time, a producer usually makes and double-checks *lists.* The type of lists needed vary from production to production. A drama needs lists that detail costumes, sets, props, and who is responsible for each. (See Figure 11.11.) An ongoing talk show needs a list of potential guests and dates when they are to appear. A game show needs a list of prizes that have been or may be acquired for free. Often the production manager draws up these lists, because they relate closely to budget determinations.

```
Date

Name
Licensing Department
Music Publishing Company
Street Address
City, State, and Zip Code

Dear Person's Name:

I am producing a student television production entitled ("Name of
Program") for which I would like to use part of your musical
composition ("Name of Music"), composed by (Name of Composer.)  I
would like to acquire a non-exclusive synchronization license for
this musical composition.

I would like permission to use this material for broadcast,
cablecast, or other means of exhibition throughout the world as
often as deemed appropriate for this stuent production and for
any future revisions of this production.  Your permission
granting me the right to use this material in no way restricts
your use for any other purposes.

For your convenience, a release form is provided below and a copy
of this letter is attached for your files.

Sincerely yours,


Your Name


I (We) grant permission for the use requested in this letter.

Signature_____

Printed Name_____

Title_____

Phone Number_____

Date_____
```

Figure 11.12

A sample of a letter you might write to obtain clearance for music.

Copyright Clearance

Producers must also keep track of **copyright.** Nothing that has been copyrighted (e.g., a poem, short story, photograph, music, videotape footage) can be used on a show unless the owner has *granted permission.* Obtaining permission involves writing letters to copyright holders and then keeping careful track of what has and has not been cleared. (See Figure 11.12.) Sometimes copyright holders specify particular stipulations, such as a special wording in a credit at the end of the program. Producers must make sure these requirements are executed.

The most commonly used copyrighted material in programs is music. Some TV stations pay **music licensing companies** (ASCAP, BMI, and SESAC), then have the right to use music represented by those companies, which is most of the popular music. However, most independent productions (including student productions) must clear copyright or use material that is not copyrighted.

Clearing copyright can be a difficult chore for the producer. Often just finding who owns the copyright can require extensive research. With music, the copyright holder could be the composer, the arranger, the publisher of the sheet music, the record company, or some combination of them. Usually when they are found, they want money, so copyright clearance can be *expensive*.

Music that is old enough to be in the **public domain** can be used without copyright clearance. Usually that means the composer has been dead at least 50 years, but sometimes a particular arrangement of a song can be copyrighted, and someone who is still alive can hold the rights to that arrangement.

A way to get around copyright clearance is to have music composed specially for the production. This, too, can be expensive if the composer is to be paid. Student productions have an advantage in this regard, because universities usually have music students eager for the experience of composing in return for a credit. There are also services that provide copyright-cleared music very inexpensively.[6] The problem with much of this music is that it is not very distinctive—it all tends to sound alike.

The producer's problems are similar when it comes to videotape or film footage. If the opening credits require a shot of an airplane taking off, you cannot simply tape a takeoff from some movie you have seen on TV and use it without permission. You could have someone take portable equipment to the nearest airport and shoot the shot, or you could acquire it from a company that supplies stock footage.

Permission to use *written material* (poems, stories, charts) can usually be obtained from the publisher of the book in which it appears, while permission to use a painting that is in an art book may require permission of the artist, the photographer who took the picture of the painting, the publisher of the book, the museum where the painting is hanging, or some combination thereof.

Record Keeping

The producer must keep careful records of legal documents (including actor contracts and performer releases), receipts for purchased supplies, damage done to sets or locations, and other paperwork that is generated during preproduction, production, and postproduction. This paperwork is necessary for a variety of reasons. First, if the producer leaves and a new producer is hired, he or she will have the necessary infor-

mation to continue production. It also supplies the cast and crew with specifics so that they can do their jobs correctly. Some of the paperwork is used for tax purposes, while some is needed in case of (or hopefully, to prevent) lawsuits or investigations.

11.6 Schedules

Scheduling is another part of the producer's duty. Sometimes this is relatively easy. An ongoing series produced in a studio is likely to tape at the same time each day or each week. The set will be the same each time, and for the most part, the cast and crew will remain unchanged. For such productions, the producer usually posts a **call sheet** (see Figure 11.13) on the studio door or somewhere that is easily accessed by cast and crew. This lists the time that everyone is to appear and gives a general idea of what will be shot. The time may generally be the same from week to week, but the call sheet takes into account aberrations. For example, if a complicated makeup job is called for in a particular episode of a series, the person being made up and the makeup person will need to report earlier than usual.

Scheduling is more complicated for a studio show that is produced only once. The producer must find a time or times when all the performers are available, often a difficult task because people appearing on a one-time-only basis are likely to have other obligations. The producer must also work with the unit manager to assure that a studio will be available at a time when all the performers are free. If a producer wants a particular crew member, such as a certain audio operator, that further complicates the scheduling process.

Shoots that cover real events, such as news and sports, have their schedule set for them. The equipment and crews must be available and in place when the event takes place. The scheduling is easiest if the time of the event is known well ahead of time. However, news, by definition, does not occur that way. For this reason, most stations and networks have equipment that is dedicated to the coverage of news events.

Most complicated of all are programs that involve field production. Multiple locations are added to the problems associated with having cast and crew avail-

```
                          CALL SHEET
    Date_____

    Program Title_____

    Episode Number_____

    Producer_____

    Director_____

    Studio Location_____
    _____
                          PERFORMERS
    NAME                POSITION                  REPORT TIME




    _____

                            CREW
    NAME                POSITION                  REPORT TIME
```

Figure 11.13

An example of a call sheet.

able. Also, everyone is usually a long distance from the studio and cannot return for something that was forgotten. For these reasons, producers draw up thorough **shooting schedules** that list all the elements needed at each location. The process of producing and shooting away from the studio is discussed more thoroughly in Chapter 13 dealing with field production.

11.7 Evaluation

Once a program is finished, the producer has another function—evaluation. The program should meet its goals. For network TV, the main evaluation process is ratings. A series with high ratings stays on the air and one with low ratings is canceled. But many other forms of programs need much more sophisticated evaluation. The producer of a cooking show designed to show people how to bake a cake should test participants after they have viewed the program to see if people really can bake the cake. Demographic studies

should be undertaken to make sure a program designed to appeal to 8- to 11-year-olds is actually watched by that age group. Interactive multimedia, in part because it is new, requires a great deal of evaluation, some of it to make sure the goals are being met and some just to make sure the program works in its entirety. Only by honestly evaluating past productions can producers create even better programming.

Discussion Questions

1. How do the duties of executive producers, line producers, and associate producers differ? Which one do you think you would prefer to be, if any?
2. Come up with an idea for a sitcom series and discuss the major points you would include in a treatment. What type of script do you think you would eventually use?

3. Come up with an idea for a video that highlights some program or event at your university. What points would you include in the proposal? What type of script would you eventually use?

4. What differences would you encounter between budgeting an action-oriented movie-of-the-week for a network and budgeting a company president's "state of the company" talk for an in-house-produced corporate video? What would be some differences in terms of casting and selecting the crew? In terms of coming up with a production schedule?

Footnotes

1. This book does not pretend to be a text in scriptwriting. What is given here is merely an overview of script forms. For more information on scriptwriting, see such books as Syd Field, *Screenplay: The Foundations of Screenwriting* (New York: Dell, 1982); William Miller, *Screenwriting for Film and Television* (Boston: Allyn and Bacon, 1998); Jurgen Wolff and Kerry Cox, *Top Secrets: Screenwriting* (Los Angeles: Lone Eagle Publishing Company, 1992); Richard A. Blum, *Television and Screen Writing* (Stoneham, Mass.: Focal Press, 1995); Edgar W. Willis and Camille D'Arienzo, *Writing Scripts for Television, Radio, and Film* (Fort Worth: Harcourt Brace Jovanovich, 1993); Ray DiZazzo, *Corporate Scriptwriting* (Stoneham, Mass.: Focal Press, 1992); and Timothy Garrand, *Writing for Multimedia* (Boston: Focal Press, 1997).

2. A large number of computer programs are available to help television writers compose their scripts. Some of the most commonly used are Movie Magic Screenwriter, The Script Thing, Final Draft, and Scriptwriter. To keep up to date on this material, refer to the Website http://www.screenwriters.com.

3. Software is available to help with the creation of storyboards. Most of it contains a large number of predrawn people and objects and can be placed in a frame and manipulated in a variety of ways—turned, made larger, made smaller, etc. One popular program is Storyboard Quick from Power Production Software—http://www.powerproduction.com.

4. For more information on wages and salaries, see *Paymaster*, a publication put out by Entertainment Partners, 3601 West Olive Avenue, 8th Floor, Burbank, CA 91505, that lists all the generally accepted minimums and working conditions.

5. Computer budgeting programs made for the television and film industries include Movie Magic Budgeting and Turbo BudgetingAD. These can be purchased from Quantum Films Software Division, 8230 Beverly Boulevard, Suite 17, Los Angeles, CA 90048. These programs and other preproduction and production software can be researched by going to http://www.hollywoodnetwork.com.

6. Some libraries that supply copyright-cleared music are Blue Ribbon SoundWorks Ltd. (404-377-1514); Canary Productions (800-368-0033); DeWolfe Music Library (800-221-6713); FirstCom Music House (800-858-8880); Killer Tracks (800-877-0078); Metro Music (800-697-7392); and Sound Ideas (800-387-3030). For more details, see "Production Music Libraries," *Mix*, August 1998, p. 78. Some of these companies have samples of their work available on CD or over the Internet.

chapter 12

Directing

Techniques and disciplines that directors use should fit their own personalities, the capabilities of the on-air talent, and the needs of the particular show they are directing. Some directors are, by nature, more authoritative than others, and give concrete direction. Others rely more on psychology and attempt to obtain disciplined performances by letting the talent and technicians feel they are the ones in charge of their own actions. Professional actors, such as those participating in a drama, require different handling than nonprofessionals who might be making a first-time appearance on a public-affairs program. A children's program with many youngsters on it requires a more patient approach than a late-night talk show.

The various techniques and discipline styles are taken into consideration as this chapter discusses:

- How the director blocks talent, marks a script, and prepares shot sheets (12.1).
- The nature of prestudio, floor, and control room rehearsals (12.1).
- How the AD uses a segment timing sheet (12.1).
- The difference between program time and body time (12.1).
- Principles related to calling commands appropriately (12.1).
- The wide shot, medium shot, close-up pattern (12.2).
- Placement of cameras (12.2).
- Aesthetic principles related to cutting ratio, jump cutting, position jumps, and the axis of action (12.2).
- The use of transitions such as cuts, dissolves, fades, defocusing, wipes, and digital effects (12.2).
- The proper timing of transitions (12.2).
- How the director must interact with people (12.3).
- What is needed to direct a discussion program (12.4).

12.1 The "Manager" Role

A director is part manager, part artist, and part psychiatrist. Directors are the ones who give instructions to cast and crew, make sure the production is aesthetically pleasing, and handle the reasonable (and unreasonable) demands or quirks of those involved with the production.[1]

As the overall "boss," the director must oversee what everyone else involved with the production does. In addition, the director has many specific tasks that are primarily his or her domain and that are part of managing the program. These include blocking the production, marking the script, preparing shot sheets, conducting rehearsals, and actually calling shots. In addition, the associate director, working with the director, must plan the exact timing procedures for the show.

Blocking

Once you, as the director, have determined the purpose of the script and are sure it is the approximate length you want (see Chapter 2, section 2.2), you should start thinking about *blocking*—placing of actors and cameras in particular spots and figuring out how and where they are going to move during the course of the show. This is more complex for dramas and comedies than it is for public-affairs programs, but all programs need some form of blocking. Think through how the actors or performers will best relate to each other.

Should the talk-show host sit in the middle of two guests or to the right of both of them? Should the husband lean against the back of the wife's chair or sit down in the chair next to her? Don't forget to think about actor comfort. An actress who has to turn her head unnaturally to see the leading man is going to be too uncomfortable to deliver her lines well.

Also think through the relationship of the actors to the cameras. Where should the daughter be positioned so that camera 2 can capture a good close-up of her reaction to her father's chastisement? On which burner of the stove should the chef stir the pudding so that camera 3 can obtain an effective shot?

Directors often draw **blocking diagrams** to help them visualize the shots ahead of time. (See Figure 12.1.) Using these diagrams, they can plan moves and think through how the people and the equipment will interact with each other. One useful blocking technique for directors is to *start blocking in the center of the program.* Pick the most crucial or difficult part of the production and figure out your camera pattern for that segment first. Once you know how that segment has to be blocked, you can figure backward to see how you will want to work your way up to that position.

In planning multicamera blocking, you must keep in mind that the action is continuous, and you will not be able to stop to readjust the prop in someone's hand. You must also keep in mind the position of all the cameras so that they are not visible in any of the shots. And you must consider the position of actors and cameras so that shots can flow appropriately from one camera to another. With single-camera shooting, you can stop, but actors must perform in exactly the same fashion over and over again so that all takes are consistent. (See Chapter 13.)

Marking the Script

Once you have thought through the blocking, you can *mark* your copy of the script so that you can call commands effectively during the program. Indicate which cameras you are going to use for which shots, what instructions the technical director and camera operators will need, where the audio cues will have to be, what cues the talent will need, and so forth. Most directors develop their own shorthand for marking their scripts, but some commonly used symbols are shown in Figure 12.2.

Depending on the program and the director's experience, scripts are marked in varying degrees. A major studio comedy special might involve hundreds of abbreviated cues, instructions, and notes. With a fairly routine ongoing program, script preparation may take no more than a few penciled reminders of unusual cues. (See Figure 12.3.) As a beginning director, you will probably feel more comfortable with a heavily marked script. Just the process of noting all the commands you will need to make will help you when you are in the director's chair.

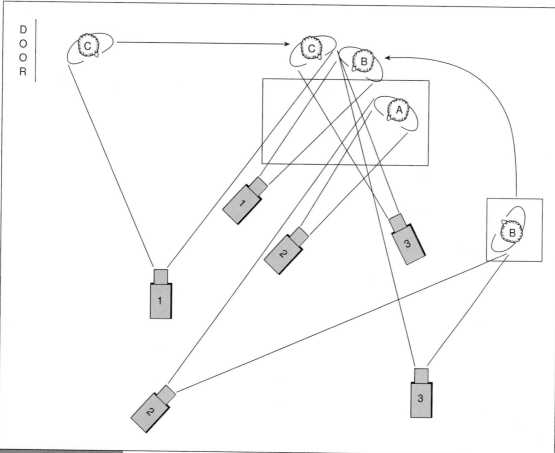

A blocking diagram as a director might draw it. In this scene, characters A and B are talking when character C comes in the door angrily and goes behind the sofa. Character B rises from the chair and goes behind the sofa where characters C and B argue. Character A reacts to the argument. Camera 1 pans with C as he moves from the door to behind the sofa and later has a close-up of B. Camera 2 shows A and B talking and then gets a reaction shot of A. Camera 3 follows B from the chair to behind the sofa and later gets a close-up of C.

Preparing Shot Sheets

Once you have thought through your camera shots and marked your script, you can prepare **shot sheets** for your camera operators. These are abbreviated descriptions of every shot that each camera has to get. A shot sheet is compact enough to be attached to the rear of the camera, where the operator can quickly refer to it. They are not particularly useful for interview shows, where the director is calling shots on the fly depending on who happens to be talking. But they are very valuable for complex, fully scripted programs, where every shot has been carefully worked

out by the director—and where the cameras will have to be moving quite a bit to get various shots as requested.

Figure 12.4 shows the three shot sheets for a three-camera drama. All the shots have been numbered in the order in which they will occur. The camera operators tape or clip these shot sheets near their viewfinders. Sometimes all the camera operators have all the shot sheets, so they know not only what they will be shooting but also what the other cameras will frame. In other instances, each camera operator would use only his or her own shot sheet.

③	Camera number three
⟨ or F.I.	Fade in
KEY or K	Key
T	Take
≷ or D	Dissolve
SD	Slow dissolve
⟩ or FO.	Fade out
Q	Cue
⌐___	At this point, cut, dissolve, or cue
D. I.	Dolly in
D.B. or D.O.	Dolly back or dolly out
PREP ②	Prepare camera 2
③ TO___	Camera 3, get ready for . . .
2-sh	Shot of two persons
3-sh	Shot of three persons
O/S	Over-the-shoulder shot
CU	Close-up shot
MS	Medium shot
LS	Long shot
ECU or XCU	Extreme close-up
MLS	Medium long shot
MCU	Medium close-up

Figure 12.2

Standard script-marking symbols.

Conducting Rehearsals

Program types differ greatly in the number and types of rehearsals they have, ranging from virtually none for live news coverage to several days for a sitcom. You want everything to be well enough rehearsed that the program runs smoothly, but at the same time you do not want to overrehearse to the extent that the material becomes stale to both talent and crew. Sometimes outside factors, such as the amount of money budgeted to pay the actors or the amount of time the studio is available, affects your rehearsal schedule. But in considering rehearsals, you may wish to think in terms of several different kinds: **prestudio rehearsals, floor rehearsals,** and **control room rehearsals.**

Pre-studio Rehearsals

For many extensive productions, especially dramas and comedies, you will want to have some rehearsals prior to coming into the studio. Studio time is too pre-cious to start from scratch with basic blocking. Using a rehearsal hall, an empty studio, or a living room, you can begin working with actors. Specific areas can be measured off and marked with masking tape or furniture to represent major staging areas, and much of your blocking of action can take place—as well as quite a bit of the dramatic interpretation and working on lines.

For nondramatic productions, there are also many good reasons for pre-studio rehearsals. Demonstration shows, educational programs, political broadcasts, and the like can benefit from having an early **dry-run** session, where the director and talent can work together on the basic staging of the program.

Studio Floor Rehearsals

When the director and the production crew start to work in the studio, the director usually spends some amount of time on the studio floor before assuming the director's chair in the control room. If the talent is particularly insecure or if the technical coordination of a production is really complicated, you might spend quite a bit of your time on the studio floor. On the other hand, if the talent is in control of the situation and the technical elements are no special problem, you probably would benefit from getting into the control room as early as you can.

The first rehearsal techniques you will most likely conduct from the studio floor will be a **walk-through rehearsal.** This might be either a *talent* walk-through (if they are not really sure of their positions and movements) or a *technical* walk-through (to explain major camera moves, audio placement, and scene changes). In many instances, the walk-through is a combination, taking both the talent and crew through an abbreviated version of the production.

Control Room Rehearsals

More complete rehearsals are usually conducted with the director calling shots from the control room. The first rehearsal may be a **start-and-stop rehearsal.** In this approach, you interrupt the rehearsal every time there is a major problem. You correct the trouble and then continue the rehearsal. It is quite a time-consuming process, although it can be effective if you have the luxury of enough studio time.

Roll opening tape **VIDEO**

  TAPE: OPENING CREDITS

Open mic

② *2-sh*
  TWO-SHOT - STEVE AND SHARON

① *MS*
  STEVE

[PREP TAPE]
Roll tape
  TAPE: FIRE REPORT

30 sec.
③ *MLS*
  SHARON

[PREP GRAPHICS]
K graphics
  GRAPHICS: MAP OVER SHOULDER

AUDIO

SOUND ON TAPE. Runs :30.
Ends with drum beat.

STEVE: I'm Steve Anderson.

SHARON: And I'm Sharon
Hendricks here with the latest
news.

STEVE: Fire fighters are still
at the scene of a three-alarm
fire on Market Street that
destroyed two buildings
earlier today. Fred White has
this report.

SOT: Runs 2:56. Ends with
"could have been a lot worse."

SHARON: The Japanese are still
trying to assess if any damage
was caused by this morning's
earthquake. The quake was
centered two hundred miles
from Tokyo and registered
7 point 1. Two strong
after shocks have been felt.

Figure 12.3

This is an example of how a novice director might mark a news script.

Another approach to rehearsing is the **uninterrupted run-through.** In this approach, the director attempts to get through the entire production (or the segment of the production that is about to be taped) with a minimum of interruptions. If time is short—and if problems are minor—you keep on plowing through the rehearsal regardless of what happens.

Finally, there is the **dress rehearsal.** Theoretically, this is the final rehearsal—a complete, uninterrupted, full-scale rehearsal after all the problems have been straightened out. In practice, this stage is rarely reached. Realities of the medium are such that there simply is never enough studio time to do as polished a job as you want. In many instances, the director

CAMERA 1	CAMERA 2	CAMERA 3
3. LS, Mary in doorway 5. LS, David in doorway 7. MS David (he walks into O/S) 9. O/S David 11. CU David 14. MS Mary (she sits) 20. Loose 2–sh. (Mary rises) 22. O/S Mary (in doorway). She walks toward David. David turns to camera. 24. CU David 28. 2–sh. Mary walks past camera. Hold on David 30. MS David. Pan to door as Alice enters 33. 3–sh., favoring Alice 36. CU Alice 39. CU Alice 42. Wide 3–sh., follow action	1. Wide Sh., Kitchen, hi-angle boom down. 4. MS Mary. Follow her 12. 2–sh., Pan L as David crosses behind Mary 15. MS David. D.B. as he comes to her. Open to 2–sh. 17. CU Mary 19. 2–sh. (tight) 21. (Crane up) Hi angle 2–sh. D.I. & crane down to single of David 25. Single David (wide). D.B., follow as he walks to Mary. Open to 2–sh. 27. CU Mary's hands 31. MS Alice 34. MS David (he sits) 37. ECU David 40. (Crane down) Loose MS Alice. Follow her to table. Follow action w/cup. Crane up & D.I.	2. CU coffee cup, pan to ash tray 6. MS Mary (she rises) 8. O/S Mary 10. CU Mary 13. MS David 16. MCU David (bust–shot) 18. CU David 23. 2–sh. as Mary turns 26. (Hook wheels) 2–sh. D.I. to ECU Mary 29. MS Mary 32. Loose 2–sh. (Mary, David) 35. Loose CU, Mary 38. ECU Mary 41. ECU Mary 43. CU of knife

Figure 12.4

Representative shot sheets.

winds up with a combination start-and-stop and dress rehearsal.

When time is short, you must economize and try to make the most efficient use of the time available. Do not stand around waiting for others to finish their jobs before starting your rehearsal; you can rehearse even while the lighting crew is still trimming the lights and while the audio technician is establishing music levels. In an abbreviated walk-through rehearsal, at least make certain you get through all the rough spots in the production; *rehearse the open and the close* and *the crucial transitions* that call for coordination of several kinds of movement. Pick your priorities; do not get hung up on small details (such as worrying about the possibility of a boom shadow) when you have only a few minutes to work out major problems (the talent doesn't know where he or she should move next).

Timing

As a director, you want to make sure that your associate director (AD) is effectively handling timing of the program. One way for the AD to do this is through the use of a **segment timing sheet.**

Segment Timing Sheet

It may take several forms and be used in different ways. One sample format is shown in Figure 12.5. In this example, there are five columns for the AD to use. The first column is for a brief description of each segment in the program. The next four columns are for timing notations of one kind or another.

"Unit" means the actual length of the *individual segment.* "Cume" is for the *cumulative time* of the program up to that point. The "Ideal" column is the estimated time that each segment *should* run; both the ideal unit-segment times and the ideal cumulative time should be figured out prior to setting foot in the studio.

The "Rehearsal" column is for jotting down the unit times as various segments are worked through in a start-and-stop rehearsal. It is difficult to get an accurate picture of the actual cumulative times at this point, but the total of the unit times should give the AD a rough picture of how long or how short the program is likely to be. This column also allows the AD to figure backtiming so that certain segments start on time.

The "Dress" rehearsal column should give the AD a clear picture of how the actual cumulative times

SEGMENT (Description)	IDEAL (Unit)	Cume.	REHEARSAL (Unit)	Cume.	DRESS (Unit)	Cume.	AIR (Unit)	Cume.
1. TEASER	(:20)	0:20	:25			:25		:25
2. OPENING TITLES	(:30)	0:50	:40			1:05		1:10
3. INTRO	(1:05)	1:55	1:30			2:15		2:20
4. CHART	(2:00)	3:55	1:50			4:00		4:10
5. DEMO.	(4:00)	7:55	4:45		(4:15)	8:15	(4:20)	8:30
6. INTERVIEW	(5:30)	13:25	6:00			13:45	(5:00)	13:30
7. WRAP-UP	(:30)	13:55	:20			14:05		13:55
8. CLOSE	(:35)	14:30	:45			14:50		14:30
			16:15					
			(+1:45 over)					

Figure 12.5

Sample segment timing sheet.

compare to the ideal times. The "Air" column is filled in as the program progresses. It lets the AD know how much to tell the talent to *stretch* or, in Figure 12.5, how much to *cut* in order to come out on time. In this program, for example, we can see that several segments ran long, so the interview segment had to be cut short (from an ideal of five and a half minutes to an actual five minutes).

There are many variations of timing sheets. Some will include *time in* and *time out* cumulative columns. Some will work with only one or two columns. This sample, however, should give the beginning AD an idea of what is needed to get the program timed accurately.

Talent Timing Cues

In many programs, such as the one illustrated in Figure 12.5, the talent would need time-remaining cues in specific segments. Thus, working from the *ideal* times, the host would get, for example, a "30 seconds remaining" cue at 3:25 into the program (as a reminder that there are 30 seconds left in the chart talk) and at 7:25 (30 seconds left in the demonstration). The talent might want time cues to get out of the interview segment on time (that is, a 30-second cue at 12:55) or simply time cues to get through with the wrap-up summary on time (that is, a 30-second cue at 13:25).

Care must be taken that the talent clearly understands what these intermediate segment cues are so that they will not be confused with time remaining in the body of the program.

Program Time and Body Time

This brings up one other point of potential confusion. The AD must be concerned both with *getting the talent wrapped up on time* and with *getting the program off the air on time*. In Figure 12.5, the talent needs a 30-second cue at 13:25 because he or she has to be completely wrapped up and finished at 13:55 (leaving the director 35 seconds for the closing credits). Also, the director has to have a 30-second cue at 14:00 in order to get the program off the air and into black at precisely 14:30.

Thus, the AD has to work with both **body time**, the actual *length of the program content* including the host's closing summary but not the show's closing credits, and with **program time,** the *total length of the show* from fade-in to fade-out.

Calling Commands

Once rehearsals are finished and you, the director, and your AD have solved any potential timing problems, you are ready to actually tape the show (or send it out live). You are the one who makes sure all the audio and video material is ready when you need it, and you make the decisions as to what happens when. In actuality, you may delegate some things to your AD, such as making sure the proper camera shots are set up, but you have the overriding authority and responsibility.

Most successful television directors work to develop a calm, articulate manner when giving commands. Whenever possible, they speak in a very casual style and even use a bit of humor. Those not used to being on the intercom should not be misled by this apparent easygoing banter. It is designed to mask the intensity and ongoing pressure under which the director and all key members of the crew are working. Good directors know that to betray anxiety is to risk losing the confidence of the crew. Inexperienced directors who speak in loud and commanding voices are very hard to put up with on a long-term basis. Crew members listen much more carefully when the director's voice is calm and assuring. All directorial commands must be delivered with practical consideration of the realities of the production. To request that any crew member do too many things in too short a time is to invite a series of problems. Once an operator falls behind in a sequence, there can be a "domino effect," which can put a whole series of production elements at risk. The wise director knows what is possible and what is not.

If the program is being taped, the first thing you need to do is start the VCR that is going to record the show. You do this by saying, "Roll record tape." When the tape has stabilized, the VCR operator will say "Speed," and you can then begin. Sometimes there are preliminary things you need to put on the tape, such as color bars, tone, and a slate. In other situations, those will already be on the tape, and you start right in with the program.

Crew Commands

Each production varies in terms of the exact commands you need to give, but a director might give different crew members the following kinds of commands:

Technical director—Various transitions, such as cuts and dissolves. The technical director will also set up special effects, but those are usually planned ahead of time because the director does not have time during production to give elaborate instructions as to what type of effect he or she desires. When the effect is needed the director will call for "effect 1" or "effect 5."

Associate director—Quick comments regarding things such as pickup shots that need editing. Actually, the associate director is more likely to be giving information to the director (such as time remaining in the program) than the other way around.

Audio operator—Fade music or other audio elements in and out; open and close mics.

Graphics operator—Change graphics and bring them in and out (unless they are brought in through the switcher by the technical director).

Video operator—Start and stop the record tape and any roll-in tapes.

Lighting director—Bring up or fade out lights if lighting changes are part of the show.

TelePrompTer operator—Usually this person rolls the script without instruction from the director, keeping pace with the talent. Commands would come only if there are problems.

Stage manager—Cues and timing information to relay to the talent.

Camera operators—Shot designations such as close-ups or wide shots and zooms or pans.

Boom operator—This person usually works independently following the talent, but the director might need to instruct the boom operator to raise the boom if it or its shadow looks as though it is going to appear in the picture.

Production assistants—These people may take their instructions through hand cues from the stage manager, or the director may need to tell them to flip charts or remove some prop.

Figure 12.6 gives examples of commands a director might give to get into and out of a talk show. It also indicates the actions these commands should bring.

DIRECTOR'S COMMAND	RESPONSE
READY IN STUDIO?	STAGE MANAGER SAYS "YES" OR SAYS "NO" AND TELLS THE DIRECTOR WHAT THE PROBLEM IS
READY IN CONTROL ROOM?	ANYONE WHO IS NOT READY SAYS WHY
STAND BY	STAGE MANAGER SAYS "STAND BY IN STUDIO"
	LIGHTING DIRECTOR MAKES SURE ALL LIGHTS NEEDED ARE ON
	CAMERAS GET ON FIRST SHOTS
	TALENT GETS IN PLACE
	MICS ARE PROPERLY POSITIONED
	TELEPROMPTER OPERATOR HAS FIRST COPY UP
	AUDIO BOARD HAS MASTER UP BUT ALL SOUND DOWN
	VCR OPERATOR GETS READY TO HIT PLAY AND RECORD
	CG OPERATOR GETS SLATE ON CG MONITOR
	SHADER MAKES SURE LEVELS ARE CORRECT
	TECHNICAL DIRECTOR PUTS SWITCHER IN BLACK
	A.D. MAKES SURE CLOCK IS AT 00:00
ROLL TAPE	VCR OPERATOR PUSHES PLAY AND RECORD AND, WHEN MACHINE IS READY SAYS "SPEED"
TAKE BARS AND TONE	T.D. PUSHES BUTTON FOR BARS
	AUDIO OPERATOR PUSHES TONE BUTTON AND MAKES SURE TONE IS AT 100%
	AD STARTS THE CLOCK AND GIVES DIRECTOR TIME CUES SO THAT BARS AND TONE ARE ON FOR 30 SECONDS
	VCR OPERATOR CHECKS TO MAKE SURE TONE IS AT 100% AND THERE IS A VIDEO LEVEL
LOSE TONE, TAKE CG SLATE	AUDIO OPERATOR PUSHES TONE BUTTON OFF
	TD PUSHES BUTTON FOR C.G.
	AD GIVES DIRECTOR TIME CUES SO THAT SLATE IS ON FOR 20 SECONDS
ROLL COUNTDOWN, TAKE VCR	VCR OPERATOR ROLLS PRECUED COUNTDOWN TAPE
	TD PUSHES BUTTON FOR VCR AND DISPLAYS COUNTDOWN TAPE UNTIL NUMBER 2 APPEARS
	CG OPERATOR GETS UP OPENING CREDITS
	AD COUNTS WITH THE COUNTDOWN TAPE AND CONTINUES WITH 2, 1
TAKE BLACK	TD PUSHES BLACK BUTTON
	VCR OPERATOR STOPS COUNTDOWN TAPE VCR
FADE IN MUSIC	AUDIO OPERATOR FADES IN MUSIC ON WHATEVER (CD, CART, CASSETTE, DAT ETC.)
	AD STARTS TIMING THE PROGRAM
FADE IN (WHATEVER—CAM 1, VCR OPENING)	TD FADES FROM BLACK TO WHATEVER
TAKE CG OPENING CREDITS	TD PUTS CREDITS OVER PICTURE
LOSE CREDITS	TD TAKES OFF CREDITS BUT KEEPS PICTURE UNDER THEM

Figure 12.6—Continued

Commands that a director might give to get into and out of a talk show. To simplify this, most of the "ready" commands have not been included. Because the equipment and configuration are different in each studio, this is just a sample of how the program might go. In some circumstances, the AD might give some of these commands, the VCR operator might not need to say "speed," the graphics might come on a different way, the bars and tone may already be on the tape, etc. However, this is a basic "script" that can be modified to fit particular circumstances.

DIRECTOR'S COMMAND	RESPONSE
FADE OUT MUSIC	AUDIO OPERATOR FADES DOWN MUSIC
STANDBY TO CUE TALENT	STAGE MANAGER GIVES TALENT STANDBY CUE
OPEN MICS	AUDIO OPERATOR RAISES MIC FADERS
CUE TALENT	STAGE MANAGER CUES TALENT AND THEY START TALKING
TAKE WHATEVER	TD TAKES WHATEVER
(CAM, 1, 2, 3)	
DIRECTOR DIRECTS THE SHOW	CAMERAS GET WHATEVER SHOTS THE DIRECTOR SAYS
	AD KEEPS TRACK OF TIME AND GIVES TIME CUES TO END
	OF PROGRAM THAT DIRECTOR PASSES ON TO STAGE
	MANAGER
	STAGE MANAGER GIVES TALENT TIME CUES
	TELEPROMPTER OPERATOR KEEPS UP WITH TALENT
	BOOM OPERATOR MOVES BOOM TO FOLLOW TALENT
	AUDIO RIDES LEVELS, ADJUSTS CONTROL ROOM MONITOR
	VOLUME, AND SETS UP AND BRINGS IN ANY NEEDED SOUNDS
	VCR OPERATOR CHECKS LEVELS PERIODICALLY AND CUES
	AND PLAYS ANY ROLL-IN TAPES
	CG OPERATOR CUES AND PLACES ON AIR LOWER 1/3RDS AND
	ANY OTHER GRAPHICS
	SHADER ADJUSTS CAMERA BRIGHTNESS LEVELS, IF NEEDED
	TD GETS THE PROPER PICTURE ON AIR AS THE DIRECTOR
	CALLS FOR IT
TAKE (WHATEVER—CAM, VCR)	TD TAKES WHATEVER
FADE IN MUSIC,	AUDIO OPERATOR BRINGS MUSIC UP ON CD OR WHATEVER
FADE OUT MICS	AND LOWERS FADERS ON MIC INPUTS
READY CREDITS	CG OPERATOR MAKES SURE CLOSING CREDITS ARE UP
TAKE CG CLOSING CREDITS	TD BRINGS IN CLOSING CREDITS
LOSE CG	TD TAKES CREDITS OFF
FADE TO BLACK	TD FADES FROM PICTURE TO BLACK
FADE OUT MUSIC	AUDIO OPERATOR FADES OUT MUSIC
STOP TAPE	VCR OPERATOR STOPS RECORD TAPE 10 SECONDS AFTER END
	OF PROGRAM
CHECK TAPE	VCR OPERATOR MAKES SURE AUDIO AND VIDEO RECORDED
THAT'S A WRAP	ALL CREW MEMBERS START TO CLEAN UP THEIR POSITIONS

Figure 12.6—Concluded

Commands that a director might give to get into and out of a talk show.

Command Principles

There is really no right or wrong way to give commands, but there are certain principles that will enable you to give directions as clearly as possible. For example, refer to talent (when talking to the stage manager) by name—"Cue Dr. Morgan," not "Cue him"—to avoid misunderstandings. Refer to camera operators, on the other hand, by numbers; you are less likely to slip up and get confused.

Make sure you use correct and precise *commands of preparation* as well as *commands of execution*. The commands of execution are those cues that directly affect what goes out over the line monitor. "Fade-in music" or "Take 2" call for an immediate action at a precise point in time. For a crew member or performer to respond with this immediate action, however, he or she needs adequate preparation time to be mentally ready and physically prepared. For this reason, commands of execution should be preceded at some point by a related command of preparation. The term "*Stand by . . .* music, announcer, VCR," and the like, is probably the most functional preparatory command. It alerts the equipment operator—and all other personnel—to listen carefully for the subsequent command of execution. Another term sometimes used for this preparatory purpose is "*ready.*" The verb "*cue*" is quite often used as the first word of a command of execution—"Cue announcer." Other commonly used verbs are "*fade*" (as in "Fade in camera 1" or "Fade out music") and "*roll*" (as in "Roll VCR" or "Roll credits").

Keeping the lag time of various equipment and personnel in mind, give your cues in a sequence designed to get things happening when you want them to. In opening your program, say "Fade in music" and then "Fade in camera 2." It always takes a second or so before the music will be heard (if it is properly cued up), but the camera is there with the push of a lever. Similarly, always cue talent before putting his or her camera on the air. "Open-mic-cue-talent-dissolve-to-two" is often given as one command of execution. By the time the stage manager reacts and throws the cue and the talent takes a breath and starts to talk, the camera will be on the air.

Watch and *listen* to your monitors. Always be aware of exactly what is going on over the air. If a picture is not what you want (what the viewer needs), then change it. The viewer watching his or her home receiver could care less about your sinus headache or your fight with the talent or the camera cable with the bad connection; all he or she knows is what comes out over the receiver, and if it is bad, it is bad. Also, always check your camera and preview monitors before calling a shot to be put on the air. Make sure the camera you want to dissolve to or the special effects you want next are prepared and ready to be put on the air. You cannot afford to get buried in your marked script while ignoring the realities of the picture and sound you are sending out.

12.2 The "Artist" Role

Many things related to managing also affect aesthetics. For example, the director must think of the aesthetics of the picture frame while planning blocking or marking the script or preparing the shot sheets. But beyond that, the director must think of artistic principles that will make a program pleasant to watch. Many of these principles involve **continuity**—a broad term that refers to keeping things the same throughout an entire program.

These principles have developed over the years as part of a language of film and television. People viewing a movie or TV program expect certain conventions, and violating them confuses the audience. However, these principles are not laws of the land. In fact, they are made to be violated, because sometimes you want to disorient (or frighten or shock) your audience. Music videos have certainly breached every camera and cutting continuity principle—and have done so effectively. But if a program is straightforward information or entertainment, a director should abide by the conventional language. In addition, understanding a principle better enables you to know how and when to violate it.

We will discuss a number of production conventions that directors should keep in mind. Although the focus of the discussion will be on multicamera production, some of these conventions also hold true for single-camera shooting or interactive media production.

Shot Juxtaposition

Early filmmakers quickly came to the conclusion that when one picture is immediately replaced by another, an interaction occurs in the mind of the viewer that communicates something more than if each picture were viewed separately. This intriguing concept obviously can have direct bearing on the process of shot selection for any television program. Each shot must be thought of as being part of a flow of images, each with a relationship to the one that precedes it and the one that follows it.

For this reason, the succession of pictures should be motivated by the basic tenet, "Give the viewers what they need to see when they need to see it." To a great extent, this is determined by a juxtaposition of *collective* shots showing the whole picture and intimate *particularized* shots giving the viewers the closer details they want. (See Figure 12.7.)

The generalities of a scene or program situation are established by the **wide shot** (also referred to as a

Comparison of wide shot and close-up. Whether in a variety show, drama, or panel discussion, the same need exists to balance wide shots (*left*) with close-ups (*right*).

long shot or **establishing shot**). Then the director cuts to a **medium shot** or a series of medium shots to give the audience particularized details. When something small or intimate needs to be seen, the director uses the **close-up.** (See Chapter 5 for more on camera shots.)

Of course, the terms *wide shot, medium shot,* and *close-up* are relative and vary from one type of program to another. The left-hand picture shown in Figure 12.7 is probably a wide shot for a discussion program. However, if this were a children's program with toys to be demonstrated flanking the four people, this shot would be considered a medium shot. Likewise, the right-hand shot in Figure 12.7 would be considered a close-up for a talk show, but for a drama in which the girl's earring played a major role, this might be the medium shot and the earring would be the close-up.

Nevertheless, the pattern of wide shot to medium shot to close-up should be observed so that the audience comprehends the total environment and can then relate to particular areas of that environment. Of course, as mentioned above, this "rule" is often violated for perfectly good reasons. Starting with a close-up of a dagger builds suspense and draws the audience into the scene. Where is this dagger and why is it sitting there? Only after the audience's curiosity has been aroused does the director use a wide shot to reveal the location.

Principles of shot juxtaposition are changing slightly with the introduction of the 16:9 aspect ratio and the greater resolution of high-definition TV. For example, a wide shot of a basketball game can cover the whole court with enough clarity for the audience to discern exactly what is happening. For this reason, there may be less need for medium shots. However, at present, most people are viewing on older sets with a 4:3 aspect ratio, so directors are generally not yet using new principles that apply to HDTV.

Camera Selection

Even with the opportunity to plan or block out the camera work in multicamera television programs such as soap operas, the ongoing production technique forces the director to make some rather quick, on-the-air editing decisions, because the exact moment of the take is crucial. With talk and game shows, of course, there is truly an ongoing series of changes in camera use every time someone new breaks in to talk. A basic challenge is to always have the proper camera ready for a shot at the exact moment the situation calls for it. On the part of the director, this requires an ability to be able to think *simultaneously* on at least two levels—what is on the air right now and what is going to be on the air next.

Thought Process

With a three-camera structure, the thinking process might work something like this: Camera 1 is on the

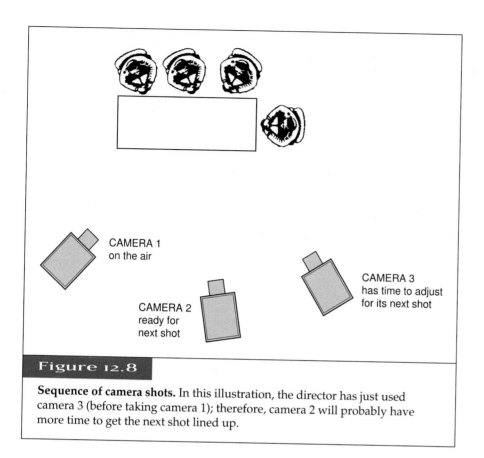

Sequence of camera shots. In this illustration, the director has just used camera 3 (before taking camera 1); therefore, camera 2 will probably have more time to get the next shot lined up.

air. You, as director, have the choice of using camera 2 or 3 for the next shot. Camera 3, however, has just been used on the previous shot. Camera 2, therefore, has more time to make a framing adjustment or even change position. (See Figure 12.8.)

It is accepted studio procedure in a three-camera setup to place camera 1 on the left, camera 2 in the middle, and camera 3 on the right. This setup allows the director to keep track easily of the relative positions of cameras on the floor and the angle of shots available to them.

Obviously, cameras usually are not employed in a repeated 1-2-3-1-2-3 rotation. In order to observe the wide shot, medium shot, and close-up requirements of any program, at least one of the three cameras at any given time will usually be designated as a wide-angle cover-shot camera. This is especially important in shooting unrehearsed programs, such as panel discussions, where there are sudden changes of the individuals speaking. The technique on such a program is to cut to a wide shot on the change of voice if a close-up of the new person is not immediately available. The director then has a chance to ascertain who is talking and call for the close-up. The most glaring error on any kind of program is for an unprepared director to be caught with a speaker or performer still on camera when that person is no longer speaking or performing.

In a rehearsed program, when the camera blocking has been worked out in advance, the director can temporarily commit all cameras to close-up shots, having planned to return to a cover shot at a later specific time. Generally, however, the wide-angle and close-up shot balance requirements are such that at least one camera is always kept on a cover shot.

Crossing Camera Angles

Another principle involving camera selection deals with *crossing camera angles.* In many staging setups, the natural pattern has two people facing each other. To frame the best headshots, cameras should shoot across each other's angles; that is, each camera should be shooting the person or object farthest away from the camera. (See Figure 12.9.) The camera on the right (camera 2) should be getting the shot of the person on the camera left, and vice versa. In this way, each

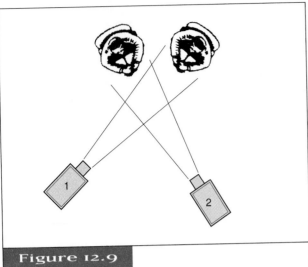

To get the best head-on shots, cameras should be set up so they shoot across each other.

camera gets a view of most of the talent's face. If camera 1 shoots the talent on the left, it will get no more than a profile of the talent. The same holds true for camera 2 if it shoots the person on the right.

Shot Relationships

When changing from one shot to another, the two pictures should relate to each other in both an informational and aesthetic setting. The subject in two successive shots should maintain continuity in that it should be *readily recognizable.* You would not want to cut to such a different angle that the viewer would not immediately recognize the subject from the previous shot.

Cutting Ratio

One of the most common errors of shot relationship involves wide shots and close-ups. If you were to cut from the left-hand shot in Figure 12.7 to a close-up of the girl's earring, most of your viewers would be totally lost, because they would not have noticed the earring in the wide shot. One good rule to follow is that you should always keep your camera cuts within a **3-to-1 cutting ratio;** that is, do not take to a shot that is *three times larger* or *three times smaller* than the preceding shot.

Jump Cutting

For aesthetic reasons, you should avoid taking or dissolving between cameras that have almost exactly the same (matching) shots. The result would be that the scene remains essentially the same, but the picture *jumps* slightly within the frame. On unrehearsed shows, the camera operators may inadvertently come up with almost identical shots; therefore, it is up to the director to watch carefully for this **jump cutting**[2] on the control room monitors.

Position Jumps

Another problem to avoid is the **position jump**—having a primary subject jump from one spot on the screen to another position in the next shot—an apparent loss of continuity. This can occur, for example, if three people are lined up facing two cameras and each camera is getting a two-shot of two adjacent persons. The center person will be on the left of one picture and on the right side of the other camera's picture. (See Figure 12.10.) This position jump can be avoided by having one camera go to a three-shot before cutting or, conversely, by cutting to a close-up single shot.

Axis of Action/Conversation

Another basic principle involves *screen direction.* In successive shots, we want to make certain that all action is flowing in the same direction and that each screen character is facing in one consistent direction. If an imaginary line is drawn extending the path in which a character is moving, we can call this the **axis of action.** As long as all cameras are placed on the same side of this axis, the action will continue to flow in the same direction. If cameras are placed on different sides of this axis of action, however, the apparent screen direction will be reversed when cutting between the cameras. (See Figure 12.11.) Directors, therefore, always try to avoid having cameras **crossing the line.**

Closely related to the axis of action is the **axis of conversation.** If the imaginary axis is drawn through two persons facing each other, all cameras should be kept on the same side of this line. Otherwise the screen direction (the direction in which a person is looking) will be reversed when you cut to the other side of the line. This imaginary line—the axis of conversation—will shift, of course, as performers move. Figure 12.12 shows two common errors in crossing the axis of conversation.

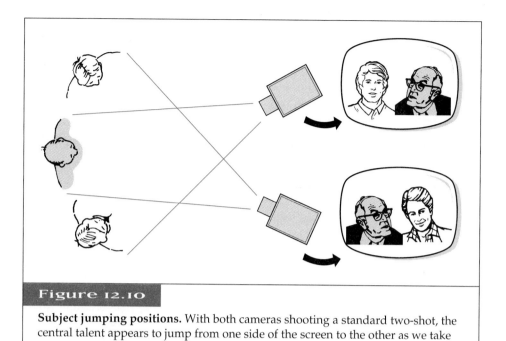

Figure 12.10

Subject jumping positions. With both cameras shooting a standard two-shot, the central talent appears to jump from one side of the screen to the other as we take between shots.

Jump cuts, position jumps, and crossing-the-line problems are all examples of mistakes that are easier to spot in a multicamera production, where the shots can be seen in relation to each other as they are being selected, than they are in the field, where shots cannot be compared. It is much easier for a director to accidentally cross the line when a long shot is recorded in the morning and its accompanying close-up is shot in the afternoon than it is for a studio director who is watching all the monitors.

Transitions

Many of the mechanics of continuity are carried out by the actual **transitions**—the manner in which the director changes from one picture to another. Over the years, these transitions have adopted meaning that audience members readily understand. The director must be aware of the psychological and visually conditioned impact of each—when to use one and when to use another. These transitions can be accomplished in postproduction editing as well as with the switcher during a multicamera studio production.

Cuts

The instantaneous **cut** or straight take replaces one picture immediately with another. It implies that there is *no change in time or locale.* It happens right now. The audience is not moved anywhere, except to a different perspective of the same scene. It is the device that the audience has accepted since the beginning of the motion-picture film for changing a point of view without making any major dramatic change. In terms of grammar, it is the end of a sentence—a period—and the beginning of a new sentence.

Dissolves

The **dissolve,** simultaneously fading out one picture and fading into another picture, creates a temporary overlapping of images. Dramatically, this implies a *change of place* or a *change in time* (usually a lapse of time). It shows a relationship with the previous shot, but there has been a change; the audience has been moved somewhere else or somewhere later in time. Grammatically, the dissolve corresponds to the end of a paragraph or possibly even to the end of a major section of a chapter.

In musical programs, the dissolve is often used purely for aesthetic reasons—a slow dissolve of a singer from a medium to a tight close-up profile, or a close-up of the dancer's feet dissolving to a long shot of the dancer. No change in time or locale is implied in this case—just a pleasant visual effect. In musical

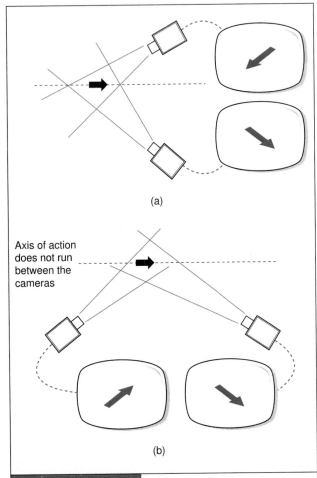

(a)

Axis of action
does not run
between the
cameras

(b)

Figure 12.11

Axis of action. (*a*) *Wrong.* If cameras are placed on both sides of the imaginary axis of action, the screen direction will be reversed when cutting between cameras. (*b*) *Correct.* When both cameras are on the same side of the axis of action, they will both perceive the action moving in the same direction.

productions, the dissolve can be used as an artistic connecting or relating transition, whereas it has the opposite effect in dramas.

Dissolves are slow and therefore have an effect on the *pace* of a program. For example, an effective series of fast camera cuts can lose its intensity if a dissolve is suddenly used. If a director does not want to lose intensity, the dissolve should not be used. If the dissolve stops for a while in the middle, creating a **superimposition,** this serves to intensify whatever is being expressed by the individual images.

Fades

A **fade** from a camera to black or a fade up from black implies a very *strong separation.* It is used in going from one segment of a program to another—from the talk-show interview to the used-car commercial. Dramatically, the fade is the curtain falling—the end of a scene or an act. Grammatically, it would be the visual counterpart of the end of a chapter or story.

Defocus

One specialized transition that can be used with no fancy electronic effects is the **defocus;** the camera on the air defocuses and is dissolved to a similarly defocused shot on another camera, which then comes back into focus. This usually implies either a *deranged state of mind* or a transition *backward in time.* As with other specialized transitions, it tends to call attention to itself and must be used very sparingly.

Wipes

The **wipe**—taking one picture off the face of the screen and replacing it with another—also calls attention to itself. Most of the time, it has no special grammatical significance except to say, "Isn't this a *fancy transition!*" Some wipes, however, have developed grammatical significance. For example, in sports productions, a wipe from the center to the sides indicates an instant replay.

Digital Effects

Digital technology has brought new dimensions to transitions. Graphics programs and digital manipulators allow for an array of bursts, flips, tumbles, and spins. These are used mainly as attention getters and are often employed during opening credits to *grab the audience.* They should be used sparingly during the body of the program because they draw attention to themselves and away from the content of the show.

Timing of the Transition

Understanding the different types of transitions helps to explain the *how* and *why* of changing cameras, but a word needs to be said about the *when.* Generally, camera changes must be adequately motivated; there has to be some reason for cutting at a particular point. The audience should want to see something else.

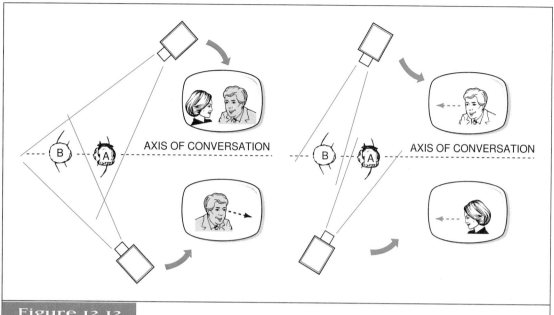

Figure 12.12

Axis of conversation. In the *left* illustration, actor B changes screen direction as we cut from one camera to the other. In the *right* illustration, both actors appear to be looking in the same direction, making it difficult for the viewer to establish the relationship between the two.

("Give the viewers what they need to see when they need to see it.") Without proper motivation, you should avoid the temptation to change the picture just for the sake of change. The following discussion on the timing of camera transitions applies equally to the timing of editing shots together in the postproduction process for a single-camera production.

One of the strongest motivations for cutting is to capture action. When the action starts, you need a wider view. When the talent walks to a new area, you need an establishing shot. When cutting on action, you should always try to cut *just prior to the action*—not too long before it nor immediately after it. Ideally, as soon as the action starts, the audience needs to see the wider shot. Cutting to a movement that is in progress creates a jarring effect similar to a jump cut.

In a similar vein, you usually should not cut to a camera that is in the *middle of movement*—panning, tilting, or zooming. Occasionally, it is acceptable to cut (or preferably dissolve) from one moving camera to another that is moving in the same way. For example, if a camera is panning right, a cut can be made to another camera that is also panning right at the same pace. Cutting to a camera panning left or zooming in or to a stationary camera would be very jarring. But, of course, there are situations where this abrupt effect is desired.

During an interview or panel program, the strongest motivation for cutting is when a speaker *starts to talk.* The ideal timing of the take is precisely between the two speakers—not three seconds after the second speaker has started. As a practical matter, cutting during an ad-lib discussion program will usually involve a delay of one second or so. To counteract this, the director has to be sensitive to the body language and facial expressions of all participants (watching the off-the-air camera monitors). Who has his mouth open? Who just leaned forward? Who just took a deep breath? Anticipate who the next speaker is going to be.

Include appropriate, judiciously spaced **reaction shots** also. How are the listeners reacting? Which listener is especially animated? In timing reaction shots, *do not* cut at the end of an obvious statement or during a break in the speaking; it will look too much like a cut to the wrong participant. Reaction shots are most effective in the middle of a speech.

During musical numbers, time your cuts to fit the music. The cuts should be crisp and clean, following a regular rhythmical pattern—cutting on the beat every four bars or eight bars—as the music dictates.

12.3 The "Psychiatrist" Role

Any video production involves the work of a team of people. You, as the director, are the team captain and must motivate people to do their best work. Sometimes this involves at least listening to problems that have nothing to do with the production at hand—the illness of the camera operator's father, a child care problem that the associate director is having.

Other personal problems that you must deal with are very much related to the production, in that they involve interactions among members of the cast and crew.

Familiarity

Cast and crew members (and college classmates) who work with each other over and over for a continuing series often become like *family*. This has the same advantages and disadvantages as other family situations. They come to know each other well and can anticipate each other's moves. However, like brothers and sisters, they get on each other's nerves and develop rivalries and incompatibilities. You, like a good mother or father, should realize that this will happen occasionally and try to make sure it has positive rather than negative outcomes. A disagreement on microphone placement between the audio person and the lighting director can be healthy, because it can lead to better lighting and better sound. However, if the antipathy between the two grows to the point where the audio person purposely places a boom microphone where he or she knows it will give the lighting director problems, the feud has gone too far.

You must be sensitive to minor problems developing between crew or cast members and nip them before they become major. Usually the best way is to sit the people involved down and have a frank, open discussion between them. Doing nothing and hoping the problem will go away rarely works.

New Relationships

When the people involved with the shoot have not worked with each other before, the director's job can be even more complicated. You must mold these people into a workable whole, taking advantage of the skills and personality traits each brings to the production. Initial rehearsals usually take longer when crew members are strangers, because all of them are trying to find their specific roles. Which of the camera operators should be given the complicated zooming shot? Should the audio operator use his or her own initiative in deciding how slowly to fade in the music or wait for specific instructions from the director? How much background information should the stage manager give the talent?

The best way for you to handle a *new* cast and crew situation is to start the rehearsal session by holding a meeting and talking through the entire program, specifying each person's role at various points. As the rehearsal proceeds, changes and discrepancies will alter these roles, but at least everyone will have had the same starting point; all people will have not only ideas about their specific roles but also a general understandings about the roles of all others.

A variation on a new situation is one in which the crew and some of the performers (e.g., the game-show host, the soap-opera regulars) are the same for each production, but others of the talent are new (e.g., the game-show contestants, an "uncle" visiting a soap-opera regular). These people must be made to feel at home so that they can perform at their best. As the director, you should welcome them and spend a little time orienting them. (See Figure 12.13.)

Directorial Style

Your style as a director can also affect the psychological makeup of interpersonal relationships. Some directors give precise instructions, such as specifying exactly how much **headroom** (the distance between the top of a person's head and the top of the frame) a camera operator should allow or telling an actress precisely when she should wrinkle her nose. Others let cast and crew members make more decisions—the actress works out her own facial expressions and the camera operator frames the shot; the director intervenes only if something is incorrect. Either method

Before production, the director spends a little time talking with two performers who have never been on camera before.

can work: The former assures quality control, but it can antagonize creative people who like to exercise their own judgment; the latter can lead to extra creative input that enhances what the director wants to do, but it can also lead to chaos if various cast and crew members run counter to each other.

Your best bet is to be yourself—but be consistent. If you feel most comfortable letting cast and crew members make many of their own decisions, do so, but don't expect initiative one moment and then clamp down on it the next.

Expectations

A director should be able to assume that the people working on a production have both the *discipline* and *technique* to do the job. If any crew members are not exhibiting one or both of these characteristics, you should have a talk with them, outlining expectations. If this does not work, you should try to remove the person from the crew. However, in union situations (and student situations), this may not be possible. The director must then use psychological persuasion to motivate the person as much as possible.

Most production situations work very well, however. Cast, crew, and director develop a sense of unity and exhilaration wherein the sum of the whole is greater than any of its parts.

12.4 Production Project: The Discussion Program

Now that we've discussed many of the elements that are needed for successful directing, let's take a look at how you, as a beginning director, might handle your first production—a fairly simple discussion show.

Staging

The majority of discussion shows use some variation of either one of two basic staging configurations: an *L-shaped grouping* that places the host on the end facing down a row of other participants (see Figure 12.14); or a *semicircle*, in which the host is generally placed in the center (see Figure 12.15). This conformity of staging is not a lack of originality on the part of the directors but rather their recognition that these seating plans provide an arrangement whereby the guests can best relate to each other and the host. At the same time they provide the director with the best camera angles of the participants.

On these programs, it is best to use four cameras. One of the cameras holds a wide shot of the entire group at all times, and another camera holds a shot of the host for use at any time in the program. The primary assignment of the other two cameras (cameras 1 and 4 in Figure 12.15) is that of providing close-up shots of those persons facing their direction—by crossing their angles. If only three cameras are available, the shoot becomes more difficult. You should always keep a cover shot of the entire group in case someone who is not on one of the other cameras starts to talk. In all probability, the cover shot will have to be alternated from one camera to another as the program progresses.

In a discussion program, the participants relate not only to the audience but also to each other and, as a result, face not to the front but in the direction of the persons to their right and left. Depending upon the role of the host/moderator, the other participants may tend to face in his or her direction during much of the program.

Figure 12.14

Typical setup for an L-shaped staging arrangement for a discussion program.

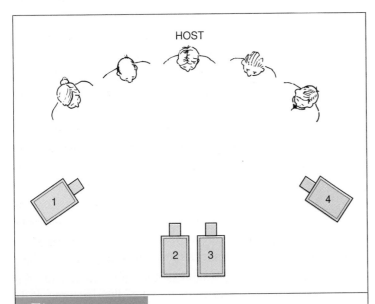

Figure 12.15

Camera pattern for semicircular staging. In this typical "talk show" camera pattern, one center camera (either 2 or 3) remains on a cover shot of the entire group while the other center camera (3 or 2) holds a close-up of the host.

Lighting

On a discussion program, care must be taken to ensure that the face, especially the eyes, is properly lit from all potential camera angles. The locations of the cameras provide a good guide to the location of the main lights in relation to the subjects. The amount of light reflected back from each subject to the camera must be individually balanced to produce an equal intensity. Differences in hair, clothing, and complexion can produce unsuitably dark or light close-up shots. When taken in succession, such shots are noticeably objectionable.

Shot Continuity

Earlier in this chapter, reference was made to *wide, medium,* and *close-up* shots in terms of their respective abilities to communicate collective or particularized program information. Wide *cover* shots are used within a program sequence to reestablish the relationship of program participants to each other and to the elements of the set. It is the *collectivizing* view of all those production values that contributes to the program as a whole.

By contrast, the medium and close-up shots are a *particularized* view of a person or object at a precisely appropriate point in the program sequence. As such, the information conveyed is selective and personal, even to the point of being intimate. The eyes and facial muscles add an important dimension to the total meaning of what a person is expressing in words. This is especially true of actors or other personalities who often speak in public or on television. For this reason, the most effective close-up shots are those in which the camera angle is not more than 45 degrees from a head-on position. (See Figure 12.16.)

Transitions

The most important production value on a discussion program is the precision with which the camera shots follow the spontaneous flow of the conversation. Each time a new person begins to speak, the camera on the air—whether a cover shot or a close-up—should include that person.

Ideally, each change of voice should be accompanied by a change of cameras to a close-up shot or one that predominately features the person talking. On a

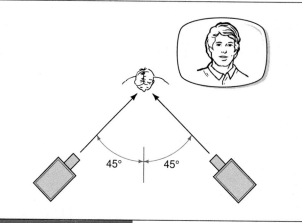

Figure 12.16

Optimum angles for close-ups. Any camera getting a close-up shot should be as perpendicular to the talent as possible. The camera should not be more than 45 degrees from a head-on shot for a good close-up.

three-camera show that features four guests and a moderator, this is not always possible. By carefully watching the panel for clues as to who may be speaking next, the director may somewhat improve the chances of having the shot ready.

Most directors solve the problem by having a cover shot of the entire group available for use at all times. When a close-up shot of a new speaker is not readily available, a take to the cover shot performs several important functions. Primarily, it includes the person who just started talking, and it gives the director a chance to be certain who is speaking before assigning a camera to the shot. In a fast-paced discussion, this alternative is the only way the director can stay with the quickly changing flow of conversation. Once the cover shot has been taken, the close-up need not be used immediately. The director can let the wide shot reestablish the collective aspect of the group while waiting for the end of a sentence as a convenient point to cut to the close-up.

During a discussion program, the situation often calls for shots other than a close-up of one participant in the total group. Shots including two or three persons not only add pictorial variety but also are quite useful when several people begin a rapid interchange of short statements or questions and answers. Smaller group shots have an added dimension—showing the silent, but often revealing, expression on the faces of persons other than the speaker. A brief close-up shot of someone moving his or her head in agreement or disagreement—a reaction shot—is especially useful when one person has been speaking for an extended period of time.

On the other hand, the director must be alert to group shots in which those persons who are not talking are looking away from the speaker. Whether or not intended, the visual effect is one of boredom and, as such, has a negative impact on the program as a whole.

Camera Blocking

The range of shots available to each camera in a program situation depends on the two interrelated variables of camera and subject position. On a discussion program, where the staging options are somewhat limited, the director generally uses the seating arrangement as a starting point in the camera blocking process. Primary camera positions can then be selected on the basis of the best angles for the close-up shots and the important requirement of wide-angle cover shots.

The direction of conversational flow may vary at different times during a program. For this reason, directors usually develop several shooting plans to cover all contingencies. Figure 12.17 shows two such plans that could be used in the coverage of an L-shaped arrangement. Plan A is designed to provide maximum close-up coverage of the three panel members, with the moderator being seen only on the wide shot on camera 1. Plan B is set up for situations in which the moderator takes a very active role in the program, and as a result, needs a close-up shot ready at all times.

Plan A has obvious limitations, but it has a basic utility in predictable situations, such as a period in the program during which the host is bringing out individual responses from each participant. The beginning and ending of discussion programs usually assume this structure.

A director would probably quickly shift over to Plan B during the more active phases of the conversation. By holding camera 3 on a cover shot, camera 1 is able to get a close-up shot of the moderator. Camera 1 also has the option of getting close-up shots of those

who turn camera left for a two-person conversation. In this situation, camera 2 then has the option of a close-up of the other person or a two-shot of both speakers. The reverse structure is also possible with camera 1 on the two-shot and camera 2 on the single of the person facing camera right.

Even taken together, these two shooting plans by no means exhaust the possibilities available within an L-shaped seating configuration. The use of camera 2 as a cover camera from either a left-side or right-side studio position opens up another series of coverage patterns. The suggestion of cameras 1 or 3 for cover shots stems from the fact that their angle to the set allows for a more interesting grouping of all participants in the frame. Each person's face occupies a larger proportion of the frame than in a wide shot from the center—which also results in empty space at the top and bottom of the frame.

In the press of a fast-moving program, the director is often tempted to give up the cover shot and use that camera temporarily for smaller group shots and close-ups. It is an option that even the most experienced directors use with considerable care. Invariably, when all cameras are committed to the three people who are dominating the conversation, the fourth (off-camera) voice suddenly starts speaking.

Calling Shots

In a discussion program, it is essential that preparatory commands always be used in conjunction with the commands of execution. An inexperienced director might be tempted to think that a needed shot can be put on the air instantaneously if only the command of execution is given. To do so, however, is to increase appreciably the possibilities for error. The spontaneous nature of talk programs makes the command of preparation doubly important. The technical director needs this lead time to be certain that the right shot is readied. Of equal importance is the possibility that the camera operators need this time for final adjustment of the framing or as a warning to hold a shot they might otherwise be in the process of changing.

A good procedure for the director on a fast-moving talk show is to give a "ready" for a probable next shot as soon as possible after the previous shot is

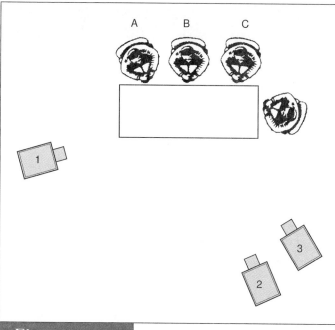

Figure 12.17

Camera patterns for L-shaped staging. Plan A: Camera 1 remains on a wide-angle cover shot. Camera 2 gets close-ups of panelists as they face camera right and two-shots or three-shots of panelists. Camera 3 gets singles of panelists as they face camera right and over-the-shoulder shots (with host in foreground). Plan B: Camera 1 gets close-ups of moderator/host, two-shots of host and panelist C, and singles and two-shots as panelists turn to camera left. Camera 2 gets close-ups of panelists as they face camera right and two-shots or three-shots of panelists. Camera 3 remains on a wide-angle cover shot.

on the line. This does not remove any option for a subsequent change in the upcoming shot; it simply aids the director in staying ahead of the action. An example of how the director can inform the crew of several probable courses of action would be as follows.

> "Ready camera 3 . . . take 3" (cover shot).
> "Ready camera 2 on a close-up of guest C
> . . . camera 1, hold the moderator close-up,
> but be ready to move over to guest B."

In this situation, guest C has just interrupted the moderator. The director can afford to wait on the cover shot to see whether guest C will continue talking or whether the moderator will start talking again. At the same time, the director has noticed that guest B is also trying to break into the conversation.

Now that you have begun to appreciate some of the basics of directing a discussion show, you and your classmates should be able to undertake such a program. The discussion format can be used for a repeated number of production exercises within the class. A minimum running time of five minutes for each exercise is suggested so that each director has an opportunity to become familiar with the pattern of the conversational flow and the related continuity of camera shots. A realistic element can be added by having the AD and the stage manager feed the moderator countdown cues for time remaining in the exercise. Directors should be prepared for the fact that the transition from the body of a program to the closing segment can be difficult unless cues and other instructions are given well in advance.

Discussion Questions

1. As a director, what jobs would you be most likely to give your AD?

2. Give some specific examples of when you might use a defocus effect. A wipe. A fade. A digital spin.

3. As a director, do you think you would lean toward giving precise instructions or toward letting the cast and crew members make many of their own decisions? Based on your answer, what might you have to watch for as danger signs that your directing was becoming ineffective?

4. If you were directing a discussion program, would you prefer to use the staging setup shown in Figure 12.7 or the one shown in Figure 12.8?

Footnotes

1. Several books that contain good advice for directors are: Ivan Cury, *Directing and Producing for Television* (Woburn, Mass.: Focal Press, 1998); Alan A. Armer, *Directing Television and Film,* 2nd ed. (Belmont, Cal.: Wadsworth, 1990); Steven D. Katz, *Film Directing Cinematic Motion* (Los Angeles: Lone Eagle Publishing Company, 1992); and Ron Richards, *Director's Method for Film and Television* (Stoneham, Mass: Focal Press, 1992).

2. When the term jump cutting is used in field production, it may mean something slightly different. The picture still jumps on the screen, but it is because something has been cut out. For example, if the mayor is talking at a press conference and the reporter edits out part of the speech, the mayor's head may appear to jump at the point of the edit.

chapter 13

Field Production

Most of what we have discussed in previous chapters has dealt with *live* or *live-on-tape multicamera* productions shot in a studio environment. However, many productions are shot totally or partially in out-of-studio locations with one camera. This technique is often called **film-style shooting,** because most motion pictures are shot with one camera that takes shots one by one from all the various angles employed in multiple-camera shoots. It is also referred to as **field production,** because it takes place in the field rather than in a studio.

There are numerous similarities between studio production and field production, mainly because much of the same equipment is used. A microphone is a microphone whether it is on a game-show set or at the scene of a fire. Pictures should be focused and well composed, and talent should maintain eye contact, whether in the studio or in the field. And yet, there are many differences in both techniques and disciplines that are caused, to some degree, by the lack of control that exists outside of the studio.

This chapter will concentrate on single-camera field production, looking at the similarities and differences between it and studio production. It is organized in a manner that is similar to the rest of the book,[1] and in doing so covers:

- Reasons for a greater need for discipline in the field (13.1).
- Different cast and crew members needed in the field as well as varying tasks that are undertaken on location (13.2).
- Handling audio problems in the field (13.3).
- Lighting for both indoor and outdoor locations (13.4).
- How cameras are used in the field (13.5).
- Functions of the recording part of the camcorder (13.6).

- The greater role editing plays in single-camera shooting (13.7).
- The lesser role that graphics and sets play in many remote shoots (13.8).
- The organizational duties a producer must perform in order to ensure a smooth production (13.9).
- How to direct on location (13.10).

13.1 Introduction

Single-camera field equipment is younger than multi-camera studio production equipment, mainly because the original TV equipment was so bulky it could not be handled in the single-camera configuration. However, with the introduction of the ¾-inch U-matic format in the early 1970s, cameras and recorders ventured out of the studio, first to cover news and then to produce other forms of programming.

Field equipment, like studio equipment, changes rapidly. With each year, cameras, microphones, and lights become smaller, lighter, and "smarter" in that they are capable of allowing their users to increase creativity and flexibility. Nonlinear editing has brought new stature to film-style shooting and has greatly increased its flexibility.

Field production, like its studio-based sister, requires both *technique* and *discipline*. It involves the development of a professional attitude and a knowledge of equipment and aesthetics. (See Chapter 1.)

Techniques

One of the reasons techniques are so important is that miles away from "home base," you cannot turn to the instructor or technician when you have a problem such as no picture in the viewfinder. This means that all crew members must know how to operate the equipment well. You and other crew members must also be well grounded in aesthetics, because you cannot see the finished product as you are taping the individual shots. You must be able to visualize how the shots will cut together.

Discipline

In some ways, field production requires more discipline than studio work because, once away from the studio, you cannot easily return for a forgotten item. You must plan very thoroughly for all eventualities. Teamwork, combined with a cooperative spirit, is a *must*. People are usually together for longer periods of time in the field than they are in the studio, especially if they commute back and forth together or stay in one location for several days. The tendency to "get on each other's nerves" must be overcome.

13.2 Cast and Crew

One of the reasons that discipline is so important is that crews are usually smaller for field productions, so it is hard to cover for anyone who is undependable.

Crew Size

One reason crews are smaller is that much less gear is involved. Only one camera is used to shoot, eliminating the need for all but one **camera operator.** With a **camcorder** configuration, this person doubles as the **video operator.** No one is needed to operate a **switcher;** the camera picture goes directly to the VTR because there is no need to cut between two or more cameras. TelePrompTers, because they are bulky, are not normally taken to shoots, eliminating the need for a TelePrompTer operator. Graphics are generally added during postproduction, not during shooting.

Because there is no control room, the director is on the location set in the midst of all the action, thus eliminating the need for a **stage manager.** Because timing is usually not crucial for scenes that are later going to be edited, an **associate director** can also be superfluous at a field shoot. However, there is often a person called a **script supervisor**[2] who keeps notes and watches for **continuity** problems so that what is shot can be effectively edited.

Some crews, especially for news, are as small as two people—one to operate the camcorder and another to hold the mic and interview talent, thus serving as producer-director-talent-script supervisor-audio operator. In fact, some "crews" are now only one person—the camcorder has a large viewfinder that pivots so that the operator can see the image while interviewing someone in front of the camera. Other shoots have larger crews that include a pro-

(a)

(b)

Figure 13.1

Crew configurations differ depending on the taping situation. For the first taping (*a*) only two crew members were needed because the footage was being shot silent to go with music during the opening credits. The director told the children what to do and the camera operator taped the material. For the second taping (*b*), which was much more complicated, five people attended—the producer, who was coordinating with the people running the children's art workshop; the director; the audio operator; the camera operator; and a combination lighting person and script supervisor.

ducer, a director, an audio operator, a camera-video operator, a lighting director, a script supervisor, and a production assistant or two to handle any other miscellaneous duties. (See Figure 13.1.)

As with most task-oriented working groups, an efficient operation must have a clearly established plan for areas of responsibility and authority. Whatever the size of the crew, each individual member of the shoot should have a *clear idea* of his or her responsibilities—but with the understanding that flexible working arrangements may find each one helping out with other jobs.

Cleanup

One of the absolute essentials that all crew members on a field shoot must handle carefully is *cleanup.* If a crew member carelessly leaves a mic cable on the floor of the studio, someone else will probably find it later and put it away. But if a mic cable is left in the middle of a park, it will quickly disappear. Everything must be conscientiously disassembled, coiled, stowed away, and neatly packed—in part as a courtesy to the next people who use the equipment and in part because such care adds to the life of the equipment. Cleanup requires discipline. It is not glamorous work, but it must be done.

Cast Considerations

Most of what applies to talent in a studio production is also true for a location shoot (see Chapter 2). Sincerity and proper projection are important to any television performer. Constantly scratching your ear will be as distracting in front of the local courthouse as it will be in front of a studio talk-show set. However, in many ways, performing at a field site is more difficult than being on camera in a studio. For starters, there probably will be no TelePrompTer, which means you must handle your own notes or script and know your lines and material well. Because there also are fewer crew members, there are fewer people to help out with talent requests.

Nonsequential Shooting

One of the hardest parts of film-style shooting, though, is that scenes are shot out of order. This can create continuity problems and difficulties for performers.

Sometimes it is necessary for an actor to *switch emotions* on and off for the convenience of a shooting schedule. Often two scenes will be shot back to back because they are at the same location, but the emotional content of two shots may be diametrically

Figure 13.2

Reporters and interviewers often have to tape reaction shots after the interviewed guest has departed. (*Left*) During the interview, the single camera would have been behind the male interviewer, focusing on the female guest answering questions. (*Right*) After the guest has departed, the camera should be repositioned to shoot the interviewer repeating the same questions for later editing.

opposed. You might be called upon to portray the emotion felt about the tragic death of a friend two days before the death of the friend has been acted out.

Even within one scene, lines are sometimes shot out of order. When actors' close-ups are shot, they deliver their lines often without benefit of cues and other lines in the rest of the scene. Frequently, the characters they are supposedly talking to are not even on the set. They may find themselves professing mad passionate love—to a camera.

Because innumerable shots are taken of one scene, you must perform the same in each take so that the material can be edited together. This means you must follow **blocking** very precisely. You cannot walk beside the sofa in the long shot and behind it in the close-up, because doing so would cause a continuity problem. Of course, there are many professional actors who have learned to perform well nonsequentially. But crew members must let them have their "space" so that they can build up to the required emotions.

Taping out of order is a problem for talent in non-dramatic shoots also. Because the camera is on the guest during an interview, the interviewer's face will not be seen. This means that after the interview has been completed, reverse-angle shots must be taped of the interviewer asking the questions over again. This is often very difficult if you are the interviewer. You

must sit there and earnestly ask questions of a camera lens—because the person being interviewed has already departed. (See Figure 13.2.)

This brings up a related *ethical* problem that reporters, in particular, must face. How much can the wording of the questions change between what was asked during the actual interview and what is asked on the reverse-angle shots taped later? The answer should be, "Not much." If the question is changed significantly, the guest's answer may take on an entirely different meaning. Networks and stations have policies regarding the need to keep the questions the same. Because of this, a continuity person should listen to the original interview and jot down the exact wording of the questions that are asked. Of course, the interviewer can also replay the camera footage so that he or she can phrase the reverse-angle questions the same as the original questions.

Sometimes even more difficult than asking questions after the fact is the need to react after the fact. In almost all single-camera interviews, shots of the interviewer listening and reacting need to be recorded—usually after the guest has departed—so that they can be edited into the interview to prevent **jump cuts.** This requires the interviewer/reporter to just sit there looking at an empty chair and smiling or frowning every once in a while; this is a difficult acting job, es-

Figure 13.3

The audio operator is positioning the boom so that it will pick up sound as well as possible without getting in the shot. *Photo courtesy of Amy Phillips.*

pecially for novices. People tend to break up into laughter or to exaggerate movements such as nods of the head.

13.3 Audio

As with other technical components, many of the elements of field production audio are the same as those for studio audio; any differences are caused primarily by the uncontrollable elements of the outside world. As a starting point, ask the same questions concerning frequency, pickup pattern, impedance, and usage categories for both studio and field productions (see Chapter 3).

Microphones

Sometimes the answers are different, however. Generally, microphones need to be more directional for field locations because of all the extraneous noise. By the same token, mics that are less sensitive (and therefore need to be located closer to the talent) are de-sired, because they will pick up less of the background noise.

Also, because of the transportation jolts and rough handling that field equipment is subjected to, mics for location shoots usually are of a more rugged design—**dynamic** rather than **condenser.** *Quality* and *frequency response* often have to be sacrificed for *dependability* and *ruggedness.*

Fishpoles and **hand mics** tend to be used most frequently in the field. Fishpoles (see Figure 13.3) are common for dramas, where the mic should not be seen in the picture. Hand mics are common in interview situations, where the presence of the mic is accepted. Another type of mic, the **shotgun,** is used in situations where the subject being taped is far from the camera and cannot be miked easily (a lion in the jungle or a man on a horse). Shotgun mics are highly directional and can pick up sound from long distances. However, because of the high directionality, they must be pointed at the subject accurately so that they pick up the desired sound. Wireless mics come in very handy when subjects need to move around a great deal.

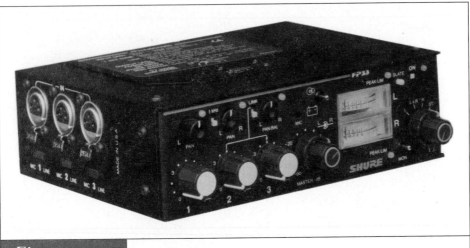

A portable audio board can help enhance the audio of a field production.   *Photo courtesy of Shure.*

At times you may want to attach the microphone to the camera to eliminate the need for someone holding it. This is usually *not* a good idea if you are recording speech, since the camera is located at some distance from the person talking and is likely to pick up noises close to the camera much more efficiently than it picks up the talent. As a rule, microphones in the field should always be as close as possible to the people talking—closer than in studio production—because of all the background and extraneous noise. A camera mic is acceptable if you are picking up crowd noises or other nonspecific sounds.

Control Equipment

The sophisticated control-room equipment that produces clean, well-balanced sound is not available at a remote site. There are no patch bays, equalizers, or separate audio recorders. The camcorder often has only a "ballpark" meter and some headphones. Audio on a location shoot is only *transduced* and *recorded*—and usually *monitored*. Channeling, mixing, amplifying, and shaping (Chapter 3) are all accomplished in postproduction, and yet great care must be taken to keep recording levels within a consistent range so that they can be matched when edited. Any differences in the levels of sounds will become very obvious when different shots are assembled in the editing process.

One way to assure consistent levels is to use the **automatic gain control (AGC)** available on most tape recorders. This automatically raises the volume of sounds that are soft and lowers the volume of loud sounds. AGC is *not* always the solution to keeping audio levels within a consistent range, however. This is because AGC can be the cause of another serious sound problem encountered with outdoor audio. The AGC cannot distinguish between desired and undesired sound; it boosts anything that is low. Therefore, when no one is speaking, the level of the background noise is automatically amplified, producing a hissing or roaring effect Because there is a built-in delay factor of one second or so, the effect is most noticeable at the beginning of segments or during long pauses. Attempts to erase this unwanted sound involve the risk of upcutting program audio.

Audio **balance** is particularly difficult if two people are talking and one has a very soft voice while the other has a booming voice. AGC cannot completely compensate. Sometimes the better solution is to record each person through his or her individual mic onto a separate track, then try to match the volumes in postproduction.

To control a large number of different audio sources that need to be recorded at the same time, you will need to take a portable audio mixer on location with you. (See Figure 13.4.) You can then feed several mics through the board, set their levels individually, and record this mix-down on the videotape. However, setting up such an audio board takes additional space and time, both of which are often unavailable on a field shoot. Also, if the shoot is taking place in a small area, you must be careful to listen for phase problems caused by placing the mics too close together.

Wildtrack

Audio operators on location should always make sure they record some separate **wildtrack** sound—background sound from the location recorded with no specific voices. Sometimes this is for a specific purpose. For example, a narrator may be standing next to a machine that is important to the story line, but the machine has a distinctive sound. In the final edited program, shots that include the machine are to have a voice-over narration, which is to be recorded later in the studio. If the director wants to have the sound of the machine as a part of the background under the narration, then a wildtrack of that sound must be recorded for a later audio mix.

At other times the wildtrack sound is just general background noise that can be used to cover abrupt transitions during postproduction editing. Good sound operators make a practice of recording numerous pieces of wildtrack sound as protection against unforeseen editing problems.

Extraneous Noise

The audio operator must also listen carefully to the sound that is occurring and being recorded while a take is being shot. The human brain *subconsciously* filters out unwanted sound. The noise of an airplane flying overhead often goes unnoticed by two people engaged in conversation; they effectively hear only each other. But this **selective attention principle** does not work with videotaped presentation. An unnoticed airplane recorded on an audio track will come through loud and clear on playback. For that reason, the audio person must listen intently and stop production if an unwanted noise is too evident.

In many ways, a person operating audio on a field shoot must have a disciplined "feel" for audio. He or she must have enough experience to know how something will sound in the final edited program.

Figure 13.5

This Lowel portable lighting kit contains the lights and supporting equipment needed for effective field production. *Photo courtesy of Lowel-Light.*

13.4 Lighting

The basic **three-point lighting** approach is appropriate for field shoots as well as in the studio. Likewise, **contrast ratio, color temperature,** and other principles of lighting (see Chapter 4) apply, at least in theory, to location work. Once again, problems occur when dealing with uncontrolled situations. In this case, the problems associated with lighting indoors are quite different from those found outside.

Indoor Location Lighting

Since lighting grids are far from common in university classrooms, corporate offices, hospitals, and other locations, the crew must bring portable lighting apparatus to the field shoot. *Portable lights* (see Figure 13.5) are usually mounted on stands that can then be placed in positions roughly approximating those of the basic **key, fill,** and **back lights.**

Often this is difficult or impossible to accomplish because of lack of space or because the light stands will show in the camera's picture. The backlight is particularly tricky, because it is essentially impossible to position it correctly without having the stand visible in a long shot. Occasionally, clip-on **internal reflectors** can be clamped onto a door or tall piece of furniture to serve as a backlight. However, many field productions are shot with only key and fill lights.

In fact, many news shoots use only one light; it is mounted on the camera and is used only for basic illumination. The result is a very flat, nonaesthetic, washed-out effect that is, nevertheless, better than shooting a silhouette.

The lighting instruments taken on a field shoot are usually limited, too. **Scoops, ellipsoidal** spots, and even **Fresnels** are too bulky to lug along. The main portable lights used are **broads** (see Chapter 4), but their beams are somewhat difficult to control.

Lighting Control

Lack of a dimmer board adds to the control problems. To increase or decrease the intensity of a light, the stand must be moved in accordance with the principles of the **inverse square law** (see Chapter 4). However, space limitations may hinder this. Space and time limitations also hinder the use of scrims, barn doors, flags, and other devices that could help diffuse or shape the light.

Power

Another big problem is securing adequate electrical power. A studio is specially wired in anticipation of the power that will be needed to meet extensive lighting demands. People's homes and offices are not. Lighting properly with key, fill, and back lights all plugged into one circuit is almost guaranteed to blow the circuit breaker.

For this reason, it is particularly important to learn ahead of time where the circuit breakers are, how many amps each circuit is rated for, and which outlets are on which circuit. You should also become familiar with the basic formula *watts = volts × amps*. (This is often referred to as the "West Virginia" formula, $W = VA$.) The watts will be written somewhere on the lamp of your lighting instrument—usually 500,

1,000, or 2,000 watts. Amperes should be indicated on the circuit breaker—usually 10, 15, or 20 amps. Voltage is regulated by the power company and in most ordinary circumstances is 110 volts. (In industrial settings, it may be 220 volts.) Therefore, if the circuit breaker is rated for 10 amps and the voltage is 110, you can plug in lights totaling 1,100 watts on that circuit. To be on the safe side, use a figure of 100 for the voltage (this also makes the arithmetic easier). So a 20-amp circuit could handle 2,000 watts.

However, you cannot assume your lights can use the whole circuit. You must take into account the total wattage of all appliances and devices on the circuit. The office copier or the home refrigerator may be using the same circuit that you want to plug into. One group of students were taping at a factory; they had been recording without problems for an hour or so when suddenly the lights went out. Lunchtime had arrived and the employees began using the company microwave oven that was on the same circuit as the lights.

Usually you must plug lights into at least two separate circuits, and generally this means using plugs in two different areas. In many homes and offices, outlets in one room are all on the same circuit, and you may have to go several rooms down the hall to use a different circuit. This means you must take along extension cords.

Safety

The use of extension cords raises another issue—the problem of safety. First of all, make sure that the extension cords you plan on using are rated for the electrical load you expect to plug into them. Using cords that are not heavy-duty will result in tripping the circuit breaker—or worse yet, overheating and starting a fire.

Also, electrical cable strung all over the floor is likely to cause people to trip, often unplugging the light and/or bringing down the light stand (as well as causing bodily injury). Where cords must be laid along the floor, cover them with a wide tape to help ensure that they will not be tripped over. Ideally, you should run the cords along the walls and up over doorjambs. (See Figure 13.6.) For these taping purposes, you must bring along heavy-duty tape—

Figure 13.6

Crew member taping a power cord above a doorway to ensure that no one will trip over it during the recording.

preferably something like *duct tape* that is a very strong adhesive. Where cords must be taped to painted surfaces, it is best to use *masking tape* that will not peel off paint when it is removed.

Lights also create a safety problem because of their heat. They should not be placed where someone is likely to bump into them accidentally. Also, they should not be placed where they are touching curtains or paper and could thereby start a fire. At the end of a shoot, they should be turned off *first* and packed away *last*. This gives them time to cool before crew members must handle them.

Available Light

One other problem associated with shooting indoors comes from available light. If at all possible, you should turn off all regular lights and just use the **quartz** or **HSF** lights from your portable lighting kit. However, sometimes available lights can be used for general illumination if they are of a color temperature close to 3,200 degrees **Kelvin** (see Chapter 4). Regular incandescent lightbulbs can usually be used, but office or home fluorescents should definitely be turned off. Not only may they result in a recording with a definite blue tint, they may also create a hum or buzz on the sound track.

Outdoor light coming through windows should also be avoided, if at all possible, because it is about 5,500 degrees K—far bluer than the 3,200-degree K quartz lights. The problem is not with the outdoor light itself but with the fact that you are *mixing* types of light—daylight and quartz. If you set the camera's filter for quartz light and some of your light source is from daylight, your footage will look blue. If you set the filter for daylight, the footage will be orange, because you are using some quartz light. **Gels** are made to place on windows to change the color temperature of the outdoor light, but they are expensive and difficult to install. A simpler solution is to avoid mixing the types of light.

Outdoor Location Lighting

If you are shooting outside, your main source of light is the *sun*. This has both advantages and disadvantages. You do not need to worry about light stands or power requirements. However, you have no control over the sun. It changes position; it can be overly intense; it darts behind passing clouds. Its color temperature changes as the day progresses so that scenes shot at noon will not match scenes shot at 5:00 P.M. Not only will these scenes have a color switch, but they are also likely to show different lengths of shadows, different molding of facial features, and different amounts of glare. This is a particular problem if long shots are taped at noon while close-ups, which are to be intercut, are not shot until 5:00 P.M.

Figure 13.8

As an example of a technique used in portable lighting, these four 12,000-watt HMI instruments were focused through a scrim to produce a soft, flat illumination for an interior scene.

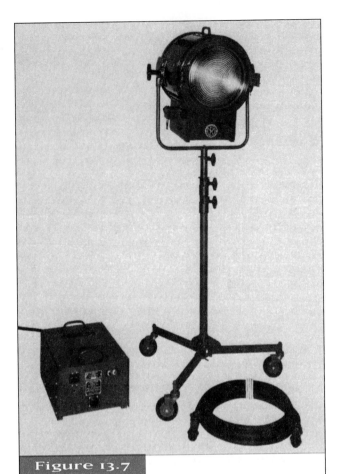

Figure 13.7

Fresnel Mole Solarspot. This 2,500-watt HMI (hydrogen medium-arc-length iodine) light is used in field production where it is necessary to match the color temperature of sunlight. The control unit known as a *ballast* protects the lamp from sudden surges of power and provides for longer bulb life. *Photo courtesy of Mole Richardson.*

Second Light Sources

Sometimes the sun is so bright that you need *extra* lights. This seeming contradiction is caused by the fact that a bright sun can wash out facial features. It acts, in essence, like a very bright key light. To counteract this, you can add artificial lights to create the effect of a fill. Of course, these lights have to be the same color temperature as daylight.

One way to do this is to cover the quartz lights used indoors with special filter gels that convert the 3,200-degree K light to 5,500-plus degrees K. However, the filters cut down on the efficiency of the light, so more lights than normal are needed. Another way is to use **HMI** (hydrogen medium-arc-length iodine) lights

that are made to produce 5,500-degree K light. (See Figure 13.7.) These lights have a separate **ballast** that protects the lamp from power surges. To minimize problems from the sun passing behind clouds and changing color temperature as the day wears on, you can actually use large HMI floods to create an artificial source of sunlight (see Figure 13.8), even for interior scenes.

If auxiliary lights are needed, getting power to them can be a problem. Powerful battery-operated lights do exist, but they are not commonly or inexpensively available. A more feasible alternative for obtaining a second light from a different direction is to use a reflector. A commercially available *foil reflector* (see Figure 13.9) can be used to bounce sunlight onto a subject's face from almost any direction. And if the sun is behind the subject (functioning as a backlight), you can place the reflector in front of the subject to provide a satisfactory key light. Even if a professional reflector is not available, you can use any large piece of white material (a white poster board, for example) in an emergency to provide some fill light from a complementary direction. Obviously, the more highly polished or reflective the surface of the reflector is, the more efficient it will be. (See Figure 13.10.)

Figure 13.9

Foil reflector. The two-sided reflector is an invaluable part of outdoor location shooting. The partitioned foil-leaf side (shown) produces a soft diffused light. A smooth silver paper surface on the other side produces a brighter, more intense light. *Photo courtesy of Mole Richardson.*

Lighting Individual Shots

Overall, lighting can be one of the biggest headaches of field production. However, there is one very distinct advantage that location lighting has over live-on-tape lighting—location lighting allows each shot to be lit individually. When a studio program is shot with three cameras simultaneously, lighting must be general enough that it will provide acceptable illumination for any camera shot. Often in multiple-camera shooting, compromises have to be made in setting the lights, and few shots are really properly lit. With location shooting, however, the camera is stopped after each shot, and the lights can be reset to light the next shot optimally.

13.5 Cameras

Most of the aesthetic principles of picture composition apply in the field as well as in the studio. So do the general principles dealing with f-stops, depth of field, lens ratio, focusing, and filters. (See Chapter 5.) However, in a studio, once cameras are set, the characteristics under which they shoot remain fairly constant. White balance set at the beginning of a studio program, for instance, can be depended upon to give accurate color throughout a taping. Such is not the case with field production.

White Balancing

White balance must be reset frequently as lighting conditions change, because the white balance control adjusts the strength of the basic video level to suit the composition of the light that is available for an individual shot. It "reads" a designated item as *white* and then readjusts the electronics associated with the other colors so that they will render true color.

As the sun peeks in and out of clouds, the light source changes, and you need to readjust the white balance. The changes in the sun's color temperature over the course of a day also require changing white balance. Going from outdoors to indoors definitely requires repeating the white balance procedure. Fortunately, white balancing is easy—just the push of a button on most cameras. In fact, some cameras automatically white-balance as changes in color temperature occur. If the camera you are using does not automatically redo white balancing, however, your main white-balancing problem may simply be remembering to do it. Also, you must remember to bring something white to the shoot to be used for **reference white**—a piece of paper, a white sweater.

Filters

A related item very easy to forget in the process of field shooting is the changing of the camera **filter.** Many cameras have four filters—for instance, one for indoor 3,200 degree K light (which also works for outdoor sunrise and sunset), one for sunny daylight, one for cloudy outdoor shooting, and one that acts as a lens cap. When you move from outdoors to indoors,

Figure 13.10

In this setup, reflectors are being used to bounce the sunlight onto the two actors sitting on the sand, providing both fill and backlight.

or vice versa, you must change the filter, or your footage will have a decided orange or blue cast. The outdoor filters are orange to compensate for the fact that quartz light is "orangish" and daylight is "bluish." The main difference between the *sunny daylight* and *cloudy outdoor* filters is the amount of **neutral density** in the filter. Neutral density lessens the intensity of the light by making the filter darker; therefore, the *sunny* filter has more neutral density than the *cloudy* filter.

Gain

Many portable cameras have dB **(decibel)** gain switches to use in instances of low light. This boosts the electronics so that the camera "sees" better in the dark. However, using this switch makes the picture grainier and also shifts the color somewhat. It should be used only when it is absolutely impossible to add light—generally in the covering of a news story.

Power

Another problem in the field is the power source for the camera. Most cameras can be operated either on regular *AC* (household alternating current) or on *bat-*

teries. AC is more reliable, but cameras do add wattage to electrical circuits that may already be taxed from your portable lights.

Batteries have a disadvantage in that they do run out of charge—usually when you are in the middle of shooting your most important scene. If you use batteries, make sure the battery is fully charged before you are scheduled to take the camera on location. While in the field, make sure you are not unintentionally discharging the battery when you are not shooting. By all means, disconnect the battery while you transport equipment from one location to another. Some cameras have a *standby* position that keeps the electronics operational but cuts down on battery use. This should be used while shots are being set up and rehearsed. Cameras differ as to how they conserve on battery power, so be sure to find out when the battery is and is not engaged on your particular camera.

Camera Mounts and Movement

Keeping a picture steady on a portable camera can be a problem. You usually do not have the luxury of the sturdy **pedestals** and **cranes** available in a studio. What you are more likely to have is a three-legged **tripod** and/or a strong shoulder. Whenever possible, use the tripod; it is steadier than the strongest of shoulders. Many student shots have been ruined because the camera operator did not want to take the time to put the camera on the tripod—thus fulfilling the axiom, "There's never time to do it right, but there's always time to do it over."

Pans, tilts, and zooms can all be executed very effectively on a tripod mount. However, assuming you do not have the benefit of a field crane, movements such as trucks and dollies do require the human body to simulate wheeled movement. Improvised dollies and trucks can sometimes be achieved with wheeled conveyances such as a child's wagon or a grocery cart.

Achieving smooth movement can be difficult, especially in a crowd. Shakiness in news footage is accepted by the audience, because the camera is being used *subjectively*. It is the audience eye, showing people what they would see were they there—including the bumping and jostling. But even so, camera operators should try to keep the picture as steady as possible at all times.

Camera operators and directors must also be willing to reposition the camera frequently for both aesthetic and informational purposes. This requires effort and muscle on the part of the person operating the camera, but it is needed for everything from reaction shots of the reporter reasking questions to low-angle shots to convey a sense of power.

Camera Care and Maintenance

Care of the camera must also be a high-priority item for the camera operator. The high level of activity and unanticipated problems on any location production occasionally mean that some of the usual equipment precautions may be temporarily forgotten. Cameras are very vulnerable to the careless treatment they may be given on a field shoot. The lens should be capped between scenes and whenever the camera is moved because stray objects such as pebbles can accidentally strike a camera.

Many types of professional location productions pose enormous engineering challenges for the opti-

mum functioning and protection of cameras and other equipment. Special housings and mountings have to be used for many adverse situations: dust protection in arid country; heaters for arctic conditions; gyroscopic mountings for helicopter shots; and underwater housings for perhaps the most adverse environment of all. (See Figure 13.11.)

In all probability, you will not be shooting in any of these extreme conditions for class projects, but if you are operating the camera, you should realize that you are in charge of an expensive piece of rather delicate equipment that must remain operational for many future projects.

13.6 Video Recording

Most modern-day field production is undertaken with camcorders, such as Betacam, S-VHS, Hi8, or DVCPRO. (See Figure 13.12.) Therefore, the camera and recorder are the same piece of equipment, and the camera operator also becomes the videotape recorder operator. A button that is easily accessible when someone is holding the camcorder turns the recorder on and off.

Setup and Connections

In a studio setting, all the video equipment is more or less permanently connected. Such is not the case in the field. It is up to crew members to know how to attach all equipment. Although a camcorder may have a microphone attached to it, audio should be routed separately from an external mic whenever possible because, as discussed previously, the microphone should be as close as possible to the talent. The VTR input for a microphone may be an *XLR* connector, a *phone* plug, an *RCA* plug, or a *miniplug*. (See Chapter 7.) Make sure you check before you leave the studio/control room to confirm that the connector on the end of the microphone cable is the same as that required by the VTR. If it is not, get an **adapter** plug that will convert from one type of connector to the other. You will also want to connect headsets into the earphone output on the camcorder, usually with a miniplug.

Monitors are sometimes attached to VTR outputs so that the director can see what the camera operator

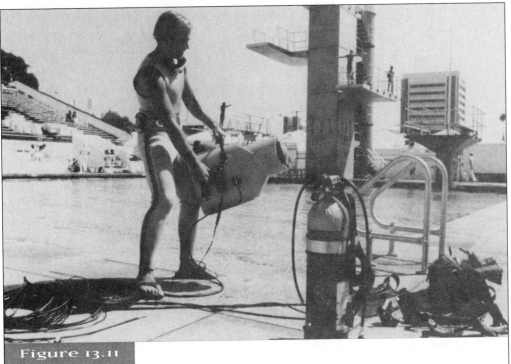

Figure 13.11

Underwater camera housing. Special equipment for underwater television coverage, such as this housing for Olympic diving events, represents an extreme in protection against environmental elements. *Photo courtesy of ABC Sports.*

is framing. The usual connectors for this are the *BNC* or *RCA,* and again you should make sure the proper cables and connectors are brought to the location to connect the VTR and monitor. Monitors can be unwieldy because, when they are connected to the camcorder, they must be moved if the camera is moved. This can inhibit the camera operator's flexibility. The viewfinder of most camcorders can serve as a viewing device. After something is shot, the tape can be rewound and played back through the viewfinder so that the director can check it. This takes time, however, so many field shoots take place without monitoring. This requires trust and complete communication between the director and the camera operator.

One good approach to the discipline of field production is to lay out all of the cables and connectors you will need for your particular assignment and then plug everything together and operate it before you leave, just to make sure you have everything.

Taping Procedures

The camcorder/video operator should set the audio level and check all controls before taping begins. It is good practice to make sure the machine has been up to speed at least 10 seconds before anything crucial is taped and, likewise, to keep the machine running for about 10 seconds after the shot is completed. The VTR should not be left in *pause* for long periods of time, because this will wear the oxide off the tape and clog the video heads.

During taping, the person in charge of recording should be watching all the "vital signs," most of which appear on indicators in the viewfinder monitor—end-of-tape warning, battery condition, low light, and so forth. In most instances, this person will also be framing shots and listening to the headphone to make sure the audio is recording properly. Because the person is doing so many tasks, he or she must be extra careful to make sure the recorder part of the camcorder is operating properly. The best of shots will be useless if they are not recorded properly and ready to be edited.

A digital camcorder. *Photo courtesy of Sony Electronics, Inc.*

13.7 Editing

Many of the options and operations of editing are the same for multicamera and field production (see Chapter 8). What is different, however, is the emphasis placed on the editing process and the expanded role of audio editing.

The Editing Process

Because much of the editing done in conjunction with studio-based production is intended to correct mistakes made during production or to put together short roll-ins to be played during production, the editing can usually be accomplished rather quickly.

Such is not the case with material shot single-camera. The program is *literally* put together during postproduction—a process that is often long and drawn out. As all professional producers know, the process of "getting into" this final phase of postproduction is a crucial time. Much of the strength—and discipline—of a good producer is an ability to generate the sense of momentum and enthusiasm needed to complete a production. In live television, the relentless clock focuses everyone's attention; in single-camera postproduction, the constant pressure of a knowledgeable guiding hand is needed.

It may be difficult to understand the time frame necessary for the editing process; an inexperienced crew may initially waste a considerable amount of energy and effort. Usually, this phase passes as crew members become more efficient at their assigned responsibilities and the leadership and organization become more evident—just as they did during the shooting process.

Although many professional editing sessions involve only the producer or the director working in conjunction with the editor (or even the editor working alone with only a detailed set of notes), student

Figure 13.13

For students, a two-person editing team can be a very efficient way to work. Many professionals, however, prefer to work alone whenever possible.

postproduction sessions should, as much as possible, become a *learning process* for the entire team. (See Figure 13.13.) Without proper organization, however, this process can drift into noisy chaos. The important thing is that there has to be someone who is acknowledged as being definitely in charge. This may be the producer, the director, or the editor, but it should be the same person who has initiated and established the basic structure of the project.

Audio Editing

For a studio production, audio is usually mixed while the program is being taped. Music is brought in at the beginning and end of the show, and sound effects are incorporated as the production is under way. Single-camera productions shot without benefit of a sophisticated audio board do not lend themselves to audio mixing during the production phase. Obtaining good dialogue, interview audio levels, or on-camera narration is all that can really be expected in the field.

As a result, for professional single-camera productions, audio editing is often undertaken separately from video editing. While one person is editing the picture and the principal dialogue shot in the field, other people are attending to music and sound effects. Dramatic productions are the most complicated from an audio point of view. Someone, often the director, must first determine where audio elements are needed. Where will the music be brought in and taken out?

What sound effects are needed? Which sounds taped in the field need to be rerecorded because they are not good enough? Once all this has been decided, a musician is asked to compose the music, someone obtains effects from sound-effects CDs, and sometimes some members of the cast are brought back into a studio where they record their lines over again—a process known as **automatic dialogue replacement** (ADR).

After all the sounds have been gathered, they are placed on a **multitrack** tape or in a computer, either one that is being used to edit the picture or one with a program to edit audio. Here the sounds are positioned so that they are heard where they are needed during the production. They are also **mixed** together so that they are in a proper volume relationship with each other. For example, the music should not be so loud that the voices cannot be heard, and the sound of a gunshot should be louder than the sound of rain in the background. The average TV drama, commercial, documentary, or top-flight industrial production has a final sound track that is the result of the skilled mixing of anywhere from 16 to 32 separate sound tracks together onto the final mix track.[3]

Most student productions do not incorporate this level of sophistication, but it is important that the preparation for the sound track start with the very first planning of the shape of the project. The director and producer should question each other continually as to the exact details of how each sound or combination of sounds (on-camera narrator, voice-over narrator, background noise, music, sound effects, and so forth) is to be achieved. Some of the sound work can be accomplished while production is still under way. For example, if you know you are going to need the sound effect of a dog barking, you can find it well ahead of the day you need to mix it with other sounds. You may have heard the phrase "We'll fix it in post." This is an invitation to audio disaster. If you have not thoroughly thought out the procedure during preproduction planning, it is often too late to fix it in postproduction.

13.8 Graphics and Sets

Pictorial elements receive less attention in field shooting than in studio shooting. Graphics are usually added after the fact, and sets are determined by the nature of the location. Nevertheless, the basics of pictorial design exist in the field as well as in the studio.

Graphics

Graphics are essentially nonexistent in actual field shooting. Some consumer cameras have built-in **character generators** so that graphics can be included during taping, but these are generally used only for slating/identification purposes. Graphics in a camera can actually be a problem. More than one student has forgotten to turn off the day/date function of a consumer camcorder and had it appear, very inappropriately, on all the footage shot for a drama. Occasionally, you may need to shoot a chart that appears on a wall or some similar graphics to use as a cutaway, but these are not likely to be designed for television, so the camera operator must frame them as well as possible under the circumstances.

If actual physical charts or illustrations are to be included in a program, they are better shot in a studio where lighting can be *controlled*. Most graphics, of course, are computer generated (see Chapter 9). All of these will be incorporated into the program during the postproduction editing.

Sets

Sets, as such, do not usually exist either. The main reason you go on a location shoot is to obtain realistic scenery and settings that are not possible with constructed sets in a studio. However, when you are scouting to find proper locations, keep in mind the *pictorial design elements* discussed in Chapter 9. For example, yellows and reds are warm colors, and greens and blues are cool colors—whether they are in a studio or out in the country. Whether you are shooting indoors or out, the principles of balance and mass, lines and angles, always apply.

Unless you find some very cooperative people or you are willing to pay a great deal of money, you cannot usually change much in a location setting. You *can* clean up someone's desk so that the clutter will not be visually distracting, but you *cannot* readily change the color of the walls, the location of trees, or the placement of windows.

When shooting interior scenes, windows do present particular problems in that they cause glare and interfere with proper lighting. The best advice is to *avoid* shooting into windows. However, it may not always be possible to avoid a passing shot of a window; perhaps it is absolutely necessary to pan with the talent while he or she walks across a room, passing in front of a window. In such a situation, you should consider disabling the automatic **iris** control; set the **f-stop** manually for the best interior (nonwindow) lighting, and keep it consistent as the talent passes in front of the window. This will result in an overexposed background through the window, but the alternative (if the automatic iris is left on) is to allow the talent to turn into a silhouette when passing in front of the window.

In one sense, the setting is much easier (and less expensive) to deal with in a remote location than in a studio, because very little, if anything, needs to be constructed. However, an improper setting can totally destroy the concept and atmosphere of your program. (See Figure 13.14.) You can wind up with the wrong colors, architecture, period furnishings, traffic flow, backgrounds, and so forth. Therefore, you may have to spend many hours scouting and searching for just the right setting.

Real locations are invariably much "busier" than studio sets; they have a lot of elements that are extraneous to what you will be taping—furniture, props, wall coverings, table objects, appliances, and so forth. As a result, you must pay particular attention to make sure you do not wind up with shots that have light switches or flower pots that look like they are growing out of someone's head.

13.9 Producing

As with studio shoots, producers are the people in charge of the *overall organization* of a field shoot. (See Chapter 2.) Their busiest time is before the shoot actually begins, but they are responsible for making sure the production finishes *on time* and *on budget*.

Scripting

The same forms of scripts can be used for field shooting as for studio shooting—**film-style scripts, two-column scripts, rundowns, outlines,** and **storyboards** (see Chapter 11). For most forms of field production,

Figure 13.14

Hallway to be considered for a location shoot. How many problems can you spot if you plan on using this hallway for a location production? How will the mixture of indoor and outdoor light affect color temperature and white balance settings? What can be done about the potential glare? How will the automatic iris function as the talent walks along the corridor, moving in and out of extremely bright spots? What will be the safest angles to use?

the script is absolutely essential before planning or production can take place. Sometimes student crews tend to place a camera on someone's shoulder and assume that the location will provide the necessary material. More than one student production team has found that all of those great ideas they thought of back in the studio just seemed to disappear into thin air once they arrived at the shooting location. The very *act* of putting things down on paper is an important test of the feasibility of the operational plan.

There are times, however, in field production when it is appropriate not to use any script at all. The most obvious example is when covering breaking news stories. But even then, you can undertake some research ahead of time. Newspeople usually keep track of the number of crimes that have been committed in a certain area, the backgrounds of the major political figures, the actions being taken by the local city council, and similar items. This material can be incorporated into what is reported from the scene.

Finding a Location

Producing a location shoot is similar to producing a studio program in that all elements must be in the right place at the right time. However, this is usually much more complex for a field shoot because everything is out of its usual habitat. Equipment logistics, travel arrangements, power supplies, and coordination of props and talent all involve extraordinary consideration.

One of the crucial initial steps a producer must undertake is to make sure someone selects and surveys the production location. For large dramatic productions requiring many locations, a person given the title of **location scout** will undertake the job of finding, visiting, and winnowing down the possible production sites. The location scout might find 10 homes where a 1940s murder mystery could be shot. But some might be a great distance from where other scenes are being shot, some might be in noisy locations, and some may not have an appropriate-looking porch. The location person will narrow down the choices and present them to the producer and/or director. At this point, most directors and some producers like to visit the potential sites to make the final selection. Having the camera operator along to give input on these location-scouting trips can also prove invaluable.

Surveying a Location

For other types of programs you know approximately where you will be doing the shoot, and you go mainly to see the lay of the land. If, for example, you are interviewing a doctor about a new medical breakthrough, you will want to shoot at the hospital where the instruments used for the procedure will be available. You go there ahead of time to see how large the room you will be shooting in is, to find out where the electrical plugs are, to determine how you can best cut out background noise, and so on. Fast-breaking news stories are another matter. Obviously, it may not be possible to check out the location for these ahead of time. However, some places where news is likely to occur, such as the city council chambers or the police station, can be "cased" ahead of time and notes made so that crews that need to go there have some idea of what they will face.

If you shoot in a studio regularly, you are aware of the location of power outlets, the positions of the cameras, the types of curtains and set pieces available, the location of lighting instruments, and other similar information. With each field shoot, these elements are different. That is why it is *essential* that the area be scouted ahead of time. If the only available plugs are out in the hallway and you have not brought extension cords for your lights, you will be faced with a major production problem. When you go to a location, it is wise to have a list of things you want to check. A general *checklist* is shown in Figure 13.15, but elements specific to each production need to be discerned.

One of the first things you should do as part of a location survey is obtain the name of a person who is in charge—someone who gives you the permission to shoot at any particular facility, someone you can contact when you arrive with equipment, and someone to turn to quickly when any unexpected problems crop up. Who has the keys? Whom do you contact when you trip a circuit breaker?

You may wish to draw up a floor plan of the location and take Polaroid or digital still-camera shots of the scene to share with other crew members and to remind you of important details as you plan specific shots. Or, better yet, take along a camcorder and tape the location.

If you are shooting outdoors, or if you are shooting indoors with any natural light, you will want to scout the location at the *same time of day* that you will be doing the shoot so that you can see exactly what you will have to deal with in terms of sunlight, shadows, and windows.

What about possible interruptions and conflicts? Do scheduled events at the location conflict with the shoot? Heavy equipment starting up? Airplanes taking off? If you are shooting on campus, for example, will the end of a class period send large numbers of people walking through the shot? What about those campus chimes? Make note of these items so that you are not in the middle of a take when any of these distractions occur. Listen for continuous extraneous noises, such as an air conditioner or telephones ringing, that will interfere with your audio. Try to obtain permission to turn them off while you are shooting. If you cannot, plan to work with more directional and less sensitive mics closer to the talent.

Stock Footage

Some productions require shots that will be in difficult or expensive locations—an airplane that has crashed on a remote mountainside, a koala bear asleep in a tree. If the principal talent does not need to be in these shots, they can be obtained from prerecorded material. Most professional producers turn to commercial companies that supply **stock footage.** The price is high (a minimum fee of $300 is not uncommon), but these companies have videotape and film to cover a wide variety of situations. News departments carefully index their old news stories on computers and file most of what they shoot for possible later use.

Students who cannot afford professional stock footage should first examine the resources of their own university. Sometimes a former student will have shot the local area from a helicopter, and this footage is made available for future student shoots. Large companies that turn out numerous public-relations films often allow use of portions of footage if

LOCATION SURVEY CHECKLIST

Type of material being shot_____

Time of shooting_____

Potential location of shooting_____

    Principal contact person_____

    Address_____

    Phone number_____

Camera:

    Where can the camera be placed?
    What, if anything, is needed in the way of camera mounting devices or platforms?
    What, if anything, is needed in the way of special lenses?
    Will any objects interfere with the camera shots? If so, how can this situation be corrected?

Lighting:

    What types of lights will be needed?
    Where can the lights be placed?
    What light stands or particular light holders will be needed?
    What, if any, special lighting accessories will be needed?
    How can any problems regarding mixing indoor and outdoor lighting be solved?
    In what ways will the sun's position at different times of day affect the shooting?
    What kinds of problems are shadows likely to cause?

Power:

    Is enough power available or will a generator be needed?
    Where is the circuit breaker box?
    Who can be contacted if a circuit blows?
    Which circuits can be used and how many watts can be run on them?
    How many, if any, extension cords will be needed?
    What power outlets can be used?

Sound:

    Are there background noises that may interfere with audio? If so, how can they be corrected?
    Where can the microphones and cable be placed?
    Are any particular microphone holders or stands needed?
    What types of microphones should be used?
    How much microphone cable will be needed?

General:

    Where is parking available?
    Where is the nearest telephone?
    If passes are needed to enter the premises, how can they be obtained?

Figure 13.15

A location checklist that is very useful when looking over an area that might be used for taping.

```
                   EQUIPMENT RENTAL FIGURES

Low-end Camcorders (VHS and Video 8)          $75 per day

Higher Grade Camcorders (S-VHS and Hi-8)      100 per day

Professional Digital Betacam or M-II          400 per day

Tripod and Head                                60 per day

Monitor                                        40 per day

Portable Light Kit with Four Lights            60 per day

HMI Light                                     175 per day

Microphone                                     15 per day

Portable Audio Mixer                           45 per day

Walkie Talkie Communication System             15 per day

Audio Sweetening                               70 per hour

Graphics Generation                            55 per hour

Cuts-only Linear Editing                       45 per hour

Linear Editing with Switcher Effects           65 per hour

Nonlinear Editing                              80 per hour
```

Figure 13.16

These are approximate costs for renting equipment and facilities.

you give them a credit. The copyright laws that govern the use of all stock footage are rather strict and should always be observed.

Budgeting

Budgeting for field production work is very similar to budgeting for studio productions, in that budgets include **above-the-line** and **below-the-line** categories. (See Chapter 11.) The main variation is that different equipment will be used and a greater emphasis will be placed on editing. Figure 13.16 gives you some equipment rental figures to help you budget for field shooting.[4]

Conceptualization and Preproduction Planning

Before a program or segment of a program is taped on location, you should conceive it in its entirety. How each individual shot is planned and executed depends on how it will be used in the final edited program. In other words, both planning and camera work must be carried out with the eventual editing process constantly in mind.

To aid in this process, video producers have developed a number of different forms. Some of the same paperwork used for studio production is used for field production. For example, you should ask performers to sign **performance releases,** and you should clear any music and other **copyrighted** material that is going to be used for the final edited production (see Chapter 11).

However, because field productions usually involve a variety of locations and their inherent uncertainties, producers must examine the scripts very carefully to determine production needs and schedules.

Breakdown Sheets

If you are planning to shoot a complex production that involves a number of individual scenes shot in different locations, **breakdown sheets** are indispensable. They

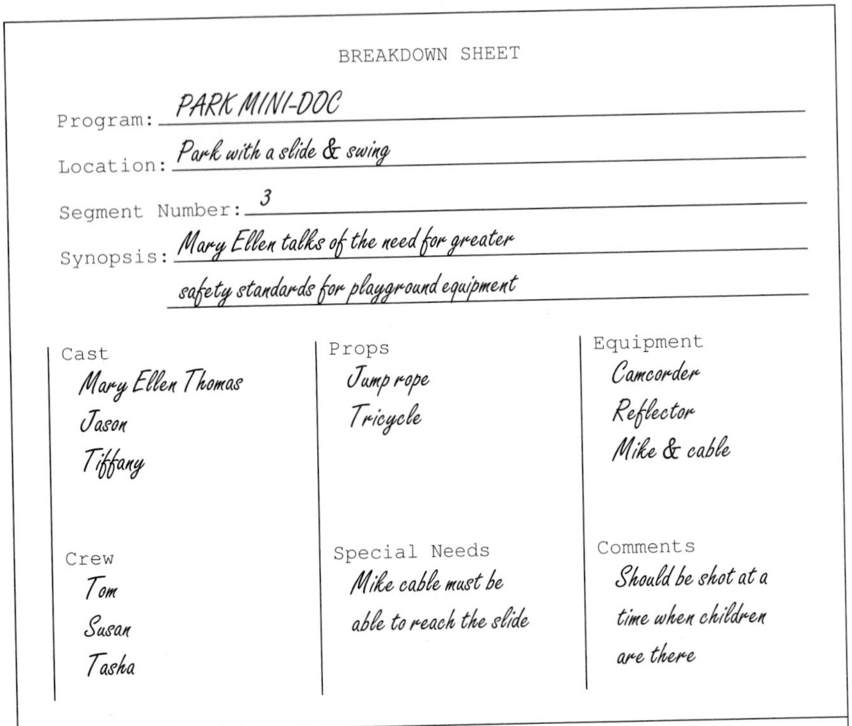

```
                    BREAKDOWN SHEET

     Program: ___PARK MINI-DOC_____

     Location: __Park with a slide & swing_____

     Segment Number: __3_____

     Synopsis: __Mary Ellen talks of the need for greater___

                __safety standards for playground equipment__

     Cast                Props              Equipment
       Mary Ellen Thomas   Jump rope          Camcorder
       Jason               Tricycle           Reflector
       Tiffany                                Mike & cable


     Crew                Special Needs      Comments
       Tom                 Mike cable must be  Should be shot at a
       Susan               able to reach the slide  time when children
       Tasha                                  are there
```

Figure 13.17

The breakdown sheet lists all the talent, crew, facilities, and other elements needed for every scene.

list—for each scene to be shot—a synopsis of the scene, the location, the people who will be needed, the props, and any special considerations. (See Figure 13.17.)

As previously mentioned, program material in extensive field productions is almost always shot out of order, so you use your breakdown sheets to juggle your production shooting and determine the order in which scenes will be shot. Usually the primary element for determining shooting order is *location*; all scenes occurring in the park will be shot at one time, even though they will be interspersed at various points throughout the program. However, sometimes the primary element for determining shooting order is the talent; if someone who is crucial to the production can only work one day, all the shots involving that person will have to be shot on that one day, even though this means traveling all over town. On rare occasions, shooting order may be determined by a prop; if you need to rent a vintage automobile, you might want to shoot all scenes with it on one day so that you can cut down on rental fees.

Sometimes it is wise to make lists of props, costumes, cast members, and so forth from these breakdown sheets. These lists are similar to what you might make for a studio shoot (see Chapter 11), but usually you need more lists because the elements needed for a field shoot are more complex. For example, one list might include all the locales that the location scout needs to find; other lists might include all the animals or all the automobiles needed. Studio productions usually do not include these elements.

Shooting Schedule

Once you have assembled all the breakdown sheets in order, you can develop a **shooting schedule.** This lists everything that is to be shot during each day, giving the description, the cast, and the location. It is used throughout the shooting and, of course, must be revised when production gets behind schedule. (See Figure 13.18.)

SHOOTING SCHEDULE

Program: *PARK MINI-DOC*

Date	Time	Description	Cast	Location
4/20	1:00	Mary Ellen discusses playground equipment and safety needs (seg 3)	Mary Ellen Thomas Jason Sorkin Tiffany Barr	Alcove Park
4/20	2:30	Mary Ellen discusses need for flowers (seg 7)	Mary Ellen Thomas Mr. Hamilton	Patterson Park
4/22	11:00	Interview with park supervisor (seg 2)	Mary Ellen Thomas Dr. Belling	Dr. Belling's office, Park building
4/22	1:00	Interview with park planners (seg 9)	Mary Ellen Thomas Mr. Loomis Mrs. Robbins	Planning offices, Park building

Figure 13.18

The shooting schedule is indispensable for coordinating location shoots on a major production.

Stripboards

Many producers (or their **production managers**) use **stripboards** to aid them with their shooting plans. Sometimes these are actual boards that can hold long strips of paper indicating the locations and characters needed each day. Computers are now heavily employed for all forms of preproduction paperwork, including stripboards. Figure 13.19 shows a stripboard made with the aid of the computer program Movie Magic. When the production needs to be reorganized because some scene didn't get shot, the strips can be moved around by clicking on them with a mouse and dragging them elsewhere. Strips of the old-fashioned paper stripboard can also be easily moved, making stripboards a very flexible production-planning device.

In addition, you can devise your own lists, forms, schedules, or pictures to help conceptualize and organize your material. Like the major multiple-camera studio production, every hour spent in preproduction planning and scripting will save countless hours of valuable crew time on the shoot. Careful script preparation and preproduction plan-

ning are perhaps the most crucial *disciplines* involved in single-camera field production.

Directing in the field is quite different from directing in the studio, mainly because the director is on the set rather than in the control room. However, a director's duties during preproduction are similar to those for a studio shoot—becoming familiar with the script and planning for equipment, cast, and crew (see Chapter 2). The main additional chores are those related to finding locations.

Rehearsals

Rehearsing for a field shoot should involve the same procedures as rehearsing for a studio program (see Chapter 12). However, because the amount of time you can use a remote facility is often limited (you can't interrupt the work on a factory floor or monopolize the merry-go-round in a park), you often do not have the luxury of rehearsal in the field—which

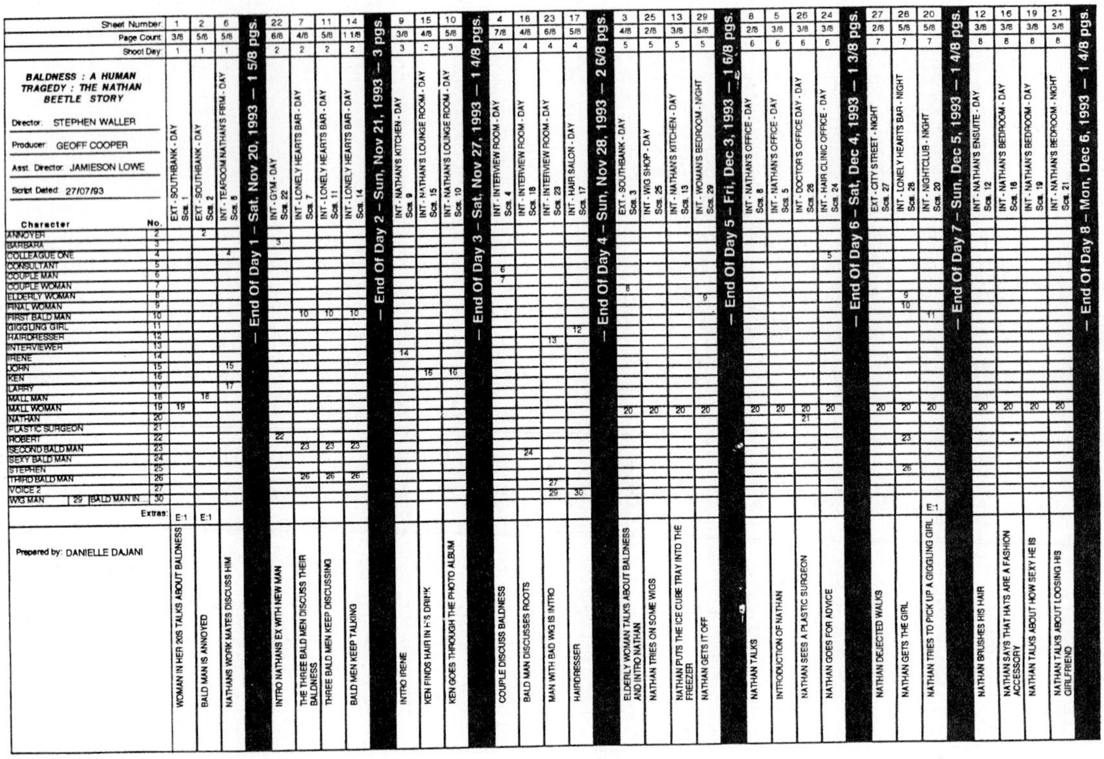

Figure 13.19

This computer-generated stripboard was produced using the program Movie Magic. *Computer work courtesy of Stephen Waller.*

BALDNESS : A HUMAN TRAGEDY : THE NATHAN BEETLE STORY

Director: STEPHEN WALLER
Producer: GEOFF COOPER
Asst. Director: JAMIESON LOWE
Script Dated: 27/07/93

Character / No.
- ANNOYER — 2
- BARBARA — 3
- COLLEAGUE ONE — 4
- CONSULTANT — 5
- COUPLE MAN — 6
- COUPLE WOMAN — 7
- ELDERLY WOMAN — 8
- FINAL WOMAN — 9
- FIRST BALD MAN — 10
- GIGGLING GIRL — 11
- HAIRDRESSER — 12
- INTERVIEWER — 13
- IRENE — 14
- JOHN — 15
- KEN — 16
- LARRY — 17
- MALL MAN — 18
- MALL WOMAN — 19
- NATHAN — 20
- PLASTIC SURGEON — 21
- ROBERT — 22
- SECOND BALD MAN — 23
- SEXY BALD MAN — 24
- STEPHEN — 25
- THIRD BALD MAN — 26
- VOICE 2 — 27
- WIG MAN — 29 / BALD MAN II — 30

Prepared by: DANIELLE DAJANI

---

suggests that you substitute other creative alternatives. Can you at least have a **run-through** with the primary talent to familiarize them with the actual location? How about rehearsing in a substitute location? A rehearsal hall? Your living room?

Production Processes

On the day of production, many events occur that have nothing in common with studio production. First, the equipment must be packed and taken somewhere. You, as the director, must make sure that all crew members *double-check* that everything needed is packed and in working order. If you get to a location site without any videotape, you are in big trouble.

Laying Bars

The taping procedure itself is quite different from that in a studio. If a camera has a **color bar generator,** at least 30 seconds of **color bars** should be recorded on the tape before anything else. This is to allow you or the editor time to adjust controls that will enable the tape to be played back with proper color balance during the editing sessions.

Slating

Each shot needs to be slated. As soon as the VTR is up to speed, one of the crew members (often the script supervisor or a production assistant) should hold a cardboard sign, small chalkboard, or professionally prepared **slate** in front of the camera. This should indicate the scene number, take number, director's name, and description of the shot.

The *scene number* should be the same as that on the script and the *take number* is the number of times that same material has been shot—take 1 for the first attempt, take 2 for the second, and so on. While this written slate is being taped, the person holding it should read the information into an open mic so

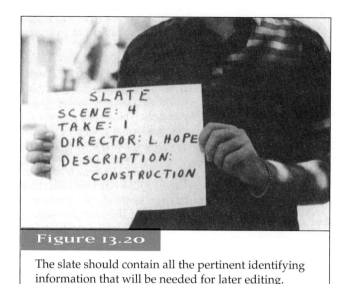

Figure 13.20

The slate should contain all the pertinent identifying information that will be needed for later editing.

that both a video and audio slate are recorded. (See Figure 13.20.)

Of course, this formalized slating procedure is not always possible, especially with fast-breaking news. If a production crew has an opportunity to record a criminal being apprehended, you certainly would not want to take a chance on missing the crucial action while you prepare a proper slate.

Taping

Once the slate is recorded, with the camera still rolling, the director should say "Action," and after waiting several beats, the talent should begin. After the segment is taped, all talent on camera should hold their positions for at least five seconds while the camera continues to roll. These beginning and ending procedures are crucial for the editing function in that they provide adequate **pads** for maintaining proper pace. If you, as the director, are satisfied with the take, you should proceed to whatever is being taped next. If the take is not acceptable, shoot it again.

Logging

Someone, usually the script supervisor, should keep a careful production log of every shot; this should include the scene number (which should be the same as the scene number on the script and the slate), take number, description, length of shot, and any special comments. (See Figure 13.21.) The script supervisor

should indicate if a take is bad so that the editor does not have to bother looking at it. Often, particularly if the taping procedure is hectic, this **logging** is done after shooting is complete.

Continuity

In a complicated shoot, such as a drama, the script supervisor's main job is keeping track of continuity. He or she makes notes concerning what the actors were wearing, where certain props were set, in which direction the action was flowing, how heads were tilted, and which hand actors used to make certain gestures. If the actor was wearing a tie when he knocked on the door in the scene shot on Monday, he should be wearing that same tie when he enters the living room in the scene shot on Thursday. If the interviewee's hand was clutching the book he was holding during the long shot, his hand should be clutching the book for the close-up that will be edited into the shot.

Shot Variety

One of the most important production techniques associated with field shooting is that of making sure enough varied shots are taken, mainly so that they can be used, if necessary, as **cutaways** during editing (to avoid jump cuts). For example, when you tape an interview, the single camera will be on the guest throughout the interview. After the interview is over, you should tape the interviewer asking the questions over again, and you should tape **reaction shots** of both the interviewer and guest listening and reacting. In addition, you might record close-ups of anything the guest talked about. Take a long shot of the location with the two people appearing to be talking. Tape some over-the-shoulder shots and zoom-in reaction shots. In general, record as many different shots as you think you might conceivably be able to use in editing. Dramatic scenes almost always include at least a cover shot of everyone involved, close-ups of each person delivering his or her lines, and reaction shots of each person.

Handling Talent

A common problem in many news or documentary shootings is people who do not want to be on television. Usually these are people who are in the news in

	Slate	Count In	Count Out	Comments
PRODUCTION Campus Parking			PAGE 2	
SHOOTING DATE 8 Nov			PRODUCER Evans	

Slate	Count In	Count Out	Comments
University Security Office Seg 3 Shot 4 Take 3	Lt. Jones. 253 "My Job...	270... this problem."	Best one
Security Office Intro. Meyer Seg 3 Shot 1 Take 1	275 "Lt. Jones...	287... no parking."	
——— Cassette #2 ———			
Parking lot student #1 Seg 4 Shot 1 Take 1	025 "Well everyday...	037... no spaces."	Stumbled over words
Parking lot student #1 Seg 4 Shot 1 Take 2	045 "Everyday...	051... really mad."	
Parking lot student #2 Seg 4 Shot 2 Take 1	059 "I don't see	071... parking ticket."	

Figure 13.21

Excerpt from sample production log.

a negative or controversial way and, as a result, try to avoid being interviewed. The degree to which these people should be pursued depends on the nature of the assignment, the context and reputation of the program, and the personalities of all involved. Some people do not want to be on TV because they know they come across poorly. If these people are not crucial to obtaining the message, they should not be used—they may be self-fulfilling prophecies. And certainly, there is little justification for pursuing an interview with the grieving relative of a person who has just been killed.

At the other end of the spectrum is the common problem of unwanted talent. Random people do not wander into a studio very often, but when a shoot is being conducted on a city street, the curious are bound to appear. If a drama is being taped, crew members (or off-duty law officers) are often hired for crowd-control purposes—placed at the edges of the scene to keep onlookers out of the shot. But there is no guaranteed way to keep people out of shots that involve fast-breaking news stories. Egomaniacs and self-proclaimed clowns who strut around in the background and make faces (or obscene gestures) at the camera can be a real nuisance. If the director deals with these people in a firm but pleasant manner, such behavior can sometimes be modified.

Handling Crew

As with a studio shoot, the director must work to build *camaraderie* among the crew members. Poor interpersonal relationships can damage a field shoot because usually people cannot get away from each other. In some instances, they are stuck together for days or weeks.

Because the director is on the set at a location shoot, he or she cannot give commands (zoom in, pan left) during taping—they would be picked up on the mic. The director and the crew must work out shot composition and other details ahead of time.

Editing Aesthetics

The directorial role during postproduction is obviously greater for field shoots than for studio productions because material shot single-camera film style must be edited. In fact, the actual show is made in the editing room. Because of the generally uncontrolled conditions during shooting, postproduction can be a tedious prospect. It can also be quite rewarding, however, if preproduction and production have been carried out effectively and the potential for a successful program is apparent.

Most of the aesthetic principles regarding design and studio camera shots (see Chapter 12) certainly apply in field shoots. However, some of them take on even increased importance. For example, the concepts of **axis of action** must be watched even more closely in the field because so many shots are taped out of order. The director must be able to envision shots that will be edited together even though they may not be taped immediately after each other. For example, if a long shot of someone running is recorded before lunch and a close-up of the person running is shot after lunch, the camera must not **cross the line** of the long shot when it is used for the close-up. Otherwise, when the two shots are cut together, the person will appear to change direction. Similarly, it is easy to shoot material that will violate the **3-to-1 cutting ratio** when you do not shoot **wide shots, medium shots,** and **close-ups** one after the other.

But the compensating factor is that when you shoot single camera, you can take the time to carefully construct each shot so that it enhances your message and appeals to the eye.

Discussion Questions

1. What are the main differences between lighting in a studio and lighting on location?
2. Give the advantages and disadvantages of a large crew versus a small crew on a location shoot.
3. How is a director's job different in the field from in the studio?

A Wrap-up

The traditional *wrap-up* is given to a performer about 15 seconds before he or she has to get off the air. It means that there is very little time left to wrap things up, quickly summarize, and say good-bye. Perhaps it is appropriate that we wrap up quickly at this point.

This text has been concerned with the *techniques* of production, both for studio productions and for field production. If it has been successful, it has also gotten into the *disciplines* of handling these various elements. Discipline has been defined in several ways throughout this text. As much as anything, it can be considered a matter of attitude.

Attitude toward learning and improving is one major ingredient of discipline. If you truly want to learn as much as you can about the business of television, you will gain quite a bit from this course. You will observe intently. You will try conscientiously. One of the most important secrets of learning in a course such as this is the ability to admit areas of temporary ignorance and then ask questions or seek experiences to fill in those areas. If you are unsure about audio patching, ask to have it explained to you. If you are insecure with the switcher, get all the experience you can as technical director. Do not try to bluff your way through; no one gets very far in that manner.

Attitude toward communication is important. Unless you have a strong feeling for the pursuit of communication—unless you really have a deep desire to succeed in communicating a message—you are in the wrong field. Television is not just a business of glamour or money or excitement. It is the business of communication. For example, every program starts with a specific purpose—a clear-cut idea of what is to be attained in the production. Until you begin program planning with this attitude, your productions may be slick and polished, but they most certainly will turn out to be meaningless and devoid of any substance.

Finally, *attitude toward a professional obligation* must be considered. The terms *professional attitude* and *professionalism* are bandied about with little thought as to their implications. We use the terms here to imply more than just a means of earning a livelihood. We challenge the student to think of professionalism in the original sense of the three learned professions (law, medicine, and theology), which carry a strong societal obligation. The true professional is one who is dedicated to high principles and a sense of community benefit. If you are committed to this kind of self-giving professionalism, you certainly will be more likely to leave your mark upon the field of video production.

Footnotes

1. There is no information that parallels Chapter 6 on the switcher, because a switcher is not used for field production. There is also no section that parallels Chapter 10 on interactive production because, although interactive production often uses

the single-camera techniques, it does not feed into field production in the same way that equipment, producing, and directing do.

2. Historically, most of the people given these jobs were female, so the term *script girl* was used in early times. For many years the script supervisor was the only woman on most film and video crews. Although the functions of script supervisor are very important, this is still a low-paying job.

3. Some professional music recording sessions use in excess of 100 different tracks. Quincy Jones, for example, has used over 200 in some sessions.

4. These prices were compiled from a number of rental catalogues, including those of: Birns and Sawyer (323-466-8211), Ametron (323-466-4321), Bexel (818-841-5051), and Raleigh (323-466-3111).

Bibliography

Alten, Stanley R. *Audio in Media.* Belmont, CA: Wadsworth, 1998.

Anderson, Gary H. *Video Editing and Post Production: A Professional Guide.* Woburn, MA: Focal Press, 1998.

Apple Computer. *Multimedia Demystified.* New York: Random House Electronic Publishing, 1994.

Armer, Alan A. *Writing the Screenplay: TV and Film,* Belmont, CA: Wadsworth, 1993.

Barr, Tony, Stephen Kline, and Edward Asner. *Acting for the Camera.* New York: HarperCollins, 1997.

Brown, Blain. *Motion Picture and Video Lighting.* Stoneham, MA: Focal Press, 1996.

Browne, Stefen E. *Nonlinear Editing Basics.* Woburn, MA: Focal Press, 1998.

Cartwright, Steve R. *Pre-Production Planning for Video, Film, and Multimedia.* Boston: Focal Press, 1996.

Compesi, Ronald J., and Ronald E. Sherriffs. *Video Field Production and Editing.* Boston: Allyn and Bacon, 1994.

Cury, Ivan. *Directing and Producing for Television.* Woburn, MA: Focal Press, 1998.

Di Zazzo, Ray. *Directing Corporate Video.* Stoneham, MA: Focal Press, 1993.

Dyas, Ronald D. *Screenwriting for Television and Film.* Madison, WI: Brown and Benchmark, 1993.

Eargle, John M. *Music, Sound, and Technology.* New York: Van Nostrand Reinhold, 1995.

Farris, Linda Guess. *Television Careers: A Guide to Breaking and Entering.* Fairfax, CA: Buy the Book Enterprises, 1995.

Filoreto, Carl, and Lynn Selzer. *How to Get a Job in TV News.* New Haven, CT: Mustang Publishing, 1998.

Fitt, Brian, and Joe Thornley. *Lighting Technology.* Woburn, MA: Focal Press, 1997.

Gates, Richard. *Production Management for Film and Video.* Newton, MA: Focal Press, 1995.

Graham, Ian S. *HTML Sourcebook.* New York: John Wiley & Sons, 1995.

Grant, August E. *Communication Technology Update.* Boston: Butterworth-Heinemann, 1994.

Gross, Lynne S., and Larry W. Ward. *Electronic Moviemaking.* Belmont, CA: Wadsworth, 2000.

Hofstetter, Fred T. *Multimedia Literacy.* New York: McGraw-Hill, 1995.

Huber, David Miles. *The MIDI Manual.* Woburn, MA: Focal Press, 1998.

Hyde, Stuart W. *Television and Radio Announcing.* Boston: Houghton Mifflin, 1995.

Kehoe, Vincent J. R. *The Technique of the Professional Make-Up Artist.* Stoneham, MA: Focal Press, 1995.

Kindrew, Gordham, and Robert B. Musburger. *Introduction to Media Production: From Analog to Digital.* Woburn, MA: Focal Press, 1997.

Kristof, Ray, and Amy Satran. *Interactivity by Design: Creating and Communicating with New Media.* Mountain View, CA: Adobe Press, 1995.

LeTourneau, Tom. *Placing Shadows: The Art of Video Lighting.* Woburn, MA: Focal Press, 1998.

Maier, Robert G. *Location Scouting and Management Handbook.* Newton, MA: Focal Press, 1994.

Mazda, F. F. *Telecommunications Engineer's Reference Book.* Boston: Focal Press, 1993.

Miller, William. *Screenwriting for Film and Television.* Boston: Allyn and Bacon, 1998.

O'Donnell, Lewis B., Philip Benoit, and Carl Hausman. *Modern Radio Production.* Belmont, CA: Wadsworth, 1996.

Olson, Robert. *Art Direction for Film and Video.* Newton, MA: Focal Press, 1993.

Pohlman, Ken C. *Principles of Digital Audio.* New York: McGraw-Hill, 1995.

Reese, David E., and Lynne S. Gross. *Radio Production Worktext.* Boston: Focal Press, 1998.

Rumsey, Francis, and Tim McCormick. *Sound the Recording.* Woburn, MA: Focal Press, 1997.

Semrau, Penelope, and Barbara A. Boyer. *Using Interactive Video in Education.* Boston: Allyn and Bacon, 1994.

Summitt, Paul M., and Mary J. Summitt. *Creating Cool 3D Web Worlds with VRML.* Foster City, CA: IDG Books Worldwide, 1995.

Tucker, Patrick. *How to Act for the Camera.* New York: Routledge Press, 1993.

Vane, Edwin T., and Lynne S. Gross. *Programming for TV, Radio, and Cable.* Boston: Focal Press, 1994.

Viera, Dave. *Lighting for Film and Electronic Cinematography.* Belmont, CA: Wadsworth, 1993.

Watkinson, John. *The Art of Sound Reproduction.* Woburn, MA: Focal Press, 1998.

Whittaker, Ron. *Video Field Production.* Mountain View, CA: Mayfield, 1996.

Wurtzel, Alan, and John Rosenbaum. *Television Production.* New York: McGraw-Hill, 1995.

Zettl, Herbert. *Sight-Sound-Motion: Applied Media Aesthetics.* Belmont, CA: Wadsworth, 1999.

Zettl, Herbert. *Television Production Handbook.* Belmont, CA: Wadsworth, 1997.

Glossary

A

A/B roll An editing system that is capable of performing dissolves, wipes, and other transitions between edits. Normally, an A/B roll system consists of at least two playback tape machines and a record machine.

above-the-line Costs for creative and performing personnel (such as the producer, writer, director, musicians, and actors).

actors TV talent who perform as someone other than themselves.

AD See *associate director*.

adapter A connector that converts from one type of connector to another (e.g., from phone to RCA).

adaptive presentations Interactive media presentations whose content can change in response to information input by the user.

AFM See *audio frequency modulation*.

AGC See *automatic gain control*.

agents People who find work for actors, writers, and others engaged in creative aspects of the media business.

air monitor (1) In video, the TV set in the control room that shows the video signal currently on the air. The air monitor receives its signal not directly from the switcher but over the air (in broadcast situations) or through an RF cable (in nonbroadcast situations). (2) In audio, the speaker that allows an operator to hear the transmitted broadcast signal.

amplify To magnify an audio or video electrical signal for mixing, distribution, and transducing purposes.

amplitude The height of a sound wave. Amplitude determines the volume of the sound. The higher the amplitude, the louder the sound.

analog A method of representing video or audio signals using a "wave" of continuously varying value.

animation A sequence of graphics that rapidly cycles to create the illusion of motion.

antenna A set of wires or rods that send a signal through the airwaves or receive a signal that has been sent through the airwaves.

aperture The opening in the camera lens that determines how much light will pass through.

arc shot A combination trucking, panning, and dollying movement in which the camera is moved in a semicircle around a subject while the camera head remains pointed toward the subject.

arm move To move the boom arm of a crane left or right.

art director A person who deals with the look of sets and other artistic aspects of a television program.

aspect ratio The ratio of the height of a television screen to its width.

assemble editing A process in which video, audio, and control track information is simultaneously recorded onto a videotape.

assistant director See *associate director*.

assistant producer See *associate producer*.

associate director The person who keeps track of timing for a program and assists the director in other ways.

associate producer A person who helps the producer with any of a number of production chores.

asymmetrical balance An informal arrangement of elements in a camera shot or graphic in which an important object placed close to the center of the picture is balanced by one or more objects of lighter visual weight some distance from the center.

audio board See *audio console*.

audio console The piece of equipment that is used to gather, mix, and amplify sounds and send them on to their next destination.

audio frequency modulation A method of recording audio on a videotape by combining it with video information in helical scan tracks. Using this method, the sound cannot be separated from video for editing.

audio operator A person who sets mics in a studio or location setting and/or operates the audio console.

audition To monitor a sound through a separate speaker that is not tied to what is being mixed by the audio console or sent over the air.

auto key A key effect in which one source is used to establish the shape of the key hole and another source or sources are then inserted into the hole.

automatic dialogue replacement Rerecording dialogue for a production after the principal shooting is over because, for some reason, it was not recorded properly when it was shot.

automatic gain control An internal control device, for either audio or video signals, that automatically increases or decreases the strength of the incoming sound or picture in order to maintain optimum signal strength.

automatic iris A camera setting that continuously alters the aperture in response to changing light levels.

automatic white balance A camera setting that automatically adjusts the camera's white balance setting for differing lighting conditions.

auxiliary send A routing bus on the audio console used to feed external processing gear or multitrack recording equipment.

axis of action An imaginary line that extends the path in which a character or object is moving, with the result that if one camera is on one side of the line and another is on the other side, cutting from one camera to another will make the person or object appear to change direction.

axis of conversation   An imaginary line that connects two persons talking to each other with the result that, if one camera is on one side of the line and another is on the other side, cutting from one camera to another will make the person appear to change position.

B

background light   General lighting on the set behind the talent.

backlight   A highly directional light coming from above and behind a subject, adding highlights, shape, and separation from the background.

backplate   The part of a condenser mic that is electrically charged.

backtime   The process of timing a piece of audio and/or video so that it can be started at a precise time and end at the properly appointed time.

balance   In audio, the achievement of the correct ratio among several sound sources; in video, a picture composition where the various portions of the screen appear to have equal weight.

balanced cables   Audio cables that have three wires, one for positive, one for negative, and one for ground.

ballast   An attachment to an HMI light that protects it from surges in power.

bandwidth   The amount of information that can be carried by a given method of signal transmission. The higher the bandwidth, the more information that can be carried.

bank   See *bus.*

barn doors   Movable metal shutters, attached to the front of a lighting instrument, that are used to limit the area of the projected light.

base light   An overall lighting that produces enough light for the cameras to yield an acceptable picture. It does not provide any

modeling or effects; it is simply illumination.

batch digitize   An automated process of digitizing a number of clips at once after all in points and out points have been selected.

batten   A counterweighted lighting grid that can be raised and lowered so that lights can be worked on near the studio floor.

beam splitter   The optical device in a color camera, consisting of a prism and mirrors, that separates the incoming visual image into the primary colors of blue, red, and green.

below-the-line   Costs for technical and production personnel and for equipment, facilities, and services.

bidirectional   A microphone that picks up sound from two directions, the left and the right of the pickup element.

bin   A storage area for clips on a nonlinear editing system.

bit   An individual unit of a digital signal that can have a value of either "off" (0) or "on" (1).

bitstream   A stream of digital information, such as video, audio, or other data.

black   (1) A synchronized video signal that contains no picture information—a blank screen. (2) To record control track and a synchronizing signal onto a videotape.

black level   The electronic adjustment of the darkest information (black) of a video signal.

blocking   The process of planning and coordinating all movement and positioning of talent and production equipment before a production begins.

blocking diagrams   Drawings made by directors to help them visualize where actors and cameras should be placed.

body time   The length of a program not including closing credits and titles.

boom   (1) Any device consisting of a movable base, an adjustable stand, and a long arm for suspending a microphone above and in front of a performer. (2) An arm of a crane that can be used to move a camera up and down or sideways.

(3) To move a camera with a boom arm.

breakdown sheets   Different pieces of paper or computer screens that list what will be needed for each shot, such as actors, props, and special effects.

brightness   An indication of where a color would fall on a scale from light (white) to dark (black).

broad   A rectangular floodlight.

browser   A program that is used to view interactive media presentations on the World Wide Web.

bus   A group of buttons on a video switcher representing the available video inputs.

button   In interactive media presentations, a graphic designed to look like a pushbutton that acts as a link.

byte   A group of digital zeros and ones that have a particular meaning.

C

cables   Coverings that contain wires that transport the signals needed for audio and video production.

call sheet   A posted list that lets cast and crew know when and where they should report.

camcorder   An integrated unit that combines a camera and a videotape or other recorder.

cameo lighting   A type of lighting where the performer is lit but the background is not.

camera control unit   The part of a studio camera used to adjust the video quality of the camera.

camera mount   The support mechanism, such as a tripod, pedestal, or crane, that holds the camera mounting head and the camera itself.

camera operator   The person who frames the shots for a production.

capacitor   The part of a condenser mic that stores electrical energy and permits the flow of alternating current.

cardioid   A microphone that picks up sound in a heart-shaped pattern.

carrier wave   A specific range of frequencies used to carry an electronic signal from a transmitter to a receiver.

cartridge An audiotape or videotape recording and/or playback tape container that holds the tape in a continuous loop on a spool.

cartridge recorder Audio or video equipment that records or plays back material on tape that is on a continuous loop in a self-contained unit.

cassette recorder Audio or video equipment that records or plays back material on tape that has both the supply reel and take-up reel in a self-contained case.

casting Deciding who will act various roles in a television program.

casting agencies Companies that can be hired to select people for various roles in a production.

cathode-ray tube A TV reception device in which an electronic beam produces what appears to be a moving picture. Commonly referred to as a "picture tube."

CCD See *charge-coupled device.*

C-clamp A metal clamp with a pivot adjustment for attaching lighting instruments to a lighting grid.

CCU See *camera control unit.*

CD player Equipment that plays back disks on which sound has been recorded digitally.

CD-ROM Compact disk/read-only memory; a computer input device that can be read but not written to.

central processing unit The part of a computer that calculates digital data. In effect, the "brain" of the computer.

CG See *character generator.*

channeling Moving signals from one place to another.

character generator An electronic device used to display lettering on the television screen.

charge-coupled device A microchip inside a camera that transduces visual energy in the form of light into electrical energy.

chroma key A special effect in which a designated color (usually green or blue) is used as a key to determine what picture information is to be cut out of the picture with the foreground image.

chrominance The color information (hue and saturation) of a video signal.

clip (1) A segment of video and/or audio stored as a discrete unit in a nonlinear editing system. (2) A digital audio phenomenon where sound that is overmodulated disappears or is intermittent.

close-up A view of a subject from a relatively short distance. A close-up of a person, for instance, might include only the person's face.

coaxial cable Standard camera and video cable with a central insulated conducting wire and a concentrically arranged outer wire.

CODEC (COder/DECoder) A device used to convert analog video or audio into digital form.

coil The part of a dynamic microphone that vibrates within the magnet, setting up an electrical charge.

cold edit An edit made without setting in or out points but by simply pressing the "record" button. It is normally used at the beginning of a videotape.

color bar generator The part of the camera or switcher or other piece of equipment that produces the basic colors—red, blue, green, yellow, cyan, and magenta.

color bars An electronically generated pattern of vertical color strips that can be used to standardize and calibrate the color values of all cameras and monitors.

color temperature The relative reddish or bluish quality of a light source, as measured in degrees Kelvin.

compact disk player See *CD player.*

complementary colors The colors produced by combining two of the three primary colors (red, blue, and green) in equal proportion: yellow, cyan, and magenta.

component A method of video signal distribution in which the signal is separated into two or more separate signals representing chrominance and luminance elements of the signal.

composite A method of video signal distribution in which the three basic video elements (hue, saturation, and brightness) are combined into one signal.

compression A process used to make digital audio or video data more compact.

compression ratio The size of the original digital signal compared to the size of the compressed digital signal. The higher the compression ratio, the more effective the compression method.

compressor An electronic device used to lessen the distance between the highest and lowest audio volume levels.

condenser A high-quality mic whose transducer consists of a diaphragm, backplate, and capacitor.

connectors Metal housings that allow audio or video or other signals to travel from one cable to another.

continuity (1) In production, maintaining a consistent and unobtrusive progression from shot to shot in terms of screen direction, lighting, props, and other production details. (2) In graphics, maintaining a consistent look among all graphics in a production.

continuous image compression A digital video effect in which a video image is shrunk to a smaller size in real time.

contrast ratio The relationship of the brightest area to the darkest area in a given camera shot, as determined by reflected light readings.

control room The area where all video signals are mixed. The director and technical director (and other crew members) control all program elements from this location.

control room rehearsals A rehearsal with the director seated where he/she will be calling the shots, rather than in the studio.

control track The portion of a videotape that contains the sync information that keeps all elements in a proper timing relationship.

convergence A term presently being used to define the coming together of technologies with previously differing applications in order to create a digitally based video system. This process involves such things as broadcasting, cable TV, telephones, satellite transmission, and a number of computer-centered applications.

cookie See *cucalorus.*

copyright The exclusive right to a production or publication.

corner insert A video effect in which one video input is placed in the corner of another video input.

CPU See *central processing unit.*

crab dolly A small studio crane that can move on tracks.

crane (1) A large camera mount with an extended boom arm for a camera and a seat for a camera operator, all placed on a large, four-wheeled base. (2) To move the boom arm of a crane up and down. (3) A shot produced by craning a camera.

crawl A graphic effect in which lettering moves horizontally across the screen.

crossfade To bring in one sound slowly while taking another out slowly.

crossing the line Having one camera shot come from one side of the axis of action/conversation and another camera shot come from the other side. If the two shots are cut together the material in the shot will appear to change direction.

cross-key A lighting technique that uses multiple key lights aimed onto the set from different directions.

cross-pair miking A stereo mic setup that uses two cardioid mics placed like crossed swords.

CRT See *cathode ray tube.*

CU See *close-up.*

cucalorus A metal or wooden cutout pattern that is placed in front of a spotlight to produce a shadow effect on a scenic background.

cue button A control on an audio board that allows an operator to hear a sound without transmitting or taping it. It is used to prepare sound before it is to be aired or taped.

cue cards Sheets of cardboard with the script written on them that are held next to the camera lens so that the talent can look at the camera and read the script.

cue monitor A small speaker within an audio board that allows the board operator to prepare sound for airing by hearing it while other sound is being transmitted.

cue tone A silent signal placed on a cartridge tape that allows it

to cue itself to the beginning of a segment.

cue track A track on a videotape that can be used to record time code or additional audio information.

cut An instantaneous change from one video source to another.

cutaway A shot edited into a program to prevent a jump cut. A cutaway shot does not show the focus of action, but rather something related to the main action. For example, a cutaway shot of the audience could be placed between two shots of a politician speaking at a podium.

cuts-only An editing system, normally with only one playback tape machine and one record machine, that is capable of performing only cut transitions between edits.

cutting for information Making a video edit in order to reveal new information to the viewer. For example, cutting from a medium shot of a magician on stage to a close-up when he holds up a particular card from a deck.

cutting on action Making a video edit at a point when some action takes place. For example, when an actor turns toward another actor.

cyc A large, continuous, smooth backing, usually made of cloth, that may cover two or three walls of a studio.

cycle per second A basic unit of frequency measurement for electromagnetic and acoustic waves; now usually referred to as *hertz.*

cyclorama See *cyc.*

D

DA See *distribution amplifier.*

daily hire Someone who is hired to work only one day or a few days at a time as opposed to someone who is a regular staff member at a particular company.

DAT See *digital audiotape.*

DAW See *digital audio workstation.*

dB See *decibel.*

decibel (1) A unit of measurement of sound that compares the relative intensity of different sound sources.

(2) A unit of measurement for video that relates to the output gain.

defocus A camera transition in which the picture on the on-air camera becomes fuzzy.

depth of field The distance between the nearest point at which objects are in focus and the farthest point at which objects are in focus in a camera shot.

diaphragm (1) The vibrating element in a microphone that responds to the compressed air molecules of sound waves. (2) The adjustable mechanism that controls the size of the lens aperture.

digital A method of representing video or audio signals that uses discrete "on" and "off" pulses. The value of a digital signal at any point can be either "off" (0) or "on" (1). Digital material can be reproduced with little to no degradation of signal.

digital audio workstation A stand-alone computer that can be used to record, store, edit, sweeten, and mix sounds.

digital audiotape Tape that gives high-quality sound because it records information in numerical data bits and bytes. It is a small tape because it records horizontally.

digital cart A piece of equipment meant to replace the analog cartridge player. It stores audio selections in files on a hard drive and can be programmed to bring up any files in any order.

digital delay A unit that holds a signal temporarily and then allows the signal to leave. It is often used for talk shows so that something a viewer says can be halted before it goes on the air.

digital versatile disk A small disk that can hold a great deal of video, audio, and/or computer data and play it back through a player or a computer equipped with a DVD player.

digital video effects Special effects accomplished through digital technology in which elements of video can be manipulated, resulting in pictures that change size, move across the screen, or are altered in other ways.

digitization   The process of converting analog data, such as an audio or video signal, into digital form.

digitizing pen   An electronic pen used to create computer graphics by "drawing" on a graphics tablet.

dimmer board   A lighting control unit, operated on the same principle as a rheostat, that determines the intensity of a light by controlling the amount of electric current flowing to the instrument.

dimmer circuit   One fader of a dimmer board that brings up one or several lights.

dissolve   A simultaneous fading out of one picture while fading in to another.

distortion   A muddy sound caused by playing a sound at a higher volume than the equipment can handle.

distribution amplifier   A power amplifier that increases signal strength as an electronic signal is traveling from one place to another.

Dolby   A noise reduction system that works by raising the volume of the program signal most likely to be affected by noise during production and then lowering it again during playback. This makes the noise seem lower in relation to the program level.

dolly   To move the camera and its mount closer to or farther from the subject.

dolly shot   A shot produced by dollying the camera.

downstream keyer   Part of a switcher used to create a key on a signal after it has gone through all other switcher manipulations.

dress rehearsal   The final, full rehearsal before the actual production take—using all sets, props, and costumes—designed to be conducted straight through without interruption.

drop frame   A mode of time code that periodically "skips" a frame number to compensate for the fact that NTSC color video actually runs at 29.97 frames per second, and not exactly 30 frames per second.

dry run   A session where the director and talent work together on the basic staging of a program without actually doing a full rehearsal.

dub   (1) To make a copy of a tape or disk. (2) A copy of a tape or disk.

DVD   See *digital versatile disk*

DVE   See *digital video effects.*

dynamic   A rugged microphone whose transducer consists of a diaphragm connected to a movable coil.

dynamic content   A characteristic of interactive media that allows a presentation to change according to a user's wishes.

E

ECU   See *extreme close-up.*

edit controller   An electronic unit used to operate the source deck(s) and record deck(s) in an editing system.

edit decision list   A computerized file containing information about edits. The file can be printed out, or used to re-create an edited program using another editing system.

editor   The person who assembles raw footage into a final program.

EDL   See *edit decision list.*

EFP   See *electronic field production.*

electronic field production   The use of a single video camera to record any kind of program on location for later editing in the postproduction process.

electronic news gathering   The use of single-camera portable equipment to record news events and other actualities.

electronic still store   A system of storing video frames in digital form, indexed for each retrieval.

ellipsoidal   A spotlight with a reflecting mirror at the back of the housing that enables it to create a very directional, well-defined beam.

ELS   See *extreme long shot.*

ENG   See *electronic news gathering.*

equalization   Emphasizing, lessening, or eliminating certain audio frequencies.

equalizer   A unit that adjusts the amount of amplification given to certain audio frequencies, such as high, middle, and low frequencies.

ESS   See *electronic still store.*

essential area   The area left after cropping 25 to 30 percent from the outer edges of the screen. Graphics and other crucial screen elements should always be placed within the essential area, as the edges of the screen may be lost by the time the image is seen by the home viewer.

establishing shot   A long shot used at the beginning of a scene or program to relate the subjects and/or circumstances to one another.

event video   The production of tapes dealing with special occasions, such as birthdays and weddings.

executive producer   A person who oversees several TV productions.

extender   An optical device placed between the lens and the camera to extend the focal length of the lens. A 2X extender, for example, doubles the focal length of a lens.

external key   See *auto key.*

extreme close-up   A very close shot of a person or object used to intensify drama or to show close detail.

extreme long shot   A shot in which the characters are so far away that they are not distinguishable as specific individuals.

F

facilities request form   A sheet that someone fills out in order to reserve studio and/or equipment time.

FACS   See *facilities request form.*

fade   The gradual bringing in or taking out of an audio or video source.

fade in   (1) For video, a dissolve transition—normally used at the beginning of a program or program segment—in which a picture gradually fades in from a black screen. (2) For audio, the gradual bringing in of a sound.

fade out   (1) For video, a dissolve transition—normally used at the end of a program or program segment—in which a picture gradually fades away to a black screen. (2) For audio, taking a sound from full up to silence.

fader   The audio console control that raises and lowers volume by controlling the amount of resistance going through the system.

fader bar   A handle unit on a video switcher that allows the operator to manually change from one bus to another.

fc   See *foot-candle*

feedback   A high-pitched squeal that results from accidentally feeding a program monitor into a live microphone, causing an instantaneous overamplification of the system.

field   In interlace scanning, one-half of a complete frame of video. NTSC interlace scans the odd-numbered scanning lines, then the even-numbered scanning lines, creating a complete frame every 1/30th of a second.

field of view   The size or scope of a shot, indicating how much is encompassed.

field production   Television production, usually consisting of single-camera recording and postproduction editing, that takes place outside of the studio.

fill light   An unfocused and diffused light used to complement the key light, coming from the side opposite the key to fill in dark areas and soften the shadows.

film-style script   A script that is organized by scene with description written the width of the paper and dialogue centered in the middle.

film-style shooting   Taping the way movie makers have traditionally filmed by using one camera and resetting the camera and lights for each shot.

filter   (1) A glass or gelatin element mounted in front of a light or in front of a camera imaging device that compensates for changes in color temperature, or in other ways changes the color of the light. (2) Equipment or code within a computer program that cuts out a particular frequency or frequency range of an audio signal.

fishpole   A small lightweight arm to which a microphone is attached, to be hand held by an audio assistant outside of the picture frame.

fixed-focal-length lens   A lens that is one specific focal length, as opposed to a zoom lens.

flag   A rectangular cloth-covered or metal frame placed in front of a lighting instrument to produce a precise shadow on one side of the light beam.

flanger   A device or part of a computer program that electronically combines an original signal with a slightly delayed one.

flat   (1) A standard staging unit, constructed of a frame covered with cloth or hardboard, often used to represent walls of a room or the exterior of a building. (2) When all audio frequencies are recorded equally well.

floodlight   A diffused light that covers a wide area.

floor director   See *stage manager.*

floor manager   See *stage manager.*

floor plan   A drawing done to scale that shows where various set flats and furniture are to be placed in the studio for a particular production.

floor rehearsals   Rehearsals where the director is in the studio rather than in the control room.

focal length   The viewing range of a given lens. The higher the focal length numerically, the narrower the field of view.

focus   To make an image look sharp and distinct.

follow shot   A camera shot in which the camera follows a moving subject, usually keeping the same distance from it.

follow spot   A light of high intensity that is most commonly used to follow a performer as he or she moves around a stage area.

font   A set of consistently designed lettering and characters.

foot-candle   A unit of light measurement equivalent to the amount of light falling upon a surface one foot away from a standard candle.

frame   A complete television picture. In NTSC television, there are 30 frames in each second of video; ATSC formats range from 24 to 60 frames.

frame rate   The number of frames in each second of video. The NTSC frame rate is 30 frames per second, while ATSC formats have frame rates ranging from 24 to 60 frames per second.

frame synchronizer   An electronic component that is used to synchronize external video sources such as satellite feeds with the synchronization created by in-house components.

free run   A time code mode in which the time code numbers continue to increment even when video is not being recorded.

freelance   Working by the hour or day on one project at a time and without being an employee of any particular organization.

frequency   The number of oscillations per second (hertz) of an electromagnetic wave that, in the audio range, determines the pitch of the tone and, in the light range, determines color.

frequency response   The range of pitches (frequencies) that any particular piece of audio equipment can pick up or reproduce.

Fresnel   A light with a well-defined lens; the beam width is varied as the bulb is moved toward and away from the lens.

front focus   The lens focus that is obtained by zooming in tightly on a subject and then focusing.

f-stop   A notation that indicates the size of the lens opening; the higher the f-stop number the smaller the opening and vice versa. The smaller the lens opening, the less light that enters the lens.

full screen   A graphic that covers the entire area of the screen.

fundamental   The main frequency of a particular sound.

G

gain   Volume of an audio signal or amount of amplification of a video signal.

gel   A thin translucent, colored material such as gelatin or plastic that can be mounted in front of lighting instruments to produce specific color effects.

generation   The term used to denote a dub made of another recording. A dub of a first generation recording, for example, is called a second generation.

giraffe A small boom that consists of a counterweighted arm supported by a tripod on casters.

graphics operator A person who creates words, drawings, and some visual effects that are incorporated within a production.

graphics tablet A pad used with an electronic pen to create drawings on a computer.

grid Pipes near the studio ceiling from which lamps are hung.

group assign switch A control on each input channel of an audio board that allows the operator to group some audio inputs together so they can be controlled separately from other audio inputs.

guide pin The part of an XLR connector that is used to line up the male and female conductors accurately.

guilds Organizations that set wages and working conditions that production companies must adhere to for people (usually above-the-line people) that they hire.

H

hand mic A microphone that a person holds to speak or sing into.

hardwired Inputs that are permanently connected, usually by soldering. For example, a DAT recorder may be hardwired to the fifth input of the audio board.

harmonics See *overtones*.

HDTV See *high definition*.

head clog A problem caused by small particles from a videotape becoming lodged in the video heads. Leaving a videotape recorder in "pause" mode for long periods of time can lead to head clogs.

headroom The space between the top of a subject's head and the upper edge of the camera frame.

headsets Ear pieces and small mouthpieces connected together. Crew members wear them so they can communicate with each other and equipment operators wear them to hear the sound from their equipment without disturbing others.

helical scan A method of videotape recording that records video and/or other information in a slanted pattern on the tape.

hertz A basic unit of frequency measurement for electromagnetic and acoustical waves, named after Heinrich Hertz.

high definition A television format with greater detail than standard definition NTSC television.

high-key lighting Lighting that is generally bright and even, with a low key-to-fill ratio.

high-speed flourescent lamp A low-energy, long-lasting light that puts out reds, greens, and blues in a consistent manner to produce 3,200 Kelvin light that oscillates between 25,000 and 40,000 cycles per second.

HMI A hydrogen medium-arc-length iodide lamp that is balanced for daylight and is often used outdoors as a supplement to the light from the sun.

home page The main menu of a World Wide Web–based interactive presentation.

horizon line The horizontal line in a camera shot that indicates that the camera is level.

horizontal sync pulse A video signal that controls the movement of a scanning beam from the right side to the left side of the screen at the completion of a line of scanning.

HSF See *high-speed fluorescent lamp*.

HTML See *Hypertext Markup Language*.

hue The color tint.

hypertext In interactive media, text that is designated as a link.

Hypertext Markup Language A text-based computer language used to author interactive media presentations for the World Wide Web.

hyphenate A person who undertakes two jobs, such as producer-director or writer-director.

Hz See *Hertz*.

I

IFB See *interrupted feedback*.

image expansion A digital video effect in which a portion of a video input is "magnified" to a larger size.

image map In interactive media, a picture that is designated as a link or series of links; different parts of a picture may trigger different links.

image stretching A digital video effect in which a portion of a video input or the entire video input is stretched to a larger size or shrunk to a smaller size vertically and/or horizontally.

impedance Opposition to the flow of an audio signal in a microphone and its cable. Low-impedance equipment allows more signal through than high-impedance equipment.

import To bring digital video, audio, or other information into a nonlinear editing system or computer program.

in point The designated start point for an edit.

incident light Light coming directly from the source of illumination.

in-house Producing a program using equipment and facilities that belong to the company desiring the production.

input selector switch A switch on a videotape recorder used to select from among inputs to be recorded.

insert editing An editing process that allows video and individual audio tracks to be recorded independently of one another.

insert track information An area of the videotape used in some formats to record data for automated functions, editing, and audio dubbing.

Instructional Television Fixed Service Television channels, usually used by educational institutions, in the 2,500-megahertz range that need a special receiver to be viewed.

interactive Methodology whereby the person operating a media program has control, to some extent, over the content of the presentation.

intercom A closed-circuit audio network connecting all production personnel with headsets.

interformat A videotape editing system that uses tape machines of two or more different tape formats.

interlace scanning A scanning method in which half of a frame is scanned at a time, creating a field. Two fields combine to create a complete frame every ⅟₆₀th of a second. Interlace scanning is used in NTSC television, and in some ATSC formats.

internal key See *self key*.

internal reflector A light with a reflector unit and focusing lens built into it.

Internet A worldwide network of computers.

interrupted feedback An audio setup that allows the talent, wearing a small earpiece, to receive instruction from the director or hear program audio.

intranet A self-contained computer network configured to operate like a smaller version of the Internet.

inverse square law A principle of physics that states that when the distance between a light (or an audio source) and its point of perception is cut in half, its intensity will be increased fourfold.

IRE units The units used to measure the brightness of a video signal on a waveform monitor.

iris The part of the lens that allows light to pass through.

ITFS See *Instructional Television Fixed Service*.

ITI See *insert track information*.

J

jack (1) A hinged stage brace attached to the rear of a flat. (2) A female connector.

Jaz disk A storage medium for computer data that uses removable disks a little larger than a standard 3½-inch floppy disk. Currently, Jaz disks are available in 1-gigabyte and 2-gigabyte capacities.

jog/shuttle knob A control on a videotape recorder used to visually search through a videotape at rapid or slow speed.

jump cut An effect—usually undesirable—in which a person or object changes position from one shot to the next.

K

K See *Kelvin*.

Kelvin The scale of measurement used to measure frequencies so that color temperature can be determined.

key A generic term for any number of special visual effects whereby video signals from two or more sources are electronically combined in such a way that one image looks like it has been cut out and placed on top of the other image.

key bus A bus on a video switcher used to select from among various key sources and create various types of key effects.

key light The primary source of illumination falling upon a subject that is highly directional and produces a definite modeling or shaping effect with well-defined shadows.

keystoning A undesirable distortion created when a camera is not precisely perpendicular to the flat object being shot. Keystoning is normally undesirable, but can be used intentionally for artistic effect.

kicker Additional light, usually a spotlight, coming from the side and slightly to the rear of the subject.

kinescope An old-fashioned film recording of a TV program made by adapting a film camera to record from the face of the TV tube.

kook See *cucalorus*.

L

lapel A small mic that can be clipped inside clothing or to a tie or lapel.

lav See *lavaliere*.

lavaliere A small mic that can be worn near the neck.

layering The process of placing video elements "on top" of existing elements during the editing process.

LCD See *liquid crystal display*.

LD See *lighting director*.

lead room Additional framing space in a camera picture on the side toward which a subject is looking or moving.

LED See *light emitting diode*.

leko See *ellipsoidal*.

light emitting diode An electron tube that puts out light that is used in audio to show the amount of volume a sound has—in this way making it a version of a VU meter.

light meter A photoelectric device that measures the amount of light falling upon a specific area.

light plot A floor plan that indicates the lighting requirements— location, type, and function of each instrument—for every staging area in the studio.

light pole A long stick that lighting crew members can use from the floor to adjust elements, such as focus, for a light that is hanging from a grid.

lighting director The person who oversees the lighting of the set and makes lighting changes, if they are needed, during production.

lighting grid See *grid*.

limbo lighting A type of lighting where the performer is seen clearly, but the background appears to be vague or nondescriptive.

limiter An electronic device used to cut off audio levels when the volume is too strong.

line level An audio amplification level for equipment, such as a videotape recorder or an audiotape recorder, that has already been amplified.

line producer A person who is on the production set representing the producer by making sure the program finishes on time and on budget.

linear Progressing in a specified order over time. Used to describe a program such as a TV show that has a specified beginning, middle, and end.

linear editing A method of video editing that uses videotape for playback and recording.

link In interactive media, an object that—when activated by the user— triggers an event.

liquid crystal display A television display composed of crystal cells that can be electrically charged to display a picture.

location scout Someone who looks for appropriate places to shoot a remote TV production.

logging Writing down what is on a videotape including the content of each shot, the in points and out points, and comments about the quality of the shot.

long lens A lens with a high focal length, creating a narrow field of view.

long shot A camera view of the subject from a relatively great distance, usually showing the subject in its entirety.

longitudinal time code A method of recording time code into one of the longitudinal tracks on a videotape.

longitudinal tracks Information tracks on a video- or audiotape that are recorded parallel to the edge of the tape.

lossless A method of compression that does not degrade the quality of the signal.

lossy A method of compression that causes degradation in the quality of the signal.

low-key lighting Lighting that is dark and shadowy with a high key-to-fill ratio.

low-power television Stations that broadcast to a limited area because the FCC does not allow their transmitters to put out very much power.

LPTV See *low-power television*.

LS See *long shot*.

LTC See *longitudinal time code*.

luminance The brightness information in a video picture.

luminance key See *self key*.

M

macro flange The part of a zoom lens used to set macro focus.

macro focus A feature found on some zoom lenses that allows the operator to focus on objects very close to the lens.

magnet The part of a microphone that creates a field that produces an electric current.

main menu The opening screen of an interactive media presentation.

manual white balance Setting white balance on a camera by aiming the lens at a pure white object, then pressing the appropriate button on the camera.

master An original videotape recording.

master control The primary engineering control center where all video and audio signals are ultimately channeled; program input, camera controls, video recording, and transmitter distribution often are handled from this location.

master fader The volume control on an audio board that is located after all the input channel controls and after any submaster controls.

M/E See *mix bus*.

medium shot A view of the subject from a comfortable distance between a wide shot and a close-up.

menu In interactive media, a screen that allows a user to choose from a series of options.

mic level The relatively low strength of an electronic signal produced by a microphone prior to several stages of later amplification.

MIDI See *musical instrument digital interface*.

mid-side miking A method of stereo miking with the mic forming an upside-down T. The stem of the T is a supercardioid mic and the top can be either one bidirectional mic or two supercardioid ones.

MiniDisc A 2.5-inch computerlike disk that can be used to record, store, and edit digital audio material.

miniphone connector A small connector with a sleeve and tip.

mix To combine and balance two or more audio signals through an audio console or two or more video sources through a switcher.

mix bus A bus on a video switcher used to set up special effects and transitions.

mix/effects bus See *mix bus*.

modem A device that allows computer-generated information to be sent over phone lines.

moiré effect Distracting visual vibration caused by the interaction of a narrow striped pattern and the television scanning lines.

monaural Sound coming from only one direction.

monitoring Listening to or viewing sound or picture as it is being manipulated.

mounting head A device used to attach the camera to the camera mount. A mounting head facilitates camera movements such as pans and tilts.

MPEG-2 A video compression system that analyzes frames and uses specially designated frames to predict the degree to which a picture will change.

MS See *medium shot*.

multimedia authoring program A computer program that is designed to produce interactive media presentations.

multiple source See *A/B roll*.

multitrack Tape or a tape recorder capable of holding a large number of audio signals, such as 8, 16, or 24, in parallel with each other.

music licensing company An organization that collects money from stations or production groups that use music and then distributes that money to composers and record companies.

musical instrument digital interface A communication protocol that allows musical instruments and other electronic devices, such as computers and tape recorders, to interact.

mute A control that turns off an assigned fader of an audio console.

N

ND See *neutral density*.

network A group of computers linked together electronically so that they can share data.

neutral density A camera filter that reduces the amount of light hitting the charge-coupled device without affecting the color temperature.

neutral shot A "head-on" shot of a moving object that can be placed between two shots in which the object's screen direction has changed.

noise Unwanted sound or static in an audio signal or unwanted electronic disturbance or snow in a video signal.

nondimmer circuit A switch that turns a light off and on but cannot adjust its brightness.

non–drop frame   A method of time code that does not "skip" any frame numbers. Using this method, one hour of video according to time code will actually be one hour + 3.6 seconds long due to the fact that NTSC color video actually runs at 29.97 frames per second and not exactly 30 frames per second.

nonlinear   Having the ability to progress independent of time constraints and in a number of different ways. Used to describe an interactive media presentation in which the user can control what parts of the program to view and when.

nonlinear editing   A method of video editing that uses computers and random-access media for recording and playback.

normalled   Having inputs and outputs of an audio patch bay permanently wired so that sound goes from one to the other if it is not sent somewhere else by a patch cord. For example mic 1 could be normalled to channel 1 of the audio board.

NTSC   The original television standard approved in the United States in the 1940s that is still in use today. The letters stand for National Television System Committee.

O

off-line   An editing mode used to create a preliminary rough cut of a product before the final product is edited using on-line editing.

off-mic   Distorted sound that occurs when noise from outside a mic's pickup area is transduced and amplified.

ohms   A measurement of impedance.

omnidirectional   A microphone that picks up sound from all directions.

on-line   An editing mode used to create a finished product.

open-ended edit   An edit in which no out points are set. At the conclusion of the edit, the operator must manually stop the tape machines.

out point   The designated ending point for an edit.

outboard equipment   Pieces of equipment that are used in conjunction with the audio board, such as CD players, DAT recorders, and cassette recorders.

outline   A general listing of what will be included within a program, usually in sentence fragment or paragraph form.

overtones   Acoustical or electrical frequencies that are higher than the fundamental tone.

P

pacing   The overall speed at which edits are made in a program. Fast pacing means there are a lot of edits.

package   A self-contained news story that includes a reporter's voice, sound bites, and video footage.

pad   (1) Extra footage at the beginning and end of a clip digitized by a nonlinear editing system. Or, in linear editing, extra material at the beginning or end of the shot that is needed to maintain sync in editing. (2) An attenuator within an audio channel or microphone that reduces the amplification.

page turn   A digital video effect transition in which one video source "peels off" the screen to reveal another video source.

paintbox   A device used to create graphics for television.

pan   (1) To turn a camera horizontally by rotating the camera mounting head. (2) The shot produced by panning a camera. (3) A rectangular floodlight.

pan handle   The handle extending toward the rear of the camera with which the camera operator controls movement of the camera.

pan knob   A control that shifts an audio signal from the left speaker to the right speaker for stereo mixing. For a mono mix it is usually placed at the 12:00 position.

patch bay   A board with numerous terminals (inputs and outputs) through which various audio, video, or lighting signals can be connected by patch cords to other channels or circuits.

patch cord   A cable with connectors on both ends that is used to go from one connector on a patch bay to another.

PCM   See *pulse code modulation*.

peak   In audio, to reach the highpoint of volume level for a particular sound sequence; the ideal place to peak is at the 0 position on the VU meter.

peaking in the red   Running volume at too high a level in that its highpoints keep going into the red part of the meter, the part that is past the 0 (or 100 percent) mark.

pedestal   See *black level*.

pedestal mount   A camera mount, usually used in studio productions, that facilitates smooth movement of the camera across the studio floor and a limited range of camera height adjustment.

perambulator   A large three-wheeled movable platform that holds a mic operator and a mic in such a way that the mic can follow action throughout a studio.

performance release   A form signed by people appearing on video giving the production company the right to distribute their performances.

performers   TV talent who are on as themselves, not acting the part of someone else.

persistence of vision   A human phenomenon whereby the brain retains images for a short period of time so that still images that are projected very quickly look like moving images.

perspective   In audio, the matching of visual and sound distance.

phantom power   Current sent to a condenser mic from the audio console.

phasing   The relationship of the positive and negative portions of the sine waves of two different electrical signals to determine to what extent their oscillations are synchronized. Sounds that are out of phase tend to cancel each other out, resulting in silence or on and off sound.

phone connector   A connector with a sleeve and tip that is used for patch bays, among other things.

pickup shots   Material recorded after an entire program or sequence is recorded that can be edited in to correct some element of what was shot.

pilot   A taped production of one representative program from a proposed series of programs.

pin   To focus the rays of a spotlight to a narrow beam of intense light.

pitch   (1) A meeting during which people with a program idea try to convince other people to buy their idea. (2) The highness or lowness of a sound, determined by the frequency of the sound wave.

pixel   One of the small, illuminating "dots" that make up a picture on a television or computer screen. Short for "picture element."

PL   See *intercom*.

playback   The process of retrieving electronic signals from a tape or disk and turning them into sound and/or images.

plug   A male connector.

pop filter   A metal or foam ball placed over the top of a mic to minimize plosive sounds.

position jump   A cut between two cameras in which a person or object appears to change position from one side of the screen to the other.

postproduction editing   The process of assembling elements of a program that takes place after the individual program segments have been produced and recorded.

pots   Round knobs on an audio board that control the volume.

preproduction   The period during which preparation and planning are undertaken for a television program.

pre-read   The capability of some digital videotape recorders to simultaneously read existing information on a tape while recording new information onto it. Pre-read allows dissolves, wipes, and other transitions to be achieved using only a single playback and a single record machine, as well as the layering of video elements.

preroll   The process by which an edit controller rewinds source and recording decks before performing an edit. This allows all machines to achieve proper speed and synchronization before the edit is performed. Normally, an edit

controller prerolls 3 to 10 seconds before the in point of an edit.

presence   The authenticity of a sound in terms of perceived fidelity and distance.

preset bus   A bus on a video switcher used to select the next video input to be placed on the air.

preset white balance   A camera setting that allows the user to select one or more predetermined white balance settings for various lighting conditions.

pre-studio rehearsals   Rehearsals with the talent in a rehearsal hall or other location before coming into the studio.

preview   To look at an edit before it is actually recorded to make sure it is correct.

preview bus   A bus on a video switcher used to set up video effects and transitions before they are put on the air.

preview line   An output of a video switcher that allows the operator to set up and view effects before they are put on the air.

preview monitor   A video monitor that shows the preview line output of a video switcher.

primary colors   Red, blue, and green.

private line   See *intercom*.

process amplifier   An electronic component that stabilizes the levels and removes unwanted elements from a video signal.

producer   The creator and originator of a television program, usually in charge of elements such as writing, music clearance, financial considerations, and hiring the director.

production   The stage during which all the shooting for a TV program is undertaken.

production designer   A person in charge of the overall look of a film or video.

production house   An organization that produces various types of video material—commercials, corporate videos, broadcast programs, educational programs.

production manager   A person who works for an independent production company who determines costs that will be incurred by a particular production.

program bus   The bus on a video switcher used to select the video input(s) that are put on the air.

program line   (1) The output of a video switcher that is the signal being put on the air or recorded. (2) A window on a nonlinear video editor used to assemble audio and video elements.

program monitor   A video monitor that shows the program line output of a video switcher.

program time   The total length of a show.

progressive scanning   A scanning method that scans a complete frame with each complete pass of the scanning beam. Many ATSC formats and most computer monitors use progressive scanning.

prop   Something on a set that is actually used or manipulated by an actor during a production.

proposal   Several written pages that describe the purpose, goals, objectives, target audience, and planned segments of a proposed TV series or program.

proprietary system   A computer unit designed specifically to perform a particular function. A proprietary system is not compatible with a standard computer operating system, such as Microsoft Windows.

proscenium arch   In the theater, the arch that separates the stage from the auditorium.

public domain   The legal condition covering copyright that says that when material is old enough it can be used without copyright clearance being obtained.

pulse code modulation   A method of sampling analog audio information and converting it to digital form. It is used in some digital videotape formats to record audio information along with video information in helical scan tracks. However, unlike audio frequency modulation, pulse code modulation allows separation of the audio information for editing.

push off   A digital video effect in which one video input pushes off the screen, usually to reveal another video source.

PZM   A flat microphone that consists of a thin pickup plate that, when mounted on a table or ceiling, uses the surface it is mounted on to collect sound waves.

Q

quantization The number of bits that each sampled unit of an analog signal is placed into. All else being equal, higher bit levels result in a digital signal that is a truer representation of the original analog wave.

quartz-halogen lamp See *quartz lamp.*

quartz lamp An efficient lamp with a tungsten filament and halogen gas in a quartz or silica housing.

R

rack focus A camera shot that starts with one object in focus, then changes to focus on another object.

radio frequency A carrier wave on which radio and television signals can be superimposed for transmission.

RAID A series of computer hard disks wired together to act as one large hard disk. Often used in video servers.

random access A storage medium that allows nearly instantaneous access to any portion of the stored data.

rate card A listing of costs for renting equipment or a facility.

RCA connector A connector with an outer sleeve and a center shaft.

reaction shot A shot that shows someone responding to what someone else is saying or doing.

record run A time code mode in which the time code numbers increment only when the video is being recorded.

recording Using audio and/or video electronic signals to arrange iron-oxide particles on the magnetic recording tape or disk or laser inputs on a disk so that they can be retrieved later.

recording head The part of an audio- or videotape recorder that records information onto the surface of the tape.

recording tab A small plastic tab on a videotape that is used to prevent accidental erasure (recording over)

of a tape. When removed or in a designated position, the tab prevents a videotape recorder from recording on the tape.

Redundant Array of Independent Disks See *RAID.*

reel-to-reel A type of audio tape recorder for which the tape must be threaded from the source reel to the take-up reed.

reference white A white object, such as a piece of paper or a T-shirt, that can be used on location to white balance a camera.

reflected light Light bounced back from the surface of an object.

remote/local switch A switch on a videotape recorder used to select how the machine is controlled. When in "local" mode, the machine responds to controls on the front panel; when in "remote" mode, the machine responds to signals coming from a remote source connected electronically to the recorder. Remote mode is used to allow an external edit controller or computer to control the videotape machine.

rendering The process by which a computer creates a complex video transition or other effect.

resolution The fineness of detail that can be produced by a given television system. The higher the resolution, the more detail that can be reproduced. Higher resolution systems use a greater number of pixels to reproduce pictures.

reverberation Sound that has bounced off a surface or various surfaces more than once or sound that has been processed so it sounds like it has bounced off surfaces.

review To look at an edit after it has been recorded to make sure it was executed correctly.

RF See *radio frequency.*

riding in the mud Operating the volume of an audio signal so low that it can barely be heard.

ripple The process by which a nonlinear editing system automatically repositions subsequent video and audio information when new information is inserted into the middle of a presentation.

robotic camera control A computerized unit that allows one or more cameras to be controlled from one location.

robotic cameras Cameras that are controlled remotely and do not have a camera operator behind them.

roll A graphic effect in which lettering moves vertically on the screen. A roll is often used at the conclusion of a program to show closing credits.

rough cut An assemblage of video and audio, created with off-line editing, that will eventually be used as the model for creating the edited master of a program with online editing.

routing switcher A simple audio or video switcher used to select from among two or more different signals.

rule of thirds A principle of composition that divides the TV screen into thirds, horizontally and vertically, and places objects of interest at the points where the lines intersect.

rundown A list of various segments that will be included in a program.

run-through A rehearsal of a production that may not involve all cast and crew.

S

SA See *studio address.*

safety chain A steel chain on a lamp housing that should always be attached to the lighting grid so that the light will not fall if it comes loose.

sampling The process used to convert an analog signal into digital form by measuring the value of the analog signal at various temporal points and converting that value into digital information. All else being equal, a higher rate of sampling results in a digital signal that is a truer representation of the original analog wave.

sandbag A heavy weight placed on the brace of a flat to hold the flat in place.

satellite   A space vehicle that orbits the earth and is capable of receiving and transmitting audio and video signals.

saturation   The strength or intensity of a color—how far removed it is from a neutral or gray shade.

scanner   A computer peripheral that can convert printed material, such as photographs or slides, into digital form.

scanning   The process of reproducing a video picture by illuminating individual pixels that make up the screen. Also, the process that a charge-coupled device uses to transduce visual energy into electrical energy.

scoop   A floodlight that contains a single bulb in a bowl-shaped metal reflector.

screen   In interactive media, the building block of an interactive presentation; the amount of information that can be displayed on a computer monitor at one time, including various media elements such as video, text, or graphics.

screen direction   The direction a subject is facing or in which a subject or object is moving.

scrim   A translucent filter, often made of fiberglass or fine screening, used in front of either a spotlight or floodlight to soften and diffuse the light quality.

script   (1) The written guideline from which a TV program is produced. (2) An HTML program.

script supervisor   A person who keeps notes during production so that continuity is maintained and the material shot can be edited properly.

search   A method of moving quickly from one point on a videotape to another while viewing the images contained on the tape.

SEG   See *special effects generator.*

segment timing sheet   A form that helps the AD keep track of the running times of various portions of a program so that they add up to the proper overall time required.

segue   To cut from one sound at full volume to another sound at full volume.

selective attention principle   The ability of the human ear to filter out unwanted noise so that a person can concentrate on the particular sound he or she wants to hear.

self key   A key effect in which the video source cutting the key is also inserted into the key hole.

serif   A small extension found on the tips of letters in some font styles.

server   See *video server.*

servo capstan   The part of a recorder that pulls the tape through the machine at the proper speed.

set designer   The person who determines the environment where the production takes place.

set dressing   Something on a set that is similar to a prop but is not essential to the action. It is there to add atmosphere or interest.

set light   General lighting on the scenery or other background behind the talent.

setup   See *black level.*

shader   A person who makes technical adjustments on a camera using a camera control unit located at some distance from the camera.

shaping   Altering an audio signal by controlling volume, filtering out certain frequencies, emphasizing upper or lower pitches, creating an echo effect, and so forth.

shooting schedule   A sheet that lists what is to be accomplished each day of production and the major elements needed in order to accomplish it.

short lens   A lens with a low focal length, creating a wide field of view.

shot log   A list of shots contained on a videotape.

shot sheets   Lists of shots in a program that can be attached to the back of a camera so that the camera operator knows what he or she will be shooting.

shotgun   A highly directional microphone used for picking up sounds from a distance.

signal processing   Changing elements of sound or picture, such as frequency response and gain, so that the resulting signal is different from the original one.

signal-to-noise ratio   The relationship of desired sound

to undesired electronic sound. The higher the ratio, the purer the sound.

silhouette   A type of lighting where the background is lit but the performers are not.

site map   A Web page that gives the user an overview of pages available on a particular Website and how they are linked together.

skew   A control on a videotape recorder that adjusts the tension on a tape to correct for when the top part of a video picture appears to "bend" to the right or left.

slant-track recording   See *helical scan.*

slate   An identification procedure whereby date, scene, segment, and other information necessary for editing are recorded at the beginning of a designated camera sequence.

sleeve   An outer part of a number of connectors, such as phone, miniphone, and RCA.

SMPTE   Society of Motion Picture and Television Engineers. Usually used in conjunction with time code.

S/N   See *signal-to-noise ratio.*

snake   A connector box that contains a large number of microphone input receptacles.

snap zoom   A camera shot that very quickly (almost instantly, in some cases) zooms in or out. Snap zooms are normally performed manually, after disengaging the zoom control's motor drive.

snoot   A circular metal object placed in front of a light in order to pinpoint the light onto a particular area of the set.

soft contrast filter   A camera filter used to create a fuzzy effect.

softlight   A lamp that has the bulb positioned in such a way that the light is reflected on the back of the lamp housing before leaving the fixture.

solo   The control on the audio console that silences all channels except the one that has been selected. It is often used during a mix rehearsal to hear individual mikes.

special effects generator   The part of the video switcher that can be used to create special electronic effects, normally through the use of digital video effects.

speech bump A frequency response characteristic of a mic that enables it to pick up speech frequencies better than other frequencies.

split screen A special effect with the screen split into two or more sections, with a picture from a different input filling each portion of the screen.

split-pair miking A stereo mic setup that uses two mics placed parallel to each other facing into the set.

spotlight (1) A concentrated light that covers a narrow area; it usually provides some means for varying the angle of the illumination by moving the bulb within the housing. (2) A special effect in which one part of the picture is lighter (brighter) than the rest of the picture; it is often used to highlight a particular portion of the screen.

spread To focus the rays of a spotlight to a relatively wide area so that the light is less intense than when the light is in the pinned position.

staff People who are employed by a particular production organization and receive regular weekly wages regardless of what project they are working on.

stage manager The director's key assistant in charge of all production concerns on the studio floor.

standard definition With the advent of ATSC (high definition) television, this term is used to refer to NTSC television. It is also used to refer to ATSC formats that have 640 × 480 resolution.

star filter A camera filter used to create a "star" effect that radiates from bright spots on the screen.

start-and-stop rehearsal A full facilities rehearsal with cameras operating, designed to be interrupted to work out problems as the production progresses.

stereo Audio that is recorded, transmitted, and played back through two separate (left and right) channels to simulate binaural hearing.

stock footage Scenes of various types that can be purchased to insert into a production.

storyboard A series of simple drawings or computer generated frames that lay out visually the content of a commercial or program.

streaming video A method that allows moving video to be viewed over the World Wide Web or an intranet.

strike Cleaning up a set after a production.

stripboards Large boards or computer-generated sheets that summarize the scenes, locations, and actors needed for each day of production.

striping The process of recording time code onto a videotape.

striplights A series of pan lights or low-wattage bulbs mounted in a row of 3 to 12 lights in one housing, used as a specialized floodlight for lighting a cyclorama or other large background area.

studio The primary room devoted to video production containing all the paraphernalia for sets, lighting, cameras, microphones, and so forth—the space where all acting or performing takes place.

studio address A public-address loudspeaker system, allowing those in the control room to talk directly to the studio floor.

studio monitor A speaker located in the studio often used for program audio or for the director to talk to the talent before actual taping.

subcode An area on a videotape used by some formats such as DVCPRO to record time code information.

submastering Controlling groups of sound inputs, such as separate inputs from each percussion instrument in an orchestra, separately from other groups of sound inputs, such as all the strings.

super See *superimposition*.

supercardioid A very narrow microphone pickup pattern, often used to record sounds that are at a distance.

superimposition A picture resulting from the simultaneous display of two pictures that are part way through a dissolve.

surround sound Audio that comes from five or six speakers placed around a room.

sweetening The process of adding pickup shots and enhanced audio information after a production has been shot.

switcher A device consisting of selection buttons and control levers that permits the selection and combining of incoming video signals to form the final program picture.

symmetrical balance A formal arrangement of elements in a camera shot or a graphic, usually with the most important element centered in the picture and other objects placed equidistant from the center.

sync generator A device that produces a synchronizing signal (sync pulse) that serves as a timing pulse to coordinate the video elements of all components in a video system.

synchronizing pulse An electronic signal used to synchronize various components of a video signal.

syndication A process by which programs are distributed to individual stations that air them when they wish as opposed to network programs that are generally aired by all network affiliated stations at the same time.

synthesizer A piece of equipment that operates with MIDI, most commonly used to create music by emulating and manipulating sounds.

T

talkback mic A microphone located in the control room that allows the director, audio operator, or others to communicate with people in the studio who can hear the studio monitor.

tally lights Small red indicators on a camera to let the talent and camera operators know that the camera is on the air or recording.

TBC See *time base corrector*.

TD See *technical director*.

technical director The production person who operates the switcher.

telecine The equipment used to transfer film to video.

telephoto lens See *long lens*.

TelePrompTer A mechanical device that projects the moving script, via mirrors, directly in front of the camera lens.

three-point lighting The traditional lighting setup that incorporates a key, a fill, and a backlight.

three-to-one cutting ratio A principle that states you should not take to a shot that is three times larger or three times smaller than the preceding shot.

three-to-one rule A microphone placement principle that states that, if two mics must be side by side, there should be three times the distance between them that there is between the mics and the people using them.

tilt (1) To pivot the camera vertically by pointing the camera mounting head up or down. (2) The shot produced by tilting a camera.

timbre A distinctive quality each voice or musical instrument has caused, to a large degree, by overtones.

time base corrector An electronic component that takes the video feed from a video recorder, encodes that signal into a digital form, and then reconstructs an enhanced synchronizing pulse and video signal for distribution and playback.

time code An address system used to assign each frame of video a unique numerical designation in the format hours:minutes:seconds:frames, such as 23:03:58:23.

time code burn-in A dub of video footage that has time code information displayed on the screen.

time code generator A device used to create running time code to record with video information. Time code generators are built in to many videotape recorders, and they are also available as separate units.

time code reader A device used to read time code information.

timeline A graphical representation used in nonlinear editing software in which small pictures of audio and/or video material are arranged along a display.

tip The end of some connectors, such as phone and miniphone.

tone generator An element in an audio board or other piece of equipment that produces a constant one kilohertz sound that can be used to set consistent volume levels on different pieces of equipment.

tracking control The control on a videotape recorder that adjusts the video head to put it in the optimum position when a tape is played back.

transducing Receiving energy in one form (sound waves or light energy) and converting it into another form of energy (electromagnetic signals).

transfer editing Any form of editing in which a signal is transferred (dubbed) from one tape to another.

transition A method, such as a cut, dissolve, or wipe, of getting from one shot to another.

transparent The term used to describe the ability of digital signals to be distributed and manipulated without loss of quality.

treatment Several written pages that describe the main premise and elements of a series or movie.

trim (1) To adjust an in or out point of an edit frame-by-frame. (2) To make final adjustments on lights.

tripod A three-legged camera mount, sometimes equipped with casters to facilitate camera movement.

truck (1) To move the camera and its mount laterally to the right or left. (2) A shot produced by trucking the camera.

tungsten-halogen lamp See *quartz lamp*.

turntable A piece of equipment for spinning records and converting the groove vibrations into electrical energy.

two-column scripts Scripts with video in the left-hand column and audio in the right-hand column.

U

ultracardioid A very narrow microphone pickup pattern, often used to pick up sound from a distance.

umbrella Shiny material in an umbrella shape that a lighting instrument is turned into so that the light is bounced off and diffused.

unbalanced cables Audio cables that have two wires, one for positive, and one for both negative and ground.

undo A feature of many computer programs and nonlinear editing systems that allows the user to "take back" the last operation or series of operations.

uninterrupted run-through The rehearsal of an entire show without stopping for anything except major problems; minor problems are fixed later.

unions Organizations that set wages and working conditions that production companies must adhere to for people (usually below-the-line people) that they hire.

unit manager A person who works for a production facility who draws up a rate card and schedules facilities.

user interaction The ability of a user to control portions of an interactive media presentation.

V

VCR See *videocassette recorder*.

vectorscope A piece of diagnostic equipment used to adjust the color qualities of a video signal using color bars.

vertical interval A brief time during the scanning process when the scanning beam turns off and is repositioned at the top of the screen to begin scanning a new frame.

vertical interval time code A method of recording time code information into the "blank" area during the vertical interval.

vertical sync pulse The portion of the sync signal that controls the movement of a scanning beam from the top to the bottom of the screen.

video capture Hardware and software that allow a personal computer to convert video into digital form.

video control A knob used to adjust the level of video coming into a videotape recorder.

video disk A round storage device that can hold video and audio signals in such a way that they can be randomly accessed.

video gain A control used to boost the overall brightness of the picture being produced by a camera.

video on demand   A system, delivered over cable or via satellite or microwave, in which a user can order a specified program at any time.

video operator   A person in charge of recording a program.

video output control   A control that increases the gain of a video signal so that a camera can obtain a picture in low lighting conditions.

video server   A computer-based unit used to store and retrieve video signals in digital form.

video split   A digital video effect in which a video input is "pulled apart" on screen, often to reveal another video source.

video track   The portion of a videotape on which video information is recorded.

videocassette recorder   A magnetic-electronic recording machine that records audio, video, and control track signals on a videotape enclosed within a container.

videotape recorder   A device used to record video and audio information onto a magnetic tape.

virtual reality   A computer simulation of a real-life event, such as flying a plane or driving a car.

Virtual Reality Modeling Language   A computer language that allows the production of interactive media presentations in which users control the presentation by moving through 3D landscapes.

virtual sets   Studio sets that are computer generated and filled in

electronically behind performers who stand in front of a blank background.

VITC   See *vertical interval time code.*

volume unit meter   A display meter that shows the relative volume of an audio signal.

VRML   See *Virtual Reality Modeling Language.*

VTR   See *videotape recorder.*

VU meter   See *volume unit meter.*

W

walk-through rehearsal   An abbreviated rehearsal, conducted from the studio floor, to acquaint the talent and/or crew with the major outline of the production.

waveform   An electronic representation of a signal.

waveform monitor   A piece of diagnostic equipment used to evaluate the brightness qualities of a video signal.

Web   See *World Wide Web.*

Web page   An interactive media screen designed for use with a Web browser.

white balance   An electronic adjustment of a camera to compensate for differences in color temperatures so that a pure white object appears as pure white.

wide shot   See *long shot.*

wide-angle lens   See *short lens.*

wildtrack   Background noise recorded at a site so that it can be mixed in with other sounds during postproduction.

windscreen   See *pop filter.*

wipe   A transition in which a geometric pattern gradually replaces one picture with another.

wireless   Any system that sends audio frequencies through the airwaves as opposed to through cables.

wireless mic   A microphone with a self-contained miniature FM transmitter built in that can send the audio signal several hundred feet, eliminating the need for mic cables.

World Wide Web   A system that allows interactive media presentations to be delivered over the Internet or an intranet.

WS   See *wide shot.*

WWW   See *World Wide Web.*

X

XLR connector   A professional-quality balanced connector with three prongs.

Z

zip drive   A computer drive that has more storage capacity than a floppy but less than a Jaz drive.

zoom lens   A variable-focal-length lens that, through a complex optical system, can be smoothly changed from one focal length to another.

Index